Peterson Reference Guide to

BIRDING BY IMPRESSION

A DIFFERENT APPROACH TO KNOWING AND IDENTIFYING BIRDS

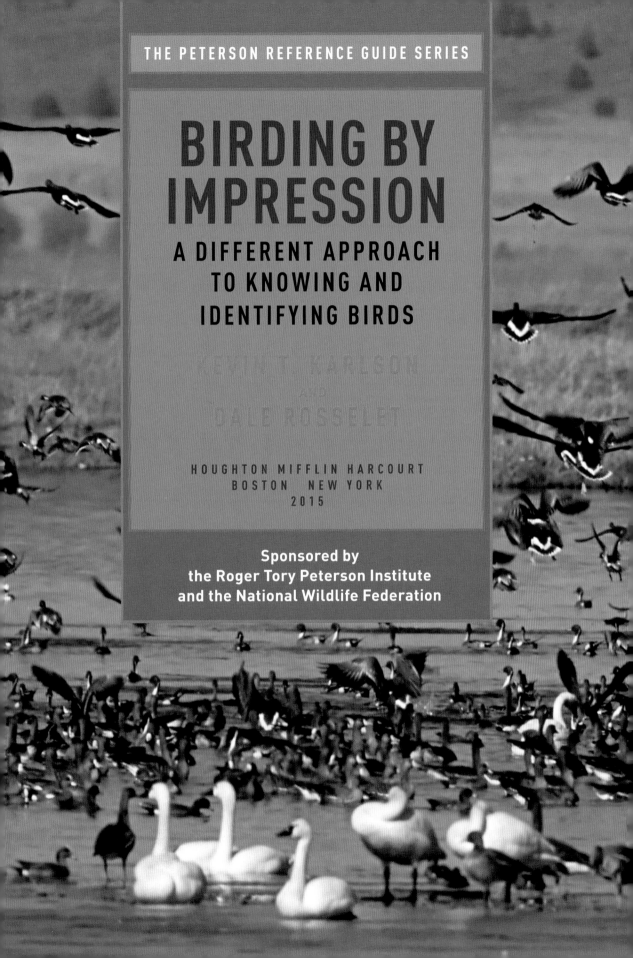

THE PETERSON REFERENCE GUIDE SERIES

BIRDING BY IMPRESSION

A DIFFERENT APPROACH TO KNOWING AND IDENTIFYING BIRDS

KEVIN T. KARLSON

AND

DALE ROSSELET

HOUGHTON MIFFLIN HARCOURT
BOSTON   NEW YORK
2015

Sponsored by
the Roger Tory Peterson Institute
and the National Wildlife Federation

The legacy of America's greatest naturalist and creator of the field guide series, Roger Tory Peterson, is kept alive through the dedicated work of the Roger Tory Peterson Institute of Natural History (RTPI). Established in 1985, RTPI is located in Peterson's hometown of Jamestown, New York, near the Chautauqua Institution in the southwestern part of the state.

Today RTPI is a national center for nature education that maintains, shares, and interprets Peterson's extraordinary archive of writings, art, and photography. The institute, housed in a landmark building by world-class architect Robert A. M. Stern, continues to transmit Peterson's zest for teaching about the natural world through leadership programs in teacher development as well as outstanding exhibits of contemporary nature art, natural history, and the Peterson Collection.

Your participation as a steward of the Peterson Collection and supporter of the Peterson legacy is needed. Please consider joining RTPI at an introductory rate of 50 percent of the regular membership fee for the first year. Simply call RTPI's membership department at (800) 758-6841 ext. 226, or e-mail membership@rtpi.org to take advantage of this special membership offered to purchasers of this book. For more information, please visit the Peterson Institute in person or virtually at www.rtpi.org.

We dedicate this book to the birds, which
provide endless fascination for those who take
the time to observe and enjoy them, and to the
many people who over the years have influenced
the way we look at birds.

Peterson Reference Guide to

BIRDING BY
IMPRESSION

A DIFFERENT APPROACH TO
KNOWING AND IDENTIFYING BIRDS

CONTENTS

FOREWORD

Now here's a rare privilege—the opportunity to write a foreword for a book in the Peterson Field Guide series. Forewords are not typically included in field guides—a point that underscores the authors' stated observation that this book is not intended to serve as a field guide. Yes, the focus is most certainly bird identification, but the information this book imparts is more akin to an avocational driver's manual than it is to the nuts-and-bolts description of individual species that are the foundation of field guides.

Back to forewords. For much of birdwatching's history, the signature characteristic of all books whose focus was birds or bird study was the sanctifying "Foreword by Roger Tory Peterson." Roger, as our tribal leader, felt duty-bound to place his stamp of approval on all avocational advances. While I do not presume to speak for RTP, I do believe Roger would have taken particular delight with this exciting new book, which is a fresh and well-conceived presentation of a simple and basic approach to bird identification not at all at odds with his famous "Peterson (identification) system," which emphasizes a focus on field marks.

What *Birding by Impression* advances is a back-to-fundamentals approach to bird identification emphasizing that a preliminary appreciation of size and shape (the cornerstones of BBI) is essential to the identification process. Plumage-based field marks, the "trademarks of nature" as Roger called them, come next. This approach is one Roger affirmed too. But generations of birders have heralded and elevated the significance of those plumage traits sanctified by Roger's trademark arrows and have, over time, given diminished regard to the fundamentals that are essential to accurate bird identification. Fundamentals that Roger himself underscored on the inside covers of the fourth edition of his famous guide, where two plates compare silhouettes by size and shape of multiple bird groups (the all-important first step in the identification process that BBI champions).

It should not be forgotten that people were identifying birds before RTP codified the elements of his "field mark"–based system in 1934—essentially an extension of the trait-based system used by ornithologists to distinguish one species from another, but modified by Roger and others to work at a distance by focusing on the traits that could be noted at a reasonable distance and in good light using optics.

Take, for example, Alexander Wilson's account of the discovery of Broad-winged Hawk (one hundred years before the publication of RTP's *A Field Guide to the Birds*). Wilson notes that he and ornithologist John Bartram came upon the hawk in Bartram's woods outside Philadelphia. As the species was "unknown" to both of them, they approached close enough to "collect" the type specimen—an adult that they then studied and described as a new species. They deduced that the bird was a species of hawk unfamiliar to them before procuring it. The only way to do this is by having a familiarity with raptors in the field.

I cannot say with certainty that Wilson was using a BBI approach when he made his initial determination, but as someone who for many years has been an advocate of looking at the big picture first and filling in the details later, I'll bet BBI principles were the foundation of Wilson's identification process. He knew it was a different species, but being a scientist (steeped in a tradition that demands verifiable evidence), he was obligated to collect the bird in order to prove his determination.

While verification does not lie at the heart of birdwatching, identifying birds accurately is central to our avocation, and being able to identify birds in the field under less than ideal conditions increases the scope and range of a birder's skill. The BBI discipline also helps birders quickly assess and sort new and uncommon species from among familiar ones, just as Wilson did with that Broad-winged Hawk.

Roger Tory Peterson was himself an able practitioner of BBI. While doing a Big Day together in 1984, we realized our list was still short Red-tailed Hawk. Stopping at a strategic power-line cut, we began scanning the crossbars of the high-tension towers. Sure enough, perched approximately 400 yards away was a raptor, but because of the long distance we were unable to note any of the textbook plumage traits that would have supported our identification of Red-tailed Hawk. However, Roger noted that the raptor staring intently at the open ground below was large, football-shaped, short tailed, and pale brown in color. All five members of the team, which also included David Sibley, Pete Bacinski, and Bill Boyle, concurred that it was a Red-tailed Hawk. "Do you think M____ and B____ would have gone with that?" I asked Roger. The ornithologists whose names I raised, while very knowledgeable about raptors, were also classically plumage-based in their approach to identification. "Probably not," Roger concluded.

Field identification has come a long way since

Snow Geese and Ross's Geese taking flight, Oregon.

Wilson and Bartram stalked the woodlands bearing fowling pieces. It took a great leap forward in 1934 with the publication of Roger Peterson's first *Field Guide to the Birds*. It continues to evolve as optics improve and the reach of our skills expands. The book in your hands both codifies and confides the limit of our skills one hundred years into the evolution of field birding.

PETE DUNNE

PREFACE

Welcome to an exciting and different approach to knowing and identifying birds. Traditional identification (ID) approaches concentrate mostly on feather details to identify birds. Birding by Impression (BBI) begins with an assessment of a bird's unchanging features, including size, body shape, structural features, and behavior. After evaluating a bird's physical profile and movements, which often takes only a short time, you can consider traditional ID details to reach a more complete and accurate ID conclusion.

Once you have reached an ID conclusion, the "knowing" aspect comes into play. Identifying a bird is just one part of the birdwatching experience, but learning more about a bird's lifestyle and behavior allows you to truly enjoy the lives of these fascinating creatures. This added awareness occurs when you watch birds in their natural habitat, which also helps the ID process by broadening your knowledge of birds' habits and typical behaviors.

In the following pages we share the basic approach to BBI, including general guidelines for how to assess important field impressions of different bird groups. BBI allows new and casual birders to build lasting ID skills that don't require constant referencing of field guides, and gives advanced birders an opportunity to take their birding skills to new levels of proficiency and enjoyment. In both cases, the end result of this approach is truly *knowing* a bird rather than just identifying it.

A PERSONAL HISTORY

The authors have been birding for more than 34 years, and used a traditional detail-oriented ID approach for much of this time. While Kevin was working on *The Shorebird Guide* (Houghton Mifflin, 2006), coauthors Michael O'Brien and Richard Crossley encouraged him to look at birds differently by consciously focusing on the features mentioned above. After much discussion and a certain amount of skepticism, Kevin agreed.

It took Kevin about a year to grasp this different ID concept and put it into practice. Being "left-brained" by nature, he critically analyzed plumage patterns and feather details to solve ID problems, and found it hard to shift to a more holistic approach. Eventually he concentrated more on birds' physical profiles and movements, and realized his birding skills were improving. Soon Kevin was intuitively identifying birds in a way he never thought possible, and at the same time building a valuable mental database of lasting impressions for comparison with less familiar species.

This was the beginning of a BBI field approach for Kevin. After reviewing various scientific studies about the brain and how it processes and stores details and impressions differently, he used these findings to explain and justify the effectiveness of a BBI approach in the ID process, which he enjoys sharing with others in workshops and field trips.

Dale's understanding and use of a similar ID approach evolved primarily from working with children and beginning birdwatchers as a teacher–naturalist for New Jersey Audubon. Countless conversations began with "Can you help me identify this bird?"—which invariably led to a description of the bird's colors. Only after Dale's probing with questions such as "How large was the bird compared with one that you already know?" or "Where did you see the bird and how was it acting?" did the ID become clearer. It was gratifying to hear the person say, "That's it, that is the bird I saw!" after looking in a field guide.

During these conversations with adults and after interacting with thousands of children, Dale realized how differently individual people process information and stimuli. She began adjusting her teaching style to address these differences so that all participants would get the most out of each class. BBI embraces these different learning styles by encouraging an evaluation of a bird's features as an important part of the ID process.

INTRODUCTION

HOW TO USE THIS BOOK

In this book we encourage you to look at birds differently by including an assessment of their physical features and behavior in your ID process. This is not a field guide, but an opportunity to learn a different approach to field identification.

The book is divided into two main sections. The first section, the introduction, provides general information about the Birding by Impression (BBI) approach and how to use it in everyday field situations. We highly recommend that you read this section to establish a familiarity with the BBI approach to bird ID.

The second section contains chapters that cover most bird groups, and shows how a BBI approach helps with the field identification of species in that group. The chapters are designed to provide helpful BBI information for birders of all skill levels; they begin with a short overview of the represented bird group and a photo composite of representative species. For most members of the group, we give a physical profile, which provides a strong foundation of unchanging features for the ID process. If there are look-alike species, we note them here as well. BBI information is next. This provides a more detailed look at ID features pertaining to individual species in the group. We compare the sizes of the smallest and largest members of each bird group with those of other common species to allow you to better visualize size parameters.

Each chapter ends with comparisons of similar species, which include advanced ID information on difficult-to-identify species. We chose these species because they represent some of the toughest ID dilemmas that birders face in the field. ID information here is separated into two categories—unchanging characteristics, and supplemental characteristics and non-BBI details—to allow a combined approach of right-brain evaluation of BBI features and left-brain analysis of plumage and bare-parts details. Photo composites of similar species accompany most of the ID comparisons to visually reinforce the information in the text.

While most ID features and details explained in the text are shown in the photos, some are not, but the information is provided to allow complete ID coverage. Some photos may also show features that appear to contradict the text, but these impressions may be a result of odd camera angles or a misleading split-second snapshot of a bird's wing, tail, or head. Not every photo is able to show every important feature or field mark, but the ones we chose show most of them. Throughout the book you will find comparative quiz photos. Here we encourage you to look for structural and plumage differences of similar species before reading the accompanying text on how to separate them. The appendix contains the answers to the ID quizzes, as well as further information about some species comparisons.

There are more than 200 photographs in the book. Some are "real-life" photos that contain more than one bird and show what you would see in the field. Others are photo composites that show similar species in comparable side-by-side postures, mostly scaled to size. Some of the photo composites include silhouettes, to encourage you to look at the physical outline of a bird—including body shape and structural features (such as legs and bill)—instead of plumage details.

Some chapters contain tables that compare a variety of BBI features and plumage and bare-parts details for different groups of birds. We cover the most commonly seen species more extensively.

Throughout the book, we use the terms "juvenile" and "immature" to describe plumage states that differ from adults. Often these terms refer to birds of different species and families that are the same age, which can be confusing (see explanation below).

Since some birds retain their juvenile feathers for a full year, while others only show juvenile plumage for a month or so, we use the term "juvenile" when the bird only has juvenile feathers, whether fresh or very worn. "Immature" is used to describe birds that have only some juvenile feathers mixed with nonbreeding or breeding feathers, or no juvenile feathers at all, but a plumage unlike full adult plumage. Most raptors and big gulls retain their juvenile feathers for about a full year, but appear very different with very worn feathers in the spring versus fresh juvenile feathers in the previous late summer or fall.

We occasionally mention a bird's subspecies in the book, which refers to members of the same species that have been separated into distinct named groups due to physical, genetic, or plumage differences. We prefer to use the familiar names for subspecies to avoid scientific confusion with some readers, such as "Eastern Willet" or "the eastern subspecies of," but at times we use the Latin names of birds for the sake of accuracy, or when there are no familiar names available.

THE PROBLEM AND THE SOLUTION

THE PROBLEM

We all have moments when we see a bird for only an instant, allowing little or no time for detailed field study. Other frustrating situations involve birds that appear superficially similar, have no outstanding field marks, are poorly lit, or are so distant that important ID information is beyond our viewing range.

These moments leave us uncertain about a bird's ID and unsure of what to look for. By the time we

FIGURE 1. COMPROMISED VIEWING SITUATIONS (QUIZ PHOTO)
Poor lighting conditions, such as heat haze or backlit birds, often result in few or no plumage details being visible to help with an ID. A careful assessment of birds' comparative sizes and structural features is helpful in these cases. If you recognize one of the shorebirds in this photo (taken in March in Texas), you can compare its size and structural features to those of the others for help in identifying it. For an expert-level quiz, try to identify all five species. (Hint: The smallest birds (#4) are Western Sandpipers.) Answers are in the appendix, page 266.

figure out how to proceed, the bird may have flown or moved out of sight. Our frustration arises because we are using a traditional ID approach that concentrates mostly on plumage and bare-parts details, and doesn't give us the kind of information we need to make a confident ID.

THE SOLUTION

BBI includes an initial evaluation of birds that uses several key unchanging characteristics, such as a bird's size, body shape, structural features, and behavior. These important characteristics create a solid foundation for the ID process because they remain constant throughout the year and are not compromised by confusing plumage variations.

You don't need to commit to memory all the fine points of feather details, but it helps to have a basic familiarity with common bird groups and their general features. A key to success with the BBI approach, however, is learning how to efficiently assess a bird's physical profile and movements by using terms that describe obvious body parts in simple ways. For example, these terms could be used to describe the Cape May Warbler in Figure 2: "small and compact with a small head; peaked or rounded crown; short, forked tail; and thin, pointed, slightly decurved bill."

With experience, using the BBI approach becomes second nature and part of your automatic thought process. Like an experienced police detective who notices and retains important aspects of a fleeing suspect, you can train yourself to quickly spot important physical features and repetitive movements by practicing your observation skills.

Using this approach over time results in the intuitive recognition of some species, and is similar to knowing a friend or family member's shape, movements, and essence at a distance without seeing any details. In these instances, you don't have to think about whom you are viewing; you just know who it is based on familiar physical features and behavioral impressions.

BBI shares some points with the familiar GISS—general impression, size, shape—style of bird identification, which relies on prior field experience with that species. While GISS also results in intuitive recognition of birds by unpremeditated absorption of their features, when using BBI you consciously assess and remember additional impressions for each species and evaluate distinctive structural features and behavioral movements. You also compare unfamiliar birds with nearby familiar ones and carefully compare similar species. This conscious, more concentrated BBI assessment of a bird's size, shape,

FIGURE 2. CAPE MAY WARBLER PLUMAGE VARIATIONS

Many birds show a variety of plumages throughout the year, but their structural features remain constant. This Cape May Warbler composite shows an adult male (L), a drab first-spring female (C), and an immature female (R). In all plumages, the thin, pointed, decurved bill; short tail; peaked crown; and small, compact size help with the ID. Note that the peaked crown is visible only on the relaxed immature female, with the other alert birds showing a rounded crown because of flattened head feathers.

structural features, and repetitive motions results in a greater awareness of a bird's physical profile and its typical posture and movements. It also allows for a more intuitive recognition of birds in future sightings because of the additional concentration on these impressions. So while BBI has its foundation in the GISS style of birding, it also takes your ID approach to greater levels of proficiency.

BBI: THE WHY AND HOW

WHY BBI WORKS

BRAIN FUNCTION AND BIRDING BY IMPRESSION

Both sides of the brain process visual information. Structured left-brain activity is analytical and uses linear thinking to form a logical conclusion using words and details. Nonlinear right-brain activity is evaluative and employs a more holistic approach by assessing three-dimensional shapes and forms as visual impressions. Repetitive right-brain evaluation of familiar faces or objects, such as birds, is responsible for your eventual instant recognition of these subjects.

When you recognize a familiar face, it is your right brain that processes this information. However, left-brain activity is needed to translate those facial features into words (though often with unsatisfactory results). Conventional bird ID employs primarily a left-brain approach, using words to describe and remember plumage details and obvious physical characteristics, such as very small or large size. This thought process is often insufficient because it does not include a more expanded assessment of a bird's shape, structural features, and motion, with the expressed intent of learning and remembering more about a bird's physical profile and behavior.

BBI adds a right-brain slant to the ID process by including your own evaluation of a bird's unchanging features. Much of this information is stored as impressions in the subconscious memory, not as words and details, which become more familiar and instantly accessible during subsequent viewings. These mental images are generally exempt from memory loss that is typically associated with word-related details. Without relying on details, these impressions are long lasting and readily accessible for future ID exercises or comparisons.

David Sibley, one of North America's most respected birders, talks about the value of using impressions for field ID in Malcolm Gladwell's book *Blink*. "Most of bird identification is based on a sort of subjective impression—the way a bird moves and little instantaneous appearances . . . all that combines to create a unique impression of a bird that can't really be taken apart and described in words . . . you don't take the time to analyze it and say it shows this, this, and this; therefore it must be this species. It's more natural and instinctive. After a lot of practice, you look at the bird, and it triggers little switches in your brain. It *looks* right. You know what it is at a glance."

DESCRIBING FIELD IMPRESSIONS
USING SIMPLE WORDS

We've all experienced the frustration of trying to explain our impressions of a bird to someone else. As we struggle to describe what we saw, the description breaks down and our words don't portray the visual image in our mind. Gladwell calls this "paralysis through analysis," whereby important visual pictures are compromised when thinking shifts from the right brain to the left brain. We mostly

FIGURE 3. RED KNOTS IN FLIGHT
These gray and white birds don't show any outstanding plumage field marks, although a strong white wing stripe and black leading edge to the wings are good supporting features. Important simple descriptions of shape and structure, including the football-shaped body, are described in the text.

communicate using words, however, so an attempt to clearly describe our impressions is important for the BBI process to work.

We recommend using simple vocabulary to describe unchanging field impressions. For example, the description of nonbreeding Red Knot in flight might be worded as "robin-sized with a football-shaped body; long, pointed wings; short to medium bill; and legs that don't extend past the tail." (See Figure 3, above.) A description of plumage could include "overall gray with a bold white stripe on the upperwing." This description is simple yet accurate for describing a bird that is notoriously difficult to identify in nonbreeding plumage. Its flight could be described as "fast and direct with quick wingbeats."

After you identify a bird by its physical profile and body language, try to determine what features were responsible for the distinctive shape or movements that you recognized. Share your ID thought process with other birders to further your understanding of a bird's physical makeup by using their feedback to fine-tune your assessment. It is important, however, to use a number of impressions and details to reach your conclusion. We occasionally change our minds after new information contradicts our initial ID, especially if it was an instant recognition. Never base your identification of an unfamiliar bird on a single impression or field mark.

HOW BBI WORKS

It is important to note that BBI is not meant to replace conventional field ID approaches, but rather to improve on them by building a foundation of unchanging ID features. A key to success with this combined approach is to initially evaluate a bird's physical profile before analyzing plumage details. This right-brain exercise allows you to form a mental picture of a bird's general size, body shape, and structural features without interference from a left-brain analysis of specific details. A careful assessment of the bird's overall shape and structural features is often sufficient to identify a bird to species, and it provides a foundation for fine-tuning your ID. Sometimes evaluating a few other BBI features is necessary to firm up your ID conclusion.

After coming to an ID conclusion, spend additional time studying a bird's movements. Observe its structural features in different postures and motions, and then compare it with nearby species. (See Figure 5, p. 7.) Also compare several birds of the same species and note any variations among them. This is how you get to really "know" a bird, and these combined impressions are a great help with future sightings.

If you're a beginning birder, you'll face more challenges with this aspect of BBI, since fewer species are familiar to you. A helpful exercise is to acquaint yourself with common birds in your backyard and local parks in addition to browsing through field guides. When you see an unfamiliar bird, take mental or written notes and describe what you see. Also try to sketch some birds, regardless of your artistic skills. All of these activities will help you remember a bird's physical profile.

The U.S. Navy and British Royal Air Force recognized the value of using visual impressions to increase the speed and effectiveness of field identification. They used a mental visualization exercise similar to BBI in World War II when training pilots to quickly recognize all aircraft encountered in the sky.

WEFT (wings, engine, fuselage, and tail) was a U.S. Navy training procedure whereby pilots were subjected to repetitive views of photographs of airplanes at a rapid pace of about 1 per 1,000th of a second. After a while, a pilot's analysis of the planes' features became overloaded and stopped functioning, at which point the visual images of these aircraft became embedded in the subconscious.

A World War II Navy pilot used the term "afterimages" for these now familiar shapes when he explained to Kevin that, because of this training, he instantly recognized virtually every plane he saw while flying missions in Europe, before he had a chance to consciously identify them.

He brought up this training to explain why Kevin quickly identified an American Golden-Plover in flight after a quick sideways glance while speaking to his birding tour group. Kevin previously had problems identifying this bird in flight, and he could not explain why he instantly blurted out the species' name when he saw it fly by. It was as if his voice belonged to someone else. The Navy pilot said that Kevin had "afterimages" of this bird in his brain, which he accessed when the plover flew past.

After asking if Kevin had viewed American Golden-Plover recently, the pilot smiled knowingly when Kevin told him that he had watched several of these birds walking and flying around a grassy field on the previous day. His casual study of their movements resulted in the intuitive recognition that occurred the next day. British pilots called their version of this training GISS (general impression, size, and shape).

During my first 24 years as a birder, I identified many American Robins but never carefully assessed their physical profile and movements. In 2008, I spent a year carefully observing robins in my yard to practice my BBI skills with a bird that few people actually take the time to study. I concentrated on both obvious and subtle impressions, especially body shape on the ground and in flight. Comparing robins with other backyard birds builds lasting impressions about how this species differs in size, shape, and behavior. (See Figure 4, below.)

I also tried to absorb the unique essence of robins by noting repeated nuances of their movements, such as their flight behavior of pulling the wings close to the body after several flaps, and pausing briefly before continuing to flap. This repetitive motion results in a distinctive flight profile and added to my intuitive recognition of this species.

FIGURE 4. AMERICAN ROBIN
The characteristic flight profile of American Robin is shown in the left photo, with wingbeats intermittently interrupted by the wings being pulled close to the body for a moment, which causes the bird to dip slightly in its strong flight path. The standing bird shows a typical robin posture of upright stance, drooping wings, lowered tail, and rounded belly.

FIGURE 5. WETLAND BIRDS COMPARISON (QUIZ PHOTO)
These four common wetland birds from Florida have very different sizes and structural features that are important to the ID process, especially for beginners. When viewing various species together like this, note the size and structural differences before concentrating on plumage details and bare-parts color. Try to identify these birds using your field guide. Answers are in the appendix, page 226.

You can study specific details of plumage anywhere, including in field guides at home, but you have to spend time in the field to fine-tune your awareness of important BBI features. After using this ID approach for several years, we have found our field skills increasing dramatically, especially in marginal or difficult viewing conditions.

It's also fun to study and enjoy birds without binoculars, which is an exercise that adds valuable information about a bird's movements that often goes unnoticed with a close-up optics view. We now first assess BBI features for every bird before conducting additional study of plumage details.

BBI BASICS

BIRDING BY IMPRESSION INFORMATION

Size, body shape, structural features, and behavior are the basic unchanging characteristics of the BBI approach.

UNCHANGING CHARACTERISTICS
Size

Determining the general size of an unfamiliar bird is a good starting point for your ID process, and a foundation for other BBI features. Many birders neglect to consciously estimate the sizes of unfamiliar birds, and this mental lapse often compromises the ID process. If you establish a rough estimate of a bird's size, you can narrow the ID possibilities in a field guide. Measurements in a field guide can be confusing, since they depict a bird's length from bill tip to tail tip, so try to determine a bird's size without allowing its body shape, bill length, or leg length to influence your general size estimate. (See Figure 6, p. 8.)

If you're a beginning birder, you may find it challenging to gauge the sizes of birds. It can be helpful to create a group of reference birds with which you are very familiar and learn their sizes. You can then compare these reference birds, such as sparrow, robin, and crow, with unfamiliar birds. As an example, if a crow is harassing a raptor, you can estimate the size of the raptor by comparing it with the crow. Crows are also useful for estimating the sizes of songbirds. (See Figure 7, p. 9.)

Challenges to Sizing Birds in Various Field Conditions

Fog and heat waves may affect your ability to accurately judge a bird's size, especially if no familiar birds are nearby. Backlit birds and silhouetted birds appear larger than they really are, as do birds viewed through optics when heat waves distort the image.

It is especially difficult to estimate the sizes of multiple birds viewed at different distances, or of a single bird at a great distance. In these cases it is best to categorize birds as small, medium, or large without determining an exact measurement. Also difficult are distant flying birds. (See Figure 8, p. 9.) We have seen a few experienced hawkwatchers struggle with a distant "raptor" before realizing it was a much closer monarch butterfly.

Body Shape and Structural Features

While the words "shape" and "structure" share similar meanings, their literal definitions and the way we apply them to the BBI approach are different. In the BBI approach, we often use the term "body shape" instead of "shape" to concentrate on just the overall shape of a bird's body.

For our purposes, *body shape* refers to the general outline of a bird's body, while *structure* includes a bird's body parts (bill, legs, neck, wings,

tail, and head) and how they combine to create a complete physical profile. (See Figure 9, p. 10.) On flying birds, the wings don't contribute to the body shape, but they greatly influence your impression of a bird's movements.

For example, a Common Loon's body shape could be described as "bulky and elongated," while a Red-throated Loon's is "slender and elongated." Adding to the body shape description is a quick assessment of the structural features, including the head, neck, and bill. Common Loon has a thick neck and bulky head with a stocky, heavy bill, while Red-throated has a slim neck and head and a slender, tapered bill. These simple descriptions help with the ID of these similar species, regardless of their plumage. (See Figure 10, p. 10.)

Keith Hansen, bird artist extraordinaire, emphasizes in his bird sketching classes the importance of capturing the overall shape of a bird by first drawing its outer body contour lines, and then filling in the details. You can use the same exercise with your field ID by assessing the outline of a bird's body, and then simply describing its shape. (See Figure 11, p. 11.) These descriptions form a part of

---

FIGURE 6. PITFALLS IN ESTIMATING SIZE

It is important to estimate the length of a bird from its head to its tail tip, and not allow leg length or body shape to influence your general size estimate. The longer legs of the Lesser Yellowlegs (top L) create a taller profile than that of the nearby sleeping Short-billed Dowitcher, and give the impression that it is larger than the dowitcher, even though they are similar in body length. While the yellowlegs has a slightly longer body, the dowitcher has a longer bill, which accounts for similar measurements. The smaller birds are Semipalmated Sandpipers (5½ in. long).

FIGURE 7. USING CROWS FOR COMPARATIVE SIZING OF OTHER BIRDS
Seeing a smaller Red-winged Blackbird (8¾ in. long) perched next to a Fish Crow (15 in. long), or an American Crow (17½ in. long) harassing a Red-shouldered Hawk (17 in. long), helps estimate the size of the unfamiliar species, and develops familiar size references for future ID comparisons.

FIGURE 8. COMPARATIVE SIZING OF BIRDS IN FLIGHT (QUIZ PHOTO)
Comparing various birds in flight can help you ID unfamiliar or distant species. The left photo shows a Bald Eagle chasing an Osprey for its food. There are only two true raptors that are much larger than Osprey (Golden and Bald Eagles), and only Bald Eagle regularly chases Osprey to steal fish, so this size comparison helps with the ID of Bald Eagle, even without its characteristic white head and tail. The right photo shows three species with distinctive wing shapes. Try to identify these poorly lit birds based on their comparative sizes and structures. Answers are in the appendix, page 266.

your ID foundation, even if other birders offer differently worded shape descriptions.

General Guidelines for Describing Structural Features

BILL: A few simple guidelines are helpful for standardizing bill descriptions. If the bill is noticeably shorter than the distance from the bill base to the nape (back of the neck), it is considered short. If it is about the same or 1¼ times longer than the head depth from bill base to the nape, it is medium in length. Two or more times longer and it is a long bill. Some birds have a bill that is many times longer than their head depth, and these may be described as extremely long. Obviously, some overlap may occur among these categories.

Bill shape is also important, and a variety of

FIGURE 9. ASSESSING COMPARATIVE SIZE, BODY SHAPE, AND STRUCTURAL FEATURES (QUIZ PHOTO)
This wetland in New York City hosts several birds with a variety of body shapes and structural features as well as different leg lengths. General size comparisons range from the large Ring-billed Gull (1; 17 in. long) to the small out-of-focus Semipalmated Sandpiper (2; 5½ in. long). Can you identify the other species? More details on these species are in the appendix, page 266.

FIGURE 10. COMMON LOON AND RED-THROATED LOON
Direct comparison of these similarly plumaged nonbreeding loons enables easy recognition of Common Loon's (L) heavier body structure with a thicker neck, bulkier head, and much heavier bill. Its heavier body structure may be hard to assess in partially submerged birds like this one, but continuous views in the field will reveal this noticeable difference. Red-throated Loon (R) often swims with its bill tilted slightly upward.

descriptions define overall shape. Typically, the length of a bill is given before its shape. For example, most plover bills are described as "short and stubby," while a Roseate Spoonbill's bill is described as "long and spatula-shaped, with a flattened tip." Looking at some common backyard birds, Northern Cardinal's bill may be labeled as "short, heavy, and conical-shaped," while a chickadee's bill is "short, thin, and finely pointed." (See Figure 12, p. 11.)

LEG LENGTH: Assigning a general value for leg length is often difficult, especially for beginning birders. If a standing bird's body appears close to the ground, or the bird moves with short, quick steps, it has short legs. Birds with short legs usually don't show any leg projection past the tail in flight. (See Figure 13, p. 12.)

Conversely, if a bird walks or runs with a slow, gawky, stiff-legged gait, or if its legs extend noticeably past the tail in flight, it has long legs. Some birds' legs are so long that they resemble stilts. Examples of very long legs include those of Black-necked Stilt (see Figure 16, p. 15) and Great Egret (see Figure 67, p. 70). Birders don't often use the term "medium-length" because of its uncertain

FIGURE 11. BODY SHAPE OUTLINE
By literally or even mentally sketching the outline of a bird, you can determine its overall body shape without distractions of plumage details and coloration. A simple description of this male Pintail's body shape is "submarine-like."

FIGURE 12. BILL SHAPE COMPARISON (QUIZ PHOTO)
These six birds have very different bill shapes, which directly influence their feeding styles and choice of foods. Can you identify these birds to general family groups (raptors, sparrows, etc.)? Next try to identify them to species. Answers to these questions and descriptions of the bill shapes are in the appendix, page 266.

meaning, but legs that are evenly proportioned compared with body size are good candidates for the term "medium-length legs."

WINGS AND TAIL: The length of a sitting or floating bird's wings may influence your impression of the bird's body shape, especially when the wingtips ex-tend past the tail. If the wings don't extend past the tail, or fall well short of the tail, as on a Loggerhead Shrike, the wings don't affect the body shape. (See Figure 156, p. 181.)

Wing length also influences a bird's flight mo-tion, with long-winged birds usually appearing more graceful and effortless in flight, and short-

FIGURE 13. LEG LENGTH ASSESSMENT (QUIZ PHOTO)
While bill length descriptions are fairly straightforward, leg length assessments often vary among birders. For a fun exercise, try to identify these three birds. From left to right are examples of short, medium, and long legs. Answers and explanations are in the appendix, page 267.

winged birds having quicker, choppier wingbeats and a more erratic flight style.

The length and shape of the tail may also influence your impression of a bird's body shape. A long, slender tail that extends past the wingtips of a sitting bird gives the impression of a more elongated body shape. When a bird's tail is covered by its wings, the tail has no effect on body shape.

Behavior

Although a bird's behavior is not part of its physical profile, its associated repetitive movements may be important to the ID process. Because of shared physical anatomy and behavioral tendencies, most members of a particular species move in a similar fashion. Recognizing birds by their body language is similar to recognizing familiar movements of a close friend or family member. After repeated observations of a bird's distinctive movements, including walking, running, flying, and feeding, you will become familiar with the body language of that species. Even though humans are built and move differently from each other, we eventually recognize familiar people because of their unique repetitive movements.

A woman once told Kevin that the first time she watched her son compete as a long-distance runner, she was not able to pick him out among other runners. After several races, however, she quickly recognized him at any distance because his running style had become familiar to her. This visual recognition is also possible with particular bird species, especially if you consciously evaluate their repetitive movements.

A bird's physical features can cause or influence behavior or body motion. Leg length, wing length and shape, and tail length all combine to create a distinct overall impression.

Other movements may not be directly related to a bird's physical structure, but instead are simply behavioral traits of that species. Dowitchers feed with a deliberate sewing-machine motion, while American Kestrels often hover over a field while hunting. (See Figure 14, below.) An example of group behavior is the tendency of some species to form large flocks during migration and winter, such as a cloud of swirling Tree Swallows.

SUPPLEMENTAL CHARACTERISTICS
Plumage patterns, general coloration, habitat use, and vocalizations vary in importance in the BBI

FIGURE 14. AMERICAN KESTREL HUNTING BEHAVIOR
Only a handful of raptors hover in place while hunting, and this American Kestrel, eating a cricket, is one of them. This small falcon can often be identified using a combination of general size estimate and hovering behavior. Merlins occasionally eat insects while flying, but not while hovering in place.

Hawkwatchers and seawatchers, more than other birders, rely on recognition of familiar physical profiles and body motion for their ID success.

Veteran hawkwatchers use subtle flight movements and wing-flap differences to identify raptors at great distances, long before they can see any details. Some of these veterans acquired subconscious familiarity with these movements over a period of time and don't try to explain why they quickly recognize distant birds. Others take the time to figure out why certain anatomical features of a bird cause the distinctive motion that they instantly recognize, and this thought process allows them to share their knowledge and flight descriptions with others.

Brian Taber, director of the Coastal Virginia Wildlife Observatory, created life-size cut-out models from Kevin's photos of raptors commonly seen at the Kiptopeake Hawk Watch. He chose typical flight shapes, superimposed the plumage details on rigid models, and painted the back sides black with no details. The purpose of these models is to teach hawkwatchers how to recognize raptors using comparative size, distinctive shapes, and field marks.

This exercise allows the left brain to process details and general shape in one view, and only the bird's size, body shape, and structural features when viewing the black models, which is an evaluative right-brain exercise. Taber realizes that many raptors are seen only in distant silhouette, and he encourages everyone to learn how to recognize these important flight impressions to increase their ID success. (See Figure 15, below.)

Seawatchers also rely strongly on the recognition of subtle, distinctive movements to identify distant seabirds speeding along the horizon. These tiny silhouettes cause most of us to look away in frustration, without hope of forming a solid ID. After watching numerous seabirds at closer range, experienced seawatchers eventually recognize the characteristic body movements of each species in flight, as well as their distinctive shapes, even at long distances.

This recognition is crucial to seawatching, since many seabirds occur offshore, and often in bad weather. Some seawatchers have so acutely refined these skills that all it takes is a single glance to correctly identify some distant birds. Unfamiliar birds set off an internal alarm and encourage extra scrutiny. These refined ID skills are proof that repetitive evaluation of body shapes and subtle movements results in quick, accurate recognition of birds without the benefit of specific plumage details.

FIGURE 15. KIPTOPEAKE HAWK WATCH MODELS (QUIZ PHOTO)
Enthusiastic hawkwatch volunteers show hawk models that depict the various sizes and shapes of regularly occurring raptors. Dark silhouettes on the reverse side allow the brain to shift from analyzing details to evaluating shapes and structural features, which is a teaching exercise at the hawkwatch. Try to identify the raptors using comparative sizing and structural features. Answers are in the appendix, page 267.

approach, depending on the bird species and field situation, so we have listed them as supplemental to the ID process. For example, many birds look very different at various times of the year with respect to plumage patterns and color, and they may be found in different habitats as well. Vocalizations are also listed in this category because many birds don't vocalize on a regular basis, or they have vocalizations that are indistinct or irrelevant to their ID. In some instances, however, vocalizations, plumage patterns, or color may be the most obvious feature or deciding factor in your ID conclusion.

Plumage Patterns and General Coloration

When you assess a bird's plumage patterns, note its general background coloration and the location of other color markings, including the bare parts (bill, legs, eye-ring, and facial skin). Also important is a lack of color or plumage shading; when color or plumage shading is hard to determine because of poor lighting, note the presence of light or dark highlights and where they occur on a bird's body.

It is also important to note the absence or presence of obvious markings on a bird, and how these markings may contribute to a recognizable plumage pattern, rather than initially analyzing specific plumage details. These markings may include spots, stripes, or bars.

One word of caution when describing colors: People see colors differently. Because of this, ID descriptions based solely on color may not translate effectively from one person to another. Additionally, plumage patterns and general color, including bill and leg color, may change for some species during the course of a year and can vary greatly among individuals of the same species at the same time of year. Juvenile, breeding, and nonbreeding plumages of some birds may also differ, and the transitions into and out of these plumages can present appearances not shown in field guides.

If you're a beginning birder, it will help to familiarize yourself with the terminology of body parts so you can effectively describe the location of important plumage patterns, coloration, and field marks.

Habitat Use

Most birds have a preference for particular habitats, so where you see a bird may be helpful to your ID conclusion. Be aware that birds are sometimes displaced from desired habitats during migration and forced to forage or rest wherever possible, so exercise caution in these situations.

The best way to become familiar with the typical habitats that various species use is to visit the same birding locations many times at different seasons. Make a list of birds that use a particular habitat, and keep this information for later use. When an unfamiliar species shows up, pay close attention to its behavior, and consult a few reference sources for information about a possible species' preferred habitat at different times of the year. If you find a bird in a totally unexpected location, such as a Reddish Egret at a far inland location, it might be an unexpected vagrant or a mistaken ID on your part.

Vocalizations

Sounds that a bird makes, including songs, calls, *chip* notes, and wind passing through feathers, can contribute to or seal a conclusive field ID. It can be overwhelming to learn all the variations of birds' calls and songs, but there are several approaches to help with this process, and patience is the key to success.

Some experts recommend onomatopoeia, or using words to describe bird sounds. A Barred Owl's call is described as *Who cooks for you, who cooks for you, who cooks for you all*, and a Chestnut-sided Warbler's song as *Pleased, pleased, pleased to MEET you*. A popular description of an Eastern Towhee's song is *Drink your teeeea*. These word descriptions are a great help to some birders, especially those who have a hard time remembering phonetics.

Another popular approach to learning songs and calls uses phonetic descriptions of the sounds. When you hear an unfamiliar call, mimic or whistle the call out loud until you recognize a pattern. Also note the number of syllables and where any inflections occur, including rising or descending patterns. Sonograms are another visual tool used to chart differences in a bird's song.

With enough experience chasing down a singer or studying recorded bird songs beforehand and putting a name to their sounds, you should find that a bird's name pops into your mind when you hear the sounds again. This is an example of the right brain recognizing a familiar sound and the left brain providing the correct name for the bird. In some instances, calls or songs are the deciding factor when other ID approaches fail to provide a conclusive field ID.

Be careful not to mistake a distinctive call or song that is given by one of the mimic bird species, such as Northern Mockingbird, White-eyed Vireo, or European Starling. A fair number of birds can perfectly mimic vocalizations of other birds, so always try to get a look at the singer.

Comparison with Nearby or Similar Species

Comparing unfamiliar birds with nearby familiar ones helps form a size estimate and allows for a comparison of structural features. Subtle differences in feeding styles or body motion of similar species are also more easily assessed with direct comparisons.

We will never forget deliberating the identities of two shorebirds we saw on a coastal New England mud-flat during our first year of birding, in 1979. After sitting in front of the first bird for 15 minutes, we could not come up with its name, despite careful searching through our field guide. This was because we were considering only plumage field marks without any evaluation of size, shape, or structural features.

Later we realized the bird was a Semipalmated Plover that had been marked with orange color on its breast, which of course was not depicted on any shorebird in our field guide. A painted breast allows biologists to find and recognize their marked bird in a crowd, and is not something you typically encounter in the field. The abnormal breast color fooled us into thinking it was part of the bird's usual plumage condition. Had we used BBI skills rather than relying solely on plumage color, we might have put a name to this relatively easy-to-identify shorebird using a simple evaluation of size, shape, and other "normal" plumage patterns.

Soon after, we identified a large shorebird in flight that showed a striking black-and-white wing pattern, which we thought resembled a Black-necked Stilt. We later determined that this shorebird was an "Eastern" Willet, which does not resemble Black-necked Stilt at all to experienced birders. While searching through our field guide for a large black-and-white shorebird, we concentrated only on the black-and-white plumage of Black-necked Stilt to compare with the black-and-white wing pattern of the Willet, and did not consider any physical features in our ID process.

These are perfect examples of beginning birders who have no experience with common species relying only on plumage details shared by several unrelated species. (See Figure 16, below.) Both experiences are a constant reminder to us of the frustration new birders can have if they consider only plumage details.

FIGURE 16. "EASTERN" WILLET AND BLACK-NECKED STILT: EXAMPLE OF MISTAKEN ID
Dale and Kevin identified an "Eastern" Willet (L) as a Black-necked Stilt (R) in their first year of birding because of the Willet's black-and-white wing pattern, even though these two shorebirds look nothing alike and a stilt does not have black-and-white wings. This is a perfect example of the pitfalls of using only plumage details for your ID conclusion, and disregarding the obvious structural differences between these birds.

A recent trip to Israel allowed us to use this comparative approach, since we saw many unfamiliar species and a few new bird families. Direct comparison of unfamiliar birds in Israel with familiar ones that occur in North America helped us establish size and shape values for the new species, and soon we had a collection of familiar foreign birds to use for comparison with unfamiliar ones.

Beginners should note distinctive structural features shared by members of a particular bird group. For example, most terns differ from gulls by having slender, pointed wings; slimmer bodies; shorter legs; and slender, pointed bills compared with the heavier bills and bodies and broader wings of most gulls. Warblers have slim, pointed bills suited for catching insects, while finches, buntings, and grosbeaks have heavier, conical bills better suited for cracking open seeds and nuts. (See Figure 12, p. 11.)

Using Photographs for Comparison Study

Photographs are helpful for comparing structural features, especially when multiple birds are shown in the same image. Establishing the size of a single bird is difficult in photographs, but when familiar birds are shown adjacent to unfamiliar ones, a general estimate of size and useful comparisons of physical characteristics are possible.

Photos of similar species shown together allow you to critically evaluate subtle differences in body shape and structural features that may not be possible in some field situations. However, care should be taken with photos that show abnormal features because of unusual or agitated behavior, or a shape altered by an odd body angle or attitude. These photos can actually be misleading rather than helpful to your ID process, and some comparative photos in this book may show one or two "abnormal" physical features, which we point out to the reader to avoid ID confusion. Looking at many photos rather than only one will help eliminate these problems.

Comparative photos of similar species—including both "real-life" and digitized composites—are rarely used in popular photographic field guides, but we rely heavily on them in this book. They allow you to assess obvious and subtle variations in body shape, structural features, plumage, and bare parts among similar species. We found a number of previously unnoticed differences between similar species when preparing photos for this book, such as the subtle differences in bill size and shape between Clark's and Western Grebes, and the very slight differences in bill and head shape between some Couch's and Tropical Kingbirds.

SAMPLE FIELD ID SCENARIOS USING THE BBI APPROACH

LOCATION 1: *Bolivar Flats, Texas, in August, by Kevin*

As an experienced BBI birder, my overall approach to bird identification is different from that of a beginner. Upon entering a coastal habitat, I casually scan the mudflats with my binoculars. Most of the birds are instantly familiar to me, even those at a distance. Within a few minutes, I recognize 20 to 30 species from several different bird families. I quickly see, process, and identify herons, egrets, pelicans, gulls, terns, sandpipers, and plovers because I know these birds from long experience watching them.

Several distinctive species allow me to establish important size and shape references for other challenging species. The enormous White Pelicans set an upper size limit as the largest birds in view, and thousands of tiny Western Sandpipers and slightly larger Dunlins and Sanderlings provide me with important size references as the smallest birds on the mudflat. Royal Tern is another great comparative species, and fairly easy to locate thanks to its medium-large size, mostly white plumage, and stout orange bill. (See Figure 119, p. 131.)

Because of my experience with this location, I expect to see about seven species of white terns. I carefully study several large groups of white gulls and terns using BBI features of size and shape, and non-BBI details of seasonal bare-parts color. I know there are distinct size parameters for most terns, and I identify Royal, Caspian, Sandwich, Gull-billed, and Least Terns using size comparisons, general shape impressions, and bill color, even at a distance. (See Table 2, p. 126.) The medium-sized terns are harder to identify, and I don't try to separate Common from Forster's Terns until I get closer. This separation often requires a combination of BBI and traditional ID approaches. (See Figure 118, p. 130.)

For the thousands of shorebirds in view, I use Marbled Godwit as a starting point for my general assessment of the sizes and shapes of medium-large to large shorebirds. Ruddy Turnstone is another good comparative species for evaluating other medium-sized and smaller shorebirds. Both are helpful to the comparative thought process at any distance, with Marbled Godwit a very large cinnamon-colored shorebird with long legs and a long, straight bill, and Ruddy Turnstone a distinctive medium-sized shorebird with a round body, chisel-shaped bill, red and black plumage, and unique herky-jerky walking motion.

I know from experience that I can quickly identify most shorebirds at this location, but that several similar species may require more detailed study. If I don't see any unfamiliar shorebirds, I begin to concentrate on these similar species.

I scan for plovers by looking for their characteristic start-stop-tilt feeding motion. Plovers forage by walking, tilting, and consistently pausing in an upright stance every few steps, similar to the way an American Robin forages. This feeding behavior differs from the continuous foraging style of other shorebirds and allows me to immediately spot several large Black-bellied Plovers and a handful of the four possible small plover species.

After locating these plovers among the thousands of similar-sized sandpipers, I begin to sort through the similar-plumaged Snowy and Piping Plovers that have pale, sandy-toned backs, and Wilson's

FIGURE 17. BOLIVAR FLATS, TEXAS
This coastal scene shows many birds of various species on an open beachfront habitat. Pelicans, gulls, and terns are in the background, and American Avocets are feeding in the upper right portion of the photo.

and Semipalmated Plovers that have darker brown backs. At a distance, these birds appear somewhat alike, but a careful assessment of structural and plumage features helps separate them. (See Figure 90, p. 99.)

Herons and egrets pose few challenges, and I quickly identify many birds without much thought using size and general coloration features. Great Blue Heron and Great Egret stand out as the largest species, while three of four medium-sized, long-legged herons and egrets are easily separated by general coloration (Cattle Egret is not typically found on mudflats). (See Figure 65, p. 68.)

A white-plumaged juvenile Little Blue Heron is an exception to this easy separation, and may require careful scrutiny to separate it from the similar juvenile Snowy Egret. (See Figure 64, p. 67.) Reddish Egret falls in between Great Egret and the four medium-sized herons in size, and a combination of its exuberant behavior and regionally dominant dark-morph plumage color usually results in a quick ID. (See Figure 62, p. 65.)

In the heat haze of Bolivar Flats, I barely make out a distant black smudge on the mudflat. From experience, I know this is a group of roosting Black Skimmers, whose very short legs and low-profile bodies create an indefinable black spot at a great distance. There are no other low-profile birds with

black upperparts that flock together and could be mistaken for Black Skimmer on this open coastal habitat.

This short field scenario shows the value of using an initial ID approach that calls on my recognition of familiar birds' sizes, shapes, and behaviors in a distant view, and a closer approach that uses a more detailed evaluation of structural features and an analysis of plumage and bare-parts details to separate similar species.

LOCATION 2: *Mixed Deciduous Woodland, Magee Marsh, Ohio, in May, by Dale*

This tight, closed habitat typically allows views of birds at limited distances, and often for only a short period of time. There is little time for leisurely scanning, with birds quickly appearing and then disappearing behind leaves and branches. If they fly to another location, it is easy to lose track of them for good.

Usually I watch an area of vegetation without focusing my eyes and wait for movement contrary to normal leaf motion. This works well to locate birds, unless it is very windy.

While it takes a great deal of practice to spot subtle movements in densely vegetated areas, it takes just as much skill to point your binoculars to the correct location. It helps to hold your binoculars

FIGURE 18. WOODLAND HABITAT
This densely wooded scene is typical of a forested habitat where warblers and other songbirds are found. It is often difficult to spot and follow songbirds in this type of habitat.

near your chin while waiting to spot movement so you can quickly raise them to your eyes.

Often I don't see the whole bird at one time, but instead build the bird in my mind by tying its parts together for an overall impression. So it becomes essential to evaluate quick glimpses of a bird's size, shape, and structural features to help narrow my choices, especially when general coloration and plumage patterns don't assist with the ID.

Without benefit of nearby familiar species for comparison, it is more difficult to establish a bird's size, but visualizing familiar birds next to unfamiliar ones helps, especially if I've recently seen the familiar bird and its image and relative size are fresh in my mind. By referencing memories of long versus short wings and tail, heavy bills versus slender ones, and bulky versus slender bodies, I quickly evaluate several important physical characteristics.

I also find that a songbird's behavior often helps with the ID process. American Redstart is especially animated in its feeding behavior, and it often acts like a flycatcher. Besides the frequent spreading of its tail and side-to-side body motion as it moves along a branch, it may fly upward, downward, or sideways in pursuit of a flying insect. (See Figure 19, p. 19.) If a small bird suddenly drops off a branch and falls toward the ground, it probably is

an American Redstart in pursuit of an insect. This feeding style is unique to American Redstart, less so for the southwestern Painted Redstart (see Figure 19, p. 19), and a quick look at their coloration and behavior is all that is needed to identify these distinctive warblers.

Scarlet Tanager, by contrast, is a slow, methodical feeder that prefers to sit quietly between forays as it scans nearby leaves for food. It may then fly to grab a bee, larger insect, or berry before moving to a secluded perch to eat. Often it remains motionless for minutes, which makes for difficult spotting. Even a bright crimson red bird with black wings can be hard to locate when it is motionless in a leafed-out tree. Leaves and branches always seem to block my view, and I often catch only glimpses of body parts. A full view of this spectacular bird always takes my breath away. (See Figure 19, p. 19.)

I also recognize about five to seven songs of warblers and other songbirds. Ovenbird, Northern Parula, Eastern Towhee, Yellow and Magnolia Warblers, and Great Crested Flycatcher are all singing at the same time, but previous experience with these calls allows for instant recognition of them all.

While scanning the woods, I spot the distinctive motion of a Black-and-white Warbler creeping along a thick horizontal branch, and the furtive

FIGURE 19. AMERICAN REDSTART, SCARLET TANAGER, AND PAINTED REDSTART
Animated tail fanning is part of American Redstart's (L) foraging behavior. A breeding male Scarlet Tanager (C) is unmistakable with its bright red body and contrasting black wings. Also note the tanager's larger size and more sedentary foraging behavior in your field study. Painted Redstart (R) is a bird of the southwestern U.S. and does not occur at Magee Marsh.

movements of a Northern Waterthrush walking along the edge of a small wet area. Most warblers hop, but both waterthrushes walk along the ground, similar to a small number of other ground-dwelling warblers. This type of body motion (walking versus hopping) may be important to the ID of some species, especially when separating Connecticut Warbler (walks) from female Common Yellowthroat (hops), which are similar in nonbreeding plumage. (See Figure 189, p. 224.)

I'm drawn to the familiar undulating flight of a Downy Woodpecker as it moves through the trees, and while I watch it hitch up a tree, a medium-sized flash of yellow appears and disappears near the outer edges of the branches. Closer examination shows that it is larger than a warbler but more slender and elongated than a tanager, and the female Baltimore Oriole eventually comes into full view for a confirmation on the ID.

Woodland birding is like doing a jigsaw puzzle: usually challenging, sometimes frustrating, but always rewarding when the pieces come together for a positive ID.

A BEGINNER'S VIEW OF A SAMPLE WOODLAND HABITAT

New birders face more challenges when visiting a woodland location. A good starting point for beginners is to locate and identify a few distinctively plumaged birds, such as male American Redstart or Scarlet Tanager. (See Figure 19, above.) Painted Redstart and male Western Tanager are similar striking western species. These birds are so distinct in color and plumage patterns that even a quick glimpse provides enough visual information to find them in a field guide.

Once you've located them in your guide, look up their sizes and study the body shapes and structural features. Then compare them with other birds on nearby pages and note sizes and structural differences. Important features include head and body shape; bill length, shape, and color; wing and tail length; and general plumage patterns and coloration. When you become familiar with a small number of birds, you can use them for size and shape comparisons with unfamiliar ones, even if the familiar birds are not in view.

ACCOUNTS

Many waterfowl species are distinctive in their size, shape, and plumage and are fairly easy to identify. Some appear very similar, however, and present formidable ID challenges. Since assorted waterfowl species often occur together, you can easily compare their size differences and physical features. (See Figure 20, below.)

Hunters share a strong appreciation of waterfowl with birders and have perfected the skill of recognizing ducks and geese using familiar impressions of size, body shape, and flight motion. They compare waterfowl flight movements to evaluate subtle differences in wing-flap speed and motion. They also rely on intuitive recognition of familiar waterfowl, even in silhouette, which is the same as the BBI ID approach.

DUCKS

Ducks are primarily aquatic birds and are generally separated into two groups. Dabbling ducks (dabblers) tip their bodies to feed on submerged vegetation in shallow water, and diving ducks (divers) swim underwater to find food. Occasionally some diving ducks search for food on the water's surface,

and dabbling ducks may submerge their bodies to reach food, but these instances are exceptions rather than the rule. Most ducks generally form small to large flocks away from breeding areas. Three species of perching ducks (Fulvous Whistling-Duck, Black-bellied Whistling-Duck, and Wood Duck) are similar to dabblers in feeding behavior, but all three perch on tree limbs and nest in cavities.

PHYSICAL PROFILE

Ducks have variably rounded, elongated bodies. Their legs are generally short, and their feet are fully webbed. Most ducks have relatively short necks and flattened bills that are rounded at the tip. (See Figure 21, p. 23.) Mergansers differ with their slender, pointed bills. Some aquatic birds have physical features that resemble those of ducks, but genetically they belong to other bird families. (See Figure 22, p. 24.)

BIRDING BY IMPRESSION INFORMATION

SIZE: Ducks range in size from Bufflehead, at 13½ in. long (slightly larger than Rock Pigeon), to the long-bodied Common Merganser at 25 in. long (about the length of Brant or Herring Gull).

FIGURE 20. MIXED FLOCK OF WATERFOWL (QUIZ PHOTO)
This image from Klamath Falls, OR, shows an assortment of waterfowl. Try to identify the birds in this photo. Hint: Swans, geese, and ducks are shown. Answers are in the appendix, page 267.

FIGURE 21. DUCKS

Four species of dabbling and diving ducks. The dabblers are a male Northern Shoveler (top L) and a female Mottled Duck (bottom L). The diving ducks are a nonbreeding male Long-tailed Duck (top R) and a male Black Scoter (bottom R).

At roughly 23 in. long, the three largest dabblers (Mottled Duck, Mallard, and American Black Duck) have noticeably larger, bulkier bodies than other dabbling ducks. Green-winged Teal is the smallest dabbler, at 14 in. long. The three teal species are visibly smaller than other dabbling ducks, which is obvious when you see them with other species.

A few diving ducks are found in the same freshwater locations as teal and range in size from slightly larger than teal (Lesser Scaup and Ring-necked Duck) to smaller (Ruddy Duck and Bufflehead).

STRUCTURAL FEATURES: The legs of dabbling ducks are situated near the middle of their body. This anatomical design makes sense since these birds use their feet mostly for casual motoring on the water's surface and walking on land while grazing vegetation. Dabblers generally have short necks and short, thick legs. Some perching ducks, such as

Fulvous and Black-bellied Whistling-Ducks, have long legs and necks. (See Figure 23, p. 24.)

Most diving ducks are heavier bodied and have smaller, more pointed wings than dabblers. Their legs are positioned closer to the rear of their bodies, which allows them to efficiently swim underwater but makes it difficult to walk on land.

Diving ducks have a wide variety of body shapes and structural features. They range from large, heavy-bodied eiders and scoters to the small, compact Ruddy Duck, Bufflehead, and Hooded Merganser. A small number of diving ducks (scaup, Ring-necked Duck, Redhead, and Tufted Duck) share similar body shapes and structural features with some dabbling ducks, but most divers have the characteristic features mentioned above.

BEHAVIOR: Ducks of similar size and wing shape exhibit distinctive flight motion. Small ducks, such as Bufflehead, Hooded Merganser, and Green-winged Teal, have short, pointed wings, fast wingbeats, and

FIGURE 22. DUCK LOOK-ALIKES (QUIZ PHOTO)
These four species look similar to ducks but are unrelated to them. Can you identify them? Answers are in the appendix, page 267.

FIGURE 23. WHISTLING-DUCKS AND HARLEQUIN DUCK
Whistling-ducks differ from other ducks in having long legs and necks, and by sexes appearing similar. A soft warm plumage and plain face result in a gentle-looking expression. Note the explosive takeoff from a floating position in the Fulvous Whistling-Duck (C); this is typical of all whistling-ducks (L, Black-bellied Whistling-Ducks) and dabblers. A male Harlequin Duck (R) running along the water typifies the type of motion that diving ducks need to take flight.

a rapid flight style. Larger ducks with longer, broader wings, such as scoters, eiders, and large dabblers, have slower wing strokes and a more deliberate flight style. Dabbling ducks and perching ducks explode into flight from a floating position, whereas diving ducks need a running start to take flight. (See Figure 23, above.)

PLUMAGE PATTERNS AND GENERAL COLORATION: Most duck species exhibit distinct plumage differences between males (drakes) and females (hens), with males being more colorful. Exceptions include Black-bellied and Fulvous Whistling-Ducks, whose sexes appear similar (see Figure 23, above), and American Black Duck and Mottled Duck, which show only minor bill coloration differences between sexes (see Figure 24, p. 25).

Identification of most male ducks is fairly straightforward due to obvious differences in plumage. Females exhibit more muted plumage patterns, however, and often appear more similar to each other.

Several species of ducks appear similar in plumage and require careful study of subtle structural features, such as head and bill shape, to help with their separation. Some hard-to-identify species include Lesser versus Greater Scaup; Common versus Barrow's Goldeneye females; Blue-winged, Green-winged, and Cinnamon Teal females; and American Black Duck versus Mottled Duck. (See Comparisons of Similar Species, p. 25.)

Redhead, Ring-necked Duck, and Canvasback females are somewhat similar in plumage tones and patterning, but a careful comparison of their different structural features helps separate these species. (See Comparisons of Similar Species, p. 26.)

HABITAT USE: During nesting season, ducks inhabit a variety of habitats, including Arctic tundra, fast-flowing streams, prairie potholes, lakes, marshes, and neighborhood ponds. In winter they move to sites that don't freeze, including shoreline habitats and large bodies of water.

While dabbling ducks are usually found in shallow freshwater locations, Green and Blue-winged Teal are common seasonal migrants offshore, where they may occur in the middle of large migrant scoter flocks. Diving ducks typically frequent deeper water, including lakes, bays, and estuaries. In fall and winter, many wild ducks are found in city parks, where they occur with domesticated ducks in small ponds and on grassy lawns.

VOCALIZATIONS: Except for a small number of species, duck vocalizations rarely play a role in the ID process. While several ducks have distinctive calls that are easily recognized, others are rarely heard away from breeding areas.

The three largest dabbling ducks (Mallard, Mottled Duck, and American Black Duck) give a loud quacking sound that most people identify as a "duck call." Female Gadwall gives a call similar to these species, but it is more nasal and less emphatic. Both whistling-ducks have distinctive wheezy, high-pitched, whistling calls.

Wood Duck gives a recognizable squeaky whistle, while male American Wigeon has a memorable two- or three-syllable, high-pitched whistled call. These are some of the more distinctive duck vocalizations, with several species giving a variety of low grunts, soft quacks, and muffled calls.

COMPARISONS OF SIMILAR SPECIES

American Black Duck and Mottled Duck

Separate geographic locations help with the ID of these similar species. American Black Duck has a more northerly range that extends south to northern Alabama in winter, while resident Mottled Duck is found through most of Florida and coastal South Carolina, and from southern Louisiana south along the Texas coast into Mexico. Black Duck breeds in and frequents saltwater marshes and bays, while Mottled breeds in and prefers freshwater habitats.

UNCHANGING CHARACTERISTICS: Size, structural features, and behavior are similar.

SUPPLEMENTAL CHARACTERISTICS AND NON-BBI DETAILS: American Black Duck is darker overall and lacks the prominent pale markings of most body feathers in Mottled Duck. Black Duck also has a grayer, less

contrasting head pattern with fine streaks on the neck and face that are absent in the warmer buff-colored head and neck of Mottled. Some "Texas" Mottleds, however, show variable fine streaks on the neck and head. Male Black Duck has a greenish yellow bill, while the female has a dark olive bill, like the left bird in Figure 24. Male Mottled has a yellow bill, like the right bird in Figure 24, while the female has an olive drab to orange bill, like the center bird in Figure 24.

Mottled Duck has a thin white border (absent in Black Duck) on a purple and black speculum (markings on the trailing edge of the inner upperwing feathers), but this white border may disappear in worn plumage. (See Figure 21, p. 23.) Mottled also has a black spot on the gape that is lacking in Black Duck. (See Figure 24, below.)

The western Gulf Coast population of Mottled Duck is often harder to separate from Black Duck, with some birds having a darker overall plumage than Florida and southeastern U.S. birds. The dark gape mark on these birds is also much smaller and is easily overlooked without conscious observation of this field mark. (See Figure 24, below.) However, the aforementioned plumage features are usually reliable.

Greater Scaup and Lesser Scaup

UNCHANGING CHARACTERISTICS: Greater Scaup is slightly larger than Lesser Scaup and has a more rounded head shape with a peak closer to the front of the crown. Some Greaters may have a rounded front and rear crown like the male in Figure 25, but the lower-profile head, with an evenly rounded shape, differs from that of Lesser, which has a taller, narrower head with a higher-profile crown. This can result in the eye being lower on the head in Lesser due to the higher crown profile.

FIGURE 24. AMERICAN BLACK DUCK AND MOTTLED DUCK

These two closely related ducks have identical physical features, so plumage details and bill markings are important to their ID. The western Gulf Coast population of Mottled Duck (C, female) is shown because some individuals appear more similar in plumage to American Black Duck (L, female) than to other Mottled Ducks. ID information is provided in the text. Note the western Gulf Coast Mottled Duck's reduced black gape marking (dark mark at base of bill), which is much less obvious than in southeastern U.S. and Florida Mottled Ducks (R, male).

The slimmer head of Lesser also has a noticeable slope to the rear crown below the peak. Be aware that these features vary depending on the duck's behavior and are best evaluated on relaxed birds. For example, the female Greater in Figure 25 shows the bump only on the forecrown because of its alert posture, and the female Lesser appears to have a larger, bulkier head than the female Greater because its neck is retracted and bulges out in the rear. (See Figure 25, below.)

Greater Scaup has a larger, wider bill, which typically has a more prominent dark nail at the tip, while Lesser has a slightly smaller, thinner, straighter bill, with a black nail that may be hard to see because it is small and narrow.

SUPPLEMENTAL CHARACTERISTICS AND NON-BBI DETAILS: Greater Scaup tends to have heavier, coarser dark barring on the back than Lesser, but we find this feature to be variable and often hard to determine in the field. While male Greater usually has a greenish gloss to the head and neck, and male Lesser a purple gloss, both can have a mix of these colors, depending on the light.

Redhead, Canvasback, and Ring-necked Duck, Females

UNCHANGING CHARACTERISTICS: Canvasback is the largest of these three (21 in. long) and has a longer neck, flatter forehead, and long, evenly sloped, pointed bill, which can resemble a ski slope. Redhead (19 in. long) has a more rounded body and head. Ring-necked Duck is smallish (17 in. long) and compact with a peaked rear crown. (See Figure 26, p. 27.)

SUPPLEMENTAL CHARACTERISTICS AND NON-BBI DETAILS: General coloration of these three ducks is similar, but female Canvasback differs with its mostly plain brown plumage. Redhead is similar to Canvasback in shading but has a slightly darker head. Ring-necked Duck has a darker brown back and crown, gray cheeks, white eye-ring, and white feathering near the bill.

Blue-winged, Cinnamon, and Green-winged Teal, Females

Female Blue-winged and Cinnamon Teal can be difficult to separate in the field, and this dilemma may

---

FIGURE 25. GREATER SCAUP AND LESSER SCAUP (QUIZ PHOTO)
Though Greater Scaup and Lesser Scaup are very similar in plumage, this composite shows the subtle structural and bill differences. Detailed ID information is provided in the text on page 25. Try to identify males and females of both species. Answers are in the appendix, page 267.

FIGURE 26. REDHEAD, CANVASBACK, AND RING-NECKED DUCK, FEMALES (QUIZ PHOTO)
While general coloration of these three diving ducks is similar, differences in size, body structure, head and bill shape, and subtle plumage details help separate them. ID information is provided in the text on page 26. Try to identify these birds. Answers are in the appendix, page 267.

FIGURE 27. BLUE-WINGED, CINNAMON, AND GREEN-WINGED TEAL, FEMALES (QUIZ PHOTO)
Recognizable differences among female teal include Cinnamon Teal's larger, more Northern Shoveler–like bill and warmer, plainer facial pattern, and Green-winged Teal's smaller head and bill and more prominent facial markings. Can you identify these birds? Detailed ID information is provided in the text on page 26, and answers are in the appendix, page 267.

be compounded by challenging viewing conditions. Female Green-winged Teal poses problems mostly for beginning birders because of its superficial similarity to the other teal species, but it differs in size, structure, and plumage. (See Figure 27, above.)

UNCHANGING CHARACTERISTICS: Cinnamon Teal has a longer, more Northern Shoveler–like bill that widens near the tip, which can be a reliable structural feature to separate it from the very similar Blue-winged Teal. Cinnamon's head is also slightly longer from front to back, but this feature can be hard to judge in the field. Female Green-winged Teal is smaller compared with other teal, and has a more compact body shape, smaller head, and smaller, thinner bill.

SUPPLEMENTAL CHARACTERISTICS AND NON-BBI DETAILS: Cinnamon Teal has a warmer, plainer facial pattern with less white feathering at the base of the bill than Blue-winged Teal. On average, Cinnamon's flanks are also plainer and warmer with less defined markings. Female Blue-winged Teal typically has more prominent white eye-arcs and a thin dark eye line. Dark facial stripes and a green and black speculum (not visible in the photo in Figure 27) in Green-

winged Teal help identify this species without too much trouble. (See Figure 27, above.)

Common and King Eiders, Females
UNCHANGING CHARACTERISTICS: Common Eider's elongated body and long neck differ from King Eider's compact body structure and shorter, thicker neck. Common has a longer head and bill than King, and shows more exposed bare bill extending up onto the forehead. Common's longer bill also slopes noticeably upward to a rising forecrown, which adds to its different head shape. Because of these features, Common's bill appears angled toward the water, while King offers a more horizontal bill impression. These different profiles are valuable when trying to identify these species in rough seas or poor lighting conditions. (See Figure 28, p. 28.)

SUPPLEMENTAL CHARACTERISTICS AND NON-BBI DETAILS: Female King Eider has more prominent white feathering around the eye and bill compared with Common Eider's plain face. Female Common has a warmer, more uniform overall plumage (except for the grayer subspecies S.m. sedentaria at Hudson Bay), including the head, while female King usually has a paler head. The curved gape and rounded

FIGURE 28. COMMON EIDER AND KING EIDER, FEMALES AND FIRST-WINTER MALE KING EIDER
The left photo shows a female (front C) and first-winter male King Eider (R) and a female Common Eider (top L). ID information is provided in the text on page 27. The two right photos show a clearer view of female Common (top) and female King (bottom) Eiders. First-winter male King Eider differs from female King Eider by its darker plumage, white chest (not visible), and pinkish orange bill.

feathering on King's bill base give it a grinning impression, while Common appears to have a more somber facial expression.

GEESE

Most geese breed in Arctic or subarctic habitats and migrate south to warmer locations, where they form large flocks during late fall and winter. Although generally found near water, geese spend more time on land while foraging for food than ducks do.

The small number of geese (eight species) that breed or occur as regular vagrants in North America are distinctive in plumage and pose few ID problems. Exceptions include separating Snow Goose from Ross's Goose and small subspecies of Canada Goose from Cackling Goose. (See Comparisons of Similar Species, p. 29.) Sexes are similar.

PHYSICAL PROFILE

Geese have heavier and more rounded bodies than ducks. They have short, thick legs and fully webbed feet. Their moderately long necks are longer than those of ducks (except whistling-ducks), and their bills are smaller and more pointed than those of ducks. (See Figure 29, p. 29.)

BIRDING BY IMPRESSION INFORMATION

SIZE: Most geese share a narrow size range (25–28 in. long), being slightly larger than Mallard and American Black Duck. "Greater" Snow Goose is larger, at 31 in. long, and some subspecies of Canada Goose are very large, up to 46 in. long.

STRUCTURAL FEATURES: Differences in bill and head shape, as well as comparative neck length, are useful structural differences when identifying geese. A small-headed, small-billed, short-necked appearance is typical of Brant and Ross's, Emperor, Cackling, and Barnacle Geese, while Canada, Snow, and Greater White-fronted Geese have larger, heavier bodies, longer necks, and larger heads and bills.

A few of the small geese (Emperor, Ross's, and "Lesser" Snow Geese) have more rounded bodies and a less attenuated rear body shape than others. (See Figure 30, p. 30.) The larger subspecies of Canada Goose have the longest necks of all geese.

BEHAVIOR: Geese are slow, lumbering birds on land, with physical features ill-suited for fast motion. They are more at home in the water, where powerful feet propel them. Geese are graceful in the air, with long, broad wings enabling powerful, steady flight. They often fly in V formation during migration.

PLUMAGE PATTERNS AND GENERAL COLORATION: All geese have mostly black, brown, white, or gray plumage tones and lack colorful feathering. They show a variety of plumage features, ranging from the all-white plumage with black wingtips of Snow and Ross's Geese (except for dark-morph birds) to Greater White-fronted Goose's brownish upperparts and black-barred belly (adults).

HABITAT USE: Geese spend a good deal of time in aquatic habitats, including lakes, ponds, and coastal bays. Many species, however, forage extensively in grassy fields and fallow agricultural areas, especially in winter, and return to roost in wetlands at night.

VOCALIZATIONS: Geese give a variety of soft to loud honking or grunting calls, especially when agitated or in flight. A few species, including White-fronted, Snow, and Canada Geese, have louder, more emphatic calls. Others, such as Brant and Emperor and Barnacle Geese, have softer, less emphatic calls.

COMPARISONS OF SIMILAR SPECIES

Snow Goose and Ross's Goose

"Greater" Snow Goose breeds in tundra locations in eastern North America and winters mostly in the Mid-Atlantic coastal region. "Lesser" Snow Goose and Ross's Goose breed in more western Arctic locations, and "Lesser" winters locally mainly across scattered portions of the southern and western United States. Ross's winters mostly in the western United States.

UNCHANGING CHARACTERISTICS: Ross's Goose is substantially smaller (23 in. long) than "Lesser" (28 in. long) and "Greater" (31 in. long) Snow Geese, and Ross's has a more rounded body shape. Ross's also has a shorter neck, steeper forehead, and more rounded head compared with Snow's longer, lower-profile, wedge-shaped head. Because of the higher crown in Ross's, its eyes sit lower on the head than on Snow. While both have stocky bills, Ross's is tinier, stubbier, and more triangular-shaped.

FIGURE 29. GEESE
Four common North American geese, *clockwise from top left:* Dark-morph "Lesser" Snow Goose, Ross's Goose, Greater White-fronted Goose, and Eastern ("Pale-bellied") Brant. Two birds are shown on land since geese forage in terrestrial habitats more than ducks do.

FIGURE 30. ROSS'S GOOSE AND SNOW GOOSE (QUIZ PHOTO—TOP)

Top: Snow Goose differs from Ross's Goose in structure and plumage, as explained in the text. Try to identify three birds of two species based on the information provided. Answers are in the appendix, page 267.
Bottom: Head shots of "Lesser" Snow Goose (L), Ross's Goose (C), and a hybrid "Lesser" Snow Goose × Ross's Goose (R). Compare the head and bill shape differences among these birds. On the hybrid, note the partially curved feathering at the base of the bill, the intermediate sloped forecrown, and the partial rounded crown that falls in between the two species in shape. Also note how the eye sits higher on the head than it does on Ross's, but lower than on Snow Goose. Ross's has a higher, domed crown and steeper forecrown compared with the lower-profile, flatter crown, and shallow forecrown on "Lesser" and "Greater" Snow Geese.

FIGURE 31. CANADA GOOSE AND CACKLING GOOSE

Left photo: A direct comparison of a Cackling Goose of the "Richardson's" subspecies (L) and a "Greater" Canada Goose (R) in Cape May, NJ, in September. Note the much smaller size; smaller bill; slightly steeper forecrown; smaller, rounded head; and duskier chest shading on the Cackling Goose. This last plumage feature is usually more pronounced than this photo shows, and Canada Goose typically shows a shallower forecrown than this bird has. *Right photo:* A direct flight comparison of Cackling Goose (below) and Canada Goose (above). Note the much smaller size and shorter neck and bill on Cackling Goose.

SUPPLEMENTAL CHARACTERISTICS AND NON-BBI DETAILS: Both species have a white overall plumage with black wingtips and pinkish orange bill. A reliable plumage feature for separating Ross's Goose from Snow Goose is the shape of the feathering line at the base of the bill. In Ross's, the feathering is mostly straight and vertical from the bottom of the bill base to the top, while Snow has a curved border to the bill-base feathering. (See Figure 30, p. 30.)

A supporting bare-parts detail not always visible in the field is a bluish cast to the bill base on Ross's, which is not present on Snow. Snow has a sizeable grin patch (dark border separating the upper and lower mandibles), while Ross's has a variably small grin patch that is often hard to see.

Moderate numbers of "Lesser" Snow Geese have a dark-morph plumage (see Figure 29, p. 29), but a dark-morph plumage is presently rare in "Greater" Snow Goose and is very rare in Ross's. The dark-morph plumage of Ross's differs noticeably from that of Snow by having a blacker back and nape and mostly white wing coverts and flight feathers (see Figures 29 and 30). Juvenile white-morph Ross's is whiter than juvenile Snow and lacks dusky tones to the head, back, and neck.

Some small "Lesser" Snows and Ross's x Snow Goose hybrids are difficult to separate from Ross's without direct comparison, or without careful assessment of the above-mentioned structural features and plumage or bare-parts differences. Hybrids often show features that fall in between those of either species, which further reinforces our recommendation that you evaluate a bird's structural features while actively comparing it with nearby similar species, all in the same thought process. This is the essence of the BBI approach. (See Figure 30, p. 30.)

Canada Goose and Cackling Goose

The Canada Goose complex is just that: complex. There are numerous subspecies, with intergrade variations resulting in a variety of plumage and structural appearances. Within the species' breeding range, Canada Geese average smaller toward the north and darker toward the west. Because of their isolated breeding ranges, subspecies of Cackling Goose do not regularly interbreed among themselves or with Canada Goose, but as numbers of both species continue to increase, hybridization between them is bound to increase. At present, however, Cackling Goose tends to have distinct physical features for subspecies rather than the great variation found in Canada Goose.

UNCHANGING CHARACTERISTICS: The four smallest former subspecies of Canada Goose now belong to a species called Cackling Goose. They are much smaller than Canada Goose and have longer wings that usually extend past the folded tail. They also have shorter necks; a steeper forehead; and very small, stubby bills compared with Canada Goose. (See Figure 31, p. 30.)

SUPPLEMENTAL CHARACTERISTICS AND NON-BBI DETAILS: Cackling Goose plumage differs from that of larger subspecies of Canada Goose by the brownish wash on the upper breast versus a whitish upper breast on Canada, but this feature is reliable only in geographic areas where "Lesser" Canada Goose does not occur. Some "Lesser" Canadas also have brownish upper breasts and closely resemble some Cackling Geese. A white lower neck ring can occur on both Cackling and "Lesser" Canada.

SWANS

Swans are the largest of all waterfowl. While typically found near water, swans often graze on vegetation in marshes and in fields or grassy areas adjacent to water bodies. Even though they walk in a clumsy fashion, swans are quick-moving on land if threatened. Sexes are similar, although males average larger than females and may have larger bills in Trumpeter and Tundra Swans. Mute Swan is a species that was introduced from Europe and Asia in the late 1800s. The population has increased dramatically since that time, posing significant ecological challenges.

PHYSICAL PROFILE

Swans have elongated, rounded, football-shaped bodies. They have heavier bodies, longer necks, and larger bills than geese. Their legs are short and thick, and their feet are fully webbed. (See Figure 32, p. 32.)

BIRDING BY IMPRESSION INFORMATION

SIZE: Swans are substantially larger than geese, with Tundra Swan averaging 52 in. long (about the size of Brown Pelican) and Trumpeter and Mute Swans being 60 in. long, which is slightly smaller than White Pelican. Trumpeter Swan is the heaviest bird in North America; some males can weigh as much as 32 lbs.

Although Trumpeter and Mute Swans may be substantially larger than Tundra Swan, this size difference is hard to notice with just one species present. Since male swans (cobs) are larger than females, a very large male Tundra Swan can be close in size to a small female Trumpeter.

STRUCTURAL FEATURES: Swans typically hold their necks fully outstretched in flight. However, Mute Swan often holds its neck angled toward the back while swimming, which creates a different appear-

FIGURE 32. SWANS

The three species of swans regularly found in North America are, *from left to right*, Trumpeter Swan, Tundra Swan, and Mute Swan. The birds shown here are all adults, but note the brownish back of a juvenile Mute Swan in the right photo.

ance from the typical straight-necked or slightly curve-necked impression of the other two species. (See Figure 32, above.) Trumpeter Swan has a longer neck and bill compared with Tundra Swan. But care should be taken with some female Trumpeters whose shorter bill and neck lengths are closer in size and proportion to those of some large male Tundras.

Mute Swan has a proportionally shorter, stockier bill with a protruding black knob just below the forecrown. Its noticeably longer tail compared with that of the other swans creates a more elongated body impression on swimming and flying birds. Juvenile Mute Swan has a similar bill shape and facial skin pattern as adults but lacks their protruding knob.

BEHAVIOR: Swans are vegetarians; they often feed with their heads submerged and pull aquatic vegetation from pond and marsh bottoms.

PLUMAGE PATTERNS AND GENERAL COLORATION: All three adult swans are white overall and lack black wingtips (as opposed to similar large white waterbirds, such as Snow Geese, which have black wingtips, and White Pelican, which has a black trailing edge to the wing). Immature swans have variably dusky plumage tones, though some juvenile Mute Swans have a mostly white plumage. Mute Swan is distinctive in adult plumage, with a bright orange bill and black facial skin border, while Trumpeter and Tundra Swans have black bills. (See Figure 32, above.) Immature Mute Swan has a dusky to pale pinkish bill. Some Tundra Swans have a yellow spot near the eye, which Trumpeter rarely shows.

HABITAT USE: Mute Swan is mostly restricted to aquatic habitats in a limited northeast Atlantic, Mid-Atlantic, and Great Lakes range and is often found in suburban and urban settings. Trumpeter and Tundra Swans occur together at a small number of wintering areas, and both species occasionally occur with Mute Swan in winter.

VOCALIZATIONS: Mute Swan is mostly silent but does give a variety of territorial calls, including hisses, grunts, and a bugling call similar to that of Tundra Swan. Trumpeter Swan is typically less vocal than Tundra but has a deep, resonant, trumpet-like call that differs from Tundra's clear hooting or barking calls.

COMPARISONS OF SIMILAR SPECIES

Trumpeter Swan and Tundra Swan

Identification of Trumpeter and Tundra Swans can be very difficult, especially with single birds. While geographic location may be helpful for separating these two species, especially in summer, both commonly occur together in the northern Pacific Coast region in winter, and small numbers of introduced Trumpeters now reside and migrate with Tundras in the Midwest and eastern United States and Canada.

UNCHANGING CHARACTERISTICS: Though Trumpeter Swan is larger than Tundra Swan and has a longer neck in direct comparison, both features are hard to evaluate with just one species present. Small female Trumpeters and large male Tundras can be close in size, and variability in neck length may reduce the effectiveness of these features in the ID process.

A somewhat reliable feature for separation of many birds is Trumpeter's longer, straighter bill versus Tundra's shorter one. On average, males have larger bills than females, so caution is advised with some female Trumpeters and male Tundras, where bill size overlap may occur. (See Figure 33, p. 33.) Another helpful feature on some birds is the higher-profile rear crown of Trumpeter, which differs slightly from the uniformly rounded head of most Tundras. This feature is best assessed on birds whose crown feathers are relaxed and not raised.

A good structural feature on standing birds is Trumpeter's much larger feet compared with Tundra's smaller ones. Evaluation of this feature, however, relies on direct comparison or familiarity with the differences in foot size.

TYPICAL BILL FEATHERING

TRUMPETER SWAN:
Male paired with bird
below in Alaska

pointed feather line

straight line of feathering

TUNDRA SWAN

rounded feather line

angled line of feathering

ATYPICAL BILL FEATHERING

TRUMPETER SWAN:
Female paired
with bird above

angled line of feathering

TUNDRA SWAN

fairly straight feathering line

FIGURE 33. TRUMPETER SWAN AND TUNDRA SWAN BILL FEATHERING AND SHAPE DIFFERENCES
This shows typical bill shape and adjacent bill feathering patterns of Trumpeter and Tundra Swans, and atypical variations that may occur. Note the larger bill on the "typical" Trumpeter Swan (male) versus a smaller bill on its mate in the "atypical" photo (female). This variable bill size can muddy an already difficult separation of these two species, especially when you compare a female Trumpeter Swan with a small bill to a male Tundra Swan with a large bill. Sex of the two pictured Tundra Swans is unknown, but the adult bird (bottom R) appears to have a similar-sized bill as the female Trumpeter Swan (bottom L). An immature Tundra Swan (upper R) is shown to illustrate possible bill feathering similarities in these two species.

SUPPLEMENTAL CHARACTERISTICS AND NON-BBI DETAILS: Trumpeter Swan normally shows a straighter line of feathering extending from the base of the lower mandible to the eye. Tundra Swan typically shows feathering that rises upward from the bottom of the bill but then angles toward the eye just above the gape. (See Figure 33, p. 33.)

While the difference in bill-border feathering is often reliable, some birds show variations of the other species' expected pattern, so a combination of pertinent field marks and structural features is recommended for separation. Another helpful plumage detail in adult birds is the shape of feathering on the forehead. In Trumpeter, the forehead has a pointed feathered border versus a rounded border in Tundra. (See Figure 33, p. 33.) These feathering lines are often clear-cut in adults, but they are not always reliable in young birds. Photo angles may also affect your assessment of the feather lines, as well as your personal understanding of the difference between variable rounded lines versus pointed feather lines.

A fairly reliable bare-parts detail useful in separating adult birds is the presence of yellow color in the lores of Tundra, which rarely but sometimes occurs with Trumpeter. (See Figure 33, p. 33.) However, not all Tundras have yellow in the loral area.

Another helpful bare-parts detail is the wider black facial skin that connects the bill to the eye on Trumpeter versus a narrower line of dark skin in Tundra. Birds on the extreme range of these parameters can be safely identified using this feature, but this detail is otherwise best left out of the ID process.

Trumpeter and Tundra Swans, Immatures

Some immature Tundra Swans may closely resemble immature Trumpeter Swans, but a few bare-parts and plumage details help separate them. Young Tundras (July through October) have a mostly pinkish orange bill with limited black at the base until late fall, when the bill appears all black, like that of the immature bird in Figure 33 (photographed in January). Young Trumpeters show extensive black at the bill base with a pinkish outer portion, and their bills are also all black by late fall. Some juvenile Trumpeters may show variations in their bill color and patterns, and Kevin has photographed a few juvenile Trumpeters in Ohio in September with all orange bills.

As the immature Tundra's bill starts to turn black in late fall, it can be difficult to pick out the differences from immature Trumpeter. Young Trumpeters retain a muted gray-brown coloration on their backs until the end of their first year (early summer), while young Tundras have a whiter back from early winter onward.

This large group of loosely related birds comprises mostly native North American species, but a number of foreign game birds that were introduced for hunting purposes and are presently on the American Birding Association (ABA) species list are also included. All species are nonmigratory, with the exception of some Arctic-breeding ptarmigans and high-elevation breeding species that have relatively short, localized seasonal movements.

TIPS FOR VIEWING UPLAND GAME BIRDS

Because game birds are hunted, they are often not as easy to observe as other species, and more planning may be required to see them. Many species form small to large flocks outside the breeding season, and several species display at communal leks during breeding season (prairie-chickens, sage-grouse, and Sharp-tailed Grouse). Some wildlife refuges provide access to viewing blinds for these displays. Many game birds, especially quails, visit feeding stations, particularly in the early morning.

When you encounter game birds in the wild, stay as still as possible. After a short time, birds will either sense that there is no danger and resume foraging, or they will start moving slowly away from you. Sudden movements cause game birds to move away quickly or explode into flight, so moving slowly will help you get a better vantage point.

PHYSICAL PROFILE

All game birds have chickenlike bodies, although some are more elongated (Wild Turkey and Plain Chachalaca), while others are compact and rounded (quails and Chukar). They have short, powerful legs suited for a fast getaway and strong, stubby bills used for cracking open seeds and nuts. Most species have short necks and tails, but several have moderate to long necks and long tails (Plain Chachalaca, Wild Turkey, Ring-necked Pheasant, male sage-grouse). (See Figure 34, below.)

BIRDING BY IMPRESSION INFORMATION

SIZE: Game birds come in a wide range of sizes, from the small Montezuma Quail, at 8¾ in. long (about the size of Sora), to the giant male Wild Turkey, at 46 in. long (about the same size as the largest Canada Goose).

Although some similar game birds are close in size, a general review of sizes will help you separate birds that occur in the same geographic area, such

---

FIGURE 34. UPLAND GAME BIRDS

An assortment of upland game birds, *clockwise from top left:* Male Dusky Grouse, male Spruce Grouse, Ruffed Grouse, Plain Chachalaca, male Wild Turkey displaying, and Ruffed Grouse drumming.

FIGURE 35. CALIFORNIA, GAMBEL'S, AND SCALED QUAILS
All quails exhibit a potbellied look, so attention to general coloration and plumage patterns is important. Male California Quail (L) has a scaled belly, spotted nape, and dark crown, while male Gambel's Quail (C) has a buff to whitish belly with a black lower belly patch, streaked nape, and rust crown. Males have more colorful plumage than females. The female Scaled Quail (R) has a plainer brown face and smaller white crest than the very similarly plumaged male (not shown), but some birds are best left unsexed.

as the much larger sage-grouse from Sharp-tailed Grouse, or prairie-chickens from smaller quails or partridges.

STRUCTURAL FEATURES: Quails share a similar rounded, upright body shape with a short tail and neck, while ptarmigans and most grouse species have slightly longer necks. A few quails have distinctive head plumes or tufts. California and Gambel's Quails have an odd head plume that resembles a forward-leaning exclamation point, while Mountain Quail has a unique and very long, straight head plume. Scaled Quail has a white head tuft resembling a small crest that is raised upward when a bird is excited or alarmed. (See Figure 35, above.)

Wild Turkey and Plain Chachalaca differ from other game birds by having long legs that are used for fast sprinting in open spaces and easier maneuvering in trees. (See Figure 34, p. 35.) Game birds have a sharp spur on the lower rear leg that they use for fighting.

BEHAVIOR: While most game birds are shy and retiring, species that reside in protected areas—where hunting is not allowed—show surprisingly tame behavior and allow great looks at close range. Most game birds remain motionless when casually threatened, but imminent danger causes them to explosively take flight. This low escape flight with stiff, snappy wingbeats is signature behavior for game birds.

Some game birds have elaborate courtship rituals in which males perform spectacular displays. Several grouse and prairie-chickens have communal courtship rituals in which multiple males perform ceremonial dances, raising ornamental feathers and inflating colorful throat sacs. Others fan their tails and bow ceremoniously. Wild Turkeys often segregate by sex, especially in winter, with males performing fancy tail-fanning displays in spring. (See Figure 34, p. 35.)

PLUMAGE PATTERNS AND GENERAL COLORATION: Birds in this group exhibit a range of earth-tone colors complemented by plumage patterns that aid in their camouflage. A few exceptions include the brightly colored Chukar and male Ring-necked Pheasant. Most species have only one year-round plumage, with the exception of ptarmigans, which molt into an all-white plumage for the snowy winter months. Willow and Rock Ptarmigans, however, retain black outer tail feathers in winter.

A good number of male game birds have more colorful and dramatic plumage patterns than females. Exceptions include Scaled and Mountain Quails, which have very subtle plumage differences between male and female, and Plain Chachalaca and Ruffed Grouse, which show no differences between sexes.

Male and female Sharp-tailed Grouse and prairie-chickens appear similar for most of the year, but males expose dramatic colorful neck sacs and showy head feathers during lek displays in spring. Chukar, Himalayan Snowcock, Gray Partridge, Sooty Grouse, and Dusky Grouse show only minor plumage differences between sexes.

HABITAT USE: Virtually every North American habitat is frequented by one or more game bird species. These varied habitats range from barren Arctic tundra to subtropical thorn forests. Although game birds are chiefly ground dwelling, Wild Turkey and

Plain Chachalaca regularly roost in trees, and some grouse and ptarmigan species move to trees when alarmed or during courtship displays.

Game birds sometimes rely on feeding stations for important winter sustenance. Species that regularly visit feeders include quails, Plain Chachalaca, Chukar, Ring-necked Pheasant, and Wild Turkey. Ring-necked Pheasant is usually found in agricultural lands near forest borders or along roadway grassy edges.

VOCALIZATIONS: Game birds make a variety of calls, including whistles, barks, hoots, clucks, and croaks. Some may also wing snap during courtship display (Spruce, Dusky, and Sooty Grouse), while others create swishing sounds by brushing their wings against their bodies (Greater and Gunnison Sage-Grouse).

Several species give explosive calls during the breeding season. Wild Turkey's gobbling sounds and Ring-necked Pheasant's startling, nonmusical

FIGURE 36. ROCK PTARMIGAN AND WILLOW PTARMIGAN

Female and nonbreeding ptarmigans present formidable ID problems. Note the larger, parrotlike bill on the breeding female Willow Ptarmigan (top R and bottom L), which helps separate this species from breeding female Rock Ptarmigan (top L and center L). Nonbreeding male Rock Ptarmigan (bottom R) shows bold black lores in front of the eye, a feature that is lacking in nonbreeding male and female Willow Ptarmigans and female Rock Ptarmigans, which are identical in plumage. Additional ID information is provided in the text.

FIGURE 37. DUSKY GROUSE AND SOOTY GROUSE, MALES (QUIZ PHOTO)
While females of these two grouse species have similar variable plumage, males show subtle plumage differences. ID information is provided in the text below. Try to separate these similar grouse. Answers are in the appendix, page 267.

two-note screech call are unlike the sounds of any other species. Ruffed Grouse produces a very loud, accelerating booming sound by beating its wings against its body. This "drumming" sound is heard at great distances. (See Figure 34, p. 35.)

COMPARISONS OF SIMILAR SPECIES

Female and Nonbreeding Rock Ptarmigan and Willow Ptarmigan

UNCHANGING CHARACTERISTICS: The best way to separate female and nonbreeding Rock and Willow Ptarmigans is by the larger, more "parrotlike" bill on Willow versus a smaller, thinner bill on Rock. This bill difference is very subtle and requires careful evaluation of both species. (See Figure 36, p. 37.)

SUPPLEMENTAL CHARACTERISTICS AND NON-BBI DETAILS: Breeding male ptarmigans are fairly distinctive in plumage and pose few ID problems. Most confusion occurs with breeding female Willow and Rock Ptarmigans and nonbreeding female Rock versus nonbreeding male and female Willows. In breeding birds, female Willow tends to have warmer plumage tones, while female Rock has a cooler overall look with some grayish highlights. (See Figure 36, p. 37.) Both species have an all-white nonbreeding plumage with black outer tail feathers, and closely resemble each other. Nonbreeding male Rock differs from nonbreeding male and female Willow and nonbreeding female Rock with its distinctive, bold black eye stripe. (See Figure 36, p. 37.)

Sooty Grouse and Dusky Grouse

In 2006 Blue Grouse was split into two species: Sooty Grouse and Dusky Grouse. Sooty is the Pacific counterpart to the interior Dusky, which occurs mainly in the Rocky Mountain region. Both species occur in a long, narrow overlap zone from southern Washington State northward through western British Columbia to southern Alaska. Sooty and Dusky Grouse are typically found singly in coniferous forests and have an overall dark plumage, with males having a deep blue-gray coloration.

UNCHANGING CHARACTERISTICS: Sooty and Dusky Grouse share similar physical features of large size (20 in. long), a moderately long neck, and a fairly long tail. Plumage details and isolated geographic ranges are the best way to separate them.

SUPPLEMENTAL CHARACTERISTICS AND NON-BBI DETAILS: Male Dusky Grouse has white spotting on the wings and flanks, while male Sooty Grouse is uniformly dark gray. (See Figure 37, above.) Females of both species share a variably gray-brown and speckled plumage and are inseparable in the field. Since Sooty and Dusky interbreed where their ranges overlap, plumage details may be unreliable for some males in these limited areas. Other male grouse in this overlap zone show distinct plumage details of each species.

Birders often think of loons and grebes as water-fowl because of similar structural features, but genetically they are more closely related to seabirds.

LOONS

Loons spend most of their lives in the water and only come to land for extended periods during the breeding season. They dive underwater for long periods while pursuing fish or escaping danger, such as Bald Eagles or powerboats. Loons breed in northern freshwater locations and Arctic tundra habitats and disperse south in winter to coastal marine locations or other large bodies of water.

PHYSICAL PROFILE

Loons have elongated, submarine-shaped bodies. They have moderately long and thick necks with smooth, rounded heads. Loons' strong legs and webbed feet are situated near the rear of their bodies and provide powerful underwater locomotion. All loons have strong, straight, pointed bills. (See Figure 38, below.)

BIRDING BY IMPRESSION INFORMATION

SIZE: Five species range from Red-throated and Pacific Loons, at 25 in. long (slightly larger than Mallard), to Yellow-billed Loon, at 35 in. long (about the size of "Lesser" [i.e., a medium-sized] Canada Goose).

STRUCTURAL FEATURES: Common and Yellow-billed Loons can be quickly separated from other loons by their larger, heavier bodies; thicker necks and bills; and blocky, flat-topped heads. Pacific and Arctic Loons have smaller, more slender bodies; thinner bills; and more evenly rounded heads. Red-throated Loon has the most slender body of all loons, a thin neck, and a slender, pointed bill that is often held slightly upward.

Loons fly with their moderately long neck outstretched, which results in a distinctive flight profile. Long, pointed, angular wings and feet that extend beyond the tail add to the streamlined flight profile, which is recognizable at long distances. (See Figure 38, below.) Common Loon's extra-large feet

---

FIGURE 38. LOONS

Loons are among the most beautiful of all waterbirds. *Clockwise from top left,* in breeding plumage: Common Loon, Pacific Loon, Red-throated Loon, and Common Loon.

help with the ID of flying birds, even at a distance. In flight, Red-throated Loon's thinner wings are angled back, and its neck droops lower from the body than on other loons. These structural characteristics help separate Red-throated from other loons in flight, as do its quicker, deeper wingbeats.

BEHAVIOR: While loons are powerful swimmers, they have trouble walking, so on land they use their feet to push themselves forward on their belly. All loons except Red-throated require a long running start to take flight, and their flight is strong and direct with measured wingbeats.

PLUMAGE PATTERNS AND GENERAL COLORATION: Sexes are similar in appearance, but there are marked plumage differences between breeding and nonbreeding birds. Loons have striking combinations of black, gray, and white feather patterning in breeding plumage. Breeding Red-throated Loon differs from the others with its bright red throat. Nonbreeding loons bear a superficial resemblance to each other, which is the reason for ID confusion. All have a darkish back, white underparts and neck, and variably grayish crown. Juveniles mostly resemble nonbreeding adults but typically have more pale fringed upperparts and less defined head and neck markings. (See Figure 39, below.) They retain their nonbreeding-like plumage throughout the first winter.

VOCALIZATIONS: Loons are mostly silent away from breeding areas, which is a stark contrast to their de-

meanor at nest locations. All give a variety of loud wailing or yodeling calls, with some resembling a mournful crying. Common and Yellow-billed Loons may give a variety of their calls throughout the year, especially migrating birds in flight.

COMPARISONS OF SIMILAR SPECIES

Nonbreeding and Juvenile Loons
Common Loon and Yellow-billed Loon

UNCHANGING CHARACTERISTICS: Common and Yellow-billed Loons are somewhat similar in size, structure, and appearance. Differences include Yellow-billed's larger overall size (35 in. long vs. 32 in. long for Common Loon) and heavier bill, with the lower mandible tapering toward the tip, giving it a slightly upturned appearance. Common has a thick, straight bill. Yellow-billed typically has a double bump on top of the head, with one over the forehead and one over the nape in profile. Common has a bump over the forehead but has a rounded rear crown in comparison. Yellow-billed also has smaller eyes and a thicker neck compared with Common.

SUPPLEMENTAL CHARACTERISTICS AND NON-BBI DETAILS: Common and Yellow-billed Loons are both dark on the crown, rear neck, and cheeks, but Yellow-billed is paler gray overall. Yellow-billed has more extensive pale markings on the sides of the neck and, similar to Common, has a partial white collar near the midneck, but this latter detail is more defined in Common.

FIGURE 39. NONBREEDING LOONS (QUIZ PHOTO)

ID information for four species of similar-appearing nonbreeding loons is provided in the text. Try to identify the four species of loons in these six photos. Three are juvenile-plumaged birds, and three are adults. Juvenile Red-throated Loon may show a smaller bill and has a duskier head and neck compared with adults during the first winter. Answers are in the appendix, page 267.

Both species have distinct white feathering around the eye, with Yellow-billed showing more extensive but less defined white feathering. Yellow-billed also has a pale yellow bill compared with Common's grayish bill. Juveniles of both species have pale barring on the back, and juvenile Yellow-billed has a paler gray head with a subtle dark cheek patch. (See Figure 39, p. 40.)

Pacific Loon

UNCHANGING CHARACTERISTICS: Pacific Loon differs from Common and Yellow-billed Loons by its smaller size and more delicate structural features, including a shorter, thinner bill and smaller, more gently rounded head compared with a larger head with flatter crown on the two larger loons. While the Pacific Loon in Figure 39 has a smaller, flat-topped look, this species typically shows a rounded crown like the Pacific Loon in Figure 38. Pacific differs structurally from Red-throated by its heavier, straighter bill; shorter, thicker neck; and larger head with steeper forehead.

SUPPLEMENTAL CHARACTERISTICS AND NON-BBI DETAILS: Compared with Common and Yellow-billed Loons, Pacific Loon has a paler nape and crown that contrasts with its darker back and forehead. Common and Yellow-billed have fairly uniformly gray shading to their upperparts. Pacific's white throat is separated from its gray nape by a blackish border, which gives its neck area a contrasting three-toned appearance that is lacking in all other nonbreeding loons worldwide except Arctic Loon. Pacific also lacks white feathering around the eye, and nonbreeding adults typically have a dark necklace of feathers below the chin. Juvenile Pacific has neat rows of white feathering on the back and often lacks the dark necklace that is present in adults.

Red-throated Loon

UNCHANGING CHARACTERISTICS: Red-throated Loon is distinctive with its small size and delicate features, which include a thin bill that is usually held slightly upward and a very slender body. Its longish neck is slimmer than that of other loons, and it lacks the steep forecrown of other loons. Juveniles in their first fall and early winter often show a shorter, stockier bill than adults.

SUPPLEMENTAL CHARACTERISTICS AND NON-BBI DETAILS: Adult Red-throated Loon is paler gray and more crisply patterned than other loons. It has a white face and neck, grayish crown and nape, and gray back with prominent white speckling.

Juvenile Red-throated poses additional ID challenges because it has an ill-defined, dusky head and neck pattern. It also has less prominent white spots on the back than nonbreeding adults. Juvenile plumage is typically held throughout the first winter. (See Figure 39, p. 40.)

Arctic Loon (not shown)

Arctic Loon is found only in a very small area in northern Alaska, and nonbreeding adults closely resemble Pacific Loon.

UNCHANGING CHARACTERISTICS: Arctic Loon is slightly larger and has a marginally longer bill, but these features are difficult to judge with just one species present. Other than its slightly larger size (27 in. long vs. 25 in. long in Pacific Loon) and longer bill (which are hard features to judge with just one species present), these two species are structurally very similar.

SUPPLEMENTAL CHARACTERISTICS AND NON-BBI DETAILS: The best feature for separating nonbreeding Arctic and Pacific Loons is the presence on Arctic of white feathering along the rear flanks that is visible above the water line on floating birds. Pacific lacks this white feathering on the rear flanks.

GREBES

Grebes are diving birds of freshwater and onshore coastal habitats. They are fast and agile swimmers that use lobed toes to help propel them underwater in search of fish and aquatic invertebrates. All seven species nest in freshwater locations and build floating stick nests in quiet ponds with emergent vegetation.

PHYSICAL PROFILE

The four smallest grebes (Least, Pied-billed, Eared, and Horned Grebes) have compact bodies with rounded backs, while Red-necked has a larger, more tapered body shape. (See Figure 40, p. 42.) Western and Clark's Grebes differ from other grebes by having more elongated bodies that resemble those of loons. (See Figure 42, p. 44.) Grebes have proportionally longer necks and shorter bodies than loons, and their rear body shows a tail-less profile. Bills range from short and pointed in the four smallest grebes to long and slender in Western and Clark's Grebes.

Grebes are heavy bodied, and their lobed feet are situated far back on their bodies, which makes walking on land difficult. Their wings are relatively short and pointed.

BIRDING BY IMPRESSION INFORMATION

SIZE: Grebes come in a wide range of sizes, from Least Grebe, at 9½ in. long (slightly larger than Sora), to Western and Clark's Grebes, at 25 in. long,

FIGURE 40. GREBES

Some grebes show a colorful breeding plumage like three of the birds pictured here, while others appear somewhat similar year-round. *Clockwise from top left,* all in breeding plumage: Eared Grebe, Horned Grebe, Pied-billed Grebe, and Red-necked Grebe.

which are similar in size to Red-throated and Pacific Loons. Males average slightly larger than females.

STRUCTURAL FEATURES: The four smallest grebes show a puffy rear body profile that is accentuated by raised flank feathers and a tail-less appearance. Red-necked Grebe has a long, daggerlike bill similar to those of loons, while Pied-billed Grebe differs from other grebes with its short, chickenlike bill. See Physical Profile, above, for more structural information.

BEHAVIOR: Outside the breeding season, the four smallest grebes are often found in small to large groups. Red-necked and Horned Grebes are highly migratory, and many spend the winter at coastal onshore locations. Pied-billed and Least Grebes can submerge their bodies "submarine style" by exhaling air and sinking in place. All grebes fly in a direct fashion with fast, steady wingbeats.

PLUMAGE PATTERNS AND GENERAL COLORATION: Red-necked, Horned, and Eared Grebes have color-ful breeding plumages consisting of red, yellow, black, and white patterns, but molt to a nondescript nonbreeding plumage of gray, black, brown, and white. Other grebes show only slight differences between breeding and nonbreeding plumage, which is reflected primarily in head and neck feather variation.

HABITAT USE: Pied-billed and Least Grebes prefer small ponds with emergent vegetation for their year-round habitats, while Western and Clark's Grebes are found in open freshwater and coastal locations. Red-necked, Horned, and Eared Grebes all nest in quiet, freshwater ponds with emergent vegetation and winter in large lakes, onshore coastal waters, and sheltered bays.

VOCALIZATIONS: Songs on the breeding grounds include a variety of loud, unmusical sounds, with Clark's and Western Grebes sharing similar vocalizations. The *Podiceps* grebes (Red-necked, Horned, and Eared) are mostly silent in winter, while others give a variety of barks, trills, and whistled calls throughout the year.

FIGURE 41. NONBREEDING EARED, HORNED, AND RED-NECKED GREBES (QUIZ PHOTO)
Differences between Horned Grebe and Eared Grebe are provided in the text below. Try to identify these two species (L and C). Answers are in the appendix, page 267. Obvious separating ID features for Red-necked Grebe (R) are its larger size (18 in. long); longer neck; and long, pointed, yellowish bill. Sometimes Red-necked Grebes are mistaken for loons because of their similar structural features.

COMPARISONS OF SIMILAR SPECIES

Nonbreeding Horned Grebe and Eared Grebe
Horned Grebe frequents deeper-water habitats in winter, especially coastal locations, while Eared prefers shallow water, including the highly saline Salton Sea and Great Salt Lake, where very large numbers occur during migration and in winter.

UNCHANGING CHARACTERISTICS: Horned Grebe is slightly larger and more heavily built than Eared Grebe. Horned has a thicker neck; larger, blockier head shape with shallow-sloping forehead; flatter crown; straighter, slightly heavier bill; and less buoyant, lower-riding rear body appearance. Because of the more fluffed rear body feathers on Eared, it often appears to ride higher above the water line, which is especially helpful when trying to identify birds at a long distance.

Eared also often has a peaked crown over the eye, while Horned's peak is behind the eye. Eared has a thinner bill that gives a slight concave impression to the upper mandible compared with Horned's straight bill. (See Figure 41, above.)

SUPPLEMENTAL CHARACTERISTICS AND NON-BBI DETAILS: Nonbreeding adult Eared Grebe has darker cheeks and duskier neck feathering than Horned Grebe, which gives Eared a darker overall front body appearance. Horned typically has a more contrasting black-and-white plumage compared with Eared's slightly browner appearance, but changing light conditions can result in Eared having a blackish appearance to its plumage, especially adults. First-winter Eared has less concentrated dark markings on the cheek and neck than nonbreeding adults.

Horned has a grayish bill with a defined pale tip, while Eared has a uniformly gray bill.

Western Grebe and Clark's Grebe
Western and Clark's Grebes have mostly similar plumage features and slight differences in their body and bill size and shapes. Subtle variations in plumage and bare-parts color are more obvious in breeding plumage (March–September) but are carefully separable in many nonbreeding birds.

UNCHANGING CHARACTERISTICS: Western Grebe averages slightly larger overall than Clark's Grebe, but this feature requires side-by-side comparison. (See Figure 42, p. 44.) Western has a slightly longer, subtly stouter bill compared with Clark's thinner one, which has a slightly recurved upper mandible.

SUPPLEMENTAL CHARACTERISTICS AND NON-BBI DETAILS: Western Grebe's dark cap extends downward and surrounds the eye in breeding plumage, while that of Clark's Grebe is narrower and does not encompass the eye. (See Figure 42, bottom photos.) Clark's also has a narrower dark nape line than Western, which is helpful for separating distant swimming birds. Clark's typically has a grayer back and whiter flanks, but these details can be variable and not always reliable.

Nonbreeding birds of both species are more difficult to ID and may have similar facial patterns that show dusky feathering around the eye, with bill color a more reliable detail to separate them. Western's bill is olive to dull yellow in color, while Clark's is bright yellow to orange-yellow. Some nonbreeding birds are best left unidentified, and this ID dilemma is compounded by hybrids.

FIGURE 42. WESTERN GREBE AND CLARK'S GREBE (QUIZ PHOTO)
These two grebes show similar plumage patterns and shading, but subtle structural differences and plumage details help separate them. Detailed ID information is provided in the text on page 43. Try to identify both species in the top and bottom photos. Answers are in the appendix, page 267.

This chapter covers a wide assortment of birds that are found in aquatic habitats, including oceans, seacoasts, and lakes. Some species are rarely seen from land, while others are often seen by bird-watchers who visit coastal shorelines and inland freshwater locations. Most breed near saltwater habitats, with the exception of Anhinga, White Pelican, Double-crested Cormorant, and Neotropic Cormorant, which breed in freshwater locations. The text is divided into several sections that loosely follow the 2010 taxonomic grouping of the American Ornithologists' Union.

TIPS FOR VIEWING SEABIRDS

Several seabird species are regularly seen from land, especially along Pacific coastlines, northern Atlantic Maritime regions, and Canadian and Alaskan rocky coastal zones. Many, however, occur far out at sea and require moderate to long boat trips for viewing. When viewing pelagic birds in challenging weather conditions, it can be very difficult to notice important plumage details. For this reason it is helpful to study all the possible birds in a field guide before you go out, and concentrate mainly on their characteristic body, wing, and bill shapes, as well as general coloration, shading, and plumage patterns.

ALBATROSSES, NORTHERN FULMAR, PETRELS, AND SHEARWATERS

Birds in these groups are highly pelagic by nature, spending most of their lives at sea except when they come to shore to breed. All species fly with stiff wingbeats and long, arcing glides. Sexes are similar.

PHYSICAL PROFILE

Albatrosses have large, heavy bodies; very long, slender, pointed wings; large heads; and big, powerful bills with hooked tips. Northern Fulmar has a stocky, compact body shape and thick neck, as well as short, rounded wings; a rounded tail; and a short, thick bill. (See Figure 43, p. 46.)

Shearwaters and *Pterodroma* petrels have elongated, streamlined bodies, but petrels have narrower and more angular, pointed wings than shearwaters. Shearwaters have heavier bodies; short tails; long, narrow wings; and relatively small to medium-length bills.

BIRDING BY IMPRESSION INFORMATION

SIZE: Albatrosses are very large seabirds. Black-footed, Yellow-nosed, and Laysan Albatrosses are 32 in. long, which is about the size of Great Black-backed Gull. Short-tailed Albatross is 36 in. long, which is slightly smaller than Northern Gannet.

Six *Pterodroma* petrels range in size from 13 to 16 in. long. Cook's Petrel averages 13 in. long (similar to Forster's Tern), while Murphy's, Herald, and Fea's Petrels are 15 in. long. Black-capped Petrel is the largest, at 16 in. long (about the size of Laughing Gull).

Northern Fulmar is 18 in. long, which is similar to Ring-billed Gull. Ten species of shearwaters range in size from Audubon's Shearwater, at 12 in. long (slightly smaller than Bonaparte's Gull), to Great Shearwater, at 18 in. long (about the size of Ring-billed Gull).

STRUCTURAL FEATURES: All species have fully webbed feet and tubes on their bills that house their nostrils. These tubes are used to secrete salt from the birds' bodies, and are the reason for this group's collective name "tubenoses."

Short-tailed Albatross has a stockier body, larger bill, and broader wings and tail than the other albatrosses that regularly occur in North America. Petrels have smaller, rounder heads than shearwaters, and more streamlined bodies. They also have elongated, tapered rear ends and very small bills. Shearwaters have longer bills than petrels and broader, more rounded tails. Short-tailed and Sooty Shearwaters have narrower, more pointed wings than other North American shearwaters. (See Figure 44, p. 47.)

BEHAVIOR: Immature birds of some larger tubenose species spend years at sea before coming to land to breed. Some shearwaters are found in large flocks of several thousand to hundreds of thousands of birds from late summer to winter.

PLUMAGE PATTERNS AND GENERAL COLORATION: All species exhibit muted plumage tones of gray, black, brown, or white, with only Short-tailed Albatross having some yellow coloration to its head and neck. Northern Fulmar and several *Pterodroma* petrels have light- and dark-morph plumage conditions.

FIGURE 43. ALBATROSSES, NORTHERN FULMAR, PETRELS, AND SHEARWATERS
Clockwise from top left: Light-morph Northern Fulmar, Cory's Shearwater, Black-capped Petrel, and Yellow-nosed Albatross.

HABITAT USE: Typical habitat for all species is deep-water oceanic environments. Breeding locations are usually offshore islands. Several species of shearwaters are regularly seen from shore in small to very large numbers (Sooty, Short-tailed, Great, and Black-vented Shearwaters), especially off the Pacific Coast.

VOCALIZATIONS: Not relevant to ID.

COMPARISONS OF SIMILAR SPECIES

Sooty Shearwater and Short-tailed Shearwater

These two species present a consistent ID dilemma off the West Coast of North America. Sooty Shearwaters greatly outnumber Short-tailed Shearwaters from spring to early fall (except in Alaska), so any sighting during this period is more likely to be a Sooty. Similar numbers of both species occur in late fall and winter, so careful evaluation of the following physical features and plumage patterns is needed during this time.

UNCHANGING CHARACTERISTICS: Sooty Shearwater is slightly larger than Short-tailed Shearwater (17 vs. 16 in. long) and averages a longer wingspan (40 vs. 38 in.). Short-tailed has a shorter neck and smaller, rounder, "dovelike" head with a steeper forehead than Sooty, which has a longer, less stocky neck and flatter head. Short-tailed also has a shorter bill compared with Sooty's, which has a thinner central portion and a noticeably longer nail. (See Figure 44, p. 47.)

SUPPLEMENTAL CHARACTERISTICS AND NON-BBI DETAILS: Both species have an overall brownish coloration with pale whitish highlights to the underwings. Some darker Short-tailed Shearwaters have very dusky underwings that lack noticeable white highlights, and these birds can be safely identified. Many birds of both species are similar in plumage, but a general guideline for separation includes the underwing pattern. Short-taileds have more uniformly pale shading to their underwings and lack the dis-

FIGURE 44. SOOTY SHEARWATER AND SHORT-TAILED SHEARWATER (QUIZ PHOTO)
ID information about these similar species is included in the text on page 46. Look for structural and plumage differences before reading the text, and then try to identify the birds. Answers are in the appendix, page 267.

tinct contrasting silvery wing panels that are present in the middle of Sooty's underwing. This detail is just a guideline, however, with some worn birds showing variations of their typical plumage.

Black-vented, Manx, and Audubon's Shearwaters
Black-vented and Manx Shearwaters are very similar in size, shape, and plumage. Geographic location is usually a reliable general guideline for these two species. Manx was formerly believed to be restricted to the Atlantic Ocean, but recent information indicates that very small numbers occur off the Pacific Coast, where Black-vented is common. Black-vented (14 in. long) does not occur in the western Atlantic, where Manx is fairly common.

Audubon's is a small (12 in. long) southern shearwater that shares Atlantic Ocean and Gulf of Mexico waters with Manx (13½ in. long). There is no overlap in range with Black-vented, and structural differences from Manx also relate to Black-vented.

UNCHANGING CHARACTERISTICS: Presently only minor physical differences help separate Black-vented and Manx Shearwaters in flight. Black-vented has shorter and wider primaries compared with Manx,

and this creates a slightly thicker and more blunt-shaped outer wing.

Audubon's Shearwater has a slighter body structure, noticeably longer tail, and shorter wings than Manx and Black-vented (27-in. wingspan vs. 33 in Manx and 34 in Black-vented). (See Figure 45, p. 48.) Audubon's also has quicker wingbeats than Manx, and tends to fly closer to the water with less gliding. Manx is much heavier than Audubon's and has a longer bill and slightly longer body projection in front of the wings. Manx also flies more like the larger shearwaters because of its larger, heavier body and longer wings. This flight style includes medium-length glides interspersed with explosive series of wingbeats and frequent dramatic banks and turns. Audubon's lighter flight style includes medium-length glides interspersed with weaker wing flaps, which result in a slower flight style.

SUPPLEMENTAL CHARACTERISTICS AND NON-BBI DETAILS:
Compared with Black-vented Shearwater, Manx Shearwater has an overall cleaner white appearance below with a more contrasting white and black plumage, white undertail coverts, and a pale crescent behind the dark cheek patch. Black-vented is

FIGURE 45. BLACK-VENTED, MANX, AND AUDUBON'S SHEARWATERS (QUIZ PHOTO)
These three similar-sized shearwaters share a black-and-white plumage but have subtle differences in plumage and structural features. ID information for separating these birds is provided in the text on page 47. Try to identify these birds. Answers are in the appendix, page 267.

darker on the underwing, has dark undertail coverts, and shows a uniformly dusky head that lacks the pale defined crescent behind the cheek. These details are easier to see in calm seas than in rough.

Audubon's Shearwater has partial dark undertail coverts compared with Manx's white ones, and is slightly grayer brown on the upperparts. Audubon's also has a broader dark trailing edge to the underwing, and a sharp contrast between its primaries and underwing coverts. A white spot in front of the eye in Audubon's is lacking in both Manx and Black-vented, but this detail is hard to see on distant birds. Audubon's lacks the distinct white crescent mark behind the ear coverts that is present in Manx.

STORM-PETRELS

Eight species of very small seabirds called storm-petrels regularly occur in North American coastal and pelagic waters. Like other tubenoses, storm-petrels spend most of their lives flying low over the water searching for prey on the surface. They come to land only at night during the nesting season. Sexes are similar.

PHYSICAL PROFILE

Storm-petrels have slender, streamlined bodies and long, narrow wings and tails that range from short and blunt-tipped to long and forked. Small, rounded heads with oddly shaped flat crowns and tiny bills complete their physical profile. (See Figure 46, p. 49.)

BIRDING BY IMPRESSION INFORMATION

SIZE: Storm-petrels are the smallest seabirds in North America and range from the sparrow-sized Least Storm-Petrel, at 5¾ in. long, to Black Storm-Petrel, at 9 in. long (about the size of Red-winged Blackbird).

STRUCTURAL FEATURES: Storm-petrels that breed in the Northern Hemisphere are structurally different than those that breed in the Southern Hemisphere. The southern-breeding White-faced, Wilson's, Band-rumped, and Least Storm-Petrels have short tails that are either squared-off or blunt, while the North American breeders (Black, Leach's, Ashy, and Fork-tailed Storm-Petrels) have longer, forked tails.

Southern breeders also have shorter, more rounded wings and longer legs, while North American breeders have longer, more angled wings and shorter legs. Wilson's and White-faced Storm-Petrels have such long legs that their exposed feet can be seen trailing behind the tail in direct flight situations.

BEHAVIOR: Each species exhibits its own flight style. Some appear swallowlike, while others glide and arc on stiff wings like shearwaters. Because of their small size and foraging styles, storm-petrels tend to fly closer to the water than other tubenoses. Be aware that flight styles often change with weather conditions and type of activity; migrating and wind-driven birds typically fly in a stronger, more direct style that includes more gliding and arcing flights.

FIGURE 46. STORM-PETRELS (QUIZ PHOTO—TOP)
Wilson's Storm-Petrel, Leach's Storm-Petrel, and Band-rumped Storm-Petrel are three similar seabirds that occur in the Atlantic Ocean and Gulf of Mexico. ID information for these birds is provided in the text on pages 49–50. Try to identify the birds in the top photos based on this information. Answers are in the appendix, page 267. The bottom photo shows typical feeding behavior of Wilson's Storm-Petrels.

When feeding, Wilson's and White-faced Storm-Petrels dangle their feet below the body and patter on the water's surface. (See Figure 46, above.) In early fall, large mixed flocks of storm-petrels of up to 10,000 birds (mostly Black and Ashy with small numbers of Leach's) occur just off the California coast.

PLUMAGE PATTERNS AND GENERAL COLORATION: All but two species of storm-petrels (Fork-tailed and White-faced, not illustrated) are brownish to blackish overall and have brown and black upperwings that have variable gray carpal bars across the inner wing. Fork-tailed Storm-Petrel is pale gray overall with dark underwing and upperwing markings. White-faced Storm-Petrel has white underparts, a pale gray-brown back, pale gray rump, and blackish tail and flight feathers. Both species are distinctive in appearance.

The absence or presence of a white rump and the shape of the rump patch are important to the ID of some dark storm-petrels. Similarly, the boldness and extent of the pale carpal bar on the upperwing helps separate similar species.

HABITAT USE: While deep-water oceanic habitats are the typical feeding areas for storm-petrels, some species may occur close to land, especially along the Pacific Coast. Breeding locations are typically offshore islands, and nest sites are underground burrows.

VOCALIZATIONS: Not relevant to ID.

COMPARISONS OF SIMILAR SPECIES

Wilson's, Leach's, and Band-rumped Storm-Petrels

These three species occur together in Atlantic Ocean and Gulf of Mexico waters and share similar coloration and plumage patterns. Different structural features, plumage patterns, and flight styles are important for separating these species. (See Figure 46, above.)

UNCHANGING CHARACTERISTICS: Leach's Storm-Petrel has some of the most distinctive features of the three species, including its slender body shape, deeply notched tail, and narrow, pointed, angled wings that are often swept back from the wrist (midpoint of the forewing). Wilson's and Band-rumped Storm-Petrels have broader, more rounded wings than Leach's and less slender overall body shapes. Compared with Wilson's, however, Band-rumped has longer, narrower wings. Leach's has the most slender wings of the three species.

Wilson's differs from the other species with its

short inner wing, which gives its wings a less angular appearance and a more straight-edged shape overall than those of Leach's and Band-rumped.

Wilson's has very long legs, and its feet trail noticeably behind the tail when it flies. This feature is not shared by Band-rumped and Leach's. Of the three, Wilson's has the most squared-off tail (although it can sometimes appear slightly notched). Band-rumped has a slightly notched tail, and Leach's has a deeper notch to its tail than Band-rumped. The slight notch in Band-rumped's tail is often hard to see, but careful evaluation of a flying bird usually reveals this feature.

Even though these birds often disappear in ocean troughs, flight style can be the most helpful feature to separate Wilson's from Band-rumped. Wilson's has a more fluttery, swallowlike flight with shallower, stiffer wingbeats interspersed with short glides versus Band-rumped's relatively steady flight style with low, banking turns. Band-rumped also glides gracefully on bowed wings versus Wilson's straighter-winged glide. Leach's typically flies in a very active style with deep, springy wingbeats and frequent changes of direction. It often arcs and glides over waves on bent wings, and may fly like a shearwater in strong winds.

SUPPLEMENTAL CHARACTERISTICS AND NON-BBI DETAILS: These species share similar coloration and plumage patterns, and the extent and shape of the white rump are helpful to their ID. Leach's Storm-Petrel has a more elongated, oval-shaped white rump with a thin, dark, dividing line on some birds. Wilson's Storm-Petrel has a large, slightly rounded white rump that is more extensive than Band-rumped Storm-Petrel's. Wilson's white rump extends into the undertail coverts and along the flanks. Band-rumped's white rump extends only slightly into the undertail coverts. (See Figure 46, p. 49.)

Leach's has the strongest pale carpal bar that extends from the rear inner wing to the wrist, but worn adult Band-rumped and Wilson's can show more prominent carpal bars that more closely resemble that of Leach's. However, they don't extend all the way to the leading edge of the forewing like Leach's carpal bar does.

ALCIDS

Alcids (or auks) are hardy seabirds that are mostly restricted to the cold seas of the Northern Hemisphere. All are oceanic by nature and come to land only to breed or to rest on exposed rocky shore-

FIGURE 47. ALCIDS
Alcids are the Northern Hemisphere's counterpart to penguins, and most inhabit cold-water locations. *Clockwise from top left* (all in breeding plumage): Tufted Puffin, Pigeon Guillemot, Kittlitz's Murrelets, and Common Murre.

FIGURE 48. COMMON MURRE: FLOCK AND ADULT IN FLIGHT

Common Murre is a colonial seabird that forms huge pre- and post-breeding flocks at far northern breeding sites (L). Note the strong, pointed wings on the flying bird (R). Alcids use their wings to propel themselves underwater when chasing fish.

lines. Alcids spend more time swimming, floating, and diving than other seabirds. Their flight is typically fast, direct, and close to the water. Sexes are similar, with males averaging slightly larger.

TIPS FOR VIEWING ALCIDS

Study your field guide to become familiar with the different sizes, shapes, and bill structures of alcids before venturing into the field. These pelagic birds are difficult to study in rough ocean waters, and often you will get only a short glimpse of them before they disappear behind another wave or dive underwater for extended periods of time. The best times to view alcids from shore are in the early morning, since some are still present after spending the night along the coastline, and during bad offshore weather conditions, when they often come close to land to take shelter along rocky shorelines.

PHYSICAL PROFILE

Alcids have low-profile, submarine-shaped bodies that vary from somewhat compact to elongate in appearance. They have proportionally large heads; short, thick necks; very short tails; and small, short, pointed wings. (See Figure 47, p. 50.) Their feet are fully webbed, and their bills vary from short to medium in length, and from stocky to slender in shape.

BIRDING BY IMPRESSION INFORMATION

SIZE: Alcids range in size from Least Auklet (6¼ in. long), which is the size of Song Sparrow, to Thick-billed Murre, at 18 in. long, which is about the size of Greater Scaup.

Size ranges are fairly consistent for similar species in the alcid family. For example, most auklets and murrelets are small, with nine species in these two groups sharing a narrow range from 9 to 10½ in. long. Rhinoceros Auklet is the larger exception at 15 in. long, and Least Auklet and Whiskered Auklet (7½ in. long) the smaller exceptions.

Horned and Tufted Puffins are 15 in. long, and Atlantic Puffin is smaller, at 12½ in. long. Common and Thick-billed Murres are 17½ and 18 in. long, respectively, while the similar-appearing Razorbill is 17 in. long.

STRUCTURAL FEATURES: Related alcids typically share similar body shapes and bill structures. Murrelets and auklets have low-riding, compact bodies, with murrelets having small, thin bills while auklets have stockier, short bills. Puffins have distinctive rounded crowns and large, rounded bills, while murres have relatively long, slender bills. Guillemots have very slender, pointed bills, while Razorbill has an oddly shaped, rounded bill. Dovekie has a distinctive plump, compact body; short, stocky bill; and large blocky head with a "no-necked" appearance.

BEHAVIOR: Alcids are expert swimmers and divers, and use their wings instead of their feet to assist in diving and to "fly" underwater in pursuit of fish. Fast flight with continuous rapid, buzzing wingbeats is typical of alcids. They may also exhibit a "cork-popping" appearance when resurfacing from a dive. Some species form very large flocks near breeding sites, especially Common Murre and Dovekie. (See Figure 48, above.)

PLUMAGE PATTERNS AND GENERAL COLORATION: Alcids have black, white, and gray plumage patterns, with several murrelet species showing brownish or gold highlights to their breeding plumage. Some auklets and all puffins have bright yellow, orange, or red bills during breeding season.

HABITAT USE: Most alcids occur well offshore, but some species are regularly seen from land at Pacific Coast locations and at their breeding colonies. A few species are regularly seen from shore in winter at northern Atlantic coastal locations. Xantus and Craveri's Murrelets occur in warm southern waters off southern California and Mexico.

Rocky cliff ledges, rock crevices, and outcrops where terrestrial predators are absent are preferred colonial breeding sites for many alcids. Exceptions include Kittlitz's Murrelet, which nests on the ground among glaciers and snowfields, and Marbled Murrelet, which nests on the ground on steep forested hillsides. A few other murrelet species nest in earthen burrows.

VOCALIZATIONS: Most alcids are silent at sea away from breeding areas, with the exception of Marbled Murrelet, which gives frequent, high-pitched squealing sounds. Alcids give a wide variety of emphatic vocalizations at breeding sites, including whistles, clucks, moans, and growls.

COMPARISONS OF SIMILAR SPECIES

Nonbreeding Thick-billed Murre and Razorbill

UNCHANGING CHARACTERISTICS: Thick-billed Murre and Razorbill share a similar size and body shape, but Razorbill has a longer, pointed tail that it often raises when floating. This long tail distinguishes it from Thick-billed Murre, which has a short tail that extends only slightly from its body. (See Figure 49, below.) Adult Razorbill has a noticeably thicker, more rounded bill than Thick-billed Murre. However, immature Razorbill has a smaller, thinner bill that is more similar to that of Thick-billed Murre.

SUPPLEMENTAL CHARACTERISTICS AND NON-BBI DETAILS: Although plumage patterns on these two species are similar, nonbreeding adult Razorbill has more extensive white feathering on the cheek than Thick-billed Murre, and it has a vertical white line on its deep, rounded bill. First-winter Razorbill lacks the vertical white line on the bill. Nonbreeding Thick-billed Murre has a white gape line that is lacking in Razorbill.

Nonbreeding Marbled, Kittlitz's, and Long-billed Murrelets

Kittlitz's and Marbled Murrelets are tiny seabirds that share the same range in Canada and Alaska. Long-billed Murrelet is an Asian species that occurs as a vagrant throughout North America. Almost all inland U.S. records of murrelets are Long-billed.

UNCHANGING CHARACTERISTICS: A smaller, shorter bill is a good structural feature to separate Kittlitz's Murrelet from the very similar Marbled Murrelet. Long-billed Murrelet has a noticeably longer and more pointed bill than Marbled. (See Figure 50, p. 53.)

SUPPLEMENTAL CHARACTERISTICS AND NON-BBI DETAILS: Nonbreeding Kittlitz's Murrelet differs from Marbled Murrelet in having more extensive white on the face, which extends above the eye, resulting in a narrow dark crown. Marbled has a broader dark crown that extends below the eye and adds to the impression of a narrow white rear collar. Long-billed Murrelet has a broad dark crown that extends slightly below the eye and a complete dark nape that lacks a white collar. Long-billed also has prominent

---

FIGURE 49. NONBREEDING RAZORBILL AND THICK-BILLED MURRE
These two black-and-white alcids can be difficult to identify at long distances and in rough sea conditions. Good looks will reveal that Razorbill (L) has a deep, rounded bill with a vertical white line and a long, pointed tail that is often raised. Thick-billed Murre (C) has a short, pointed bill with a white gape line and a more extensive black crown. Immature Razorbill (R) lacks the bulbous bill of adults and shows whiter feathering toward the nape.

FIGURE 50. NONBREEDING LONG-BILLED, MARBLED, AND KITTLITZ'S MURRELETS (QUIZ PHOTO)
These tiny alcids have somewhat similar nonbreeding plumages and are often hard to view because they constantly disappear behind small waves and frequently dive for food. Detailed ID information is provided in the text. Try to identify these birds based on this information. Answers are in the appendix, page 267.

white eye-arcs that are lacking in Marbled, but this feature is hard to see at a distance.

TROPICBIRDS

Tropicbirds are ternlike seabirds that are typically found over warm waters far offshore, except during the nesting season or when they're driven to shore by storms. Tropicbirds fly in a more direct fashion than terns and have stiffer, shallower wingbeats.

PHYSICAL PROFILE

Tropicbirds have slender, streamlined bodies; small, rounded heads; short, pointed bills; and very short legs with small webbed feet. Wings are long, slender, and angular. Adult birds have very long tail streamers. (See Figure 51, below.)

BIRDING BY IMPRESSION INFORMATION

SIZE: White-tailed Tropicbird is the smallest species, at 15 in. long without tail streamers (slightly larger than Forster's Tern), while Red-billed Tropicbird measures about 18 in. long (slightly smaller than Royal Tern).

STRUCTURAL FEATURES: The larger Red-billed Tropicbird has a longer wingspan (44 vs. 37 in.) and a bigger bill than White-tailed Tropicbird.

BEHAVIOR: Tropicbirds plunge-dive to catch their diet of fish, and they often rest on the water.

PLUMAGE PATTERNS AND GENERAL COLORATION: Tropicbirds are white overall with distinctive black markings on their wings and upperparts. Bill color differs in adults and juveniles, with adults having red (Red-billed) or orange (White-tailed) bills, and juveniles having yellowish bills.

HABITAT USE: After breeding on tropical islands outside the mainland United States, tropicbirds frequent far offshore pelagic waters. Two of the three species worldwide regularly occur in southern North American waters, with the third species, Red-tailed Tropicbird, a rare vagrant in far offshore California waters.

VOCALIZATIONS: Generally silent at sea, tropicbirds give harsh, ternlike calls near their breeding sites.

FIGURE 51. TROPICBIRDS
Somewhat similar body and wing shapes and long tail streamers are offset by distinctly different plumage in these adult tropicbirds (see text for details). White-tailed Tropicbird (L) and Red-billed Tropicbird (R).

COMPARISONS OF SIMILAR SPECIES

Red-billed Tropicbird and White-tailed Tropicbird

UNCHANGING CHARACTERISTICS: White-tailed Tropicbird has a more buoyant flight style than Red-billed Tropicbird, including quicker, more flicking wingbeats.

SUPPLEMENTAL CHARACTERISTICS AND NON-BBI DETAILS: Adult Red-billed Tropicbird differs from White-tailed Tropicbird by its red rather than yellowish orange bill. Red-billed also has a finely black-barred back and inner upperwing, while White-tailed has a white back and upperwing with striking angled black lines that extend from the rear inner wing to the leading edge of the mid-forewing. (See Figure 51, p. 53.)

Juveniles pose more formidable ID problems, with both species having yellowish bills and black barring on the upperparts. Red-billed differs by having denser dark upperparts barring and a black eye line that connects across the nape. Juvenile White-tailed has less extensive black barring on the upperparts and a short grayish eye line. Juvenile Red-billed also has black upperwing primary coverts versus white ones in White-tailed.

MAGNIFICENT FRIGATEBIRD, BOOBIES, NORTHERN GANNET, CORMORANTS, ANHINGA, AND PELICANS

This diverse mix includes five bird families that are grouped in several taxonomic orders. All are found in aquatic habitats.

Magnificent Frigatebird, Boobies, and Northern Gannet

All species in these groups are powerful fliers that are found in near coastal or offshore pelagic waters. Northern Gannet and boobies plunge-dive for fish, while frigatebirds either harass gulls, terns, and other seabirds for their food or pick small prey from the water's surface while flying.

PHYSICAL PROFILE

All of these birds have fairly heavy, streamlined bodies and are generally similar in structure, with long, narrow wings and strong bills. Boobies and Northern Gannet have long, powerful, pointed bills, while Magnificent Frigatebird has a long, narrow bill with a hooked tip. (See Figure 52, p. 55.)

BIRDING BY IMPRESSION INFORMATION

SIZE: At 40 in. long, Magnificent Frigatebird is a very large seabird with a wingspan of almost 8 ft., which is almost a foot longer than that of Bald Eagle. Northern Gannet (37 in. long) is larger than all boobies and has a 6-ft. wingspan. Boobies range in size from Red-footed Booby, at 28 in. long, to Masked Booby, at 32 in. long, which is slightly larger than Great Black-backed Gull.

STRUCTURAL FEATURES: Magnificent Frigatebird has the longest wings in relation to its body weight (3 1/3 lb.) of all birds, which allows it to soar endlessly. It is reminiscent of an ancient pterodactyl with its long, narrow wings; long, slender, but powerful hooked bill; and long tail with two extended tail feathers.

Northern Gannet and boobies have strong, pointed bills; relatively long necks; and long, pointed tails and wings. They also have long, narrow, angular wings, and smoothly rounded heads that resemble those of loons when birds are floating.

BEHAVIOR: Northern Gannet and boobies fly with a steady flap-and-glide fashion either low over the water or high in the sky. Sudden, dramatic falls from the sky culminate with spectacular plunge-dives into the water to catch fish and squid. While all species can vary their diving styles, gannets usually dive perpendicular to the water, while Brown, Red-footed, and Masked Boobies typically dive at an angle. Blue-footed Booby dives range from vertical to angled, which may be related to water depth or the location of fish underwater (see Figure 54, p. 57), and Masked Booby occasionally plunges into the water with a vertical dive.

Magnificent Frigatebird soars endlessly, often without flapping, but can fly swiftly and agilely while chasing terns and other seabirds to steal their food. Boobies and Northern Gannet nest colonially on rocky cliffs and islands, while Magnificent Frigatebird builds stick nests in trees and shrubs on tropical islands.

PLUMAGE PATTERNS AND GENERAL COLORATION: Magnificent Frigatebird shows a variety of plumages depending on age and sex. Adult males are all black with a red throat pouch and dark feet. Adult females have a dark head, body, and wings with a white upper breast and yellow-orange feet. Juveniles and immatures in their second year resemble females but have a completely white head and neck. (See Figure 53, right photo, p. 55.) Both females and juveniles/immatures have a whitish carpal bar on the upperwing.

Adult Northern Gannet and Masked Booby are superficially similar in plumage—white overall with black wingtips—but Masked Booby differs by having dark secondary flight feathers. (See Figure 52, p. 55.) The other three booby species have a mixture of brown and white feathering, and Red-

FIGURE 52. MAGNIFICENT FRIGATEBIRD, BOOBIES, AND NORTHERN GANNET
All of the birds in these groups are very large. *Clockwise from top left:* Adult Masked Booby, adult Northern Gannet, male (all dark) and female Magnificent Frigatebirds, and adult Brown Booby. (Frigatebirds are not scaled to size.)

FIGURE 53. ADULT LONG-TAILED JAEGER AND IMMATURE MAGNIFICENT FRIGATEBIRDS
We identified immature Magnificent Frigatebirds (R) in Key West, FL, in 1979 as Long-tailed Jaegers (L) during our first year of birding because of similarities in black-and-white plumage and long tail streamers. Noting the dramatic size and wingspan differences of these species would have helped us identify them correctly (15-in. length, 43-in. wingspan for Long-tailed Jaeger; 40-in. length, 90-in. wingspan for Magnificent Frigatebird). Photos are not scaled to size; frigatebirds are much larger.

footed has several color morphs, including dark, light, and intermediate. Juvenile and immature Northern Gannet and boobies have variable combinations of dark and light feathering on underparts and upperparts.

HABITAT USE: All species frequent deep offshore waters, but Northern Gannet and Magnificent Frigatebird are regularly seen from shore. While Northern Gannet is a northern, cold-water species, boobies and Magnificent Frigatebird are tropical species that reside in warm to cool-water locations. Brown Booby is often seen from shore in tropical locations outside the United States where nest colonies occur.

VOCALIZATIONS: Not relevant to ID.

COMPARISONS OF SIMILAR SPECIES

Northern Gannet and Boobies

UNCHANGING CHARACTERISTICS: Northern Gannet is slightly larger than Masked, Nazca, and Blue-footed Boobies, but noticeably larger than Brown and Red-footed Boobies. Nazca Booby, which occurs mainly outside of U.S. waters, was recently split from Masked Booby and differs mainly in its orange bill color versus pale yellow in Masked. Northern Gannet's larger size and longer, heavier wings are good structural features to help separate it from all boobies. (See Figure 54, p. 57.) Northern Gannet often sits on the water for longer periods after surfacing from a successful plunge-dive, while boobies do not.

While boobies regularly sit on buoys, trees, rocks, or beaches away from breeding areas, Northern Gannet rarely does so, preferring to rest on the water for extended periods. Masked Booby usually sits on level ground but occasionally joins Brown and Red-footed Boobies in trees or on offshore buoys. Blue-footed Booby prefers to sit on rocks.

SUPPLEMENTAL CHARACTERISTICS AND NON-BBI DETAILS: Adult Northern Gannet is most similar to Masked and Nazca Boobies in its overall white plumage with black wingtips, but it lacks the black secondary flight feathers and dark tail tip that are present in Masked and Nazca Boobies. Masked has a greenish yellow bill and Nazca an orange-pink bill, while Northern Gannet's is gray. Juvenile and immature boobies and Northern Gannet may have plumage similarities, and careful assessment of their variable underwing patterns is helpful to their ID.

Immature Northern Gannet and Masked Booby have whiter bellies than juvenile and immature Brown Boobies, which have a noticeably darker hooded appearance that contrasts with a lighter brown to tan belly. Juvenile Red-footed Booby has mostly dark underwings, which differs from all other boobies. Adult Red-footed has several plumage morphs, including white and dark.

Adult Blue-footed Booby has a white body and head, with fine dark streaks on the head and neck. Juveniles are mostly brown above, with a brown-hooded appearance contrasting with white underparts. Subtle plumage differences from Brown Booby include a white (versus brownish) belly and grayish blue (versus yellow) feet. Another helpful tip is the usual lack of overlap in the normal ranges of Blue-footed and Brown Boobies.

Cormorants and Anhinga

All members of these groups are fish-eating birds that swim underwater in pursuit of food. While cormorants grab fish with their powerful bills, Anhinga often spears fish with its pointed bill. All regularly perch on rocks or snags while holding their wings out (vulture-style) to dry, which they need to do because, unlike other birds, they lack oil on their feathers.

PHYSICAL PROFILE

Long gooselike bodies are a shared feature among cormorants, with Anhinga being more slender overall. Cormorants have long necks and slender but powerful hooked bills. Anhinga's neck is longer and more snakelike than those of cormorants, and its bill is pointed and daggerlike. All have short legs and webbed feet that help propel them underwater. (See Figure 55, p. 58.)

BIRDING BY IMPRESSION INFORMATION

SIZE: Great Cormorant is the largest of this group, at 36 in. long (about the size of Northern Gannet), while Neotropic Cormorant is the smallest, at 25 in. long (about the size of Red-throated Loon). Anhinga is 35 in. long, but a good part of this measurement is its long tail and neck; its body is about the same size as Neotropic Cormorant's.

STRUCTURAL FEATURES: While swimming, cormorants resemble ducks and geese, but when out of the water they sit in an upright fashion because of their leg placement near the rear of their bodies and thus front-heavy weight distribution. They have long, rounded wings and stocky heads with rounded crowns. Anhinga has long, pointed wings and a longer rounded tail than cormorants.

BEHAVIOR: Cormorants and Anhinga are colonial-nesting birds, but nonbreeders are found either singly or in small to medium-sized groups in winter. Large groups of cormorants and Anhingas often fly high in V formation during migration.

PLUMAGE PATTERNS AND GENERAL COLORATION: Adult cormorants are black overall and have variably colored bare facial skin (yellow, orange, red, or blue). Great and Neotropic Cormorants have white feathering bordering their facial skin. Immature cormorants range from brownish black to pale brown overall.

Juvenile Great Cormorant has a grayish head and white belly, while some juvenile Double-cresteds have a whitish upper breast and dusky belly. An-

FIGURE 54. NORTHERN GANNET AND MASKED, BROWN, AND BLUE-FOOTED BOOBIES

Northern Gannet and three booby species in typical plunge-dive behavior. Northern Gannet (top L) usually plunge-dives in a vertical fashion, while the three boobies often use a more angled approach. These are only guidelines, however, with Blue-footed Booby regularly diving vertically, and Masked Booby sometimes diving vertically. *Clockwise from top left:* Immature Northern Gannet, immature Masked Booby, adult Brown Booby, and adult Blue-footed Booby.

hinga has bold white wing markings and a black lower body. Adult males have dark heads and necks, while females and immatures have buffy ones. Immatures lack the bold white wing markings.

HABITAT USE: Double-crested and Neotropic Cormorants breed at inland freshwater locations but may be found in winter at inland lakes or along saltwater coastlines. The other cormorants are residents of saltwater coastal areas, with Great Cormorant found along the northern Atlantic Coast and Brandt's, Pelagic, and Red-faced Cormorants along rocky Pacific coastlines. Red-faced is found only in Alaska. Anhinga is a resident of southern freshwater wooded ponds and swamps.

VOCALIZATIONS: Cormorants are generally silent except at their breeding colonies, where they give a variety of grunts, croaks, and guttural sounds. Anhinga is quite vocal and gives a mixture of croaks and froglike grunts when perched.

COMPARISONS OF SIMILAR SPECIES

Anhinga and Cormorants

UNCHANGING CHARACTERISTICS: Anhinga is similar to cormorants in appearance and behavior but differs structurally by having a long, straight bill rather than a hooked one, and a head that is the same width as the neck, resulting in an odd, bow-and arrow-like appearance in flight. Pointed wings and a very long, fan-shaped tail are good features

FIGURE 55. CORMORANTS AND ANHINGA

An assortment of typical cormorant and Anhinga views. *Top:* Double-crested Cormorant wing-drying (L) and swimming (C), and Brandt's Cormorant resting on a Pacific Coast cliff (R). *Bottom:* All Anhingas. A breeding female (L), a female and male on the nest (C), and a wing-drying male (R).

FIGURE 56. ANHINGA AND DOUBLE-CRESTED CORMORANT IN FLIGHT (QUIZ PHOTO)

Double-crested Cormorant is a migratory species that is regularly seen high overhead and is sometimes mistaken for Anhinga. Try to identify each species after reviewing ID information in the text. Answers are in the appendix, page 267.

to separate a soaring Anhinga from cormorants, which have slightly more rounded wings and shorter tails. Cormorants have fairly large heads that are obvious at the end of long, thin necks when you see them overhead in flight. (See Figure 56, above.)

Anhinga is known casually as "the snake bird," since it often swims with just its neck and head above the water and resembles a water snake. Cor-

morants swim with their bodies above water, similar to diving ducks.

SUPPLEMENTAL CHARACTERISTICS AND NON-BBI DETAILS: Since adult cormorants and Anhinga both have mostly black underparts, there are no outstanding plumage traits that are useful for separating these species in flight overhead. However, a few subtle field marks may be helpful to your ID. Anhinga has

FIGURE 57. DOUBLE-CRESTED CORMORANT AND GREAT CORMORANT, IMMATURES
The differences between these two similar species in immature plumage are provided in the text below.
Top: Immature Double-crested Cormorants. *Bottom:* Immature Great Cormorants.

bright yellow feet that are visible unless a bird is flying very high, and Double-crested Cormorant has bright orange facial skin that may also be visible on low-flying birds. A buffy tail tip is also visible on Anhinga, but this feature is hard to pick out unless the sun is shining through the pale feathers from above.

Great Cormorant and Double-crested Cormorant

UNCHANGING CHARACTERISTICS: Great Cormorant is the largest and bulkiest of all cormorants, with an 11-in.-longer wingspan than Double-crested Cormorant (63 vs. 52 in.) and a much heavier body (7¼ vs. 3¾ lb.). Great's heavier body and longer wings result in a different flight style of slower, heavier wingbeats and a larger overall physical profile. (See Figure 57, above.)

SUPPLEMENTAL CHARACTERISTICS AND NON-BBI DETAILS: Several plumage details are helpful for separating these two species. Breeding Great Cormorant has distinctive white patches on the rear flanks and a large white border beneath the limited pale yellow facial skin just below the bill. Double-crested Cormorant lacks the white feathering below the bill and has more extensive orange facial skin, including a larger orange chin patch that extends upward to its eye and loral area, unlike Great, whose yellowish orange bare facial skin is restricted to the area behind and below the bill.

Immature Great has a clean white belly that contrasts with a brownish neck and upper breast, while young Double-crested has a pale brownish neck and breast with a slightly darker lower belly. This difference is easy to notice on both perched and flying birds. Some young Double-cresteds may have whitish underparts with a darker lower belly, but all lack the sharp dividing line between brown neck and white belly that is present in immature Great. Immature Great also has whitish feathering on the chin that is lacking in immature Double-crested.

Double-crested Cormorant and Neotropic Cormorant

With a continuing expansion of Neotropic Cormorant's range into the southern United States, these two species are now seen together in greater numbers in Texas and Louisiana. In recent years (2011–present) Neotropic has moved into Florida and has bred with Double-crested. In 2014 Kevin observed several hybrids breeding with pure Double-crested and Neotropic Cormorants in Boynton Beach, FL. Continued interbreeding, and the hybrids resulting from it, will surely result in further ID confusion.

UNCHANGING CHARACTERISTICS: Neotropic Cormorant is noticeably smaller than Double-crested Cormorant, but its small size is often difficult to discern unless the two species are near each other. Neotropic also has a longer tail, smaller head, shorter bill, and slightly thinner neck. A helpful ID feature for

FIGURE 58. DOUBLE-CRESTED CORMORANT AND NEOTROPIC CORMORANT

Top: See text for differences between Double-crested Cormorant (L and top R) and Neotropic Cormorant (C and bottom R). *Bottom:* The two species flying together. Note the smaller size, thinner neck, smaller bill, and longer tail on the Neotropic Cormorant (L).

flying Neotropic is the almost equal projection of the head and neck in front of the wings compared with the rear body and tail extension behind the wings. Double-crested has noticeably less extension of the rear body and tail behind the wings compared with its longer neck and head extension in front of the wings. These differences in structural features create a "plus sign" flight shape for Neotropic versus Double-crested's reverse "cross" shape in overhead flight. (See Figure 58, above.)

SUPPLEMENTAL CHARACTERISTICS AND NON-BBI DETAILS: Breeding Double-crested Cormorant differs from Neotropic Cormorant by the presence of a larger amount of deep orange facial skin with a rounder rear border versus narrower yellowish orange facial skin with a pointed rear border in Neotropic. A good distinguishing feature is the more extensive orange facial skin in Double-crested that extends above the bill into the loral area and continues to the eye. On most Neotropics the paler orange facial skin is located beneath the bill and does not extend to the loral area. A few individuals have a slight amount of bare orange skin above the bill, but it is nowhere near as extensive as on Double-crested.

Immature Neotropic is somewhat similar in plumage to immature Double-crested, but it has a uniformly darker brown breast compared with Double-crested's pale brown upper breast with darker lower belly. Immature Neotropic also has a pointed gape behind the bill.

Pelicans

Pelicans are among the most recognizable birds in the world because of their large size and unique, large, shovel-like bills.

PHYSICAL PROFILE

Both pelican species have heavy, rounded, yet elongated bodies. Unmistakable long, heavy bills with expandable pouches are the pelicans' trademark feature. They also have long necks and long, powerful wings. (See Figure 59, p. 61.)

BIRDING BY IMPRESSION INFORMATION

SIZE: White Pelican is one of the largest birds in North America, at 62 in. long and with a 9-ft. (108-in.) wingspan. Brown Pelican is 52 in. long with a 79-in. wingspan, which is about the size of Tundra Swan.

FIGURE 59. PELICANS
Brown Pelican (L) is much smaller and weighs less than American White Pelican (R), and their size difference shows when they occur together (C).

STRUCTURAL FEATURES: Both species have short, thick legs and large, powerful webbed feet. See Physical Profile (p. 60) for additional structural features.

BEHAVIOR: Brown Pelicans plunge-dive for fish, often in loose groups. They also course low over the water in lines without flapping their wings for extended periods. White Pelicans swim in groups and herd fish into lake corners or shallow water, where they scoop them up with their massive bills. White Pelicans often soar very high for long periods in large groups. Pelicans breed in colonies, and form small to large groups away from breeding areas.

PLUMAGE PATTERNS AND GENERAL COLORATION: White Pelicans are white overall with black wingtips and a black trailing edge to the wings. They have a bright orange bill and legs. Young birds have a grayish wash to their backs and necks. Adult Brown Pelicans have a gray back, brown underparts, and a whitish to yellow neck and head. The bill is brownish to gray with a pale upper mandible. Pacific-breeding birds have a bright red throat pouch, while Atlantic and Gulf Coast birds have a dark brown pouch. Juveniles are mostly brown overall with white underparts.

HABITAT USE: Brown Pelican is a coastal breeding species that is found on many temperate U.S. coastlines. White Pelican breeds on lakes at western prairie locations and winters in southern locations, both inland and along coastlines.

VOCALIZATIONS: Not relevant to ID.

Wading birds are some of the most visible birds in the world, and their stately body language and graceful flight make them favorites for birders everywhere. Though cranes and Limpkin are taxonomically grouped in the same order with rails, they are included in this group because their body structure and behaviors are similar to those of wading birds, and they use the same habitats.

HERONS, EGRETS, AND IBISES

Herons, egrets, and ibises are usually found in aquatic or intermittently wet habitats because of their food preference of fish, crustaceans, and aquatic insects or invertebrates. Most species nest and roost in medium-sized to large colonies in trees adjacent to wetlands. While the majority of species forage in or adjacent to water bodies, some also forage regularly in grassy fields, suburban lawns, and agricultural sites (Great Egret, Cattle Egret, and Great Blue Heron).

TIPS FOR SEPARATING SIMILAR WHITE-PLUMAGED HERONS AND EGRETS

Size, foraging behavior, and body posture can collectively help separate the six species of white egrets and herons, especially young birds, which appear more similar to each other than adults.

White-morph Great Blue Heron is very large and has a heavier body and bill than the smaller Great Egret. (See Figure 67, p. 70.) Both move more slowly than other herons and egrets when foraging, and often appear stately in their stalking behavior.

Snowy Egrets either hunt actively while running around or crouch quietly without moving until a fish swims past. They also run through the water while flapping their wings and snatch fish as they run. (See Figure 60, p. 63.) Immature white-plumaged Little Blue Heron walks slowly while foraging, with its neck outstretched and bill pointing toward the water or ground, and Reddish Egret sprints around frenetically chasing fish with wings outstretched. Reddish Egret also stands quietly in shallow water with its wings held out like an umbrella waiting for fish to seek shelter in its wing shadow. (See Figure 62, p. 65.)

PHYSICAL PROFILE

Herons, egrets, and ibises have elongated, football-shaped bodies and share similar structural features, with the exception of their bills. Many have long necks that form an S shape when retracted and long legs that allow them to forage in fairly deep water.

Herons and egrets have powerful long, straight, pointed bills suitable for spearing fish, while ibises have curved bills that they use to probe into mud for food. (See Figure 60, p. 63.) The long wings of wading birds enable sustained flights in migration and during daily hunting forays.

BIRDING BY IMPRESSION INFORMATION

SIZE: Species range from Green Heron (18 in. long), which is about the size of an oystercatcher, to Great Blue Heron, at 46 in. long (similar in size to Sandhill Crane).

Nine of the 13 North American heron, egret, and ibis species share a narrow size range from 20 to 26 in. long, with Green Heron (18 in.), Reddish Egret (30 in.), Great Egret (39 in.), and Great Blue Heron (46 in.) occurring outside this range.

STRUCTURAL FEATURES: Most herons and egrets have long legs and necks, but these features vary among different species. Great Blue Heron and Great Egret have exceptionally long legs and necks, while Reddish Egret has slightly shorter legs and a shorter, stockier neck than Great Egret. (See Figure 66, p. 69.) Green Heron has the shortest legs and neck, and a stocky body shape.

A group of four medium-sized, long-legged herons and egrets (Snowy and Cattle Egrets and Tricolored and Little Blue Herons) have somewhat similar physical features but have subtle to obvious differences in the structure of their body parts. Detailed descriptions of these differences are covered in the text on p. 66 and illustrated in Figure 65.

Three species of ibises (White, Glossy, and White-faced) are similar in size, shape, and leg length to Snowy Egret and Little Blue Heron, but their bills are decurved and longer than those of all herons and egrets.

BEHAVIOR: Herons and egrets are often seen standing in water stalking fish, frogs, and other aquatic animals. Hunting styles vary by species but generally fall into two categories: walking deliberately or running aggressively after fish and other small prey, or standing quietly near the water's edge waiting for fish or crustaceans to come by. Both stalking behaviors culminate with a quick thrust of the long neck and a spearing or grabbing of prey items.

Species that actively stalk prey include Great, Reddish, Snowy, and Cattle Egrets and Tricolored, Little Blue, and Great Blue Herons. Reddish Egret exhibits a different and more animated feeding behavior than other herons and egrets. (See Figure 62,

FIGURE 60. HERONS, EGRETS, AND IBISES
This diverse group of birds is represented by a variety of species. *Clockwise from top left:* Great Blue Heron, Yellow-crowned Night-Herons displaying, Snowy Egret fly-fishing, Cattle Egret in breeding plumage, White Ibis, and Black-crowned Night-Heron in breeding plumage.

p. 65.) Species that typically sit and wait for prey to come to them include Green Heron and Black-crowned and Yellow-crowned Night-Herons. Yellow-crowned also actively stalks small crabs and other prey on open beachfronts and in mangroves.

Ibises forage in a different fashion. They probe in soft mud and shallow water habitats by using their long bills to reach deep into the substrate. While fish are a major food source for most herons and egrets, small crustaceans and insect larvae make up a good portion of the ibis diet.

PLUMAGE PATTERNS AND GENERAL COLORATION: In addition to the four white egrets and white-morph Great Blue Heron, herons and some egrets show a variety of plumage colors and patterns. While many young herons and egrets have a plumage similar to that of adults, some have a distinctly different juvenile and immature plumage that remains for a year or more.

Young Black-crowned and Yellow-crowned Night-Herons have a brownish to grayish plumage with spots on the upperparts and streaks on the underparts (see Figure 63, p. 66), while immature Little Blue Heron is mostly white for much of its first year (see Figure 64, p. 67).

Immature dark-morph Reddish Egret has a grayish buff color instead of the rich reddish neck and deep gray body shading of adult birds, while immature white-morph Reddish Egret is similar in plumage to adults. Both color morphs lack the shaggy head and neck feathers of adult birds for the first two years of life.

Glossy Ibis and White-faced Ibis have an all-dark plumage that includes rufous necks, wings, and bellies in breeding birds. Nonbreeding birds have a brownish plumage that includes streaked heads and necks. (See Figure 68, p. 71.) Increased interbreeding now occurs in some southern locations around Louisiana, and resulting hybrids show a variety of plumage appearances that resemble either species or a combination of features from both. White Ibis is all white with black wingtips, and adult birds have a red bill and legs. Immature White Ibis has brownish wings, a brown-streaked neck, white underparts, and a white slash up the back. The bill and legs on immature birds are pale orange to pink.

HABITAT USE: A few members of this group are reliably found in specific habitats, and their suspected presence in other locations should cause extra scrutiny. For example, Reddish Egrets are found primarily in coastal zones, and although Cattle Egrets are sometimes found in wetland habitats, they are typically seen in grassy fields feeding on insects flushed by or attracted to cattle and other large mammals. They also sit on the backs of livestock and pick off pesky flies, with full endorsement by their larger hosts. If you see white egrets around cattle, it is a good bet that they are Cattle Egrets. (See Figure 61, below.)

VOCALIZATIONS: Although the nonmusical, guttural, raspy calls of herons and egrets may initially sound similar, there are slight differences in tonality and pitch. Over time you may detect slight dif-

ferences for each species. The sharp, rising *wok* calls of both night-herons differ from those of other wading birds by the lack of raspy tones. Green Heron also differs with its short, sharp, higher-pitched call. Great Blue Heron has a deep, harsh croaking call that differs from the smaller species' grating calls. Reddish Egret is mostly silent, but it gives softer, less harsh groans, similar to those of Tricolored Heron.

COMPARISONS OF SIMILAR SPECIES

Adult Dark-morph Reddish Egret and Adult Little Blue Heron

Adult dark-morph Reddish Egret and adult Little Blue Heron have similar plumage colors but differ in their size and structural features.

UNCHANGING CHARACTERISTICS: Reddish Egret is noticeably larger (30 in. long) than Little Blue Heron (24 in. long) and has a longer neck and legs. (See Figure 62, p. 65.) Feeding behaviors also differ, with Reddish Egret often running around frenetically, intermittently raising its wings while feeding, while Little Blue walks slowly and deliberately with its bill pointed at the water.

SUPPLEMENTAL CHARACTERISTICS AND NON-BBI DETAILS: Reddish Egret has a rust-colored head and neck, while adult Little Blue Heron has a purplish red color to these areas. While both species have a black-tipped bill, the base of Little Blue's is grayish to blue, and that of adult Reddish is pink. Immature Reddish Egrets can have a similar gray-based bill with a black tip. Adult Reddish also has shaggy feathers on its head and neck that are lacking in Little Blue, and Reddish has dark legs while Little Blue's are yellow.

FIGURE 61. CATTLE EGRETS WITH CATTLE

This small white egret is the only North American heron or egret that regularly associates with cattle and other large four-legged mammals. It feeds on insects and other small creatures flushed by or attracted to these animals, and often sits on their backs while looking for bugs.

FIGURE 62. REDDISH EGRET BEHAVIOR AND COMPARISON WITH ADULT LITTLE BLUE HERON

Top: Reddish Egret extends its wings outward to create a shadow in the water, which attracts small fish (L). "Sky dancing" is Kevin's term for an exuberant display of Reddish Egrets wherein they appear to run in the sky during low flights (R). *Bottom:* Adult Little Blue Heron (L) is often mistaken for adult dark-morph Reddish Egret (R) because of plumage similarities, but they differ in several ways. ID information is provided in the text.

Immature Black-crowned and Yellow-crowned Night-Herons, and American Bittern

The two night-herons share somewhat similar body shapes and structural features and have comparable immature plumages for most of their first year. With careful study, you will notice subtle differences in body and bill shape as well as plumage features. Juvenile plumage may be referred to as immature plumage after August because of a slightly different appearance caused by feather wear, even though the feathers are the same.

UNCHANGING CHARACTERISTICS: Yellow-crowned Night-Heron has a longer, thinner neck and more slender body. Combined with a stocky bill of a different shape, this creates a distinctly different profile than Black-crowned Night-Heron's.

Black-crowned's thick-based bill tapers to a fine point with a slightly decurved upper mandible and straight lower mandible. This differs from juvenile Yellow-crowned's stocky bill, on which the upper and lower mandibles are similar in shape. With careful comparison, Yellow-crowned's different bill shape combined with its smaller head becomes a reliable and recognizable physical impression, especially with silhouetted birds.

Compared with both night-herons, American Bittern is much larger and has a noticeably longer neck and bill. It also has a thin head that seems to be an extension of its neck, unlike both night-herons, which have defined head shapes. (See Figure 63, p. 66.)

SUPPLEMENTAL CHARACTERISTICS AND NON-BBI DETAILS: Immature Black-crowned Night-Heron's bill is mostly yellowish, especially the lower mandible, while immature Yellow-crowned Night-Heron has a mostly blackish gray bill that is often washed

FIGURE 63. BLACK-CROWNED NIGHT-HERON AND YELLOW-CROWNED NIGHT-HERON, JUVENILES, AND AMERICAN BITTERN (QUIZ PHOTO)
Structural differences are pointed out in the text, but subtle plumage differences between juvenile Yellow-crowned and Black-crowned Night-Herons include sparser, finer streaking and spotting against a grayer background on Yellow-crowned. American Bittern is larger with a longer neck that has bold brownish neck stripes against a pale background. Try to identify these birds. Answers are in the appendix, page 267.

whitish by salt in coastal locations. During a Yellow-crowned's first few months of life, its evenly proportioned bill has a yellowish lower mandible base similar to Black-crowned's, so care should be taken when evaluating this detail during summer months.

Subtle plumage differences are helpful in separating these two birds. Black-crowned is browner than the grayish-toned Yellow-crowned and has large, elongated white spots on the wing coverts, compared with finer ones on Yellow-crowned. Black-crowned also has broad, blurry streaks on the underparts compared with narrow, sparser, more defined spots in Yellow-crowned.

American Bittern shows slight plumage similarities to both juvenile night-herons and is often found in the same wetland habitats. It has a uniformly unstreaked brownish crown, nape, and back; buff cheeks; and complex, fine markings on its wing coverts. Its underparts and neck are more heavily streaked, with greater pale background than on both immature night-herons, and its yellow iris differs from orange ones in night-herons. (See Figure 63, above.)

Snowy Egret and Little Blue Heron, Juveniles
While adult and older immature birds of these two species are easily separable by plumage, young juveniles can be problematic. A few subtly different structural impressions and plumage details help distinguish juveniles of these two species.

UNCHANGING CHARACTERISTICS: Careful comparison shows that Snowy Egret has a longer, thinner neck and more slender, daggerlike bill compared with Little Blue Heron's shorter, bulkier neck and thicker bill (which has a slight decurve to the upper mandible). Little Blue also has somewhat thicker legs and a stockier body structure than Snowy, which further adds to a different physical impression. Snowy's longer legs extend farther beyond the tail in flight than Little Blue's shorter legs do. (See Figure 65, p. 68.)

SUPPLEMENTAL CHARACTERISTICS AND NON-BBI DETAILS: Young juvenile Snowy Egrets and Little Blue Herons have an all-white plumage and may have similar greenish yellow legs and variably gray- to pinkish-colored bills with dark tips. As Snowy matures, its legs turn blackish, while Little Blue's legs remain greenish yellow. At a young age (1–3 months), Snowy may have pale yellowish lores, while Little Blue has pale grayish, pink, or yellowish lores. Small dark tips to the outer primary flight feathers are distinctive for juvenile Little Blue, but these are often hard to see. (See Figure 64, p. 67.)

Medium-sized Herons and Egrets in Flight
While the four medium-sized, long-legged herons and egrets appear somewhat similar with respect to body shape and structural features, they have subtle, yet recognizable differences. When the birds are seen in silhouette, the differences become clearer.

FIGURE 64. SNOWY EGRET AND LITTLE BLUE HERON, JUVENILES (QUIZ PHOTO)
Several different structural features give Little Blue Heron a subtly different physical appearance than Snowy Egret. The dusky primary tips on juvenile Little Blue Heron are hard to see in the field. Try to identify all four birds to species after reading the ID information in the text. Answers are in the appendix, page 268.

UNCHANGING CHARACTERISTICS: Cattle Egret has the stockiest, most compact body shape and the shortest legs of all four species. It also has a short, thick bill and short neck. These features result in a compact flight silhouette with only the feet and a little leg extending beyond the tail and a greatly reduced retracted neck projection compared with the other species.

Little Blue Heron has the second shortest legs, which extend moderately past the tail in flight, and

FIGURE 65. MEDIUM-SIZED HERONS AND EGRETS IN FLIGHT (QUIZ PHOTO)
Four medium-sized herons and egrets may be identified in flight using a combination of body shape and structural features. Can you identify the species in real life and in silhouette? Detailed ID information is provided in the text, and answers are in the appendix, page 268.

a shorter, thicker neck than Snowy Egret, resulting in a smaller retracted neck profile. A thicker-based, more tapered bill gives Little Blue a different profile than both Snowy Egret and Tricolored Heron. Little Blue also has slightly broader wings than Snowy.

Snowy has longer legs than both Little Blue Heron and Cattle Egret, and they extend noticeably past the tail, with the ankle joint (midpoint of the leg) almost reaching the tail tip. Snowy also has a long, thinner, daggerlike bill, and its long neck creates a distinct elongated U-shaped retracted neck projection in flight (C-shaped in silhouette).

Tricolored Heron has the longest, thinnest neck of all, which creates a deeper retracted neck profile in flight. Its bill is also longer and thicker-based than Snowy's, and when combined with the longer neck creates a distinctive flight profile. The long

neck retracted in flight is reminiscent of a drainage trap from a kitchen sink. Leg length projection past the tail is similar to Snowy's or slightly longer.

SUPPLEMENTAL CHARACTERISTICS AND NON-BBI DETAILS: The distinctive colorful plumages of adult Little Blue and Tricolored Herons of all ages are helpful in identifying these medium-sized herons and egrets in flight. If light conditions are good, Snowy and Cattle Egrets share similar all-white plumages, as does immature Little Blue.

Snowy Egret, Great Egret, and White-morph Reddish Egret

A recurring problem for birders involves the identification of immature white-morph Reddish Egret that doesn't have a shaggy crest, throat, and nape.

FIGURE 66. WHITE EGRET COMPARISON
This interesting photo of three white egret species illustrates obvious structural differences in Snowy Egret (the numerous smallest birds) and Great Egret (rear center left). White-morph Reddish Egret (rear center right) falls in between the other two species in size and structural features. ID information about physical differences is provided in the text.

When seen alone, it is often overlooked as a large Snowy Egret or a small Great Egret because of similarities in plumage, bill, and leg color. When seen together, a few size and structural differences become clearer.

UNCHANGING CHARACTERISTICS: Reddish Egret (30 in. long) is in between the size of Snowy Egret (25 in. long) and Great Egret (39 in. long). Reddish has a noticeably longer neck than Snowy and a shorter, thicker neck than Great. Its legs are much longer than Snowy's, yet slightly shorter than Great's long legs. Reddish has a longer and thicker bill than Snowy, and a bill that is superficially similar in thickness and length to Great's. (See Figure 66, above.)

SUPPLEMENTAL CHARACTERISTICS AND NON-BBI DETAILS: Gray lores and a variably gray to pink bill with a well-defined black outer portion on young Reddish Egret differ from Snowy Egret's yellow lores and all-black bill, and from Great Egret's yellowish to green lores and yellow bill with variably black culmen and bill tip. Leg color is grayish to black in Reddish, black in Great, and yellowish black with yellow feet in immature Snowy.

Great Egret and White-morph Great Blue Heron
Great Blue Heron has two plumage morphs, one of which is mostly white. This white morph resembles Great Egret in plumage and general shape but oc-curs only in south Florida. Occasional intergrades occur with dark-morph Great Blue, and the offspring typically have bluish bodies and whitish heads. This intergrade was formerly considered a separate species known as Würdemann's Heron.

UNCHANGING CHARACTERISTICS: Great Blue Heron is larger than Great Egret (46 vs. 39 in. long) and has a much heavier, straighter bill with a narrowing of the upper mandible near the tip compared with Great Egret's thinner bill.

SUPPLEMENTAL CHARACTERISTICS AND NON-BBI DETAILS: White-morph Great Blue Heron has buff, pinkish, or grayish legs versus Great Egret's black legs. Great Egret has showy rear body plumes, while white-morph Great Blue has short, stiff lower neck and rear body plumes and a few wispy white plumes on the back of its head (adults). First-year birds and nonbreeding adults lack these rear head plumes. Breeding white-morph Great Blue has blue facial skin in the loral area, while Great Egret has green to yellow skin. Both species can show colorful facial skin in nonbreeding adults that are transitioning to breeding condition but have not yet acquired showy breeding plumes and feathers.

Nonbreeding Glossy Ibis and White-faced Ibis
Immature and nonbreeding Glossy Ibis and White-faced Ibis are difficult to separate, with only subtle differences in plumage and bare-parts color. Glossy

FIGURE 67. GREAT EGRET AND WHITE-MORPH GREAT BLUE HERON (QUIZ PHOTO)
These two similar wading birds are found together in south Florida, but a few structural differences can be combined with differences in leg color and location of breeding plumes to reach a solid ID. Try to ID these birds after reading the information in the text. Answers are in the appendix, page 268.

is an eastern counterpart of the western-breeding White-faced. Recent expansion of Glossy to western Gulf Coast locations has resulted in increasing numbers of hybrids with White-faced.

UNCHANGING CHARACTERISTICS: White-faced Ibis averages slightly larger than Glossy Ibis, but this subtle difference is best seen in direct comparison and is very difficult, if not impossible, to distinguish with single species. (See Figure 68, top photo, p. 71.)

SUPPLEMENTAL CHARACTERISTICS AND NON-BBI DETAILS: Nonbreeding adult White-faced Ibis has a red iris and pinkish facial skin in the loral area, while Glossy Ibis has a dark iris and grayish facial skin bordered by thin white to bluish lines. Adult White-faced also has pale reddish legs versus gray legs in Glossy. Juvenile White-faced may not show any red color to the legs from late summer to early winter, but typically shows a dull red eye at these times. Glossy may have reddish ankle joints in late winter to early spring, with breeding Glossy showing variable amounts of reddish color on its legs. Nonbreeding White-faced also has paler rosy greater wing coverts and tertials than Glossy. (See Figure 68, p. 71.)

WOOD STORK, ROSEATE SPOONBILL, BITTERNS, FLAMINGOS, CRANES, AND LIMPKIN

These six groups of birds pose few ID problems. All of these species forage and nest near wetland habitats.

PHYSICAL PROFILE

All of these species have rounded yet elongated bodies that taper at the rear. They have long, thin legs, although Least and American Bitterns have proportionally shorter legs. Necks are long and slender, with Wood Stork and Roseate Spoonbill having the shortest necks and Greater Flamingo having the longest and thinnest. Both bitterns have long necks that are usually retracted, with American Bittern having a noticeably longer, thinner neck. Bills are variable and very different in shape. (See Figure 69, p. 72.)

BIRDING BY IMPRESSION INFORMATION

SIZE: The majority of birds in these groups are large, ranging from American Bittern, at 28 in. long, to Greater Flamingo and "Greater" Sandhill

FIGURE 68. NONBREEDING GLOSSY IBIS AND WHITE-FACED IBIS (QUIZ PHOTO)
Two nonbreeding dark ibises photographed in Texas in March appear very similar but show subtle differences. Detailed ID information is provided in the text. For an expert-level quiz, try to identify the ibises in all three photos. Two mottled white and brown immature White Ibises (L and C) share the top photo along with two smaller Blue-winged Teal. The bottom photos show a closer view of these two species. Answers are in the appendix, page 268.

Crane, at 46 in. long (similar to Great Blue Heron). The oddball is the tiny Least Bittern, which at 13 in. long is the smallest wading bird in North America.

STRUCTURAL FEATURES: Bill length and shape are among the most obvious differences in these birds. Wood Stork has a fairly long, stout bill that tapers and decurves near the tip, while Roseate Spoonbill has a unique long, flat bill that is shaped like a spoon. American and Least Bitterns have moderately long, straight, powerful bills that taper to a point at the tip, while Greater Flamingo has one of the most unusual bills, shaped like an inverted scoop with a point at the end.

While body shape is mostly similar among these groups, Sandhill and Whooping Cranes have a unique bustle of feathers at the rear, and Greater Flamingo has very long, sticklike legs and a moderately long tail and wings that extend beyond its body. Wood Stork's hunched foraging posture is distinctive.

BEHAVIOR: Differences in foraging behavior are marked in these groups. Wood Stork inserts its slightly agape bill into shallow water and stirs up food by vibrating its foot underwater. Roseate Spoonbill swishes its bill from side to side in the water to trap fish and other prey items. Least Bittern typically sits quietly close to the water and grabs fish with a quick thrust of its long neck, while American Bittern walks slowly in marshes or grassy areas, like a Great Egret, while stalking its prey of crawfish, large insects, and other aquatic invertebrates. Flamingos swish their odd bills from side to side and upside down in the water while straining diatoms, algae, and invertebrates. (See Figure 69, p. 72.)

Cranes forage by walking deliberately and stately with their necks raised. When they spot prey, they tip their bodies and thrust their long necks to grab their food. Limpkin has a very restricted diet of apple snails and other crustaceans, which it finds by probing its long bill into shallow-water substrates.

FIGURE 69. WOOD STORK, ROSEATE SPOONBILL, BITTERNS, FLAMINGOS, CRANES, AND LIMPKIN
Birds in these six groups are residents of aquatic or marshy habitats, although cranes and Wood Stork also forage in fields. *Clockwise from top left:* Wood Stork, Roseate Spoonbill, male Least Bittern, Limpkin, Sandhill Crane, and Greater Flamingo.

PLUMAGE PATTERNS AND GENERAL COLORATION: Most of these groups share no similar plumage color or patterns, with the exception of Roseate Spoonbill and Greater Flamingo. Both have a rich, pinkish orange color and reddish to pink legs. (See Figure 70, p. 73.) The others birds have distinctive color, shading, or plumage patterns. Whooping Crane differs from Sandhill Crane with a white versus gray plumage. Female and immature Least Bitterns have brown versus black backs and upperwing borders like the male shown in Figure 69. Juvenile Roseate Spoonbill and Greater Flamingo may appear whitish overall.

HABITAT USE: While all species are regularly found in wetland habitats, several are exclusive to aquatic environments throughout the year (Least Bittern, Limpkin, Roseate Spoonbill, and Greater Flamingo). American Bittern and both cranes can be found in grassy areas adjacent to wetlands, with cranes also frequenting agricultural fields. Some Wood Storks have become so accustomed to people in Florida that they can be found accepting food at close range in backyards. Wood Stork, Roseate Spoonbill, and Greater Flamingo nest colonially, while the others are solitary nesters.

VOCALIZATIONS: Wood Stork is mostly silent, except for bill clattering and grunting near its nest, while Roseate Spoonbill gives muffled grunting sounds similar to those of ibises. Greater Flamingo gives a gooselike honking sound in flight and a low gobbling sound while feeding. American Bittern gives a deep, repetitive gulping sound during breeding season, while Least Bittern has a low, cooing sound. Cranes give a loud, bugling call year-round, while Limpkin has a loud, wailing call that sounds like someone screaming in agony.

FIGURE 70. ROSEATE SPOONBILLS WITH OTHER SPECIES

Striking pink and white coloration and a long, spatula-shaped bill are prominent features of Roseate Spoonbill. Size, shape, and structural differences are obvious when comparing Black-necked Stilts (black-and-white shorebirds), immature White Ibises (large waders at right with long, decurved, orange bills), and numerous Blue-winged Teal (background).

Nine of 12 species in the order Gruiformes are covered in this chapter. Three species not covered (Sandhill Crane, Whooping Crane, and Limpkin) are included in the previous chapter because they share physical features and behavior with species in that group.

RAILS

Rails are secretive birds that are more often heard than seen. When seen, the bird is usually scooting through vegetation or marsh clearings. A positive ID may require a careful assessment of size and structure along with habitat type. Elevated boardwalks or impoundment dikes can be reliable places to see these birds, since they don't feel as threatened and are somewhat acclimated to human presence.

PHYSICAL PROFILE

The two smallest rails (Yellow Rail and Black Rail) are plump and rounded with very short tails and necks and short, stubby, pointed bills.

The other four species have longer, oval-shaped bodies with distended bellies, longer necks, and longer tails that are often cocked upward. Three of the four species (Virginia, King, and Clapper Rails) have long, slender pointed bills, while Sora's bill is short and stubby. (See Figure 71, below.)

BIRDING BY IMPRESSION INFORMATION

SIZE: The six species of North American rails range from the sparrow-sized Yellow Rail, at 6 in. long, to Clapper Rail, at 14 to 15 in. long, which is close in size to Common Gallinule. They fit neatly into three size categories: small (Black and Yellow Rails), medium (Virginia Rail and Sora), and large (Clapper and King Rails).

STRUCTURAL FEATURES: Rails have proportionally short, rounded wings and strong, thick legs. Leg length ranges from short in the small rails to medium-long in the two large rails. Toes are very long, which allows rails to move easily on and through marsh vegetation, and also to climb in dense tangles. Laterally compressed bodies allow rails to squeeze through narrow openings in vegetation.

BEHAVIOR: Rails often run quickly to escape danger, but they can also swim and dive underwater to avoid predators. Flight is slow and weak in local movements, often with the legs dangling. During migration, flight is fast and direct, with the legs pulled into the body.

PLUMAGE PATTERNS AND GENERAL COLORATION: Most rails have earth-tone coloration and cryptic plumage patterns. A few species have bright rust coloration on their breasts and necks (Virginia, King, and some subspecies of Clapper Rail).

HABITAT USE: Rails are residents of marshes and wet meadows and spend the majority of their time in dense vegetation. Yellow and Black Rails are occasionally found in wet, short-grass meadows during migration and in winter.

VOCALIZATIONS: A wide variety of vocalizations are given by rails, even within the same species. Yellow Rail's call sounds like two stones clicking together, while Clapper and King Rails give a series of loud, dry *kek-kek-kek* notes at different cadences. Virginia, King, and Clapper Rails give somewhat similar harsh grunting sounds, especially in winter. Sora has a unique whinnying call and a plaintive two-note rising call that mimics its name. It also gives just the distinctive first note of the two-note call, but mostly in winter.

FIGURE 71. RAILS

Rails are secretive birds that inhabit aquatic habitats. *From left to right:* Black Rail, Sora, Clapper Rail ("Atlantic Coast" subspecies), and immature Virginia Rail.

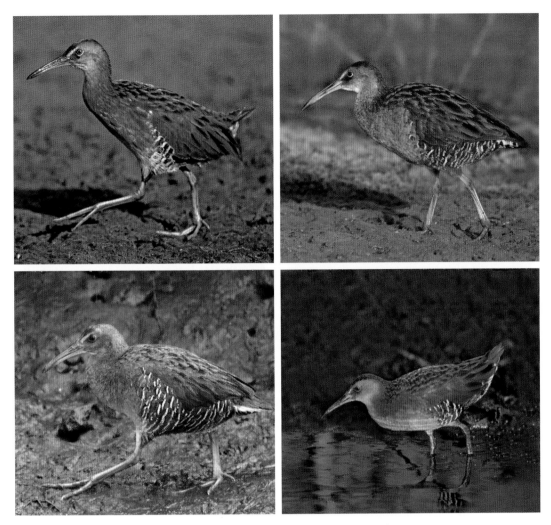

FIGURE 72. VIRGINIA, CLAPPER, AND KING RAILS (QUIZ PHOTO)
A female King Rail and two subspecies of Clapper Rail ("Gulf Coast" and "California") are shown, as well as an adult Virginia Rail. Try to identify these similar birds after reading the ID information in the text. Answers are in the appendix, page 268.

COMPARISONS OF SIMILAR SPECIES

King, Clapper, and Virginia Rails

Clapper Rail is mostly associated with brackish and saltwater marsh habitats, while King Rail is primarily a freshwater counterpart, although both species may breed in the same area where fresh- and saltwater habitats exist. Hybridization is a normal occurrence in these overlap zones, and identification of some birds is best left unresolved. A small population of Clappers ("Yuma" subspecies) occurs inland in freshwater habitats near the California–Arizona border, but far from any breeding or winter range of King. Virginia Rail is found mostly in freshwater habitats.

UNCHANGING CHARACTERISTICS: King Rail and Clapper Rail are similar in size, body shape, and structural features, with males averaging larger than females in both species. Virginia Rail (9½ in. long) is much smaller than both Clapper and King, which average 14½ and 15 in. long, respectively. Virginia has a shorter neck, more compact body shape, and shorter legs than both King and Clapper. It also has a more slender decurved bill. (See Figure 72, above.)

King and Clapper Rails have a similar tonal quality to their songs, with Clapper usually slowing in cadence toward the end and King having a uniform series of dry *kek-kek-kek*... notes. Clappers may be confused with King when they perform nocturnal flights near breeding areas and give a song similar to King's that involves a series of *kek* notes that don't slow down near the end.

SUPPLEMENTAL CHARACTERISTICS AND NON-BBI DETAILS: Some Clapper Rail subspecies can be very similar in plumage to King Rail. Males of both species are brighter than females, with a dull female King closest in appearance to a bright male "Gulf Coast" Clapper. California Clapper is the brightest and deepest orange of all Clapper subspecies, but it does not overlap in range with King Rail, which it closely resembles. (See Figure 72, p. 75.)

Distinctive plumage details include a deep orange color to King's underparts and a clear orange foreneck versus a grayish wash to the foreneck and upper breast of "Gulf Coast" and "Atlantic Coast" Clapper Rails. Male King has distinct, dark streaks to the sides of its neck, while females may have indistinct streaks. Dark flank markings are also bolder and more contrasting in King, which averages less gray shading in the face.

Virginia Rail's rich orange underparts and crisply marked black flanks with white stripes make it more similar to King than to Clapper. Bright orange legs and bill, especially in breeding season, help separate Virginia from King, which has duller yellow-orange legs and bill and a contrasting gray face with variably orange cheeks. Juvenile and early first-winter Virginias are duller overall and lack the orange breast and deep reddish legs and bill. They differ from King Rail with a completely gray face and duller orange underparts. (See Figure 71, p. 74.)

Upperpart feather edges are typically rustier on King compared with duller, more olive-colored edges on "Gulf Coast" Clapper. "Atlantic Coast" Clappers are drabber overall with grayish upperparts and a combination of gray and buff underparts. This subspecies does not resemble King's brighter plumage, and poses few ID problems. (See Figure 71, p. 74.)

Yellow Rail and Juvenile Sora

UNCHANGING CHARACTERISTICS: Sora is larger than Yellow Rail (8¾ vs. 7¼ in. long) and has a longer neck, wings, bill, and tail, which is typically held upward.

SUPPLEMENTAL CHARACTERISTICS AND NON-BBI DETAILS: Important differences include vertical white lines on Sora's back versus horizontal white lines on Yellow Rail, and broad, bright buff vertical stripes on the back of Yellow Rail. (See Figure 73, below.) The face and underparts of Yellow Rail are deeper yellow than the buff to grayish color on juvenile Sora. Other separating features include a dark mask and dark central crown that contrast with a broad yellowish supercilium on Yellow Rail (adult only). Juvenile Yellow Rail has a dark crown with white spotting and a muted mask, while juvenile Sora has a wide plain brown crown and narrower buff to grayish supercilium.

FIGURE 73. YELLOW RAIL AND JUVENILE SORA

Juvenile Sora (L) can closely resemble Yellow Rail (R) from midsummer to late fall, depending on hatching dates. This Sora was photographed in late fall; younger birds—in summer and early fall—show slightly buffier plumage features that are more similar to those of Yellow Rail. ID information is provided in the text.

FIGURE 74. GALLINULES AND AMERICAN COOT
These gallinaceous birds are often mistaken for ducks, since they have some ducklike features and occur in aquatic habitats. They also have conical-shaped bills and extremely long toes. *From left to right:* Common Gallinule, American Coot, and Purple Gallinule.

GALLINULES AND AMERICAN COOT

Although they're genetically related to rails, coots and gallinules are more cosmopolitan in nature and are easier to see feeding in open habitats, including parks and neighborhood ponds.

PHYSICAL PROFILE

Common and Purple Gallinules have oval-shaped bodies, while American Coot has a chunky, rounded body shape. All three species have stubby, pointed bills; medium-length, thick necks; small, rounded heads; and strong, stocky legs with very long toes. Short, stiff tails are often cocked upward. (See Figure 74, above.)

BIRDING BY IMPRESSION INFORMATION

SIZE: All three species share a narrow size range that is similar to that of Green-winged Teal. Purple Gallinule is 13 in. long, Common Gallinule averages 14 in. long, and American Coot is 15 in. long.

STRUCTURAL FEATURES: All three species have stocky, rounded wings, with Purple Gallinule and American Coot having longer wings than Common Gallinule. Purple Gallinule has longer legs and very long toes, which it uses to walk on lily pads and to climb emergent vegetation. American Coot has lobed toes that it uses to paddle in shallow water and to help with tipping feeding behavior.

BEHAVIOR: Common Gallinule and American Coot are not shy birds and are often seen floating duck-like on ponds and lakes. They mostly forage on submerged aquatic vegetation, which they access by tipping their bodies forward or using shallow dives. American Coots form large flocks in winter, and they often graze on grass adjacent to bodies of water. Purple Gallinule is shier and more terrestrial. It inhabits vegetation adjacent to water and often feeds on seedpods and flowers above the water line.

Unlike the other two species, American Coot runs on the water during takeoff flights. All three species have direct and fast flight with quick wingbeats.

PLUMAGE PATTERNS AND GENERAL COLORATION: Adult birds are distinctive. (See Figure 74, above.) Juvenile Purple Gallinule has a pale brown head and neck with greenish back and lacks the colorful bill of adults. Juvenile Common Gallinule and American Coot are dull grayish brown overall, with Common Gallinule having darker gray underparts. Juvenile Common Gallinule has a dark gray bill with yellow tip, while American Coot has a pale gray bill.

HABITAT USE: All three species inhabit freshwater ponds and lakes with emergent vegetation.

VOCALIZATIONS: Purple Gallinule gives a long series of nasal honking sounds, while Common Gallinule and American Coot give a similar series of short, clucking sounds. All give a short, sharp call note.

Raptors are a popular group of birds that capture the interest of birders and nonbirders alike. Hawk-watchers rely on a BBI approach to identify raptors in flight, especially distant birds and those with no visible field marks. A good place to start your raptor ID is to assess the general size and shape of a flying bird, noting physical features such as wing and tail shape and how they contribute to the bird's overall profile. (See Figure 75, below.)

While these profiles help narrow your ID choices, they are influenced by a bird's behavior or flight style, including an aggressive power flight or a relaxed glide. A raptor's flight profile can quickly change to show a handful of different body and wing shapes based on flight styles. While this seems a bit confusing, there are only several different looks for each species, and you will develop a comfort zone of recognition for each profile over time. A comparison of different flight profiles of Merlin is shown in Figure 76.

EAGLES AND BUTEOS

These two groups of raptors represent the largest birds of prey in North America, and they share several physical features. Two species of eagles are regularly seen in North America, as well as 10 buteos and 2 additional hawks that are grouped with buteos (Harris's Hawk and Common Black-Hawk).

PHYSICAL PROFILE

Eagles are heavier and bulkier than all other raptors. They have very large heads and bills; long, broad wings; and short, wedge-shaped tails. Their legs are short, and their feet are very large with huge talons.

Most buteos and buteo-like hawks have elongated, robust body shapes. They have somewhat large heads and bills, and short legs with strong, powerful talons. Their wings are long and broad, and their tails are typically short and slightly rounded in flight. (See Figure 77, p. 80.)

BIRDING BY IMPRESSION INFORMATION

SIZE: Bald Eagle and Golden Eagle are larger than buteos and vultures and very close in size to each other (30 in. long), with wingspans of 79 to 80 in. Buteos and buteo-like hawks range in size from Broad-winged Hawk, at 15 in. long (about the size of Fish Crow), to Ferruginous Hawk, at 23 in. long (slightly smaller than Common Raven).

FIGURE 75. RAPTOR FLIGHT PROFILES (QUIZ PHOTO)

Raptors in various groups typically show similar physical features, including body, wing, and tail shapes. Five common raptor groups are represented here, and the silhouettes illustrate typical flight profiles. Note the different structural features on these birds and try to identify each raptor group as well as each species of raptor. Answers are provided in the appendix, page 268.

FIGURE 76. MERLINS IN VARIOUS FLIGHT STYLES
Raptors can show several flight profiles based on different behavior or weather conditions. Here are three typical flight styles illustrated by Merlins: a soar, a glide, and a power flight. The female at top left with very broad wings shows a relaxed glide profile with wings spread. The male at top right has narrower wings that are pulled back in a fast power flight. The male at bottom left shows the spread wings and tail typical of a soaring or banking bird. The male at bottom right is in a relaxed glide but shows a fanned tail used to change directions. Note that the gliding female is larger, bulkier, and has broader wings than the gliding and soaring males.

Four species (Broad-winged, Red-shouldered, Gray, and Short-tailed Hawks) are noticeably smaller and have shorter wingspans than other buteos. These size differences are helpful when viewing flying or sitting buteos.

STRUCTURAL FEATURES: Bald Eagle has a noticeably larger head and bill than Golden Eagle, which is discernible even in distant flying birds. Bald also has straighter wings with a proportionally narrower outer half (hand) compared with Golden's uniformly broad wings with more bulging secondary flight feathers. Golden shows a slight dihedral shape to its wings in flight, similar to but not quite as obvious as on Turkey Vulture.

Harris's Hawk differs from most buteos by having long legs and a long tail. (See Figure 77, p. 80.) Some buteos have larger heads and bills than others, while some have longer wings that taper toward the tip, which are helpful ID features in flying birds. Many juvenile raptors have longer tails and wings than adults (since a juvenile's tail and wing feathers are replaced with shorter ones after about one year), and these slight differences can change their flight profile and movements enough to cause additional ID problems.

FIGURE 77. EAGLES AND BUTEOS

Some of the largest raptors in North America. *Clockwise from top left:* adult Red-tailed Hawk (buteo), adult Harris's Hawk (buteo-like raptor), adult female Rough-legged Hawk (buteo), adult Bald Eagle, immature Bald Eagle, and adult Red-shouldered Hawk (buteo).

BEHAVIOR: Bald Eagles either kill live prey or scavenge dead carcasses. Golden Eagle is a powerful hunter that kills live prey with fast, stooping dives. Buteos hunt either from the sky or from exposed perches. A few species, including Swainson's and Red-shouldered Hawks, forage on the ground for large insects, lizards, snakes, and frogs. For a comparison of hunting styles and prey preferences, see "Behavior" in Table 1, p. 92.

PLUMAGE PATTERNS AND GENERAL COLORATION: Golden Eagle is mostly brown overall with a golden head at all ages. First-year birds have a white tail base and variable white wing spots. Bald Eagle has mostly brown upperparts and variable white mottled underparts, underwings, and tail for the first few years. It begins to show a white tail and head and pale eye in its third year, and has a completely white head and tail by its fourth year.

A wide variety of plumage patterns and color morphs exist among buteos and buteo-like hawks. Buteos have a juvenile plumage that is held for most of their first year. It differs dramatically from adult plumage in some species, and only slightly in others. Those with markedly different juvenile plumages typically show a combination of streaks and spots on the underparts, and brownish upperparts.

HABITAT USE: Eagles and buteos use a wide variety of habitats. See Table 1, p. 92, for more information.

VOCALIZATIONS: Golden Eagle gives a weak, two-syllabled yelping call, while Bald Eagle has a series of chirping, stuttering whistles. Buteos give a variety of calls that range from high-pitched screams to piercing whistles. Red-shouldered Hawk differs by having a loud, emphatic call that is often imitated by jays and sounds similar to a distressed Laughing Gull. Harris's Hawk has a loud, raucous call that lasts for several seconds.

COMPARISONS OF SIMILAR SPECIES

Broad-winged Hawk and Red-shouldered Hawk, Juveniles

Juvenile Red-shouldered and Broad-winged Hawks can have very similar plumage, and careful evaluation of their structural features is helpful for a confident ID.

UNCHANGING CHARACTERISTICS

FLIGHT: Red-shouldered Hawk has a larger head and more pronounced neck extension than Broad-winged Hawk, and a longer, less compact body structure. These structural differences are best evaluated in an overhead view and may be hard to assess

FIGURE 78. BROAD-WINGED HAWK AND RED-SHOULDERED HAWK, JUVENILES (QUIZ PHOTO)
These two similarly plumaged hawks are often confused for each other in flight. ID information is provided in the text. Can you identify these three birds after consulting the text? See the appendix, page 268, for answers.

from side views. Red-shouldered also has a longer tail projection past the undertail coverts and longer, more rounded wings than Broad-winged. Broad-winged lacks the pronounced bulging secondaries of most other buteos and has a straighter appearance to the trailing edge of the wings, but this feature is best seen in soaring or gliding birds. In flight, also note the four distinct separate emarginated primaries on Red-shouldered versus three on Broad-winged. (See Figure 78, above.)

Broad-winged often resembles several other raptors in its different flight styles. When it flies with a head or tail wind and its wrists are thrust forward, a juvenile Broad-winged—which averages longer tail feathers than adults—can suggest a large female Cooper's Hawk; however, in a relaxed glide or soar, it appears similar to a Red-shouldered Hawk, which has a proportionally long tail for a buteo.

PERCHED: When looking at a perched bird, note the length of the tail and how it compares with the tip of the wings. Red-shouldered Hawk has a proportionally longer tail that may give an accipiter-like impression, with wings that fall short of the tail tip. Broad-winged Hawk has a shorter tail that is more buteo-like, but it exhibits a somewhat similar wing-to-tail ratio as Red-shouldered because of its shorter wings. Broad-winged often shows a "no-necked" appearance and more compact body shape when perched, which contrasts with Red-shouldered's "hunch-shouldered" impression and lankier body shape. With a longer neck, Red-shouldered often cranes to look at the ground directly below, which creates a visual impression that is recognizable even in silhouette.

SUPPLEMENTAL CHARACTERISTICS AND NON-BBI DETAILS: Generally, juvenile Red-shouldered Hawk has heavy streaking across the upper breast and finer streaks or spots into the lower belly. Juvenile Broad-winged Hawk is highly variable, with some birds showing heavy underpart streaks and spots and others having very limited, sparse markings. The streaks on juvenile Broad-winged tend to be heavier on the sides of the breast compared with the uniformly distributed breast streaks on juvenile Red-shouldered, but some birds with heavily marked underparts don't conform to these guidelines. (See Figure 78, above.)

Juvenile Red-shouldered typically shows a wide, bold, dark line down the center of the throat that is usually absent in juvenile Broad-winged, which has a cleaner, paler throat, though this field mark is not always consistent. Some juvenile Broad-wingeds may show a thin dark line on the throat, but the throat area on these birds averages paler than on juvenile Red-shouldereds.

While all juvenile buteos show some translucent feathering on their primaries, Red-shouldered has a narrow crescent-shaped line of pale feathering at the base of the outer primaries. This feature is best seen during top-lit views when the sun shines through the translucent feathers, and may not be obvious on some underwing views. The reddish-toned underwing coverts in the eastern subspecies of Red-shouldered Hawk are distinctive among juvenile buteos, although some juvenile Broad-wingeds can show this feature as well. (See Figure 78, above.)

Red-tailed Hawk and Ferruginous Hawk
Juvenile Red-tailed Hawk and "Krider's" Red-tailed Hawk can somewhat resemble juvenile Ferruginous Hawk in plumage.

FIGURE 79. RED-TAILED HAWK AND FERRUGINOUS HAWK (QUIZ PHOTO)
These two large buteos can show somewhat similar plumage and structural features, especially juveniles. ID information is provided in the text. For an expert-level quiz, try to identify all four birds to age, species, and subspecies (two photos). Answers are in the appendix, page 268.

UNCHANGING CHARACTERISTICS: Ferruginous Hawk is larger (23 in. long) than Red-tailed Hawk (19 in. long) and has a longer wingspan (56 vs. 49 in.), but since female raptors can be noticeably larger than males, these size differences may not be obvious in some birds. Ferruginous has wings that are narrower (particularly in the outer half) and more pointed than Red-tailed's, as well as a straighter trailing wing edge that lacks the bulging secondary flight feathers that Red-tailed displays. Ferruginous also has a larger head and heavier bill, but these features are more noticeable on sitting birds.

SUPPLEMENTAL CHARACTERISTICS AND NON-BBI DETAILS: A few distinctive plumage marks set adult Ferruginous Hawk apart from light-morph juvenile Red-tailed Hawk. Rufous leg feathers and a whitish tail that appears translucent when backlit are distinctive for adult Ferruginous. (See Figure 79, p. 82.)

Juvenile Ferruginous is harder to identify because it lacks rufous leg feathers, and its tail shows faint barring on the outer half, similar to that of juvenile Red-tailed. Juvenile Ferruginous may also appear almost fully white on the underparts, closely resembling "Krider's" Red-tailed. A dark patagial mark on the leading edge of "Krider's" inner underwing, however, separates it and other Red-taileds from juvenile Ferruginous Hawk. Ferruginous of all ages lack this patagial bar. (See Figure 79, p. 82.)

Most Red-taileds, including juveniles, have a variable series of dark markings across the lower belly (belly band), which separates Red-tailed from Ferruginous of all ages. "Krider's" Red-tailed, however, may not have a belly band, and "Eastern" Red-taileds with "Krider's" traits may have only a small amount of barring on the sides. They may also have a brownish hood similar to that of Ferruginous

(see Figure 79, p. 82), so care should be taken when viewing these birds.

ACCIPITERS AND NORTHERN HARRIER

Accipiters are represented in North America by three species of forest-dwelling hawks. Northern Harrier, while not an accipiter, is an open-country hawk that shares a few physical features with accipiters.

PHYSICAL PROFILE

Accipiters and Northern Harrier have tapered, elongated bodies. The accipiters have long tails and legs; relatively short, rounded wings; and small heads and bills. Northern Harrier has longer, more tapered wings than accipiters but shares the other structural features mentioned here. (See Figure 80, below.)

BIRDING BY IMPRESSION INFORMATION

SIZE: Accipiter and Northern Harrier females are larger than males. Sizes range from male Sharp-shinned Hawk, at 9 to 11 in. long (about the size of Blue Jay), to female Northern Goshawk, at 21 to 24 in. long (with a wingspan of 41 to 45 in.), which is slightly smaller than Red-tailed Hawk. Northern Harrier ranges from 16 to 20 in. long, with a wingspan of 38 to 48 in.

STRUCTURAL FEATURES: Adult accipiters average stockier than juveniles of the same sex and have shorter wings and tails (since the feathers are replaced as they age). Northern Harrier has long wings that almost reach the tail tip on perched birds, unlike accipiters, whose shorter wings extend

FIGURE 80. ACCIPITERS AND NORTHERN HARRIER
All three species of North American accipiters, *from left to right:* Adult female Sharp-shinned Hawk, second-year male Cooper's Hawk (similar to adult plumage but eye is orange, not red), and adult Northern Goshawk. An adult female Northern Harrier is on the far right.

only slightly past the base of the tail. (See Figure 80, p. 83.)

BEHAVIOR: Accipiters feed mostly on birds, although Cooper's Hawk regularly preys on small mammals. Both Sharp-shinned and Cooper's Hawks frequent backyard bird feeders and may be found perched above feeders or in nearby trees waiting for unsuspecting birds. Sometimes they fly directly into dense shrubbery in pursuit of their prey. The flight style of Northern Harrier is distinctive even from a distance as it dips and turns when coursing above marshes and fields in search of small mammals and birds. See Table 1, p. 92, for more information.

PLUMAGE PATTERNS AND GENERAL COLORATION: Adult Sharp-shinned and Cooper's Hawks have similar plumage, with a few subtle shading and color differences between sexes. Northern Goshawk has a distinctive grayish plumage. Juvenile accipiters have a plumage that is very different from that of adults but similar to each other. (See Figure 81, p. 85.) Adult male and female Northern Harriers look nothing alike, with males having a striking gray plumage (see Figure 75, p. 78) and females somewhat resembling juveniles without the orange underpart and upperwing coloration.

HABITAT USE: Accipiters are hawks of forested areas, but they often hunt in open clearings adjacent to woodlands. Northern Harrier frequents open fields and marshes at all times of the year.

VOCALIZATIONS: Accipiters give a series of short, sharp notes, with that of Sharp-shinned Hawk sounding somewhat insectlike, and those of Cooper's and Northern Goshawk having a deeper, nasal quality. Northern Harrier is mostly silent away from breeding areas unless agitated, when it gives a high, piercing whistle or dry clucking notes.

COMPARISONS OF SIMILAR SPECIES

Sharp-shinned Hawk and Cooper's Hawk

These two similar species cause more trouble with field ID than most other raptors do. Since males and females differ noticeably in size, it is relatively easy to separate small male Sharp-shinned Hawks from large female Cooper's Hawks. Problems occur when trying to separate small male "Coops" and large female "Sharpies," which are more similar in size and shape.

UNCHANGING CHARACTERISTICS

FLIGHT: The larger head and longer neck of Cooper's Hawk are useful features to separate flying birds, but be careful when evaluating this feature on female Sharp-shinned Hawks whose wings are strongly angled in flight, since they may seem to have large heads because of the forward-thrusting wrists. Focus more on the amount of neck projection off the body when assessing this structural feature, with Cooper's—especially females—showing slightly to obviously more neck extension than Sharp-shinneds. (See Figure 82, p. 86.) This structural difference is obvious in the perched birds in Figure 81. The flying birds don't show this difference because of a slightly different angle in the male Cooper's photo and because the difference can be very slight with some small male Cooper's. These photos illustrate why juvenile male Cooper's and juvenile female Sharp-shinneds consistently present ID problems for many birders.

PERCHED: Female Cooper's Hawks are much larger than female Sharp-shinned Hawks, and have distinctive structural features that are very different from those of Sharp-shinned. Male Cooper's can be quite similar to female Sharp-shinned, however, but careful assessment of perched birds reveals subtle structural differences. Sharp-shinned has a smaller, more rounded head, compared with Cooper's larger, deeper head, which has a squarish rear profile. Cooper's also has a larger bill and longer neck. (See Figure 81, p. 85.) Sharp-shinned's forehead rises abruptly from the base of the upper mandible, while Cooper's forehead follows the same line of curvature of the upper mandible, giving it a "Roman-nose" appearance. A combination of these features helps separate perched birds of all ages. The last feature is obvious in the relaxed adult birds in Figure 80, but not as obvious in the alert immatures in Figure 81 because of a flattening of head feathers.

Cooper's has a proportionally longer, uniformly wider tail than Sharp-shinned, whose slender tail may have a narrower base, especially in females, which average longer tails than males. A rounded tail tip in Cooper's versus a squarish tip in Sharp-shinned is a useful feature, but one that is often unreliable in juveniles and molting or worn birds. Cooper's outer tail feathers have an angled outer tip, while Sharp-shinned has a square one, and these dissimilarities add to the overall tail shape differences. While Sharp-shinned may sometimes have a rounded tail shape, because of uneven growth of tail feathers in juveniles (see Figure 81, upper photo) and molting in adults, Cooper's rarely has a square one. This is because the angled outer tail feathers in Cooper's consistently give a rounded impression to the outer tail, even when the other tail feathers are equal in length. Cooper's thicker legs and larger feet differ from Sharp-shinned's sticklike legs and smaller feet, but these may be hard to assess with just one bird present.

FIGURE 81. JUVENILE ACCIPITERS
All three juvenile accipiters perched and in flight, and scaled to size. The flight photo shows a female Sharp-shinned Hawk and a male Cooper's Hawk to more closely approximate potential ID problems with similar-sized accipiters. Detailed ID information is provided in the text. *Top, from left to right:* Female Sharp-shinned Hawk, male Cooper's Hawk, and Northern Goshawk, sex unknown because of the close size range of male and female goshawks. *Bottom, from left to right:* Sharp-shinned Hawk, Cooper's Hawk, and Northern Goshawk.

COMPARISON OF FEMALE COOPER'S HAWK AND SHARP-SHINNED HAWKS IN FLIGHT: Draw an imaginary line that connects the bird's wrists (halfway point on the leading edge of the wing) and note where the line passes through the head. If it cuts through or just behind the eye, the bird is probably a Sharp-shinned Hawk. If the line is well behind the eye or through the neck, it is a Cooper's Hawk. While this may be hard to do with some flying birds whose wing position doesn't allow this mental exercise, it helps with many others. (See Figure 82, p. 86.)

In a glide or relaxed flight, Sharp-shinned's wings come off the body at a slight forward angle, which creates a U-shaped profile close to the body. Cooper's wings come off the body at a right angle in these instances, which results in a straight leading edge to the wing in soaring or relaxed gliding birds. (See Figure 81, above.) Cooper's proportion-ally longer and more round-tipped wings that often give a paddle-shaped impression are also straighter along the rear edge compared with Sharp-shinned's broader secondaries and tapered primary flight feathers, especially in a soar or a glide. (See Figure 81, above.) This wing shape difference in Sharp-shinned is more pronounced in females.

A helpful feature for birds flying away from you is the shape of the tail. A male Cooper's uniformly wide tail differs from a female Sharp-shinned's thinner, narrow-based tail that may widen slightly near the tip. This uniformly wide tail profile in Cooper's is surprisingly effective when other features are not visible.

Differences in flapping motion are fairly easy to see in female Cooper's Hawk, which has a slower, deeper wing stroke. The differences between female Sharp-shinned and male Cooper's wing flaps

FIGURE 82. COOPER'S HAWK AND SHARP-SHINNED HAWK, JUVENILES (QUIZ PHOTO)
ID information for shape, structural differences, and plumage is provided in the text. Can you identify these birds? Answers are in the appendix, page 268.

are much harder to assess, and this requires a good amount of careful comparative observation. A male Cooper's flap is a bit heavier, shallower, and stiffer than a female Sharp-shinned's, whose deeper and slightly quicker wing flaps are more fluid and show more independent movement at the wrist and outer half.

SUPPLEMENTAL CHARACTERISTICS AND NON-BBI DETAILS:
Plumage color and patterns are similar on adult Sharp-shinned and Cooper's Hawks, with only subtle differences helpful for separating them. (See Figure 80, p. 83.) Cooper's darker gray to black cap that contrasts with a paler nape and mantle (upper back) differs from Sharp-shinned's bluish gray crown and similar-colored nape. Another helpful field mark is the cheek color. Adult female Sharp-shinned has an orange cheek, while the slightly larger adult male Cooper's has a grayish cheek with

orange edges. The mostly adult-plumaged male Cooper's in Figure 80 is a second-year bird, and thus its cap is not as contrastingly dark as that of a full adult, and the cheek still has some orange highlights. Female Sharp-shinned also has a drabber bluish back color than male Cooper's in fresh plumage, but this color shading may be influenced by lighting and feather wear.

Plumage color and patterns on juvenile accipiters are very similar, with a few details helpful in separating them. Streaking on Cooper's underparts is usually heaviest on the upper breast and thins out to narrow streaks on the belly, while Sharp-shinned has denser streaks that extend farther down into the belly and vent area. A prominent clean, white vent is a reliable feature for juvenile Cooper's, although small numbers show streaks in this area.

The shape of the streaks on the underparts is a reliable ID feature. On Cooper's, the dark, thin streaks resemble swimming polliwogs or inverted teardrops, with a rounded bottom and a thin, tapered tail at the top of each streak. Sharp-shinned has coarse, dark streaks on the upper and central breast, and often ill-defined blobs on the lower flanks, especially on females. (See Figure 81, p. 85.) These field marks are visible even on flying birds.

A supportive field mark is the bolder, white tail band on juvenile Cooper's versus a gray tail band on Sharp-shinned. This feature usually remains useful until late fall, when feather wear causes the narrow, pale tail band to wear off or become duller. Sunlight passing through the pale terminal band may cause it to appear whitish on both species (see Figure 81). Another helpful plumage detail is the warmer buff color of juvenile Cooper's head versus a mostly brownish gray shading on Sharp-shinned, but small numbers of each species may resemble the other. Cooper's also has more buff or rust feather edges on the back than Sharp-shinned, and a browner lower wing panel compared with a grayish one in Sharp-shinned.

Juvenile Northern Goshawk and Juvenile Female Cooper's Hawk

UNCHANGING CHARACTERISTICS: Size differences between male and female Northern Goshawk are not as dramatic as in other accipiters, and some may not be separable in the field. Male Northern Goshawk averages 18 to 20 in. long with a wingspan of 38 to 41 in., while female Cooper's Hawk averages 16 to 19 in. long with a wingspan of 31 to 34 in., so you can see how close in size these two birds can be.

However, Northern Goshawk is the largest and bulkiest accipiter, and in soaring flight is often mistaken for a buteo because of its broad wings and proportionally shorter tail compared with a large female Cooper's. (See Figure 82, p. 86.) A perched Northern Goshawk is noticeably heavier bodied than the lanky female Cooper's, and the goshawk's wings extend farther down its proportionally shorter tail.

A few structural features help separate these two birds in flight. Northern Goshawk has noticeably broader inner wings, and its outer wings taper considerably more than Cooper's. This gives the goshawk's wings a more angular appearance, especially the outer half. The goshawk also has the proportionally longest hand, or outer wing, of all accipiters, and this, combined with its tapered shape, gives the wings a longer, narrower appearance in a glide. (See Figure 81, p. 85.)

SUPPLEMENTAL CHARACTERISTICS AND NON-BBI DETAILS: Juvenile Northern Goshawk's plumage differs from juvenile Cooper's Hawk's in having heavier dark streaks on the underparts that extend into the lower belly, and a buff wash on the chest compared with a mostly white background on Cooper's. Goshawks also have dark markings on the undertail coverts and lower vent. (See Figure 81, p. 85.) Both species can have the inverted teardrop-shaped markings on the underparts, but Northern Goshawks typically have other heavy, undefined dark markings on their underparts that are lacking in Cooper's. Goshawks, however, have a defined line of buff spots on the trailing edge of the upperwing that is lacking in Cooper's.

The brown back of Northern Goshawk is speckled with white and buff color versus rust feather edges in Cooper's, and a whitish supercilium, pale eye, and pale face in the goshawk contrast strongly with a darkish rear cheek. Juvenile Cooper's has a fairly uniform buff color to the entire head. Goshawk has narrower, uneven dark tail bands against a grayish background compared with Cooper's wider and more uniformly dark bands.

KITES AND OSPREY

Five species of kites breed in North America, and they all have different shapes and habits. Each also belongs to its own genus. Osprey is a large raptor that lives near aquatic habitats and eats fish. See Table 1, p. 92.

PHYSICAL PROFILE

Most kites have long, slender bodies; long, tapered wings; and small, rounded heads with tiny bills. Hook-billed Kite and Snail Kite differ with their slightly heavier bodies; broad, rounded wings; and larger heads with long, hooked bills.

Osprey has a long and slender body as well, but its long, tapered, angled wings create a distinctive flight profile. (See Figure 83, p. 88.)

BIRDING BY IMPRESSION INFORMATION

SIZE: Kites range in size from Mississippi Kite (14 in. long, 31-in. wingspan), which is about the size of a male Cooper's Hawk, to Swallow-tailed Kite (22 in. long, 51-in. wingspan), which is similar in size to Red-tailed Hawk. Osprey (23 in. long, 63-in. wingspan) is slightly smaller than Turkey Vulture.

STRUCTURAL FEATURES: Hook-billed and Snail Kites have unique hooked bills that are suited for extracting snails from their shells. Swallow-tailed Kite has an unmistakable, long, forked tail and very long, slender wings. Mississippi Kite (not shown in Figure 83) has a slender body and long, pointed wings. White-tailed Kite has the slenderest and most pointed wings of all kites, and often holds them in a dihedral shape in flight. (See Figure 83, p. 88.) See Table 1, p. 92.

Osprey has a small head compared with its large

FIGURE 83. KITES AND OSPREY (QUIZ PHOTO)

Five species of North American kites (four of which are shown here) show very different physical features. Osprey is one of the most familiar of all raptors. Try to identify these birds. Answers are in the appendix, page 268.

body and long wings, and this feature is especially helpful when viewing distant or poorly lit perched birds. It also has short, thick legs and very strong, powerful toes and talons.

BEHAVIOR: Snail Kite resides year-round in subtropical shallow lake habitats, where it feeds exclusively on aquatic snails. Hook-billed Kite is a shy resident of tropical thorny brush habitats, where it feeds on terrestrial snails. White-tailed Kite hunts by hovering in place, or sits on an exposed perch while scanning for rodents or large insects. Mississippi Kite is an aerial hunter of large insects but also hunts from perches for insects, small mammals, and birds. Swallow-tailed Kite is a graceful aerialist that eats flying insects and plucks amphibians and reptiles from treetops. See Table 1, p. 92.

Osprey feeds exclusively on fish, which it obtains by plunging feet-first into water and grabbing fish that are close to the surface. After catching a fish,

it retires to an exposed perch to feed. Osprey often hovers in place while searching for fish in the water below, and this behavior is also helpful when identifying distant birds.

PLUMAGE PATTERNS AND GENERAL COLORATION: Each species of kite has distinctive plumage and patterns. Osprey has distinctive black, brown, and white plumage features. (See Figure 83, above.)

HABITAT USE: Kites use a wide variety of habitats, including forests, lakes, grasslands, and marshes. Osprey is found near large bodies of water that contain ample fish.

VOCALIZATIONS: Calls range from a variety of whistles by most kites to cackling notes by Snail Kite and a rapid series of short notes by Hook-billed Kite. Osprey gives a memorable series of easily mimicked whistles.

FALCONS AND CRESTED CARACARA

Falcons and Crested Caracara inhabit a variety of open spaces. Falcons are fast-flying raptors that pursue and capture their prey with a combination of speed and agility. Crested Caracara feeds mostly on carrion, which it finds by flying low above its territory, but it also takes lizards, small mammals, and amphibians.

PHYSICAL PROFILE

Falcons have long, pointed wings and fairly long tails. Their head shapes are blocky with large eyes and small to medium-length hooked bills. Their legs are short with powerful feet and talons. American Kestrel, Merlin, and Aplomado Falcon have slender, tapered bodies, while Prairie and Peregrine Falcons have heavier body structures. Gyrfalcon is bulkier than all other falcons.

Crested Caracara has a long, tapered body with long, straight wings that are rounded at the tip. Its head is large with a massive, hooked bill. The legs are long and unfeathered. (See Figure 84, below.)

BIRDING BY IMPRESSION INFORMATION

SIZE: Falcons range from the small American Kestrel (9 in. long, 22-in. wingspan), which is about the size of American Robin, to Gyrfalcon (22 in. long, 47-in. wingspan), which is about the size of a male Red-tailed Hawk. Crested Caracara averages 23 in. long with a wingspan of 49 in.

STRUCTURAL FEATURES: Aplomado Falcon differs from other falcons with its very long tail, which when combined with its long, slender wings gives it a unique flight profile. Gyrfalcon has a heavy, bulky body and proportionally longer tail than Peregrine Falcon, which is a helpful feature to note on perched birds. A Gyrfalcon's wings don't come close to the tail tip like a Peregrine's do.

Crested Caracara's long neck and large head are obvious structural features on both perched and flying birds. Its paddle-shaped wings with separated primary tips are helpful to its flight identification.

FIGURE 84. FALCONS AND CRESTED CARACARA (QUIZ PHOTO—TOP)

Top: Three falcons with different shapes and plumages. Try to identify the birds in this photo. Answers are in the appendix, page 268. *Bottom:* The Aplomado Falcon in the left photo is carrying its dragonfly food. Crested Caracara is in the middle and on the right.

BEHAVIOR: American Kestrel differs from most other falcons with its preference for eating large insects, especially during migration and winter, although Aplomado Falcons and Merlins supplement their diet with insects, especially dragonflies. American Kestrel also differs from other falcons by its typical hovering flight style when searching for crickets, grasshoppers, and other large insects on the ground. (See Figure 14, p. 14.) Kestrels often sit on wires while searching for insects, which other falcons infrequently do, except for the occasional resting Merlin or Aplomado Falcon.

Aplomado Falcon is a powerful, fast flier that often steals food from other falcons and raptors by chasing them down in flight and forcing them to drop their prey. Merlin is another aggressive falcon that attacks other raptors, including eagles, for no apparent reason other than its ornery nature, but it is no match for Aplomado Falcon in the raptor pecking order.

Crested Caracaras are gregarious birds that often feed on carrion in large groups. Falconers value them for their high intelligence.

PLUMAGE PATTERNS AND GENERAL COLORATION: Falcons have a wide variety of plumage colors, tones, and patterns. Male and female American Kestrels and Merlins differ from each other, and juveniles of Gyrfalcon and Peregrine Falcon differ from adults by their streaked underparts and brownish upperparts (except for dark-morph adult Gyrfalcon). Adult Crested Caracaras are darker bodied than immatures, which have a brownish plumage. Adults also have yellower legs and brighter orange facial skin. (See Figure 84, p. 89.)

HABITAT USE: American Kestrels typically hunt in fields and grasslands, while other falcons use a variety of open-country habitats, including deserts, coastlines, marshes, and grasslands, to hunt for birds and small mammals. Gyrfalcon is a bird of tundra habitats, where it hunts large birds such as ptarmigans. Crested Caracara is a bird of arid savannas, grasslands, and deserts.

VOCALIZATIONS: Falcons give a series of repetitive, piercing notes on different pitches. Caracara is usu-

FIGURE 85. FALCONS IN FLIGHT (QUIZ PHOTO)

Four of the most common North American falcons, with silhouettes to better show their shapes and structural features. ID information is provided in the text. Try to identify these four falcons. Answers are in the appendix, page 268.

ally silent but will give a low croaking sound when agitated.

COMPARISONS OF SIMILAR SPECIES

American Kestrel, Merlin, Prairie Falcon, and Peregrine Falcon

The two smallest falcons (American Kestrel and Merlin) are somewhat similar in size and shape, and often confuse birders when their distinctive plumage is not visible.

UNCHANGING CHARACTERISTICS: American Kestrel's hand (outer wing) is proportionally longer and distinctly narrower than Merlin's, because of more tapered flight feathers.

Merlin's wings are broader based, and have outer primaries that are less tapered than American Kestrel's. This results in a different wing shape on gliding and soaring birds. (See Figure 85, p. 90.) While both species thrust their wrists forward in fast, direct flight, American Kestrel's wrist projection is more noticeable, partly because of the narrower primaries and longer outer wing. One of North America's finest hawkwatchers, Frank Nicoletti, often referred to kestrels as "banana wings" because their distinctive wing profile suggests a banana's shape. This simple yet valuable impression is hard to forget, and it helps many birders separate these two species.

Peregrine Falcon is much larger and has longer, broader-based wings than Merlin and American Kestrel. Peregrine also has a very long hand, which results in a "floppy" yet powerful impression in a relaxed flight. Because of the longer hand, the outer wingtip of Peregrine snaps upward after its upstroke in a glide. This distinctive wing-flick helps hawkwatchers and other birders identify Peregrines at great distances, even head-on birds.

A heavy, stocky body adds to the powerful impression of Peregrine in flight, as does the slight uplift of the long wingtips in a head-on view of gliding birds. Peregrines with a fully folded tail could also be described as having a spoon-shaped tail tip.

Prairie Falcon is about the same size as a Peregrine and has a similar wingspan, but it is a more slender bird with less pointed wingtips.

SUPPLEMENTAL CHARACTERISTICS AND NON-BBI DETAILS: Adults of all four species have distinctive plumage features that pose few ID problems. American Kestrel has a dark vertical cheek spot and a thin, dark mustachial stripe against a pale face. Immature and female Merlins and Peregrine Falcons share somewhat similar plumage, with brownish upperparts and streaked underparts, but a strong, dark "mustache" or dark cheek helps separate Peregrine from Merlin, which has a weak facial stripe and a streaked cheek. Adult Prairie Falcons are pale gray above and lightly streaked below. Immatures are brownish above and heavily streaked below, and have a buff supercilium and malar region with a dark mustache. Dark wingpits are a defining field mark for Prairies of all ages.

VULTURES AND CALIFORNIA CONDOR

Turkey and Black Vultures and California Condor fly endlessly while searching for carrion, often without wing flaps. They have acute eyesight and sense of smell, which are used to locate food and to spot other birds on carcasses. Vultures and Condors are scavengers and not birds of prey.

PHYSICAL PROFILE

Both vultures have fairly heavy, elongated bodies, while California Condor has a large, bulky body shape. All three species have long wings with separated primary feathers that give the impression of fingertips, though California Condor has especially long, separate outer primaries. (See Figure 86, p. 92.)

BIRDING BY IMPRESSION INFORMATION

SIZE: Vultures are large birds that surpass all other raptors (except eagles and California Condor) in size and wingspan. Turkey Vulture is slightly larger than Black Vulture (26 vs. 25 in. long), and has a longer wingspan (67 vs. 59 in.). Both species may be mistaken for eagles in flight. California Condor is huge, at 46 in. long, with a wingspan of 109 in., almost double that of Black Vulture.

STRUCTURAL FEATURES: Turkey Vulture has longer, more angular wings and a longer tail than Black Vulture, which results in a different profile on perched and flying birds and a dihedral wing shape in flight. Flying Black Vultures show more head extension; they have shorter wings and a much shorter, wedge-shaped tail. California Condor has long, broad wings with exaggerated "fingered" primaries.

BEHAVIOR: Some differences in flight styles are helpful to identify vultures when plumage details cannot be seen. Turkey Vulture often rocks back and forth while gliding. Its wingbeats are slower, deeper, and heavier than those of Black Vulture, which flies with a flat-winged profile when soaring and a slightly bowed profile when gliding.

When initially taking flight, Black Vulture has very quick, shallow wingbeats that give the impression of a bird in a hurry to get up in the air. Turkey

FIGURE 86. VULTURES AND CALIFORNIA CONDOR
The distinctive shapes and plumage features of Turkey Vulture (L), Black Vulture (C), and California Condor (R). Photos are scaled to size, so note the much larger size of California Condor.

Vulture takes slow, lazy wing strokes and appears in no hurry at all to take flight. Black Vultures sometimes drop the tips of their wings to almost touch each other during flight, which Turkey Vulture does not do.

PLUMAGE PATTERNS AND GENERAL COLORATION: Bodies and upperwings are black to dark brown (the latter in worn Turkey Vultures) in all species, but adult Turkey Vulture has a red, unfeathered head while Black Vulture has a gray one. Adult California Condor has a red head and neck. Juveniles of all species have dark gray to black unfeathered heads.

Underwing patterns differ in all three species. Turkey Vulture has pale flight feathers and dark underwing coverts, while Black Vulture has black underwings and bold, whitish outer primaries. California Condor has black underwings with a bold white slash on the leading edge of the underwing.

HABITAT USE: The two vultures and California Condor are found in a wide variety of habitats. California Condor often soars near exposed cliff faces, where it often perches to rest.

VOCALIZATIONS: All are mostly silent.

TABLE 1—QUICK COMPARISON GUIDE: RAPTORS				
Species	Size	Body Shape	Structure	Behavior
Eagles Golden Eagle and Bald Eagle	Largest of all raptors (except California Condor); bigger than vultures and buteos.	Heavy, elongated.	Large heads and bills; broad, powerful wings; massive feet and talons.	Soar on long, broad wings; stoop in fast, direct dives while hunting prey; Bald Eagle also scavenges food.
Buteo Hawks Broad-winged, Short-tailed, Gray, Red-shouldered, Swainson's, Red-tailed, White-tailed, Zone-tailed, Rough-legged, and Ferruginous Hawks	Crow sized to marginally smaller than Common Raven.	Variable, but elongated and robust in many species; smaller species are more compact.	Generally large heads; powerful bills; broad wings and short tails; powerful legs and talons.	Visual hunters from perches or soaring; wing flaps slow and heavy for larger species, quicker for smaller ones; "stoop" flight is used to capture prey on ground; prey includes mammals, birds, reptiles, amphibians.
Buteo-like Hawks Harris's Hawk and Common Black-Hawk	Slightly smaller than Red-tailed Hawk.	Tapered and elongated in Harris's, compact and bulky in Common Black.	Harris's has long legs and long tail; Common Black has relatively long legs, very broad wings, and short, rounded tail.	Harris's may hunt in packs and share prey; Common Black eats a variety of food, including crabs and shellfish.

TABLE 1 CONT.—QUICK COMPARISON GUIDE: RAPTORS

Species	Size	Body Shape	Structure	Behavior
Vultures Black Vulture, Turkey Vulture, and California Condor	Much larger and longer winged than crows; vultures are slightly smaller than eagles, condor is much larger than eagles.	Heavy, elongated.	Relatively long wings with separated primaries; short tails; small, unfeathered heads; strong bills for tearing carrion; lack powerful talons.	Scavengers; hunt carrion by sight and smell while soaring; perch in groups, often with wings extended for drying; often feed in groups.
Osprey	Slightly smaller and more slender than Turkey Vulture.	Elongated, slender.	Long, gull-like wings taper at outer half and often bend back at wrist; strong legs, talons, and hooked bill.	Hunts fish by hovering or slow-flying; dives into water feet-first to capture fish with talons; eats fish while perched.
Kites Swallow-tailed, Mississippi, White-tailed, Hook-billed, and Snail Kites	Larger and longer winged than crows.	Slender and tapered, except in Hook-billed and Snail, which are heavier and have less tapered bodies.	Long winged and long tailed; small heads and bills; variably shaped tails and wings; several have long, rounded wings (Hook-billed and Snail), others have long, tapered, pointed wings.	Variable; some hunt aerial insects, others amphibians, snails (Snail), or mammals; some hover; Hook-billed forages on ground or in trees.
Northern Harrier	Larger and longer winged than crows; noticeably smaller than Turkey Vulture.	Slender, tapered.	Small head and bill; long, tapered wings, often held in a dihedral; long tail and legs.	Flies buoyantly over open areas while hunting; dips and drops toward ground during flight; migratory flight is high, direct, and with deep wing strokes.
Accipiters Sharp-shinned Hawk, Cooper's Hawk, and Northern Goshawk	Slightly smaller (males) to larger (females) than Blue Jay (Sharp-shinned) to slightly larger (female Cooper's) to noticeably larger (Northern Goshawk) than American Crow.	Tapered and elongated, except in Northern Goshawk, which is heavier.	Long tails (proportionally shorter in Northern Goshawk); relatively short to longish, rounded wings; small heads with relatively small but powerful bills; long, slender legs.	Short, fast, direct flight suited for chasing down avian prey in forests or clearings; wing flaps fast and snappy for smaller accipiters, heavier for larger ones.
Crested Caracara	About the same wing-span as Red-tailed Hawk. Body and tail length is longer than Red-tailed.	Slender.	Large head with massive bill; long, unfeathered legs; long neck; long, hawklike wings with rounded tips and separated primaries.	Feeds chiefly on carrion, snakes, small mammals, and lizards; often in large packs at carrion feed; soars on broad, flat wings; flaps with slow, heavy, deep strokes.
Falcons American Kestrel, Merlin, Peregrine Falcon, Prairie Falcon, Aplomado Falcon, and Gyrfalcon	Shorter bodied but longer winged than Blue Jay (American Kestrel) to larger and longer-winged than crows (some female Peregrines, Gyrfalcon).	Variable, from slender and elongated (American Kestrel, Merlin, and Aplomado Falcons) to heavy bodied (Prairie, Peregrine and Gyrfalcon).	Large head and eyes; long, powerful, pointed wings; generally long tail; strong feet and talons.	Fast, powerful flight is used to pursue and catch prey in open habitats, with birds often hunting from open perches; American Kestrel also hovers while hunting.

Shorebirds are a diverse group of birds typically associated with wet habitats, including coastlines, marshes, and tidal mudflats. They represent some of the planet's longest-distance migrants, with some species crossing several continents in their bi-annual migrations.

In North America, shorebirds are taxonomically grouped into four families: plovers, stilts and avocets, oystercatchers, and sandpipers. Because plumage similarities among species can create identification problems, a careful assessment of structural features and behaviors can help narrow your ID choices. A few specialty guides are devoted entirely to shorebirds, including *The Shorebird Guide* (Houghton Mifflin, 2006), of which Kevin is a co-author.

TIPS FOR VIEWING SHOREBIRDS

Shorebirds are often seen in open spaces, so using a spotting scope is helpful. This higher magnification optic allows you to see distant birds without disturbing them, as well as others that are impossible to approach because of water or muddy substrates.

Some shorebirds are adequately seen with just binoculars. These tamer birds usually occur where they have become accustomed to people. In these situations, it is often easier to assess comparative size and shape differences using binoculars instead of a telescope, as the binoculars will give you a broader perspective of multiple birds instead of close-up scrutiny of just one species. (See Figure 87, below.)

When approaching shorebirds in open spaces, do not hurry onto the scene. Instead, walk slowly, stopping every few minutes to allow these perceptive birds to get used to your presence. This slower pace will enable you to approach the birds without flushing or disturbing them.

PLOVERS

Plovers are distinguished from other shorebirds by their unique foraging style, which includes a start-stop-tilt foraging behavior similar to that of American Robin. Some species breed in the Arctic tundra and migrate to South America for the winter, while others are residents or short-distance migrants of temperate coastal locations.

PHYSICAL PROFILE

Most plovers have stocky bodies with a rounded undercarriage (lower body profile), blocky heads, rounded crowns, short and stubby bills, short tails, and short to medium-length legs. Killdeer differs

FIGURE 87. ASSORTED SHOREBIRDS
Three species of shorebirds. Red Knots (breeding and nonbreeding) are the largest, round-bodied birds; nonbreeding Short-billed Dowitcher (second from left) has a longer, heavier bill with a slight kink near the tip; and Semipalmated Plover (second from right) has the typical blocky head and stubby bill of plovers.

FIGURE 88. PLOVERS
Four species of plovers, *clockwise from top left:* Breeding male Black-bellied Plover, breeding male American Golden-Plover, Killdeer, and breeding Mountain Plover.

slightly with its more slender body, smaller head, and longer wings and tail. (See Figure 88, above.)

BIRDING BY IMPRESSION INFORMATION

SIZE: The nine species of plovers most often seen in North America range in size from Snowy Plover at 6 in. long (about the size of Song Sparrow) to Black-bellied Plover at 12 in. long (slightly larger than a scrub-jay or Blue Jay).

Plovers can be divided into three groups based on size. Four small plovers share a narrow range of 6 to 7¾ in. long (Snowy, Piping, Semipalmated, and Wilson's Plovers). Medium-sized plovers include Mountain Plover at 9 in. long and Killdeer at 10¼ in. long, but Killdeer's longer measurement is mainly due to a longer tail and not a larger body size. The three large species (Black-bellied, American Golden-, and Pacific Golden-Plovers) share a narrow range of 10¼ to 12 in. long.

STRUCTURAL FEATURES: The three large plovers and Mountain Plover have stockier, heavier body shapes and larger heads than other plovers, and longer legs than the four small plovers. Subtle structural differences help separate the three large *Pluvialis* plovers (shown in Figure 89, p. 97) and four smallest *Charadrius* plovers (shown in Figure 90, p. 99). Killdeer has a noticeably longer tail, more slender, angular wings, and a smaller head than other plovers, while Mountain Plover has a larger, more rounded body and longer legs than the four smallest *Charadrius* plovers.

BEHAVIOR: Feeding style is a very helpful way to separate plovers from sandpipers in large flocks of actively feeding shorebirds. After taking a few steps, plovers stop and stand upright to visually search for food or to feel with their sensitive feet for worms retracting into the soil. If they spot prey or feel worm motion, they tilt their bodies forward to pluck the food from the surface, or wait patiently for the worm to resurface. After feeding or standing still for a few seconds, plovers continue their distinctive start-stop-tilt feeding behavior.

Most plovers form small to large loose flocks during migration and winter. All species perform animated distraction displays near their nest.

PLUMAGE PATTERNS AND GENERAL COLORATION: All three large plovers (Black-bellied, American Golden-, and Pacific Golden-Plovers) have boldly marked breeding plumage, with a black face and underparts and brightly spangled upperparts. Non-breeding birds are muted in plumage and feather patterning, with juvenile birds somewhat similar in appearance. (See Figure 89, p. 97.) Black-bellied Plover has black wingpits, or axillaries, which help separate it in flight from the similar American Golden- and Pacific Golden-Plovers in juvenile and nonbreeding plumage.

The four small plovers share muted sandy or darker brownish upperparts throughout the year, which helps them blend in with beachfront or marsh habitats. All have white underparts and either full or partial dark collars in breeding plumage, and muted shadows of the collars in nonbreeding condition. (See Figure 90, p. 99.)

Mountain Plover is sandy colored throughout the year, which helps it blend in with the fallow fields and prairie habitats it frequents. While Killdeer has predominantly brown upperparts, it sometimes has a strong rust-tinged color to its feathers. Its diagnostic two black neckbands separate it from the similarly plumaged but smaller Semipalmated Plover, which has only one dark neckband.

HABITAT USE: All three large plovers and Semipalmated Plover breed in Arctic tundra or subarctic habitats. Black-bellied Plover uses a variety of habitats in migration and winter, including shorelines, mudflats, grasslands, and agricultural fields. American Golden-Plover frequents short grassy areas and sod farms during migration, while Pacific Golden-Plover forages in grassy areas or mudflats adjacent to coastlines in winter.

Wilson's Plover, the Atlantic Coast subspecies of Piping Plover, and the Pacific and Gulf Coast subspecies of Snowy Plover spend their entire lives at saltwater coastal areas or adjacent salt flats. Great Basin Snowy Plovers and the midcontinent subspecies of Piping Plover breed at inland freshwater locations and migrate to coastal areas in winter. Mountain Plover breeds in short-grass prairies and winters in fallow agricultural habitats, while Killdeer breeds in suburban or rural locations on grassy lawns, fields, and gravel driveways.

VOCALIZATIONS: Black-bellied Plover gives an easily mimicked, slurred whistle call, while American and Pacific Golden-Plovers may be separated by subtly different whistled calls. The four small plovers have somewhat distinctive, whistled calls, while Killdeer's explosive call is quickly recognized by most birders. Mountain Plover gives a short, coarse call note, or a series of grating *ji, ji, ji* notes. Flight songs of all plovers vary in tone and cadence.

COMPARISONS OF SIMILAR SPECIES

American Golden-Plover, Pacific Golden-Plover, and Black-bellied Plover, Juveniles

American Golden-Plover and Pacific Golden-Plover

These two very similar species present one of the most challenging ID dilemmas for birders worldwide and were considered a single species (Lesser Golden-Plover) until the late 1900s. Careful evaluation of plumage and structural features is needed for a confident ID of some birds, especially juveniles and nonbreeding adults.

UNCHANGING CHARACTERISTICS: American Golden-Plover has a smaller, pigeon-like head and slighter, more slender bill than Pacific Golden-Plover, which has a larger, blockier head shape and a slightly to noticeably longer, heavier bill. Pacific Golden also has a more "chesty," front-heavy body structure than American Golden, which has a more slender, bottom-heavy body shape. Because of these features, Pacific Golden often has a more upright stance when relaxed. These differences impart an overall structural impression for Pacific Golden that more closely resembles that of the bulkier Black-bellied Plover. (See Figure 89, p. 97.) Pacific Golden also has longer legs on average, which creates an overall lankier appearance.

SUPPLEMENTAL CHARACTERISTICS AND NON-BBI DETAILS: Juvenile Pacific Golden-Plover has bolder, more golden upperpart markings and a buff wash to its head and upper breast compared with smaller, daintier, gold and white upperpart markings on American Golden-Plover. Pacific Golden has a buffier overall appearance, especially on the face and upper breast, and a buff supercilium that typically widens past the eye.

Head and breast markings are sparser on Pacific Golden, and the coarse markings on the upper breast that contrast with the pale, mostly unmarked buff belly and vent differ from American Golden's evenly diffused, blurry underpart markings against uniformly grayish underparts. (See Figure 89, p. 97.) Legs and bill base may be pink tinged in Pacific Golden, dark in American Golden.

FIGURE 89. BLACK-BELLIED PLOVER, AMERICAN GOLDEN-PLOVER, AND PACIFIC GOLDEN-PLOVER, JUVENILES (QUIZ PHOTO)
These three large juvenile plovers present consistent ID problems for all birders. Try to identify the three species in this photo composite. A fourth bird shown is a presumed American Golden-Plover × Pacific Golden-Plover hybrid. Detailed ID information is provided in the text, and answers are given in the appendix, page 268.

First-year Pacific Golden has brighter gold upperpart markings in early spring compared with American Golden's whitish upperpart markings with some gold feathers.

Molt strategy may also be helpful in deciding the ID of first-year birds in spring and early summer. First-year Pacific Golden does not replace its juvenile primary flight feathers until late summer or early fall of its second year, which coincides with a complete molt to first adult nonbreeding plumage. Juvenile American Golden replaces all of its flight feathers in late winter.

Juvenile Black-bellied Plover
UNCHANGING CHARACTERISTICS: A larger, blocky head shape; long, heavy bill; and chest-heavy body pro-

portions with husky shoulders are good physical ID traits for juvenile Black-bellied Plover. This species is larger and heavier overall than the two golden-plovers.

SUPPLEMENTAL CHARACTERISTICS AND NON-BBI DETAILS: Some juvenile Black-bellied Plovers have a golden tone to their plumage and more closely resemble American and Pacific Golden-Plovers in appearance (see Figure 89, above), but most have a black-and-white plumage with checkered upperparts. Black-bellied differs by having little or no pale supercilium, defined coarse streaking on the upper breast, and a contrasting clean white vent. It also retains a good portion of its juvenile plumage through the first winter. Dark-centered upperpart feathers

American Golden-Plover's primary flight feathers are longer than Pacific Golden-Plover's and extend farther past the tail on standing birds. Another traditional ID feature is the number of exposed primary wingtips that extend past the longest tertial on standing birds: adult and first-winter Pacific Goldens typically show three exposed primary tips past the longest tertial tip, while American Goldens usually show four or more exposed primary tips. This comparison, however, is sometimes unreliable with juvenile birds whose flight feathers are not fully grown (especially the tertials), which may result in more or fewer exposed primary tips than usual in both species. First-spring Pacific Goldens, which retain their juvenile primary flight feathers but replace tertials in late winter, may have shorter replaced tertials and longer retained primaries, resulting in more than three exposed primary tips.

with crisp, pale edging separate juvenile from adult Black-bellied Plovers, which have mostly plain, unmarked grayish upperparts.

Piping, Snowy, Semipalmated, and Wilson's Plovers

You can quickly narrow your ID choices for the four small plovers by noting the birds' back color. Semipalmated and Wilson's Plovers have darker brown upperparts compared with the pale gray-brown or sandy-toned to whitish gray upperparts of Piping and Snowy Plovers. This general plumage description is especially helpful for new birders but also allows an immediate separation into two groups.

Semipalmated Plover and Wilson's Plover

UNCHANGING CHARACTERISTICS: Semipalmated Plover has a small, rounded head and short, stubby bill with an orange base, while Wilson's Plover has a larger, blocky head and a very large, thick, black bill. Semipalmated also has a more slender body structure and a more elongated, tapered rear body compared with Wilson's bulky, chest-heavy body structure, which often results in a more vertical resting posture.

SUPPLEMENTAL CHARACTERISTICS AND NON-BBI DETAILS: Wilson's Plover has dull pink legs, while Semipalmated Plover's are orange. Wilson's also has a broader dark neckband than other small plovers, especially males like the bird shown in Figure 90 (p. 99). The neckband is variable, however, with females often having a smaller and sometimes incomplete band, and juveniles and some nonbreeding birds having a pale shadow of a neckband. The shape and extent of the neckband change with the bird's posture, with a larger band visible when the neck in raised and a smaller band visible when the neck is retracted. A white forecrown is also more extensive in Wilson's compared with the other small plovers.

Piping Plover and Snowy Plover

UNCHANGING CHARACTERISTICS: Piping Plover has a rounder head and more uniformly rounded body shape than other *Charadrius* plovers, and its large eye and plain face convey a surprised expression that is lacking in other small plovers. Piping also has a short, stocky bill that differs from Snowy Plover's longer, thinner bill. Snowy has a less uniformly rounded head than Piping, and its front-heavy, chesty body structure with more weight distributed in front of the legs differs from Piping's evenly balanced, rounded body shape. (This head-shape difference is not shown well in Figure 90 but is obvious in real-life viewing conditions.)

SUPPLEMENTAL CHARACTERISTICS AND NON-BBI DETAILS: Piping Plover differs from Snowy Plover by having orange legs and a partial to complete neckband. Snowy has grayish to pinkish legs and only a narrow dark slash on the sides of the upper breast in breeding plumage, and a shadow of this neck slash in juveniles and some nonbreeding birds. While all Piping and Snowy Plovers have pale gray to sandy-colored backs, the Snowy Plover subspecies from the eastern side of the Gulf of Mexico (not shown) has a very white plumage, and the Atlantic Coast subspecies of Piping Plover (not shown) is also paler white. This results in Florida Snowy Plovers and migrant Atlantic Coast Piping Plovers being similar in plumage tones and shading.

SUBSPECIES SEPARATION OF SNOWY AND PIPING PLOVERS: Great Basin–breeding Snowy Plovers have slightly darker backs than the pale eastern coast of Gulf of Mexico subspecies, and far-western-breeding Snowy Plovers have slightly darker backs than Great Basin birds. Compared with the Atlantic Coast Piping Plover, the inland subspecies of Piping Plover (*Charadrius melodus circumcinctus*) has a slightly darker back, darker cheek, dark lores, and often a few black flecks in the forecrown and loral area, especially on adult birds. It also has a complete neckband in breeding adults and partial muted band in first-winter birds. Atlantic Coast Piping Plovers typically have an incomplete band in adults, although some males have thin complete bands.

FIGURE 90. PIPING, SNOWY, SEMIPALMATED, AND WILSON'S PLOVERS (QUIZ PHOTO)
Four small plovers in the genus *Charadrius* have subtly different structural features and plumage traits. Can you identify the four species shown here? ID information is provided in the text. Answers are in the appendix, page 269.

Nonbreeding and first-winter Atlantic Coast birds have a muted partial neckband on the sides of the upper breast.

AVOCETS, STILTS, AND OYSTERCATCHERS

These species are all large, fairly easy to identify, and do not migrate long distances. All are conspicuous and have distinctive plumage and structural features. Four species in two families occur in North America.

PHYSICAL PROFILE

American Avocet and Black-necked Stilt have long, slender bodies with tapered rear ends. American Avocet has fairly long legs, a relatively long neck, a small head, and a needlelike bill that curves upward near the tip (more so in females). Black-necked Stilt has exceptionally long legs; a long, thin neck; a small head; and a straight, needlelike bill.

Both oystercatchers (Black and American) have heavy, football-shaped bodies with short, thick legs;

stocky necks; rounded heads; and long, thick bills that resemble carrots. (See Figure 91, p. 100.)

BIRDING BY IMPRESSION INFORMATION

SIZE: All are large shorebirds. Black-necked Stilt is the smallest species at 14 in. long, while American Avocet is the largest at 18 in. long. Both oystercatchers average 17½ in. long, and represent the heaviest shorebirds in North America.

STRUCTURAL FEATURES: American Avocet has a heavier body structure than the very slender, attenuated Black-necked Stilt. Both species have slender, pointed, angular wings, and Black-necked Stilt has legs that extend far past the tail in flight, resulting in a very distinctive flight profile.

Both oystercatchers have broad, powerful wings that are suited for fast, localized flight. Their bills are laterally compressed and perfectly shaped for prying open bivalves.

BEHAVIOR: American Avocet feeds by swishing its thin, slightly agape bill from side to side in shallow water and often feeds in large groups by herding

FIGURE 91. AVOCETS, STILTS, AND OYSTERCATCHERS
These four large shorebirds have unique plumage and structural features and typically don't pose any ID problems. *Clockwise from top left:* Black-necked Stilt, breeding American Avocet, Black Oystercatcher, and American Oystercatcher.

small fish. In winter avocets form small to very large groups of more than 10,000 birds. At shared breeding sites they are very aggressive toward Black-necked Stilts, with which they share similar microhabitat nest locations.

Black-necked Stilt frequents quiet, freshwater ponds, where it walks slowly while picking or stabbing at the water's surface. It is usually seen in small to medium-size groups when not breeding, and exhibits noisy, frenetic behavior when disturbed.

Stilts are social by nature away from breeding areas, and commonly bicker with their neighbors.

American Oystercatchers are noisy, gregarious shorebirds that may be found in large flocks in the winter, while Black Oystercatchers are more subdued in nature and often found in pairs, although they may form small flocks in winter. During the breeding season, small groups of American Oystercatchers posture and strut together on the beach. This usually leads to a group of birds flying in syn-

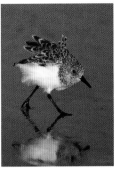

FIGURE 92. SANDPIPERS

Sandpipers come in all sizes and shapes, and this assortment shows some of the many (35 regular breeding) species in North America. *From left to right:* Displaying Buff-breasted Sandpiper, breeding female Ruddy Turnstone, breeding male Sanderling, and breeding male Hudsonian Godwit. Photos are roughly scaled to size, although in real life Hudsonian Godwit is larger compared with the others.

chrony while loudly vocalizing. American Oyster-catchers often use their powerful legs to run instead of fly from casual danger.

PLUMAGE PATTERNS AND GENERAL COLORATION: Three of the four species exhibit bold black-and-white plumage patterns with varying degrees of other colors. Black Oystercatcher differs with its uniformly blackish brown coloration. American Oystercatcher is unmistakable with its brownish "smoking jacket" look, bold white wing stripe, and white rump. Breeding American Avocets have cinnamon heads and necks, but nonbreeding birds have white or grayish heads and necks. Juvenile Black-necked Stilt differs from adults with its pale nape and brownish wash to the back and crown.

HABITAT USE: American Avocets breed in freshwater prairie habitats, but many spend the winter in shallow saltwater bays and the highly saline Salton Sea as well as other shallow freshwater locations. Black-necked Stilts are found mostly in freshwater locations but occasionally use estuarine habitats and other brackish water sites while foraging.

American Oystercatchers are found mostly on sandy beachfronts and coastal marshes but occasionally use rocky jetties for feeding and resting, especially in winter. Conversely, Black Oystercatchers are typically found on rocky jetties and headlands as well as gravel beaches, and seldom use vegetated habitats.

VOCALIZATIONS: American Avocet has a plaintive, melodic piping call that often goes unnoticed, except when a flock of several thousand birds vocalize. Black-necked Stilt gives a distinctive "yipping" call, which is repeated frequently when a bird is agitated. Both oystercatchers give a series of emphatic,

high-pitched, descending whistled notes and a sharp alarm note that resembles Long-billed Dowitcher's call note.

SANDPIPERS

Thirty-five species of highly variable sandpipers in 16 genera in the family Scolopacidae occur as North American residents. Another eight species are regular to rare vagrants.

Feeding, flocking, and nesting behaviors vary widely among sandpipers, although most feed with a constant picking or probing motion that differs from that of other shorebirds. Migratory behavior also varies widely, with some species traveling up to 20,000 miles each year and others moving only a short distance to more productive feeding areas in winter.

PHYSICAL PROFILE

Sandpipers' body shapes vary from thin and tapered to heavy and stocky, but generally birds in the same genus share similar physical features. Likewise, leg length and thickness vary greatly, as do bill length and shape. Many sandpipers have long, pointed wings suitable for long-distance migration, and all but Sanderling have a nonfunctional hind toe. (See Figure 92, above.)

BIRDING BY IMPRESSION INFORMATION

SIZE: Sandpipers range in size from Least Sandpiper at 4½ in. long, which is the smallest shorebird in the world and slightly larger than Ruby-crowned Kinglet, to Long-billed Curlew at 24 in. long, which is about the size of Glossy Ibis. Sizes listed in most field guides represent the length from bill tip to tail tip, so don't allow body shape, bulk, or leg length to influence your size estimate. (See Figure 6, p. 8.)

FIGURE 93. ESTIMATING SIZE USING DIRECT COMPARISONS
A relatively small Sanderling (8 in. long, bottom C) next to the largest shorebird in North America, a Long-billed Curlew (23–26 in. long, bottom R). The Herring Gull (23–25 in. long, top L) is about the same length as the curlew but is larger and heavier bodied than the nearby Ring-billed Gull (17 in. long, top R).

By comparing a familiar shorebird such as Sanderling to a much larger shorebird such as Long-billed Curlew, you can establish a working range of sizes for multiple shorebird species, as well as other nearby birds. (See Figure 93, p. above.)

STRUCTURAL FEATURES: Since sandpipers vary greatly by genus, there is no typical structural description. Small *Calidris* sandpipers have tapered bodies; small, pointed bills; and short to medium-length legs. Dowitchers have bulky, compact bodies; longish legs; and long, straight, thick bills. Curlews have long, decurved bills and large, elongated, football-shaped bodies, while godwits have long, straight bills; large, slender bodies; and long legs and necks. It is better to initially familiarize yourself with the typical structural features of each genus than to try to remember all the various structural features of each species.

BEHAVIOR: Feeding behavior varies among sandpiper groups, and even among species within a genus. Most sandpipers actively feed while constantly moving, picking, and probing the substrate as they walk on land or in shallow water. Bill length and leg length often determine where a particular bird is able to forage successfully, and this behavior is often helpful to its ID.

Dowitchers, Stilt Sandpiper, and Greater Yellowlegs often feed in deeper water, while "peeps" (Least, Semipalmated, and Western Sandpipers) generally feed at the water's edge or in shallow water. Baird's and White-rumped Sandpipers also feed near the water's edge and are sometimes referred to as "peeps" as well, but in worldwide taxonomy they are considered stints.

Several species of sandpipers may form very large flocks away from breeding areas, and distant views of these flocks may narrow your ID choices. Red Knot, Dunlin, Semipalmated Sandpiper, and Western Sandpiper are species that reliably form large flocks during migration and in winter.

PLUMAGE PATTERNS AND GENERAL COLORATION: While some sandpipers have plumage patterns and coloration that remain consistent throughout the

FIGURE 94. PACIFIC COAST SHOREBIRDS

These three medium-sized, round-bodied shorebirds—Black Turnstone (L), Rock Sandpiper (C), and Surfbird (R)—are found only near rocky Pacific Coast habitats when not on their breeding grounds. Note the different bill shapes and plumage patterns on these nonbreeding birds, and subtle differences in body shape and size.

year, others show marked variation between their breeding and nonbreeding plumage. Many sandpipers have a striking combination of rust, gold, and black feathers and a variety of complex feather patterns in breeding plumage, but they revert to a dull, nondescript gray to brown nonbreeding plumage in winter.

Some sandpipers, including Least and Stilt Sandpipers, have a juvenile plumage that is different from both breeding and nonbreeding appearances, but this juvenile plumage typically lasts only a month or two, and then is replaced by a plumage similar to that of nonbreeding adults.

HABITAT USE: Most sandpipers are found in a wide variety of open habitats adjacent to water. Smaller numbers forage and breed in grasslands and wet pastures, and American Woodcock lives in forests and breeds in adjacent tall-grass fields. Some species breed in Arctic tundra habitats and migrate long distances to wintering areas in South America, while others migrate short distances to rocky coastlines and jetties for the winter months. (See Figure 94, above.) Red and Red-necked Phalaropes breed in Arctic tundra locations and winter far offshore in deep ocean waters.

VOCALIZATIONS: Sandpipers have a wide degree of variation in their calls. Some are loud and distinc-tive, such as those of Whimbrel and Long-billed Curlew, while others are short, muted, and easily missed, such as those of Red Knot, Buff-breasted Sandpiper, and Stilt Sandpiper. Many of the smaller sandpipers have short, "gritty" calls that, to the untrained ear, sound similar.

A few species have distinctive, unforgettable calls, including Greater Yellowlegs, Willet, Least Sandpiper, and both turnstones. Sandpiper songs, which are heard near breeding areas, may involve a complex series of whistles, buzzy notes, and clear, ringing notes.

COMPARISONS OF SIMILAR SPECIES

Greater Yellowlegs and Lesser Yellowlegs

Single birds present persistent challenges, thanks to very similar plumage combined with bill-size variation, especially with small-billed male Greater Yellowlegs and long-billed female Lesser Yellowlegs.

UNCHANGING CHARACTERISTICS: Greater Yellowlegs and Lesser Yellowlegs are easy to separate by size when seen together. Greater averages 11½ to 14 in. long, while Lesser is 9¼ to 10 in. long. In both species, males average smaller than females.

Subtle body shape and structural features are helpful to the ID of a single yellowlegs, especially distant birds. Lesser's gently rounded body contours, evenly balanced body structure, and shorter, more evenly proportioned neck and head differ from Greater's rangy, angular body contours, longer neck with a prominent "Adam's apple–like" bulge on resting birds, and bulkier, front-heavy body structure. (See Figure 95, right.)

Carefully assess these features with many yellowlegs to become familiar with subtle structural differences. More obvious structural differences include Greater's longer, heavier bill, which appears upturned near the tip on females, compared with Lesser's finer, thinner, more pointed bill. Greater's bill averages 1½ times the width of its head, while Lesser's is usually equal to or slightly longer than its head width, but variations in bill length by sex may cause some confusion with these ratios. While the bill of some male Greaters may be close in length to an extra-long female Lesser Yellowleg's bill, the shape of Greater's bill is thicker with a bulkier tip compared with Lesser's thinner bill with a more pointed tip.

SUPPLEMENTAL CHARACTERISTICS AND NON-BBI DETAILS: Breeding Greater Yellowlegs has more extensive dark markings on its underparts than breeding Lesser Yellowlegs, especially the lower flank barring. Birds in transition to and from breeding plumage may appear similar, like the birds in Figure 95, top photo. Nonbreeding birds of both species have very similar plumage. Juvenile plumage is somewhat similar, but Lesser differs by having a brownish wash to the upper breast and head in young birds, and diffused brown streaks on the upper breast in older juveniles. Greater does not have this brownish wash in juvenile plumage, but has defined upper breast streaking against white underparts. Also note Greater's more pronounced eye-ring and more extensive pale grayish bill base versus Lesser's slightly yellow-based or all-dark bill.

Solitary Sandpiper and Lesser Yellowlegs

Solitary Sandpiper is another medium-sized sandpiper in the genus *Tringa* that superficially resembles Lesser Yellowlegs in size and plumage features.

UNCHANGING CHARACTERISTICS: Solitary Sandpiper is slightly smaller than Lesser Yellowlegs, with shorter legs and a more foreshortened, less tapered rear body, which is accentuated by Solitary's shorter wings. Solitary also has a slightly shorter neck and shorter, thicker-based bill on average than Lesser Yellowlegs. (See Figure 96, p. 105.)

SUPPLEMENTAL CHARACTERISTICS AND NON-BBI DETAILS: Solitary Sandpiper's yellow-green legs are not as bright as the yellow-orange legs of breeding Lesser Yellowlegs, but they are variable and can be bright yellow in spring. A darker cheek in Solitary versus

FIGURE 95. GREATER YELLOWLEGS AND LESSER YELLOWLEGS (QUIZ PHOTO)

Top: Greater Yellowlegs (L) and Lesser Yellowlegs (R) in mostly breeding plumage. Note the size, body shape, bill length and shape, and structural differences in these two species. *Bottom:* Plumage and feather patterns are very similar in these closely related juvenile shorebirds: Greater Yellowlegs (L) and Lesser Yellowlegs (R). ID information is provided in the text and answers are given in the appendix, page 269.

a streaked cheek in Lesser highlights a bold white eye-ring on Solitary, and a darker brown, less spotted wing panel is distinctive in all plumages for Solitary. A black border to the lower wing edge is also helpful to its ID. Brown upperparts with white spots on Solitary differ from the black-, white-, and brown-checkered look of the upperparts on Lesser Yellowlegs.

Semipalmated Sandpiper and Western Sandpiper

A comparison of these two species is shown in Figure 97 (p. 105), with silhouettes provided to allow you to assess the structural differences without distracting plumage features.

UNCHANGING CHARACTERISTICS: Western Sandpiper's wider, puffier head and bulkier chest and neck are helpful structural features for separating it from Semipalmated Sandpiper in all plumages. Semipalmated has a smaller, evenly rounded head that lacks the squarish rear shape of Western's larger, deeper head. Because of its rounded, "half-domed" head

FIGURE 96. SOLITARY SANDPIPER AND LESSER YELLOWLEGS (QUIZ PHOTO)
Can you identify the breeding Lesser Yellowlegs and Solitary Sandpiper? ID information for separating these species is provided in the text. Answers are in the appendix, page 269.

FIGURE 97. WESTERN SANDPIPER AND SEMIPALMATED SANDPIPER (QUIZ PHOTO)
Top: Semipalmated Sandpiper and Western Sandpiper are very similar small shorebirds that pose major ID problems in transition, juvenile, and nonbreeding plumages. Can you identify these transition-plumage birds? The silhouettes in the top right photo can help you assess subtle structural differences. ID information is provided in the text, and answers are in the appendix, page 269. *Bottom:* Juvenile Semipalmated and Western Sandpipers can have similar plumages, but a few structural features and plumage details help separate them. Try to ID these birds. Answers are in the appendix, page 269.

shape, Semipalmated often imparts a "no-necked" look on resting birds. The less evenly rounded head shape of Western is hard to assess in birds that have their necks fully retracted.

A larger portion of Western's body weight is distributed in front of its legs, which results in a more imbalanced, front-heavy body profile versus Semipalmated's evenly balanced profile with equal weight distribution in front of and behind its legs. This even weight distribution often results in

a more horizontal body posture on relaxed, foraging, and resting birds versus an angled-back look to Western. With a chest-heavy body weight distribution, Western often tilts its front body upward for balance when resting.

Field guides often stress bill shape as a reliable feature for separating these two species, with Semipalmated's straight, blunt-tipped bill differing from Western's decurved, fine-tipped bill. These guidelines work fine for male Semipalmateds and female

FIGURE 98. WHITE-RUMPED SANDPIPER AND BAIRD'S SANDPIPER (QUIZ PHOTO)
Baird's Sandpiper and White-rumped Sandpiper are similar in size and show a long rear body structure and long wings. Try to identify these three birds (two juveniles and one nonbreeding bird) in photos taken in September. ID information is provided in the text. Answers are in the appendix, page 269.

Westerns whose bills never overlap in length or shape, but are unreliable for some female Semi-palmateds that breed in eastern Canada and small-billed male Westerns.

These eastern Semipalmateds can have long bills with fine, drooping tips that overlap with or are slightly longer than a male Western's bill, and some of these Semipalmateds have distinctly finer-tipped bills than male Westerns do. Male Westerns can have relatively short bills that lack the fine drooping tips of female Westerns, and that closely resemble some female Semipalmateds' bills. In these cases, bill length and shape are unreliable for ID purposes. (See Figure 97, bottom photos, p. 105.)

SUPPLEMENTAL CHARACTERISTICS AND NON-BBI DETAILS: Nonbreeding Semipalmated and Western Sandpipers are very similar in plumage, but Semipalmated tends to have a darker cheek and lores and more prominent, smudgier streaks along the sides of the upper breast. Western has less extensive and more defined streaks on the sides of the upper breast. Nonbreeding Western has a whiter overall appearance to the face than Semipalmated, and a less contrasting cap.

Juvenile Semipalmated differs by having a dark (often reddish) cap and paler nape versus Western's uniformly grayish plumage in these areas with only a slightly darker cap than nape. Juvenile Westerns have a line of bright rusty scapular feathers on the sides of the upper back that contrast with the rest of their upperparts. (See Figure 97, bottom photos, p. 105.) Juvenile Semipalmateds are extremely variable, but most have uniformly whitish-, ginger-, or rust-edged upperpart feathers that lack the strong, contrasting rust scapulars of juvenile Western. Some juvenile Semipalmateds have straw-colored legs that lack dark pigment. Adults of these two species are usually distinctive in plumage, with Western having strong rusty upperpart feather edges and basal markings, and Semipalmated having ginger-colored fringes to the upperparts.

Baird's Sandpiper and White-rumped Sandpiper
These two *Calidris* sandpipers are noticeably larger than the three "peeps" (Least, Semipalmated, and Western Sandpipers) and share similar size and body shape features with each other. A comparison of juvenile Baird's and White-rumped and a nonbreeding White-rumped is shown in Figure 98 (above).

UNCHANGING CHARACTERISTICS: Both species are longer winged and have noticeably more attenuated rear body shapes than the three "peep" sandpipers, but a few subtle structural differences help separate them. White-rumped Sandpiper is heavier overall compared with Baird's Sandpiper, and has a bulkier chest and shoulders and a larger, puffier head shape, but some birds may appear quite similar because of lower body weight and fat reserves on some White-rumpeds. (See Figure 98, above.)

Baird's is slender and streamlined in structure, and has a proportionally smaller head compared with White-rumped. Baird's wings are also longer than White-rumped's and typically cross behind the tail when a bird is standing. These very long wings contribute to Baird's more streamlined body profile. White-rumped's wings often extend beyond the tail without crossing, and a small number of birds have wings that project just beyond the tail tip in standing birds. (See Figure 98, above.)

White-rumped's bill is short and pointed, but it averages thicker than Baird's and often has a slight decurve near the tip. Baird's has a very slender, short, straight bill with a narrower, finer tip than White-rumped's. Both species have an evenly balanced, horizontal body profile, but Baird's often stands and walks upright with its neck extended.

SUPPLEMENTAL CHARACTERISTICS AND NON-BBI DETAILS: Breeding birds are fairly distinctive, with Baird's Sandpiper having dark-centered upperpart feathers with buff fringes in early spring and silvery edges in summer. Crisp, dark underpart streaking is limited to the upper breast and neck. White-rumped Sandpiper has bold, rufous upperpart feather edges and heavy streaking on the face, neck, upper breast, and flanks, with the flanks showing chevron-shaped markings.

Since Baird's replaces only a small number of its breeding feathers prior to migrating to South America, adults migrating in summer mostly resemble worn breeding birds. The majority of Baird's seen in late summer and fall along both coasts are juveniles, with adults migrating south through the Great Plains and West-Central United States. Juveniles have an overall buffy appearance, with buff to whitish feather edges to brownish-centered upperpart feathers and a neat bib of fine, dark streaks on the buffy upper breast. Baird's retains its juvenile plumage throughout fall migration and molts to nonbreeding plumage in South America.

Juvenile White-rumped has a scaly look to its upperparts thanks to pale white and rust fringes, and differs from Baird's by having a grayer overall appearance with a reddish cap and cheek versus a uniformly buffy look to Baird's. Adult White-rumpeds replace a good number of their head and body feathers on the Arctic tundra breeding grounds prior to migrating to South America, so late-summer and fall migrants have a mostly nonbreeding plumage. Nonbreeding and fall adults are mostly gray overall, and differ from the similar juvenile Baird's by having a stronger, pale supercilium and a lack of buff to the upper breast. Fine streaks often extend down the flanks, unlike on Baird's. (See Figure 98, p. 106.)

Nonbreeding Stilt Sandpiper and Dunlin

Both of these species have somewhat similar nonbreeding and transition plumages.

UNCHANGING CHARACTERISTICS: Both species can be similar in body size and bill shape and length, so caution is advised, especially when only one species is present. Stilt Sandpiper's longer legs versus Dunlin's shorter legs are a reliable ID feature. Dunlin's larger, puffier head and shorter, thicker neck are other useful separating structural features. Stilt Sandpiper has a smaller head with a sloping forehead and rounded rear crown and a longer, thinner neck versus Dunlin's puffier head and shorter, thicker neck. Bill length is variable on both species and often not a useful ID feature, although Dunlin typically shows a thicker bill toward the tip.

SUPPLEMENTAL CHARACTERISTICS AND NON-BBI DETAILS: Dunlin has black legs, while Stilt Sandpiper has yellowish green legs. Stilt Sandpiper also has a pronounced whitish supercilium compared with Dunlin's uniformly streaked head, but some Dunlins can have a muted pale supercilium. Stilt Sandpiper typically has more defined upper breast streaks against a uniformly pale background versus Dunlin's diffused streaks against a gray-washed upper breast in nonbreeding birds. Transition birds in early spring, however, can appear similar in plumage. (See Figure 99, below.)

Long-billed Dowitcher and Short-billed Dowitcher

These two similar species have long been regarded by experts as unidentifiable in many field conditions unless their distinctive calls are heard. Recent careful assessment of subtle differences in structure and bill shape has allowed us to identify most birds in all plumages.

UNCHANGING CHARACTERISTICS: A husky, front-heavy weight distribution, thick neck, and different head

---

FIGURE 99. DUNLIN AND STILT SANDPIPER (QUIZ PHOTO)
Nonbreeding and transition plumages can be similar in these two species. Try to identify these birds after reading the ID information in the text. Answers are in the appendix, page 269.

FIGURE 100. LONG-BILLED DOWITCHER AND SHORT-BILLED DOWITCHER (QUIZ PHOTO)

Identification of these two closely related shorebirds can be very difficult. In nonbreeding plumage (top photos) and transition-plumage birds (bottom photos, April), a combination of body shape, structural features, and plumage details is often required for a confident ID. Can you identify these birds? Complete ID information is provided in the text. Answers are in the appendix, page 269.

shape contribute to a physical profile on Long-billed Dowitcher that differs from Short-billed Dowitcher's more even weight distribution, thinner neck, and more evenly rounded head. While both dowitchers can have a rounded upper body shape, Long-billed has a deeper, more egg-shaped lower body carriage (profile) compared with Short-billed's straighter undercarriage. (See Figure 100, above.) These differences in body shape can also be seen on some flying birds.

Care should be taken with juvenile and under-nourished Long-billed Dowitchers that don't exhibit the typical egg-shaped lower body, but instead have a slender undercarriage similar to that of Short-billed. (See Figure 100, above.) In these cases, a careful assessment of body weight distribution, thicker neck, bill length and shape, and pertinent plumage features will help with the ID of Long-billed.

The front-heavy body structure causes a weight imbalance in Long-billed that requires it to adjust its body angle and tilt upward when sleeping or resting. This back angle may be as extreme as 40 degrees in

large females and differs noticeably from the more evenly balanced Short-billed Dowitcher, which has a horizontal or slightly angled back in a resting posture. Sleeping birds are more easily identified using this back-angle difference, unless a strong headwind causes both species to lean forward.

The combination of rounded back and slightly rounded, egg-shaped undercarriage on Long-billed creates a "swallowed a tennis ball" profile on many relaxed feeding Long-billeds, especially females. Short-billed lacks this "tennis ball in the belly" impression because of its straighter undercarriage. The more rounded body shape on Long-billed is also obvious in head-on and tail-on views, with Short-billed showing a more elliptical body shape.

Female dowitchers are larger bodied, longer billed, and longer legged than males, and these differences are especially noticeable in Long-billed. Female Long-billed is easier to ID because of its especially long bill and legs, and extra chest-heavy body structure. Male Short-billed is easier to ID because of its especially short bill and small, slender, compact body. It is the female Short-billeds and male Long-billeds that can appear similar in size, structure, and bill length, with most male Short-billeds and female Long-billeds having no overlap in size or bill length.

Short-billed has a bill that is thicker overall with a fairly blunt tip and a deeper base. This deeper base is a helpful feature for identification of some Short-billeds, and is not present in Long-billed. Many Short-billeds also have a distinct "kink" in the bill near the tip, as if it got caught in a closing door. Long-billed has a uniformly tapered bill that flattens near the tip and has a shallower base. Some Long-billeds (mostly females) have a uniformly downward arch to the outer bill half (not illustrated) that superficially suggests the "kink" near Short-billed's bill tip, but the longer downward arch versus a localized kink in Short-billed is different.

SUPPLEMENTAL CHARACTERISTICS AND NON-BBI DETAILS: NONBREEDING PLUMAGE: Plumage is darker gray overall in Long-billed Dowitcher, with its head and neck often appearing as if they'd been dipped in a bucket of soot. Some Long-billeds may show less concentrated gray shading on the upper breast. A bold white lower eye crescent is obvious on Long-billed and is accentuated by a uniformly darker face. Short-billed Dowitcher has a paler head and neck and a whitish upper breast with variable gray spotting. (See Figure 100 top, p. 108.) It also shows a whiter upper breast with scattered gray spots.

Upperpart feather shafts are darker in Long-billed, with dusky shading adjacent to the central shaft in many birds adding to the darker impression, especially in adults. Short-billed has paler upperpart feathers and less prominent dark central feather shafts, especially in the subspecies *Limnodromus griseus hendersoni,* which gives it a lighter appearance overall, especially from a distance. Two other subspecies of Short-billed Dowitcher (*L. g. griseus* and *L. g. caurinus*) have darker upperpart feathers and shafts in nonbreeding plumage, but are still paler than Long-billed. The dark tail bands on Long-billed are noticeably wider than the thinner white bands. Short-billed usually has white and dark bands of equal width, or slightly wider white bands.

TRANSITION AND BREEDING PLUMAGE: Upperpart markings and feather fringes on Short-billed Dowitcher are typically more orange in color and wider than Long-billed Dowitcher's narrower rust-colored feather fringes, which creates a more contrasting and colorful appearance in breeding Short-billed, and gives the impression of a mostly orange back with black feather centers. Long-billed also has narrow white fringes to upperpart feathers into the

summer months, while Short-billed has only white fringes in early spring.

Long-billed's black feather centers and very narrow rusty fringes give the impression of a blackish back with minimal rusty highlights. Both species may show similar upperpart fringes in fresh transition and breeding plumage (see Figure 100, p. 108), but late-spring and summer breeding–plumaged birds appear very different overall in terms of upperpart feather edge color width, scapular fringe color pattern, and proportion of dark internal shading.

Underpart coloration is more brick red in Long-billed versus orange in Short-billed, and only the prairie subspecies of Short-billed (*L. g. hendersoni*) has orange color that extends to the undertail, similar to Long-billed. Both, however, can show slightly white rear vents in breeding plumage. The other two subspecies of Short-billed have distinct white vents and do not resemble breeding Long-billed.

Differences in breeding *hendersoni* include lighter spotting on the central upper breast compared with Long-billed's denser, heavier spotting, and dark bars on the upper and lower flanks of Long-billed compared with mostly spotting on Short-billed. These dark bars on the upper flanks in Long-billed also have distinct white fringes, while Short-billed's spots or bars typically do not. Late-summer transition Long-billed and *hendersoni* Short-billed can be almost identical in plumage when the flank and upper breast markings wear off, and structural differences are more important in these instances. (See Figure 100, p. 108.)

"Eastern" and "Western" Willets

These two subspecies will most likely receive full species status in the coming years.

UNCHANGING CHARACTERISTICS: "Eastern" Willet differs from "Western" Willet by its smaller average size, and by a noticeable lack of sexual dimorphism compared with "Western's" dramatic size difference between larger females and smaller males (up to 20 percent size difference). While female "Easterns" may occasionally be slightly larger than males, their body proportions are mostly similar. Female "Westerns" have much longer legs and necks, and appreciably longer, more tapered bills, than males. These longer bills may have a slight upward curve near the tip, and are longer and more tapered than any "Eastern" Willet bill, which is stockier, blunt-tipped, and may have a slight droop to the outer half.

"Western's" body structure is longer and more graceful compared with "Eastern's" stockier, more foreshortened body, but these differences are not obvious in some male "Westerns." "Western" also averages longer-legged than "Eastern," although

FIGURE 101. WILLET COMPARISON (QUIZ PHOTO)

"Eastern" Willet and "Western" Willet are presently considered one species, but this designation is slated for review. ID information is provided in the text to separate these two similar subspecies. The left two photos show one subspecies, the right two photos the other subspecies. The top photos show mostly nonbreeding and transition-plumage birds in mid-March, while the bottom photos show juvenile birds. Answers are in the appendix, page 269.

some male "Westerns" can have similar leg length and have a body and bill shape somewhat similar to that of "Easterns." (See Figure 101, above.) In most cases, "Eastern's" bill can be separated from "Western's" by its blunter tip and more uniform thickness along the entire length versus a more tapered tip on male Western.

SUPPLEMENTAL CHARACTERISTICS AND NON-BBI DETAILS:
Breeding "Eastern" Willet differs from "Western" Willet by having denser, browner barring on the underparts and a brown cast to the head and back versus "Western's" grayish tone. Breeding "Eastern" has a pinkish cast to the inner half of the bill, while "Western" has an all-dark bill in breeding birds. Worn breeding "Eastern" appears very dark brown overall, while worn "Western" has a distinct grayish to brownish cast. Breeding "Eastern" has pinkish-colored legs compared with "Western's" dark gray legs.

Juveniles are distinctly different in plumage, with "Eastern" having very dark brown scapulars with prominent buff spots that contrast strongly with paler wing coverts. Juvenile "Westerns" are pale gray and buff overall with pale cinnamon feather fringes and dark subterminal markings on their upperpart feathers. These cinnamon fringes wear to whitish after a month or so. (See Figure 101, above.) "Western's" scapulars show little to no contrast with the wing coverts. Worn juvenile "Eastern's" are more difficult to ID, with some lacking the above contrasting plumage details. In these cases, a careful assessment of structural features is necessary, especially the incompletely formed thick, blunt-tipped bill.

Nonbreeding differences are poorly known by

North American birders because "Eastern" Willet does not occur in the Northern Hemisphere in nonbreeding plumage. A small number of mostly nonbreeding "Easterns" may be found in Texas in mid-March, just after their arrival from South America. (See Figure 101, p. 110.) Nonbreeding "Western" is mostly pale gray overall with white underparts, neck, and lower cheek. The legs are dark, and the bill has a mostly gray basal half and a dark tip. Nonbreeding "Eastern" is browner overall, with a brownish wash to the neck and entire cheek, and darker scapulars that contrast with paler wing coverts. Some nonbreeding "Easterns," however, can appear very similar to "Westerns" from October to January. The legs are pale to pinkish colored, and the bill has a pinkish-colored base with a dark tip.

These three groups of birds were formerly listed together in the family Laridae, and they share similar physical attributes of long, powerful, pointed wings; relatively small heads and bills; and webbed feet. New taxonomic listings show a distinct family for each of these groups.

GULLS

Gulls are highly visible birds that often congregate in open areas where food is available, and at favorite roost sites. Found mostly near aquatic habitats throughout the year, they often float and paddle on the water's surface while resting, but some can also be seen in parking lots or near landfills, where they scavenge for all manner of food.

Few things are more intimidating to birders than a mixed flock of different-aged gulls. Though gulls typically sit still for long periods and allow close scrutiny, they remain the dreaded "G word" for many casual birders, who often don't try to identify them.

TIPS FOR IDENTIFYING GULLS

If you're a beginning birder, start by becoming familiar with the most obvious gull species, which you can then use to compare with other gulls. Most North American locations have only a handful of regularly occurring gulls, and this list is further reduced during the summer breeding season. After you become familiar with the size and overall structure of a common gull in your area, other unfamiliar gulls will be easier to evaluate with respect to comparative size and structure as well as plumage patterns and shading.

A recent change in bird aging terminology uses the term "cycle" to describe a typical plumage condition that occurs in each year of a gull's life. Rather than relying on a calendar dating system, it concentrates on the molt cycle timing during which a plumage condition is present. This allows you to compare specific plumage appearances rather than seasons or times of the year to describe what a gull looks like.

For example, a second-cycle gull represents the plumage condition that is present from the approximate end of a gull's first year of life to the end of its second year, including its breeding and nonbreeding conditions. Juvenile gulls are still referred to as being in juvenile plumage, however.

A problem with identifying gulls is their tendency to interbreed with other similar-sized gulls. While some bird families have occasional hybridization between species, larger gulls interbreed on a more regular basis, with two common Pacific Coast species (Western Gull and Glaucous-winged Gull) having hybrid offspring that are more common than their predecessors in certain areas of the Pacific Northwest coastal zone. Some hybrids resemble rare vagrant gulls, so be careful when studying an unusual gull.

Gull ID is one of the most challenging aspects of birding, and entire books are dedicated to the process, including *A Reference Guide to Gulls of the Americas* by Steve N. G. Howell and Jon Dunn (Houghton Mifflin, 2007). Since gull taxonomy has recently undergone major changes, we have grouped the gulls according to general size parameters using plumage patterns as supporting criteria. (See Figure 102, p. 113.)

PHYSICAL PROFILE

All gulls have fully webbed feet, fairly short legs, and short, squarish tails (Ross's Gull differs with a wedge-shaped tail). (See Figure 103, p. 114.) Bills are short and range from slender and fine-tipped in smaller gulls to stocky and blunt-tipped in larger gulls. Wings are generally long, tapered, and variably pointed. Male gulls typically have a larger bill and heavier body structure than females, although this difference may be obvious in some birds and subtle in others. (See Figure 106, p. 117.)

BIRDING BY IMPRESSION INFORMATION

SIZE: Gulls range from Little Gull at 11 in. long, about the size of Merlin, to Great Black-backed Gull at 30 in. long, which is the same length as Bald Eagle but with much shorter wings (80 in. for Bald Eagle vs. 65 in. for Great Black-backed Gull). Male gulls are slightly larger than females.

Gulls generally fall into two groups: small and large. Small gulls include nine North American breeding species that range in size from Little Gull to Ivory Gull, which at 17 in. long is slightly larger than Laughing Gull. Large gulls include 14 species that range in size from Mew Gull, at 16 in. long, to the imposing Great Black-backed Gull, which is the largest gull in the world.

Mew Gull and Ring-billed Gull (17 in. long) are included in the "large" gull group even though they overlap with a few species in the "small" group (Ivory Gull and Black-legged Kittiwake, both 17 in. long) because they are part of the large white-headed gull complex, members of which share similar structural features and plumage details.

STRUCTURAL FEATURES: The small gulls have more delicate features than the large white-headed gulls,

FIGURE 102. GULLS

Two large white-headed gulls and two smaller hooded gulls in breeding plumage. *Clockwise from top left:* Herring Gull, Western Gull, Laughing Gull, and Sabine's Gull.

including smaller heads and bills and more stream-lined body shapes. Small gulls have proportionally long wings; slender bodies; and small, thin bills. An exception is Ivory Gull, which has a portly body shape. (See Figure 103, p. 114.)

The large gulls have heavier body structures; longer legs; longer, thicker necks; and larger heads and bills. Body structure and bill shape are more slender and streamlined in the smaller species in this group, and these features increase in size proportionally with the larger gulls.

Mew Gull and Ring-billed Gull differ from other large gulls with their streamlined body structures and smaller heads and bills, and may resemble some small gulls. The remaining large gulls share a superficially similar heavier body structure, larger head size, and bulkier bill shape, which is why field ID of these species can be so challenging. Wing

length and its projection past the tail are helpful features for separating gulls.

BEHAVIOR: Many of the smaller gulls, especially the pelagic species, feed on small fish and aquatic inver-tebrates found near the water's surface. They are ag-ile fliers and make quick turns and dips to the water to catch their meal. This buoyant flight style is simi-lar to that of most terns, except it doesn't culminate with a plunge-dive. Smaller gulls don't scavenge for food as much as the larger gulls do, with the excep-tion of Ivory Gull.

Two of the five species of small hooded gulls (Lit-tle and Bonaparte's Gulls) forage for fish and inver-tebrates in near-shore coastal waters and freshwater inland lakes, while Franklin's Gull feeds mostly on terrestrial and flying insects at prairie breeding sites before moving to oceanic environments for the

FIGURE 103. IVORY GULL AND ROSS'S GULL

Ivory Gull (L) is the rarest breeding gull in North America and a highly regarded species. The bird shown here is in first-winter plumage. Breeding Ross's Gull (R) is one of the most sought-after species for all birders because of its stunning plumage, delicate features, and remote, year-round Arctic range.

winter. Hooded gulls "flycatch" for flying insects over fields and marshes in mid- to late summer.

Larger gulls regularly kill live prey, including seabirds and their nestlings, unwary smaller birds, and even other gulls. During the winter, a good number of larger gulls occur at landfills and coastal locations where food is abundant. This is one reason why the conventional term "seagull" is incorrect—many of these gulls don't occur near the sea, but breed or winter near inland freshwater lakes or at Arctic tundra locations.

Most gulls migrate to other locations after breeding, although some move only short distances to productive feeding areas. Among those that do migrate, some go moderate distances within North America, while others go very long distances to South America or open oceanic waters.

PLUMAGE PATTERNS AND GENERAL COLORATION:
All gulls share a combination of white, black, or variable gray or brown plumage patterns, with only a few species having an all-white plumage (adult Ivory Gull and some first-cycle Iceland and Glaucous Gulls).

Gulls have a variety of plumage conditions until they reach full adulthood, which is two to four years depending on the species. White-headed gulls (except Heermann's, Mew, and Ring-billed Gulls) take three to four years to attain full adult plumage, and they retain an increasingly worn juvenile plumage through the first winter. Smaller gulls typically take two years to reach adulthood, though some have a somewhat adultlike plumage after one year.

To add to the confusion, plumages vary during the transition from one plumage cycle to the next, with feather wear further compounding the issue. These mixed-plumage conditions are responsible for added ID confusion since birders concentrate mainly on plumage details and disregard valuable unchanging physical features and comparative size.

All adult gulls except Heermann's have white underparts, and many have pale to dark gray upperparts. (See Figure 104, p. 115.) Five species have black or very dark gray upperparts (Great and Lesser Black-backed Gulls, Western Gull, Slaty-backed Gull, and Yellow-footed Gull), which helps narrow your ID choices. Bill color in adult white-headed gulls is yellow with variable red and black tips (except Heermann's, which has a red bill with black tip). Leg color varies from pinkish or pale reddish to yellow, gray, or black.

Six species in the "small" gull group have dark hoods in breeding plumage and variable dark markings on their heads in winter. Bill color changes from red to black in nonbreeding Laughing and Franklin's Gulls. Leg color may also change with elevated breeding hormones (including red legs in some breeding Laughing and Franklin's Gulls). These hooded gulls show adult nonbreeding plumage early in their second cycle, except for Laughing Gull, which has a slightly different second-winter plumage from adult birds. All have adult breeding plumage in the spring of their second cycle. Other hooded gulls include Bonaparte's, Little, Sabine's, and Black-headed Gulls. The last is a regular vagrant to North America.

FIGURE 104. BREEDING HEERMANN'S GULL

This medium-sized gull (19 in. long) is one of the most beautiful of all gulls. Heermann's breeds in Mexico around the Gulf of California and then disperses as far north as British Columbia. Its typical wintering range is central and southern California coastal areas. Juveniles are chocolate brown.

HABITAT USE: All gulls are found mostly near aquatic habitats throughout the year, and they rely on these for breeding sites and nonbreeding roost locations. Many gulls nest on islands or inaccessible coastal habitats, such as rocky cliffs and coastal or freshwater marshes. Others are Arctic or subarctic breeders that use tundra habitats and boreal forests for nest sites. Mew and Bonaparte's Gulls occasionally use abandoned stick nests in trees for breeding.

VOCALIZATIONS: Gulls have a wide variety of calls, with many of the larger gulls giving loud, repetitive bursts of melodic to nasal sounds with a buglelike quality. Some of the smaller gulls give raspy, tern-like calls, while Laughing Gull gets its name from its piercing, laughing-like call. Other than Great Black-backed Gull, which gives a deep, flat, muffled series of notes, many of the large gulls' vocalizations are compared with those of Herring Gull for better understanding, and have only subtle differences in tonal quality.

COMPARISONS OF SIMILAR SPECIES

A number of gulls, especially the larger ones, present complex ID problems for birders of all skill levels. Some of these challenges are the result of plumage variation in one species that resembles another species, especially in the first and second cycles, while a small number are the result of hybridization with other species.

Ring-billed Gull and Mew Gull

Ring-billed Gull and Mew Gulls are cosmopolitan by nature and can regularly be found in a wide variety of locations, including parks and the parking lots of malls and waterfront restaurants. Ring-billed overlaps with Mew only in the Pacific coastal zone (lower British Columbia and south to Mexico) from fall to spring, where direct comparison is possible.

UNCHANGING CHARACTERISTICS: Ring-billed Gull (17½ in. long) is slightly larger than Mew Gull (16 in. long) and has a longer, heavier bill; longer, broader, more pointed wings; and a bulkier body structure. (See Figure 105, p. 116.) Mew has a rounder head shape with a larger eye compared with Ring-billed's wider head with a shallower sloping forehead.

SUPPLEMENTAL CHARACTERISTICS AND NON-BBI DETAILS: Breeding Mew Gull has a slender, all-yellow bill compared with adult Ring-billed Gull's yellow bill with a black ring. Mew has dark eyes versus yellow eyes in Ring-billed, more prominent white wing-tips, and slightly darker gray upperparts than Ring-billed. First-cycle Mew has a pinkish bill with a dark tip. Second-cycle Mew has a yellow bill with a black ring, and nonbreeding adults have a yellow bill with a faint, dusky ring.

Wing patterns differ on adults, with Mew having larger and more extensive white spots on the upperwing outer primary tips. Ring-billed has mostly black primaries with small white spots near

FIGURE 105. RING-BILLED GULL AND MEW GULL (QUIZ PHOTO)
These two closely related gulls are somewhat similar in size and plumage patterns, but they have subtly different body shapes, structural features, plumage shading, and bill patterns. Try to identify these gulls to species using the information in the text. One species is on the left (top and bottom), the other on the right. Answers are in the appendix, page 269.

the tip. (See Figure 105, above.) Ring-billed has a less prominent white trailing edge to the wing and finer, more distinct head markings in nonbreeding plumage.

Both species retain complete juvenile plumage for only a short time (mainly July and August, with a few birds retaining some juvenile body plumage until early winter). Both retain their boldly patterned juvenile wing feathers until the following summer, which gives them a distinct two-toned appearance when perched or in flight. This molt strategy occurs only with these two white-headed gulls, and is a good way to separate them from larger first-cycle gulls.

First-cycle Mew and Ring-billed Gulls are fairly straightforward in their plumage differences. Mew has an overall dusky brownish appearance, while Ring-billed has a whitish look, especially in the underparts. First-cycle Mew also has an all-brown tail band with heavy brown barring on the uppertail coverts versus a dark tail band and mostly whitish uppertail coverts on Ring-billed. Upperwing mark-

ings on Mew are more muted with less contrasting markings than on Ring-billed through the first winter.

Laughing Gull and Franklin's Gull
UNCHANGING CHARACTERISTICS: Laughing Gull (16½ in. long) is larger than Franklin's Gull (14½ in. long) and has longer, more pointed wings; a longer, heavier bill that droops more at the tip; and a proportionally longer, more streamlined body structure with a longer neck than Franklin's. Because of its longer, more pointed wings, Laughing flies with deeper wing strokes on strongly angled wings compared with Franklin's stiffer, shallower wingbeats and less angled wings.

SUPPLEMENTAL CHARACTERISTICS AND NON-BBI DETAILS: Although overall plumage features are superficially similar, there are a few reliable differences. Some of these include Franklin's larger, bolder white primary tips (adults) and thicker, bolder white eye crescents. Franklin's also has more extensive white

FIGURE 106. LAUGHING GULL AND FRANKLIN'S GULL (QUIZ PHOTO)

Top: This early April scene shows subtle yet distinct plumage and structural differences between breeding Laughing Gull and Franklin's Gull. For an expert-level quiz, try to identify these gulls using the ID information in the text. Can you also identify the sleeping bird at left? Hint: Use the size of the gulls to help you. Answers are in the appendix, page 270. *Bottom:* Nonbreeding adult Laughing Gull and Franklin's Gull. Note the larger size, bulkier body structure, and larger bill on the male gull of one species compared with the adjacent female of the same species. Identify these gulls to species using information in the text. Answers are in the appendix, page 270.

feathering between a gray back and black primaries from first summer onward. (See Figure 106, above.)

Nonbreeding plumage is mostly straightforward, with first-cycle and adult Franklin's having a fairly well defined dark "half-hood" or helmeted appearance that highlights the bold white eye crescents. Laughing has a dark smudge behind the eye and variable head smudging, with a less prominent white eye-ring. Similarities between Franklin's and Laughing occur from January onward, when Laughing has an expanded black hood similar to Franklin's, with new dark breeding head feathers molting in.

The black underwing primary tips of Franklin's are noticeably less prominent than Laughing's large dark wedge on the outer primaries. A clean white underwing on first-winter Franklin's differs noticeably from first-winter Laughing's mottled underwings. First-winter Franklin's also has a partial, narrower tail band that does not extend to the outer tail feathers compared with Laughing's wider, complete tail band. The upperwings of first-winter Laughing have brownish inner wings and black outer wings, while Franklin's has a mostly gray upperwing with contrasting brownish wing coverts and less extensive black wingtips.

First-cycle Western Gull and First-cycle California Gull

These two Pacific Coast gulls are not usually problematic for experienced birders, especially when seen side by side, but their first-cycle plumages can be similar and can cause ID problems if structural features are not carefully evaluated, especially with single birds.

FIGURE 107. CALIFORNIA GULL AND WESTERN GULL (QUIZ PHOTO)
The first-cycle gulls shown here share similar plumage color and patterns but differ in body size, structural features, and subtle plumage shading. ID information is provided in the text. Can you identify these two species? Answers are in the appendix, page 270.

UNCHANGING CHARACTERISTICS: Western Gull is larger than California Gull (25 in. long vs. 21 in. long on average), but a large male California is closer in size to a small female Western. Western has a noticeably bulkier body structure with a heavier, mostly dark bill that shows a distinct thick, drooping tip. This last feature is helpful for separating Western from all similarly plumaged large gulls. In flight, Western's wings look heavier and broader compared with California's relatively long, narrow, pointed wings.

Important structural features used to separate California Gull at all ages from Western, Herring, and Thayer's Gulls include California's more slender body structure; proportionally longer, narrower wings; and especially long, slender bill. While common at inland locations in the western United States in summer, California is found primarily along coastal and adjacent inland Pacific locations in winter.

SUPPLEMENTAL CHARACTERISTICS AND NON-BBI DETAILS: First-cycle Western Gull has a more evenly shaded dark head and neck compared with California's pale head, which contrasts with a darker back. California's black primaries also contrast with a paler inner wing compared with Western's mostly uniform brownish wings. California's slender bicol-ored bill with a pink base and black tip differs noticeably from Western's heavier, all-dark bill. (See Figure 107, above.)

Worn First-cycle "American" Herring Gull and Great Black-backed Gull

UNCHANGING CHARACTERISTICS: Great Black-backed Gull averages much larger than Herring Gull (30 vs. 25 in. long), but a large male Herring can almost approach the size of a small female Great Black-backed. (See Figure 108, p. 119.) Structural differences include a much larger, blockier head and massive bill in Great Black-backed, and a bulkier, chestier body structure. Herring has a proportionally longer, more slender bill and a smaller head with a less sloping forehead.

SUPPLEMENTAL CHARACTERISTICS AND NON-BBI DETAILS: First-cycle Great Black-backed Gull differs from Herring Gull by its white head and mostly white underparts with variable fine streaking, and by its spangled black-and-white upperparts that impart a "salt-and-pepper" appearance. Wing coverts typically have a "piano-key" appearance, with alternating black and whitish bars.

First-cycle Herring shows a creamy brown to dark brown appearance, but late-first-cycle birds in spring can have a worn, bleached-out look that

FIGURE 108. "AMERICAN" HERRING GULL AND GREAT BLACK-BACKED GULL
Though larger in size, worn first-cycle Great Black-backed Gulls (L) may pose ID problems when seen alone or in the presence of large male Herring Gulls (R), such as this one. This worn Great Black-backed Gull shows checkered wing coverts and a noticeably bulkier body shape. Some worn, late first-cycle "American" Herring Gulls may have white heads, but they lack the checkered wing coverts. Additional ID information is provided in the text.

somewhat resembles that of Great Black-backed, and can cause ID problems when only one species is present. In these instances, concentrate on the more slender, two-toned, pink-based bill of Herring and the checkered wing coverts of Great Black-backed. (See Figure 108, above.) Herring typically has a two-toned bill after midwinter, while Great Black-backed has an all-dark bill.

Glaucous Gull and Iceland Gull

UNCHANGING CHARACTERISTICS: Glaucous Gull is one of our largest gulls and averages larger than Iceland Gull. Glaucous has a heavy, bulky body structure with a relatively short wing projection compared with Iceland's more slender body structure and noticeably longer wing projection, which extends well past the tail tip. Glaucous has a large head and long, heavy bill, while Iceland has a smaller, evenly rounded head and a small, slender bill. (See Figure 109, p. 120.)

SUPPLEMENTAL CHARACTERISTICS AND NON-BBI DETAILS: First-cycle Glaucous and Iceland Gulls have an overall white to pale brown plumage, though Iceland has more distinctly patterned body markings compared with Glaucous's muted ones. Glaucous has white primaries compared with Iceland's brownish-washed ones. Glaucous also has a distinct bicolored bill with a pink base and black tip versus Iceland's mostly black bill.

In second-cycle birds, Iceland's back is gray while Glaucous has all-whitish plumage. Adult birds are more similar in plumage, but the "Kumlien's" subspecies of Iceland Gull typically has dusky primary bars while Glaucous has pure white primaries. Some "Kumlien's" may have pure white primaries, and structural differences are more reliable for ID purposes in these cases. Iceland Gull typically has darker pink legs at all ages.

Black-legged Kittiwake and Red-legged Kittiwake

Black-legged Kittiwake is regularly seen at various North American locations, while Red-legged Kittiwake is a restricted local breeder and year-round resident in the Bering Sea of Alaska.

UNCHANGING CHARACTERISTICS: Both species are medium-sized, somewhat delicate, pelagic gulls with long wings and small, slender to stubby bills. Black-legged Kittiwake is slightly larger and has longer legs, and a longer, thinner bill, while Red-legged Kittiwake has thinner and proportionally longer wings. Black-legged has a small, rounded head and Red-legged a squarish head. Black-legged has black

FIGURE 109. FIRST-CYCLE GLAUCOUS GULL AND ICELAND GULL (QUIZ PHOTO)
These two "white-winged" gulls have similar plumage but differ in size, structural features, and bill size and shape. Try to identify them using the ID information in the text. Answers are in the appendix, page 270.

FIGURE 110. BLACK-LEGGED KITTIWAKE AND RED-LEGGED KITTIWAKE
Note the smaller bill, squarer head with larger eye, and darker gray back on the breeding adult Red-legged Kittiwake (two right photos). Compared with the breeding adult Black-legged Kittiwake (second from left), the first-cycle Black-legged Kittiwake (far left) shows distinctive markings on its wings and tail that are absent in first-cycle Red-legged Kittiwake (not shown). Additional ID information is provided in the text.

legs, while Red-legged has red ones, and both have yellow bills. (See Figure 110, above.)

SUPPLEMENTAL CHARACTERISTICS AND NON-BBI DETAILS:
Breeding plumage of these two species is fairly similar. Slight differences include a darker back on Red-legged Kittiwake (close to the darker gray color of Laughing Gull) versus a paler gray back on Black-legged Kittiwake (closer to the mantle color of Herring Gull). Another difference is the gray underwing primaries on Red-legged versus white on Black-legged.

First-winter plumage is very different, with Black-legged showing a distinctive black M pattern on the upperwings and a black tail band (see Figure 110, above), while Red-legged has gray upperwings with a contrasting white triangle on the wing's trail-ing edge, black wingtips, and a plain white tail. The wing pattern on first-cycle Red-legged is similar to that of Sabine's Gull. First-winter birds have dark bills.

Nonbreeding birds are similar to breeding adults but have a gray smudge behind the eye. Leg color is the same in winter as it is in the breeding season.

JAEGERS AND SKUAS

Jaegers and skuas are highly pelagic birds, spending most of their lives in offshore oceanic waters, except during the breeding season. They have a gull-like physical makeup and share many attributes with gulls, including powerful flight; long, pointed wings; and relatively small but strong bills. The name "jaeger" is used only in North America;

in worldwide taxonomic terminology, jaegers are referred to as skuas.

PHYSICAL PROFILE

Jaegers' body shapes range from slender and tapered (Long-tailed Jaeger) to fairly heavy and stocky (Pomarine Jaeger). Parasitic Jaeger averages in between these extremes. (See Figure 111, below.) Skuas have heavy, bulky, foreshortened bodies with slightly rounded backs. All species have short legs and necks, relatively small bills, and fully webbed feet. (See Figure 113, p. 123.)

BIRDING BY IMPRESSION INFORMATION

SIZE: Three species of jaegers range from Long-tailed Jaeger at 15 in. long (slightly smaller than Laughing Gull) to Pomarine Jaeger at 18½ in. long, which is similar to Ring-billed Gull in length but much bulkier and broader winged. Long-tailed and Pomarine Jaegers may reach 23 in. long during the breeding season, but this measurement includes long tail streamers. South Polar Skua and Great Skua are 21 in. and 23 in. long, respectively, or about the size of a bulky Herring Gull.

STRUCTURAL FEATURES: Jaegers have relatively small heads, while skuas have large, blocky heads. Jaegers' wings are slender and angular, though Pomarine has noticeably broader wings. Skuas have very broad wings that are less angular than those of jaegers. Jaegers have somewhat long tails with extended tail streamers in breeding birds, while skuas have very short, wedge-shaped tails.

BEHAVIOR: All jaegers and skuas steal food from gulls, terns, and other seabirds by vigorously chasing them and forcing them to drop or regurgitate their food (mainly fish). On their far northern breeding grounds, jaegers and Great Skuas feed on lemmings, birds, and insects, while South Polar Skuas steal chicks from penguins and other seabirds in their Antarctic breeding locations. Parasitic is the one jaeger most often seen from shore on both coasts during the fall, and less commonly in spring. Skuas are almost never seen from shore.

PLUMAGE PATTERNS AND GENERAL COLORATION: Jaegers have several color morphs. See "Comparisons of Similar Species," next page, for detailed plumage information. Skuas range mainly from light to dark brown, although the color range differences are minimal. South Polar Skua also has a pale grayish plumage with dark wings and tail.

HABITAT USE: Jaegers breed in Arctic tundra habitats, while Great Skua breeds on far northeast Atlantic islands. South Polar Skua breeds in the Antarctic and disperses to North American waters after breeding. Away from breeding areas, all species are typically found in offshore oceanic waters.

VOCALIZATIONS: All species are generally silent away from their breeding grounds, though Pomarine Jaeger may give barking calls in winter.

FIGURE 111. LONG-TAILED, PARASITIC, AND POMARINE JAEGERS

Note the adult Long-tailed Jaeger's (L) more slender body shape, smaller head and bill, and longer tail feathers. Parasitic Jaeger (C) has a larger head and bill and more bottom-heavy body structure. Pomarine Jaeger (R) has a bulkier-chested appearance and a much larger head and bill. Additional ID information is provided in the text. Flight photos of each species appear underneath.

FIGURE 112. POMARINE JAEGER AND PARASITIC JAEGER UNDERWING PATTERNS
Besides a much broader wing shape, note the more extensive white feathering at the base of the primary flight feathers on Pomarine Jaeger (L). Also note the presence of white feathering at the base of Pomarine's greater underwing coverts, which results in a double row of white feathering on the outer underwing. This feature is often helpful in identifying distant flying birds.

COMPARISONS OF SIMILAR SPECIES

Long-tailed, Parasitic, and Pomarine Jaegers

UNCHANGING CHARACTERISTICS: Long-tailed Jaeger has the most slender, delicate body structure of all jaegers, and the most slender wings as well. The result of these slight physical features and a longer hand (outer wing) is a lighter, more buoyant flight style than that of other jaegers. Parasitic Jaeger has a slightly heavier body structure than Long-tailed, with a rounder lower body shape. Its broader wings and shorter hand result in a more powerful, direct flight style, somewhat similar to that of a Laughing Gull in a power flight.

Pomarine Jaeger has the heaviest body structure of all jaegers, with a bulky, chest-heavy shape and long, broad wings (especially the inner wing). It has a powerful flight style that exhibits a slower, heavier wing stroke than seen in other jaegers, similar to that of a Herring Gull.

Long-tailed has a tiny, rounded, pigeonlike head; a thin neck; and a very small, delicate bill. Parasitic has a slightly larger head with a peaked crown, a thicker neck, and a longer, heavier bill than Long-tailed. Pomarine has a large, deep, rounded head with a rear peak, a thick neck, and the stockiest bill of all jaegers. (See Figure 111, p. 121.)

Breeding tail streamers in Long-tailed are extremely long and pointed, while nonbreeding birds have short, blunt-tipped tail feathers that extend just beyond the tail. Breeding Parasitic has shorter, pointed tail feathers, while nonbreeding birds have short, slightly pointed ones. Breeding Pomarine has odd, fairly long, spoon-shaped projecting tail feathers, while nonbreeding birds have either very small nubs or no projecting tail feathers.

SUPPLEMENTAL CHARACTERISTICS AND NON-BBI DETAILS: The three jaeger species have somewhat distinctive adult plumages, with obvious differences in the shape of their dark caps. All light-morph adults have variable gray-toned wings and backs, whitish breasts, darker lower bellies and vents, small dark caps, and yellowish sides of the neck. Pomarine and Parasitic Jaegers have dark-plumage morphs, represented by a mostly uniform, dark brown plumage. (See Figure 111, p. 121.) Some birds (mostly Parasitic) exhibit intermediate plumage features of light- and dark-morph conditions.

A good separating feature for breeding adult Long-tailed Jaegers (March to October) is their pale gray upper inner wing and back that contrast noticeably with a dark outer upperwing. They also have uniformly dark underwings that lack the white inner primary feathering of other jaegers. Upperwing primaries are mostly dark in Long-tailed, with crisp white shafts on only the outer three primaries. The underparts show a clean white neck and upper breast and a dusky lower belly and vent.

Adult light- and dark-morph Parasitics have broader but less defined black caps than Long-tailed, and most have narrow, pale feathering at the

FIGURE 113. GREAT SKUA AND SOUTH POLAR SKUA
These large seabirds are pelagic by nature and not often seen by many birders. *From left to right:* South Polar Skua, South Polar Skua (pale variant), and Great Skua.

base of their blackish bills. Light-morph adult Parasitic has a variable dark breast-band, or just dusky breast sides, and yellowish neck sides.

Juvenile Parasitic is typically warmer toned (pale to rich brown) than juvenile Long-tailed, with broad, buff tips to its upperpart feathers. Juvenile Long-tailed has grayish-toned to brownish upperparts with whitish tips. Parasitic also has short, pointed tail feathers, while Long-tailed's are blunt-tipped.

Light-morph adult Pomarine has the most extensive black cap of all jaegers—it extends below its bill gape—and more extensive, defined dark barring across the upper breast and flanks. Some pale adults lack a dark breast-band and have limited barring along the flanks. Nonbreeding adults are typically more heavily marked on their underparts. Pomarines of all ages have heavy, strongly demarcated pale pinkish bills with dark tips.

Juvenile and adult Pomarines have bold white feathering at the base of the underwing primaries and the primary wing coverts. The pale feathering of the underwing coverts creates a double pale underwing pattern separated by darker, outer underwing coverts. This pattern is easiest to grasp when seen. (See Figure 112, p. 122.)

Great Skua and South Polar Skua
UNCHANGING CHARACTERISTICS: The size, body shape, and structural features of Great Skua and South Polar Skua are very similar, and the features that do differ are subtle and not easily separable in the field, especially on flying birds. Shared structural features include large, bulky, gull-like bodies; long, broad, pointed wings; short, slightly rounded tails; large,

blocky heads; and short but powerful, stocky bills that are noticeably longer and stouter than those of jaegers. (See Figure 113, above.)

SUPPLEMENTAL CHARACTERISTICS AND NON-BBI DETAILS: Separating the two skuas in the field is not an easy task, with only slight differences in overall body color. Great Skua is more commonly seen in winter, while South Polar Skua is a regular visitor to North America from May to October. Both species have light and dark plumage morphs, but they are not as dramatically different as those of jaegers.

Great Skua is best distinguished by its overall warmer plumage with large, pale spots on the back and inner upperwing. South Polar typically has a colder, grayer body tone. Lighter adult South Polar shows strong contrast between a pale gray body and head and dark upper- and underwings. Dark-morph South Polar is uniformly dark gray overall, with a pale buff to yellow nape.

Darker adult Great Skuas are not as uniformly dark as South Polar, with warm brown bodies and darker upperwings that have pale buff feather tips and large pale spots. Lighter adult Greats (rare) have more contrast between paler streaked underparts and darker wings.

Juveniles of both species have uniformly dark plumages, with Great Skua typically showing obvious cinnamon tones to the breast and upperpart feather edges. South Polar juveniles have a colder gray-brown overall plumage. Some adults and juveniles are best left unidentified, even with good looks and photographs, because of the variability in plumage in both species.

Terns are aerial masters that are connected to aquatic habitats for food gathering and lifestyles. While they're sometimes confused with gulls, most terns plunge-dive into water to reach fish just below the surface; gulls don't do this. Like gulls and terns, Black Skimmer is a member of the Laridae family (2010 American Ornithologists' Union taxonomy). It is unmistakable in appearance, and often seen skimming the water's surface with its lower mandible inserted to catch fish. All nest in loose to tight colonies.

PHYSICAL PROFILE

Terns and Black Skimmer have relatively slender, elongated bodies, although a few tern species are noticeably bulkier than others. They have short legs and fully webbed feet. Wings are typically long, angular, and tapered, and necks are very short. Most terns have short to medium-length, finely pointed, slender bills, while Black Skimmer has an odd bill that is long and slightly decurved. (See Figure 114, below.)

BIRDING BY IMPRESSION INFORMATION

SIZE: The 16 species of North American terns range from the tiny Least Tern, at 9 in. long (about the size of Sanderling), to Caspian Tern, at 21 in. long (about the size of California Gull). (See Figure 115, below.) Black Skimmer is 18 in. long. Terns fit into three size groups: small, medium, and large, with a few species straddling the medium and large categories. See Table 2, p. 126.

STRUCTURAL FEATURES: The majority of terns differ from gulls by having more streamlined, tapered body structures and noticeably shorter legs. They generally have more delicate bills than gulls, although Caspian and Royal Terns have longer and heavier bills than other terns and most gulls. See Table 2, p. 126, for structural information on all terns and Black Skimmer.

BEHAVIOR: While most terns plunge-dive for food, exceptions include Aleutian Tern and the freshwa-

---

FIGURE 114. TERNS

From left to right: Least Tern and chick, breeding Black Tern, breeding Royal Tern, and Black Skimmer "skimming" for food.

FIGURE 115. TERN SIZE COMPARISON

Left: The large-bodied, heavy-billed Caspian Tern (L) is the largest tern in the world (21 in. long), and looks huge next to the medium-sized (13 in. long) nonbreeding Forster's Tern (R). *Right:* The Forster's Tern (L) in its spring transition to breeding plumage looks very large compared with the diminutive Least Tern (C; 9 in. long), one of the smallest terns in the world. A Sanderling (R; 8 in. long) is bulkier than Least Tern, but Least Tern's long wings and tail give it a longer bill-tip-to-tail-tip measurement.

FIGURE 116. GULL-BILLED TERN
This elegant tern is a favorite among birders. Its long wings and very long outer primaries result in an overall curved, tapered impression to the wings. It also has a stocky, gull-like bill and short tail. Fresh juveniles (R) have buff-colored back feathers and crown, but these feather edges wear off quickly (by early August), resulting in the clean, whitish gray look of the center bird, which resembles nonbreeding adults but has a yellowish bill and paler gray upper primaries. The bird on the left is a breeding adult.

ter marsh–breeding Black Tern, which pick small fish, insect larvae, and small aquatic invertebrates from the water's surface or adjacent shorelines. Gull-billed Terns swoop from high above the ground and adeptly pluck small crabs and other prey items from the ground. They also steal fish from other terns at colonial nest sites. (See Figure 116, above.)

Tropical terns forage by flying low over warm waters (often in groups) and dipping down to pluck fish and other aquatic prey from the water's surface. The four species of tropical terns and noddies (Bridled Tern, Sooty Tern, Brown Noddy, and Black Noddy) differ from temperate terns by their highly pelagic behavior in the nonbreeding season. (See Figure 120, p. 132.) They spend their time flying, feeding, and resting on the water in deep, offshore waters and come to land only to breed, where they nest in large colonies on offshore islands.

The flight style of terns is usually related to their physical structure. Least Terns fly with rapid wingbeats because of their tiny size and short, narrow wings, while Roseate Terns fly with incredible grace, thanks to their long and angular wings, very long tails, and slender bodies. Caspian Terns often fly with their bills pointed straight down at the water, searching for fish, and flap their broad wings with slow, heavy, gull-like strokes, similar to a hunting buteo, while the similar Royal Terns fly with quicker wingbeats because of their more slender, angular wings.

PLUMAGE PATTERNS AND GENERAL COLORATION:
Most North American terns share similar plumage patterns and shading, which includes various tones of gray on their backs, black crowns, and white underparts. This plumage similarity is what makes terns challenging to birders. Exceptions include the tropical terns and breeding Black Tern, all of which show darker gray to black upperparts compared with most other terns, and the distinctive Black Skimmer.

HABITAT USE: All terns are found near aquatic habitats, which provide them with their main food source of fish. The particular habitat that a tern uses during the breeding and nonbreeding seasons can be helpful to your ID. For example, some species, such as Roseate Tern and Royal Tern, are found only at coastal or near-coastal locations, while others, such as Forster's Tern and Caspian Tern, frequent freshwater inland locations as well. These are general guidelines, however; some coastal terns are regularly found at interior freshwater locations during migration or when these inland water bodies are connected to the coast by canals or estuaries.

VOCALIZATIONS: Many terns give somewhat similar high-pitched, raspy calls, while others give calls with a distinctive tonal quality. Caspian Tern gives a rising, guttural, raspy call that is among the most nonmusical of all bird vocalizations. After you've been startled by this call a few times, it will remain with you forever. Many terns give more than one call, especially near breeding areas, but most species typically give a single representative call.

SMALL TERNS

Species	Size	Body Shape	Structural Features	Bill and Legs: Shape and Color	General Coloration
Least Tern	Length: 9 in. Wingspan: 20 in.	Slender, elongated.	Long, narrow wings; short tail.	Breeding adult has slender, slightly decurved yellow bill; juvenile and nonbreeding adult have black bills. Legs are yellow at all ages.	Gray and white overall; black cap with white V-shaped forecrown in breeding adult; irregular white forecrown in juvenile and nonbreeding adult; masked look to juvenile and first-year birds.
Black Tern	Length: 9¾ in. Wingspan: 24 in.	Rounded, with elongated rear end.	Long, broad wings; very short tail.	Small, slender, black-pointed bill in all ages. Very short legs are black in breeding adult; dull red in nonbreeding adult; orangish in juvenile.	Body and head are blackish; wings and back are gray in breeding adult; underparts and head are whitish in juvenile and nonbreeding adult, and both show dark rear crown with dark ear spot connected to cap.

MEDIUM-SIZED TERNS

Species	Size	Body Shape	Structural Features	Bill and Legs: Shape and Color	General Coloration
Common Tern	Length: 12 in. Wingspan: 30 in.	Elongated, streamlined; more slender and less "chesty" than Forster's.	Long wings; head is more rounded than Forster's but less rounded than Arctic's; tail is typically shorter than wingtips.	Breeding adult has thin orange-red to deep red bill with a dark tip; bill is thinner than Forster's; juvenile has orange to black bill; nonbreeding adult has black bill. Legs are red in breeding adult; black in nonbreeding adult; yellow-orange in juvenile.	Gray upperparts and grayish-white underparts; white cheek; white forecrown in juvenile and nonbreeding adult.
Arctic Tern	Length: 12 in. Wingspan: 31 in.	Elongated, streamlined; "no-necked" look at rest; "chestier" than Common.	Long wings; short legs (shorter than on Common and Forster's); tail typically extends just past wingtips; head is more rounded and with steeper forecrown than on Common.	Breeding adult small, thin, dark red bill is shorter than in other medium-sized terns; juvenile and nonbreeding adult have black bills. Legs are red in breeding adult; black in nonbreeding adult; orange in juvenile.	Gray upperparts and whitish underparts; white forecrown in juvenile and nonbreeding adult is more extensive than on Common.
Roseate Tern	Length: 12½ in. Wingspan: 29 in.	Slender, tubular; less "chesty" than other medium-sized terns.	Long tail projects well past wingtips; small head has a rounded shape.	Breeding adult has thin, black bill, often with a deep reddish base; bill is more daggerlike than in other medium-sized terns; juvenile and nonbreeding adult have black bills. Legs are dull red in breeding and nonbreeding adult, black in juvenile.	Very white and pale gray overall; young juvenile has dark forecrown; older juvenile has white forecrown similar to that of Common.
Forster's Tern	Length: 13 in. Wingspan: 31 in.	Elongated, streamlined; chest and shoulders huskier than in other medium-sized terns.	Generally slender and long-winged; blockier head than other medium-sized terns.	Breeding adult has slender, orange bill with black tip; heavier than in other medium-sized terns; juvenile and nonbreeding adult have black bills. Legs are orange all year but brightest in breeding adult.	Pale grayish upperparts and white underparts; white head and black mask are obvious in juvenile and nonbreeding adult; outer upperwing is whiter than inner wing on adults in all plumages; first-winter birds have black primaries and carpal bar.

MEDIUM-LARGE TERNS

Species	Size	Body Shape	Structural Features	Bill and Legs: Shape and Color	General Coloration
Gull-billed Tern	Length: 14 in. Wingspan: 34 in.	Larger and heavier than medium-sized terns.	Bulky, front-heavy body structure; long wings extend well past short, forked tail at rest.	Adult has short, black, stocky gull-like bill; juvenile has blackish bill with mostly yellowish lower mandible. Longish legs are black all year.	Pale gray upperparts and white underparts; black cap in breeding adult; white head with dark ear spot in juvenile and non-breeding adult.
Sandwich Tern	Length: 15 in. Wingspan: 34 in.	Slender, elongated; similar to Royal.	Short tail; adult has shaggy rear crest.	Adult has long, black, daggerlike bill with yellow tip; much more slender than Royal's bill; juvenile has blackish bill with indistinct pale tip. Legs are black all year.	Pale gray and white overall; white forecrown in nonbreeding birds; full black cap in breeding adult.

LARGE TERNS

Species	Size	Body Shape	Structural Features	Bill and Legs: Shape and Color	General Coloration
Elegant Tern	Length: 17 in. Wingspan: 34 in.	Similar to Royal but less attenuated in rear.	Proportionally larger head and bulkier chest than Royal; longer, more drooping shaggy crest than Royal.	Adult has reddish to orange bill, which is longer, thinner, and more decurved than Royal's; juvenile has yellowish bill. Adult legs are black all year; juvenile has yellowish legs.	Gray and white overall; white forecrown in nonbreeding birds.
Royal Tern	Length: 20 in. Wingspan: 41 in.	More slender and streamlined than Caspian.	Slender but powerful body structure; long wings are more slender and angular than Caspian's; short, shaggy crest.	Adult has orange to reddish bill, which is thinner and longer than Caspian's; juvenile has yellowish bill. Adult legs are black all year; juvenile has yellowish legs.	Gray and white overall; juvenile has dark markings on upperparts and wings; white forecrown in nonbreeding adult and juvenile is more extensive than in Elegant.
Caspian Tern	Length: 21 in. Wingspan: 50 in.	Heavy, gull-like.	Broad wings; thicker neck, bulkier chest, and shorter tail than Royal.	Adult has heavy, red bill, thicker than Royal's; juvenile has orange bill. Legs are black all year.	Gray and white overall; juvenile has dark mottling on upperparts; nonbreeding birds have white and black streaking on forecrown.

TROPICAL AND OTHER TERNS, including Black Skimmer

Species	Size	Body Shape	Structural Features	Bill and Legs: Shape and Color	General Coloration
Aleutian Tern	Length: 12 in. Wingspan: 29 in.	Elongated, streamlined, with rounded chest.	Similar to Arctic, but with a deep, bulky chest and very short neck; pointed wings are slender, angular, and extend well past the very short tail in resting birds; very short legs; round head is slightly deeper than Arctic's.	Short, straight, very thin black bill is slightly longer than Arctic's. Legs are orange in juvenile, black adults.	Black cap with triangular-shaped white forecrown; gray upperparts and grayish underparts in breeding adult; gray upperparts, white forecrown, and white underparts in nonbreeding birds.
Black Noddy	Length: 13½ in. Wingspan: 30 in.	Slender, tubular; shorter, less attenuated, stockier, and with a rounder chest than Brown Noddy.	Smaller, rounder head than Brown Noddy; thin neck; wings are relatively short and extend just past tail; rounded tail shape is similar to that of Brown Noddy. (See Figure 120, p. 132.)	Longish, straight bill is black in all ages, very thin, and extremely pointed. Legs are very short, and black in all ages.	Adult is blackish overall with a white cap and gray nape; immature is blackish brown with pale wing coverts and a sharply defined white cap.

TROPICAL AND OTHER TERNS, including Black Skimmer

Species	Size	Body Shape	Structural Features	Bill and Legs: Shape and Color	General Coloration
Brown Noddy	Length: 15½ in. Wingspan: 32 in.	Slender, tubular, with somewhat bulky chest.	Blocky head; thick neck; wings are shorter and less pointed than Sooty's and just reach tail tip; tail is long with an odd, rounded tip when folded; open tail has compound rounded feathers of different lengths.	Medium-length bill is slender, pointed, and slightly decurved; bill and legs are black in adult and juvenile.	Adult is brownish overall with a small white forecrown that blends into a grayish-brown crown and nape; immature is brownish with pale wing coverts and narrow white forecrown.
Bridled Tern	Length: 15 in. Wingspan: 30 in.	Slender, streamlined.	Slighter structure than Sooty; slightly shorter angular wings and longer, forked tail than Sooty; short neck; very short legs.	Short, slender, pointed bill; bill and legs are black in adult and juvenile.	Gray upperparts and black cap with triangular-shaped white forecrown in breeding adult; upperparts paler than Sooty's; nonbreeding adult has irregular white forecrown; juvenile is dark overall with white spots on upperparts.
Sooty Tern	Length: 16 in. Wingspan: 32 in.	Somewhat slender, tubular; overall shape is heavier and bulkier chested Bridled's.	Long wings extend slightly past long tail; very short neck; short legs; bigger head than Bridled.	Slender, pointed bill is longer than Bridled's; bill and legs are black in adult and juvenile.	Black upperparts and wings; white forecrown, cheek, and underparts; darker tail than on Bridled.
Black Skimmer	Length: 18 in. Wingspan: 44 in.	Slender, tubular.	Short, slightly forked tail; extremely long, pointed wings; deep, rounded head; medium-length neck; very short legs.	Odd bill with long, thin, recurved lower mandible and shorter, thicker decurved upper mandible; bill is reddish orange with a black tip in adult, dull orange in juvenile. Legs are pale orange in juvenile, red in adult.	Black upperparts and crown; white underparts; pale nape in nonbreeding birds; juvenile has checkered brown and white upperparts and brownish streaked crown.

COMPARISONS OF SIMILAR SPECIES

Common, Arctic, and Roseate Terns

One of the most difficult ID challenges with North American terns involves separating these three very similar medium-sized terns. While Arctic Tern and Common Tern are similar in breeding plumage, all three species present formidable ID problems in nonbreeding and juvenile birds.

UNCHANGING CHARACTERISTICS: Because differences among these species are subtle, BBI features are further separated below to focus on specific physical features.

BODY STRUCTURE: Arctic Tern has a proportionally bulkier look to its chest and shoulders than do Common and Roseate Terns. Common, however, has a heavier overall body structure than Arctic, with a less attenuated appearance to the rear body.

Roseate has a longer, more slender, tubular-shaped body than both Arctic and Common, which gives it a more streamlined look. Don't let the differences in wing length affect your accurate assessment of the different body shapes of these similar terns.

WING-TO-TAIL COMPARISON: An important difference to note is the length of the wings compared with that of the tail on sitting birds. Roseate Tern has an extremely long tail that extends noticeably past the wings on sitting birds, while Arctic Tern's tail extends just past the folded wings. Common Tern has a tail that is slightly shorter than its wings. Be aware that these generalizations may be compromised by molting birds with wings and tails that are incompletely grown.

BILL LENGTH AND SHAPE: Bill length and shape also differ among these birds. Roseate Tern's bill is distinctly longer and more daggerlike than either

FIGURE 117. COMMON, ARCTIC, AND ROSEATE TERNS, NONBREEDING (QUIZ PHOTO)
Detailed ID coverage of these three very similarly plumaged terns is provided in the text. All photos were taken in June. The plumage of nonbreeding terns is similar to that of late first-cycle terns, with subtle differences in wing patterns and molt timing. Note differences in bill size and shape, body and head shape, and wing and tail length to confidently ID these species. Answers are in the appendix, page 270.

Common or Arctic Tern's. This feature is one of the most reliable ways to separate Roseate from the other two species. Common's bill, while noticeably shorter and thicker than Roseate's, often shows a distinct downward arc to the upper mandible. It is longer and often thicker-based than Arctic's short, straightish bill. (See Figure 117, above.) Some Arctics, though, show a slight decurve to their bills.

LEG LENGTH: Roseate and Arctic Terns have shorter legs than Common Tern, but this feature is best evaluated when birds are sitting next to each other. Be careful when assessing leg length, as birds may be crouching, sitting in a slight depression, standing in shallow water, or fluffing their body feathers, which may hide some of the leg length.

HEAD SHAPE: Arctic Tern has a steeper forehead and more evenly rounded crown than Common Tern, which has a shallower forehead and crown as well as a deeper head profile from front to back. Arctic also has a shorter neck that imparts a "no-necked" impression to relaxed sitting birds. Roseate Tern has a small, rounded head with a peaked crown.

These features are best evaluated on birds in a relaxed sitting posture, since agitated birds may flatten their feathers and temporarily alter typical body structure and head shape. Pay attention to these variations particularly when studying similar terns in the field, and especially in photos, where only one posture may be misleading rather than helpful.

SUPPLEMENTAL CHARACTERISTICS AND NON-BBI DETAILS: Roseate Tern has an overall paler gray and white plumage with less contrast in shading between gray upperparts and whitish underparts than either Common or Arctic Tern. (See Figure 117, above.)

Common has a bold, black carpal bar on the folded wing, while Arctic has a variable pale dusky carpal bar. Roseate has little or no visible dark car-

pal bar. Common typically has dark primaries in first-year and nonbreeding birds, with similar-aged Arctics having uniformly pale gray primaries. Some subadult Arctics, however, can show dark primaries. Nonbreeding Roseate has dusky outer primaries, but white edges to inner primaries. All of these hard-to-visualize features can be seen in Figure 117.

A helpful plumage feature for nonbreeding Arctic is a heavier concentration of black feathering in front of and around the eye, which when combined with a whiter forecrown gives a "punched-in-the-eye" appearance. (See Figure 117, above.) Common also shows a defined lower white eyelid that is lacking in Arctic.

Common Tern and Forster's Tern
These two similar species occur together from spring to fall at numerous North American locations.

UNCHANGING CHARACTERISTICS: On standing, relaxed birds, Forster's Tern has a slightly larger, deeper, blockier head with a squarish rear profile compared with Common Tern's smaller and more evenly rounded head. Forster's also has a more chest-heavy body structure compared with Common's slightly more slender, evenly proportioned body shape. Forster's typically shows a heavier, thicker bill versus a longer, thinner one on Common, but these features vary in some birds and do not always conform to the norm. (See Figure 118, p. 130.)

Forster's has longer legs than Common, which is noticeable in direct comparison but not easy to recognize in single-species views. Less obvious structural differences for separating these two species are Forster's broader wings, which contribute to a more powerful flight motion with shallower wingbeats and a less graceful impression than Common gives. Common's thinner wings and more streamlined body contribute to its more buoyant flight impression. These differences are subtle but result

FIGURE 118. COMMON TERN AND FORSTER'S TERN (QUIZ PHOTO)

Top: These two similarly plumaged terns have different body shapes and structural features when sitting, but these differences are difficult to notice in fast-flying birds. Several plumage features are reliable for separating these birds. Can you identify these two terns in flight? ID information is provided in the text, and answers are in the appendix, page 270. *Bottom:* Transition-plumage birds are the most difficult to identify, so structural and plumage features are especially important in their ID. Try to identify both standing terns. Use the Laughing Gull in the background for size comparison. ID information is in the text, and answers are in the appendix, page 270.

in a slightly different flight motion, which is best assessed when both species are seen flying near each other. The actual physical differences are very difficult to assess in flight, with concentration on wing width and body shape necessary for any success.

SUPPLEMENTAL CHARACTERISTICS AND NON-BBI DETAILS:
Adult Forster's Tern has whitish wings and upperparts, with the outer part of the upperwing whiter than the slightly grayer inner wing and back. A white rump is only slightly lighter than a pale gray back. Whitish underparts blend with white wing linings and cheek and impart an overall white impression underneath.

Common Tern has uniformly darker gray upperwings with a variable black wedge on the outer primaries, and a grayish back that contrasts with a white rump. A dusky chest contrasts with a white cheek, and the underwings show a distinct black wedge near the tip. In spring, fresh-plumaged birds have restricted black markings to their more silvery primaries, which darken as flight feathers become worn into the summer months.

The plumage of juvenile birds is distinctly different, with Forster's briefly showing very rust tones to the upperparts versus more brownish tones in Common. Juvenile Forster's also has a characteristic black mask similar to that of nonbreeding birds, versus a partial dark rear crown in Common.

Nonbreeding Forster's has a black mask behind the eye versus a partial dark rear crown in Common, and lacks the distinct black carpal bar present

FIGURE 119. CASPIAN, ROYAL, AND ELEGANT TERNS
ID coverage of these three similar large terns is provided in the text. Note the larger, bulkier body structure and heavier, stockier, reddish bill of Caspian Tern (most birds in right photo). Royal Tern (second from right in right photo) is more slender and streamlined with shorter legs and a whiter forecrown. Elegant Tern (L) has a proportionally larger head; very long, daggerlike bill; and shaggier crest than both Royal and Caspian.

in Common. First-spring Forster's may closely resemble Common in plumage when its partial dark crown blends with the dark mask; in such cases, structural features and leg length can be helpful to your ID. (See Figure 118, p. 130.)

Caspian, Royal, and Elegant Terns

These three "crested" terns are similar in plumage patterns and occasionally bill color, and all have a crested look to the rear of their black crowns. There are several structural and plumage features that help separate them, even when only one species is seen. Recent sightings of Elegant Tern in Florida, the southeast Atlantic coastal states, New Jersey, and New York may result in hybridization between Royal and Elegant Terns.

UNCHANGING CHARACTERISTICS: Caspian Tern is the largest (21 in. long), heaviest, and bulkiest tern in North America, and has a noticeably different body and bill profile than the other two crested terns with orange to red bills. Reliable structural features for separating Caspian from Royal and Elegant Terns include a bulky chest and neck; large, blocky head; and very heavy bill. (See Figure 119, above.)

Compared with Caspian's bulky, big-headed profile, Royal is slightly smaller (20 in. long) with a more slender body, smaller head, and shorter legs. Elegant is even smaller (17 in. long) than Royal and has shorter wings and a shaggier rear crest. Size and structure differences are dramatic enough to make Elegant and Caspian difficult to confuse.

Caspian's wings are much broader and longer than those of Royal and Elegant, and its resulting flight impression is one of slower, heavier wingbeats, similar to those of a large gull. Royal and Elegant have shorter, narrower, more angular wings and a snappier wing stroke during their powerful, direct flights.

Caspian has a thick, massive bill compared with Royal's long, slender bill with decurved upper mandible and straight lower culmen. Elegant has a longer, thinner bill than Caspian and Royal, with a very fine tip and noticeable droop to the outer half. Some large Caspians appear only slightly smaller than nearby small female Herring and California Gulls because of their bulky body structure, which is not the case with the streamlined Royal Tern and smaller Elegant Tern.

SUPPLEMENTAL CHARACTERISTICS AND NON-BBI DETAILS: Caspian Tern has the least defined black rear crest of the three; Royal Tern's is shaggier, and Elegant Tern's is very long and shaggy. Nonbreeding Caspian does not have a white forecrown like the other two crested tern species, and instead has a finely streaked black forecrown with white speckling. Compared with Royal, Elegant has a more extensive black cap in nonbreeding birds.

Caspian's blood red bill (orange in juveniles) has a dusky tip, while Royal's bill is all orange (yellow in juveniles; red in some breeding birds). Elegant's bill is orange to red (yellow in juveniles) and paler at the tip. Breeding adult Caspian has dark underwing primary feathers compared with pale ones in both Royal and Elegant, but nonbreeding Caspian can be more similar to Royal and Elegant because of plumage variability in this area.

Sooty Tern and Bridled Tern

Sooty Tern is by far the most common tropical tern in the United States, with about 80,000 birds breeding in Florida's Dry Tortugas (72 mi. west of Key West). Bridled Tern does not breed in the United States, but numerous birds disperse north into the Gulf Stream along the Atlantic Coast and in the Gulf of Mexico.

FIGURE 120. BLACK NODDY, BROWN NODDY, SOOTY TERN, AND BRIDLED TERN
Four North American tropical terns. *Clockwise from top left:* Brown Noddy, Black Noddy (immature), Sooty Tern, and Bridled Tern. Note Black Noddy's smaller, more compact slender body; smaller head; and longer, more slender bill compared with Brown Noddy. Most vagrant Black Noddies are worn first-cycle birds, like this one, with brownish plumage tones and worn wing coverts. Sooty Tern is a large (16 in. long), stocky, black-and-white tern. Bridled Tern is smaller (15 in. long) and more slender than Sooty Tern, and it has brownish gray upperparts, a white nape, and contrasting black cap. Additional ID information is provided in the text.

UNCHANGING CHARACTERISTICS: Sooty Tern is a large, bulky tern that differs from Bridled Tern by having a larger, heavier body structure; bigger, blockier head shape; and longer bill. Bridled has a smaller head; shorter, heavier bill; and longer, more forked tail. (See Figure 120, above.) Sooty has longer, broader wings compared with Bridled's thinner, more angular wings, and this difference results in Sooty having a more powerful flight style and the ability to maneuver more effectively in very strong winds, such as in a hurricane.

Bridled flies with lighter, more buoyant movements. Both species are highly pelagic and rarely seen from shore unless driven in by storms. While Bridled often rests on flotsam and driftwood, Sooty rarely does so.

SUPPLEMENTAL CHARACTERISTICS AND NON-BBI DETAILS: Adult Sooty Tern has all-black upperparts and crown with a white forehead. Adult Bridled Tern has dark gray upperparts and a contrasting black crown with white forehead that extends back over the eye in breeding birds. Both species have clean white underparts.

Sooty has a mostly dark tail with narrow white borders, while Bridled has a white tail with a gray central stripe and wider rear edge. Bridled's paler gray upperparts and wings with an extensive white tail offer a different overall impression from Sooty's black upperparts and wings and mostly black tail.

Brown Noddy and Black Noddy

Brown Noddy is reliably found in North America only on the Dry Tortugas, FL, where it occurs as a breeding species from March to late summer. Black Noddy is a rare vagrant from South Pacific tropical islands and occurs in very small numbers on the Dry Tortugas in most years. Black Noddies in the Dry Tortugas are mostly first-summer birds (like the one in Figure 120) and are found roosting among the many Brown Noddies.

FIGURE 121. MIXED TERNS (QUIZ PHOTO)

There are five species of regularly occurring North American terns here. Focus on size, shape, and structural features, as well as bill color and shape and subtle plumage features. Hint: The smaller terns in the front of the main group are in transition plumage, and one is a first-spring bird. Answers and ID information are provided in the appendix, page 270.

UNCHANGING CHARACTERISTICS: Both species have slender, tubular bodies, but Brown Noddy is bulkier overall with a thicker neck, while Black Noddy has a more compact, less attenuated shape overall with a bulky upper chest. Brown Noddy also has a broader, deeper head compared with Black Noddy's smaller, more rounded head that has a peak near the rear crown. The bills of these two species are noticeably different, with Brown Noddy having a much thicker bill that has a slight decurve to the upper mandible, while Black Noddy has a longer, very thin, straight, daggerlike bill.

SUPPLEMENTAL CHARACTERISTICS AND NON-BBI DETAILS: Brown Noddy is mostly brownish with a whitish forecrown that blends into a light grayish brown rear crown and upper nape. Black Noddy adult is black overall with a crisply defined white forecrown that extends only to the midcrown region. First-summer Black Noddies, like the bird in Figure 120, have blackish brown bodies with worn, paler wing coverts and mostly blackish heads, and a similar white crown pattern as adults. Both species have black bills and legs.

Pigeons are the larger species in the family Columbidae, while the smaller ones are doves. Otherwise there is no scientific distinction between them, and the shape and structural features of some larger doves are similar to those of pigeons. All are strong, fast fliers that eat mostly seeds and fruits, which they access primarily as ground feeders (except for Red-billed and White-crowned Pigeons, which are mostly arboreal).

Two species of doves occur only as regular rare vagrants (Key West Quail-Dove and Ruddy Ground-Dove). Two more species represent isolated populations that resulted from escaped or released foreign species (Spotted Turtle-Dove and Ringed Turtle-Dove). Ruddy Ground-Dove has bred in the southwestern United States in small numbers.

PHYSICAL PROFILE

All species are relatively plump. Pigeons and most doves have tapered, elongated rear bodies, while some doves have more compact, stocky body shapes (ground-doves, White-tipped Dove, Key West Quail-Dove). Pigeons have longer, more pointed wings than the shorter, rounded wings of doves. All have small, rounded heads, short legs, and small, stubby bills. Tails range from short and square to long and pointed. (See Figure 122, below, and Figure 123, p. 135.)

BIRDING BY IMPRESSION INFORMATION

SIZE: Four pigeons share a narrow size range, from Rock Pigeon at 12½ in. long (similar to Northern Flicker) to Band-tailed Pigeon and Red-billed Pigeon at 14½ in. long (slightly smaller than Fish Crow).

Ten species of doves can be grouped into two general sizes: small and large. The three small doves include Common Ground-Dove and Ruddy Ground-Dove (6¾ in. long), which are only slightly smaller overall than Inca Dove (8¼ in. long), whose long tail accounts for its extra length. The remaining seven species of large doves are 12 to 13 in. long, which is similar to Blue Jay.

STRUCTURAL FEATURES: The three species of native pigeons are very similar in overall structure (see Figure 122, below), while the introduced Rock Pigeon has longer, more pointed wings and a shorter neck and tail. Three small doves (especially the ground-doves) have shorter legs and shorter necks than larger doves. Mourning Dove differs from all larger doves with its long, pointed tail (see Figure 123, p. 135), although the introduced Spotted Dove has a relatively long, square-tipped tail.

BEHAVIOR: The ubiquitous Rock Pigeon is a familiar sight in urban and suburban areas, especially in city parks, where it feeds on crumbs at people's feet. Native pigeons tend to be quite shy, although Band-tailed Pigeons that occur in urban and suburban West Coast locations may be extremely tame. White-crowned Pigeons in Key West, FL, are easily seen and more tolerant of people, thanks to a lack of hunting pressure and constant human presence, but birds in rural areas are extremely shy.

Doves that have colonized cities and suburban areas are much tamer than rural birds, while ground-doves and White-tipped Doves are shy by nature and don't allow close approach. Key West Quail-Dove is a very rare vagrant to Florida, where

---

FIGURE 122. PIGEONS

These three large pigeons have distinctive plumage and feather patterns but occupy widely separate geographic ranges. ID information is provided in the text. *From left to right:* Band-tailed Pigeon, Red-billed Pigeon, and White-crowned Pigeon.

FIGURE 123. DOVES

Mourning Dove (L) has the most slender shape of all North American doves, with narrow, pointed wings and a long tail. White-winged Dove (C) has a heavier body, with a square tail and distinctive white wing-slash, but this bird appears slender because it is alert and stretched out. Eurasian Collared-Dove (R) has a heavy body structure, square tail, and pale overall plumage with black neck-slash.

it hides in dense thickets. With most species being on seasonal hunting lists, hunting is one reason that pigeons and doves in wild areas are more difficult to see.

All species can explode into flight from a sitting position, similar to quails. Several pigeons and doves perform territorial breeding flights, including Mourning Dove, which flies with stiff wingbeats and a sustained glide that gives an impression of a Sharp-shinned Hawk. Many a birder has mistaken a Rock Pigeon for a falcon because of its powerful, direct flight on broad, angled wings.

PLUMAGE PATTERNS AND GENERAL COLORATION: Pigeons are generally muted in coloration, although there is much variation among Rock Pigeons because pigeon fanciers have bred them to show specific colors and characteristics. Native Rock Pigeons are mostly gray with a white rump and black wing bars. Doves also have muted earth-tone colors, with White-winged Dove the only one with any bold markings.

HABITAT USE: Most rural pigeons and doves occur in dense to open forested areas, but some are found in arid desert habitats and along sea-cliff faces. Other pigeons and doves have adapted to urban and suburban areas, where they nest in backyards and city parks and on buildings. Only one dove is widespread in the United States and lower Canada (Mourning Dove); the others all occur in southern areas of the United States or in a few very local, isolated populations.

VOCALIZATIONS: Pigeons and doves give a wide variety of cooing and hooting calls, often repeated in a rhythmic fashion. Some calls have a mournful, somber quality.

COMPARISONS OF SIMILAR SPECIES

Ruddy Ground-Dove and Common Ground-Dove

Common Ground-Dove is a permanent resident of extreme southern portions of the United States, while Ruddy Ground-Dove is an uncommon to rare vagrant to Texas, Arizona, and California, with sporadic localized nesting and resident populations in some of these areas.

UNCHANGING CHARACTERISTICS: Both species are small, plump doves, but Ruddy Ground-Dove is slightly larger overall and has a noticeably longer tail and marginally longer neck than Common Ground-Dove. (See Figure 124, p. 136.)

SUPPLEMENTAL CHARACTERISTICS AND NON-BBI DETAILS: One of the best ways to separate these two species is the plain nonpatterned breast and nape on Ruddy Ground-Dove versus the scaly breast, nape, and rear crown on Common Ground-Dove. (See Figure 124, p. 136.) Other helpful details include the narrow blackish markings on the scapulars and tertials of Ruddy (absent in Common), with both species showing dark markings on the wing coverts. Male and female Ruddys also have grayish bills versus pink to red-based bills on Commons.

Male Ruddys of the eastern subspecies have a rich, red plumage and a blue-gray crown, which is diagnostic for the species. With their pinkish brown body color, male Ruddys of the western subspecies and female Ruddys of the eastern subspecies are superficially similar to male Common Ground-Dove of the eastern subspecies. However, a plain silvery gray crown on Ruddy and scaling on Common's nape and breast help separate these two species.

Adult females of both species in the western United States have mostly gray plumage, with structural features and the aforementioned plumage differences the best way to separate them.

FIGURE 124. COMMON GROUND-DOVE AND RUDDY GROUND-DOVE (QUIZ PHOTO)
Our two smallest doves share somewhat similar plumage features. ID information is provided in the text. Can you identify these birds and their sex? Answers are in the appendix, page 270.

Unlike many cuckoos in other parts of the world, North American cuckoos are not brood parasites, which means they lay their eggs in their own nests and incubate the young. Sexes are similar. All three groups here are members of the family Cuculidae.

PHYSICAL PROFILE

Cuckoos have long, slender, tapered bodies with small heads and short, thin, slightly decurved bills. Wings are long and rounded, and the long, slender tails have graduated feathers. (See Figure 125, p. 138.)

Anis also have long bodies, but they have bulky chests; large, blocky heads; and odd-shaped, rounded bills. Other features shared by the anis include short, thick necks and long, rounded tails with graduated rectrices.

Greater Roadrunner is unmistakable, with a very long body with a rounded chest and flat back. Other distinguishing features include an extremely long tail; bushy crest; powerful, unfeathered legs; and a long, strong bill. (See Figure 125, p. 138.)

LOOK-ALIKE BIRDS

Anis generally differ from grackles by having larger heads, thicker necks, and much heavier bills. (See Figure 126, p. 139.)

BIRDING BY IMPRESSION INFORMATION

SIZE: Three species of cuckoos and two anis are fairly large and all fall within a narrow size range of 12 to 14½ in. long (slightly larger than Common Grackle). Very long tails account for almost half of these measurements. Greater Roadrunner is a large bird that averages 23 in. long, with its long tail accounting for about half of its measurement.

STRUCTURAL FEATURES: The three cuckoos show only slight structural differences (see Comparisons of Similar Species, right-hand column). The two anis are also very similar in structure (see Figure 126, p. 139). Greater Roadrunner is unmistakable, and its short, broad, rounded wings are well suited for short flights in its nonmigratory range.

BEHAVIOR: Cuckoos are typically shy and avoid interaction with humans. They are fairly solitary birds that are more often heard than seen, preferring to sit in dense vegetation, even when vocalizing. Movements are measured and deliberate. Anis are social creatures that live in noisy, animated groups. They often breed cooperatively, with several females using the same nest and multiple adults feeding the nestlings. Anis may be hard to see at times

because of their preference for dense weedy habitats and thickets.

Greater Roadrunner is a ground-dwelling species that preys on lizards, small mammals, large insects, and small birds. It can achieve speeds of up to 15 mi. per hour when sprinting along the ground. When pursuing prey or escaping danger, the roadrunner lowers its head and tail to the same horizontal plane, which gives its body an arrowlike impression. Greater Roadrunners sometimes visit feeders and backyards in search of food, especially in winter, and often become quite tame in these circumstances.

PLUMAGE PATTERNS AND GENERAL COLORATION: Cuckoos share brownish backs and white underparts; Mangrove Cuckoo has a buffy wash on its lower belly and vent. All cuckoos have white spots underneath the folded tails, with Black-billed Cuckoo having the least obvious spots. Yellow-billed Cuckoo has an obvious rusty upperwing color in flight. Anis are all black. Greater Roadrunner is boldly streaked with a small bluish bare skin patch behind its eye.

HABITAT USE: Cuckoos inhabit dense forest habitats and mangroves, while anis frequent dense thickets and tall grass. Greater Roadrunner is a bird of open, arid habitats in the southwestern United States.

VOCALIZATIONS: Cuckoos give a variety of loud guttural or whistled notes during the breeding season but are silent the rest of the year. Smooth-billed Ani gives a rising, whining *quee-lick* call, while Groove-billed Ani has a liquid *tee-ho*. Both also give soft clucking notes in flight. Greater Roadrunner gives a series of descending, low *coos*.

COMPARISONS OF SIMILAR SPECIES

Mangrove, Black-billed, and Yellow-billed Cuckoos

The most common and widespread cuckoos are Yellow-billed and Black-billed Cuckoos, which occur across most of the eastern two-thirds of the United States. Mangrove Cuckoo is a resident of mangrove habitats in coastal southwest Florida and the Florida Keys, and a vagrant to coastal Texas.

While Mangrove is basically nonmigratory in Florida, northern-breeding birds move south in winter, where any Mangrove is hard to find because of their secretive behavior and silent nature. They are easier to locate in spring to early summer when they vocalize loudly and frequently.

FIGURE 125. BLACK-BILLED, MANGROVE, AND YELLOW-BILLED CUCKOOS (QUIZ PHOTO—TOP)
Three species of cuckoos found in North America. ID information for separating these birds is provided in the text. Try to identify the three birds in the top photo using this information. Answers are in the appendix, page 270. Greater Roadrunner is in the bottom photo.

UNCHANGING CHARACTERISTICS: Mangrove Cuckoo has the stoutest body structure and heaviest bill of all three cuckoos, although Yellow-billed Cuckoo has only a slightly slimmer body and moderately thinner bill. Black-billed Cuckoo has the most slender body structure of all, and a very thin, pointed bill compared with the other two species. (See Figure 125, above.) Black-billed imparts an overall smaller impression than Yellow-billed, with flying birds offering a smaller, shorter-tailed, more slender-winged look than the similar Yellow-billed and Mangrove.

Vocalizations are distinctive for each species. Yellow-billed gives a long series of hard, guttural notes that resemble a gulping sound (*kuk, kuk, kuk,* *kuk...*) that usually slows and descends into a *kaka-kowlp-kowlp* ending. Black-billed gives a repeated series of two or three clear, high-pitched whistled notes that resemble the cuckoo's name phonetically (*cu-cu, cu-cu-cu, cu-cu-cu*). On the breeding grounds after nesting is established, Yellow-billed often gives a series of single-note *cuu-cuu-cuu* sounds, but they are monosyllabic in nature, slower and more drawn out, and lower pitched than similar multi-syllabled Black-billed calls. Mangrove gives a distinctive, very guttural call, *gaw, gaw, gaw, gaw,* in a deliberate cadence.

SUPPLEMENTAL CHARACTERISTICS AND NON-BBI DETAILS: Mangrove Cuckoo most closely resembles Yellow-

FIGURE 126. SMOOTH-BILLED ANI AND GROOVE-BILLED ANI (QUIZ PHOTO)

Smooth-billed Ani (top left) has a typical bill shape with a high, flared upper mandible. Groove-billed Ani (top right) has broader bare facial skin, noticeable grooves on the bill, and a shallower, uniformly curved upper mandible. In the field, Kevin misidentified the ani in the bottom left photo because it was not listed in the field guide as possible for Veracruz, Mexico. Try to identify this ani to species. Answers are provided in the appendix, page 270. A look-alike species (male Boat-tailed Grackle) is shown in the bottom right photo, but note its longer, slender bill and smaller head.

billed Cuckoo but differs by having buff-colored versus white underparts, and a noticeable black mask on the cheek versus a uniformly brown cheek with a muted dark mask in Yellow-billed. Mangrove lacks the rufous color in the primaries that is present in Yellow-billed.

Black-billed Cuckoo differs from both Yellow-billed and Mangrove by its all-gray bill with limited black tip versus a blackish bill with mostly yellow lower mandible on the other two cuckoos; by a reddish eye-ring on adult Black-billed versus yellow on the other two species (immature Black-billed has a yellowish green eye-ring well into the first winter); and by the presence of small white and black tips to mostly gray undertail feathers on adult Black-billed versus bold white spots against a black background on the other two species. This last field mark is also obvious in flying birds if the undertail is visible. Black-billed also has off-white underwings versus bright white ones in the other two species.

Immature Black-billed differs from the similar immature Yellow-billed by its somewhat warmer, buff throat and undertail and by pale fringes to the wing coverts and tertials that are lacking in Yellow-billed. Immature Black-billed also has a mostly gray undertail pattern with only small, pale tips to each graduated feather, while immature Yellow-billed has large white spots and edges to each tail feather. (See Figure 125, p. 138.)

Groove-billed Ani and Smooth-billed Ani

These two tropical residents of brushy habitats occur only in very small, localized regions of south Florida (Smooth-billed) and south Texas (Groove-billed). Smooth-billed is a rapidly declining species in Florida, with only a few known birds present in early 2012. Groove-billed is a summer resident in south Texas, with small numbers occurring in winter.

UNCHANGING CHARACTERISTICS: "Typical" birds are fairly easy to identify, with Smooth-billed Ani showing a high, flared upper mandible that lacks any horizontal grooves and steeply rises up from the bill tip and descends back to the forehead. Groove-billed Ani has a low, gently rounded upper mandible that rises gradually from the tip and joins the forehead in a fairly continuous line. Most Groove-billeds have distinct horizontal grooves on the upper and lower mandibles. (See Figure 126, p. 139.)

Major ID problems occur with immature Smooth-billeds that have smaller, gently rounded bills, or with young Groove-billeds that lack noticeable grooves. In these cases, the two species resemble each other. Other problems occur with Smooth-billed adults that have smaller, rounded bills that lack a pronounced flared upper mandible, or with Groove-billed adults that have bills with a higher, flared upper mandible and reduced visible grooves. In these cases, a few additional features are important to note.

The shape of the lower mandible differs very slightly between these species, and it requires close observation or a good photo to evaluate this feature. The lower mandible on Groove-billed typically lacks the strong gonydeal (midpoint on the lower mandible) angle of Smooth-billed, which results in a straighter edge to the lower mandible of Groove-billed versus a protruding lower mandible angle on Smooth-billed. Most adult Groove-billeds, however, have some grooves in their bills. (See Figure 126, p. 139.)

SUPPLEMENTAL CHARACTERISTICS AND NON-BBI DETAILS: Groove-billed Ani tends to have broader bare facial skin around the eye than Smooth-billed Ani. Adult Groove-billed typically has narrower and more bronze-colored, glossy edges to its head feathers than adult Smooth-billed.

While not genetically related, species in these three groups are typically nocturnal or crepuscular (active at dusk and dawn).

OWLS

Most owls are nocturnal counterparts to diurnal birds of prey. Some are active and hunt during the day, including far northern owls that experience little to no darkness in the summer months. Most owls hunt from familiar perches, where they watch and listen for prey with incredibly accurate eyesight and hearing.

TIPS FOR FINDING AND WATCHING OWLS

There is often no easy strategy for locating and viewing owls, but a few simple tips will increase your chances for success. A good starting point is to visit appropriate nesting, wintering, or year-round habitats and listen for owl vocalizations during their courtship and early breeding seasons. If you hear vocalizations at night (or during the day, for diurnal owls), you have found their territory.

When you hear protracted fussing of songbirds in wooded areas, this may indicate that an owl is present. Walk quietly into the area and scan nearby trees and bushes for owls. Sometimes snakes, raptors, and ground predators elicit similar mobbing behavior, so be vigilant for these creatures as well. Look for whitewash excrement under trees or on tree trunks, and search for owl pellets scattered on the ground. These compact indigestible parts of an owl's meal often indicate the presence of an owl's daytime roost.

When you see an owl in an open space, use a telescope (if possible) to view it from a distance. Owls are very sensitive to human disturbance, so try not to flush the bird, which may hinder its ability to obtain food. Walk directly away from the owl after a satisfactory viewing.

Diurnal owls are easier to find and study because of their daytime hunting habits. Nocturnal owls are more difficult to find, even after hearing their vocalizations, although Great Horned Owl is often seen well before dusk in familiar hunting locations. Screech-owls nest and roost year-round in cavities, so be sure to check old woodpecker holes or nest boxes if there are fresh scratch marks around the opening in winter or early spring.

Nocturnal owls, including Long-eared, Saw-whet, and Boreal Owls, are typically hard to locate since they often sit close to the trunk of a coniferous tree. They are easier to find in winter in suitable coniferous roost habitats, stunted cedars, or bramble thickets by searching for telltale white-wash or pellets.

PHYSICAL PROFILE

All owls except Barn Owl have variable, elongated, rounded body shapes. Barn Owl has a slender, elongated body shape. Generally, owls have relatively large, rounded heads; very short necks; and short, feathered legs with strong toes and sharp talons. Most owls have short, rounded tails that are the same length as their wingtips when they're sitting on the ground or perched. Exceptions are described below in Birding by Impression Information. (See Figure 127, p. 142, and Figure 128, p. 143.)

BIRDING BY IMPRESSION INFORMATION

SIZE: Nineteen species range from Elf Owl, at 5¾ in. long (about the size of White-breasted Nuthatch), to Great Gray Owl, at 27 in. long (slightly smaller than Golden Eagle at 30 in. long).

Owls fall neatly into two general size categories, large and small. Large owls include 9 species that range from 15 to 27 in. long, while small owls include 10 species that range from 5¾ to 10 in. long, with most being 7 to 8 in. long.

Three species (Northern Hawk Owl, Northern Pygmy-Owl, and Ferruginous Pygmy-Owl) have long tails that contribute to their size measurements, and their bodies appear smaller than those of owls with similar field guide measurements and shorter tails.

STRUCTURAL FEATURES: Body shape and structural features are similar among members of the same owl genus, but they vary slightly among owls of different genera. A large, rounded facial disc is shared by "typical owls," which include all owls except Barn Owl, which has a heart-shaped facial disc. Barn Owl also differs from "typical owls" by its long, feathered legs; bare toes; small eyes; and short, square tail. (See Figure 129, p. 144.)

A handful of owls have ear tufts on the sides of their crown. These include Great Horned, Long-eared, and three species of screech-owls (Eastern, Western, and Whiskered). Ear tufts are not related to hearing. They are often raised when owls are surprised or agitated, which gives the birds an imposing appearance.

The 10 small owls can be separated using a combination of body shape and structural features. Burrowing Owl is unique with its long, unfeathered lower legs and ground-dwelling habits. The three screech-owls are distinctive because of the presence of small but obvious ear tufts and yellow

FIGURE 127. LARGE OWLS

Clockwise from top left: Great Gray Owl, Snowy Owl, Barred Owl, and Northern Hawk Owl.

FIGURE 128. SMALL OWLS
Clockwise from top left: Ferruginous Pygmy-Owl, Western Screech-Owl, Eastern Screech-Owl (Mexican subspecies), and Burrowing Owl.

eyes. Flammulated Owl belongs to the same genus as screech-owls but has a longer, tapered body shape; short ear tufts; and dark eyes. Two species of pygmy-owls (Ferruginous and Northern) have long tails, short wings, and proportionally large, rounded heads without ear tufts. (See Figure 128, above.)

Two species of small, deep-forest owls, Boreal and Saw-whet Owls, are similar to screech-owls, with compact, rounded body shapes, but have proportionally larger heads and lack ear tufts. They are close in size to each other but have subtle structural and plumage differences. (See Figure 132, p. 147.) Elf Owl is one of the world's smallest owls and has a relatively small, rounded head and tapered body.

FIGURE 129. BARN OWL AND SHORT-EARED OWL
Barn Owl (L) and Short-eared Owl (R). These two pale owls often hunt during daylight hours by flying low over marshes and fields and dipping to the ground when they spot prey. Both have a ghostly facial appearance.

BEHAVIOR: While most owls are heard rather than seen, some owls have distinctive behaviors that help with their ID. Elf Owl is so small that it gives the impression of a large moth with fluttery wingbeats as it chases insects during nighttime hours. Short-eared Owl flies low over open marshes and fields with distinctive, stiff, shallow wingbeats that are also often described as "mothlike." Barn Owl hunts by flying low over open spaces as well. Both Barn Owl and Short-eared Owl may be seen at dawn or dusk or on cloudy days.

Snowy Owl is a ground-dwelling predator that sits on raised areas in open spaces when hunting. Burrowing Owl has a unique behavior of using its underground burrow for nesting, sleeping, and as a safe haven from danger.

Northern Hawk Owl is a diurnal hunter of open woodlands that often perches at the tops of tall trees. Northern and Ferruginous Pygmy-Owls are also active daytime hunters; Northern is most active at dawn and dusk.

Many owls are cavity nesters, with smaller ones often using abandoned woodpecker holes. While all small owls nest in cavities, many large ones use large abandoned stick nests, natural tree cavities, or simple ground nests. Snowy and Short-eared Owls nest on the ground, while Barn Owl nests and roosts in old buildings, abandoned mine shafts, and natural cavities.

PLUMAGE PATTERNS AND GENERAL COLORATION: Owls are earth-toned and have barring, streaks, spots, and blotches to help with camouflage. Some are unmistakable, including the largely white Snowy Owl and the uniformly gray Great Gray Owl, which shows a large, circular facial disc with alternating dark and light lines and a white and black chin that resembles a bow tie. (See Figure 127, p. 142.)

Barn Owls are distinctive with their buff-colored upperparts and whitish face and underparts (see Figure 129, above), while Long-eared Owl has obvious long, tawny-orange facial discs with dark vertical stripes that border the inner edge and transect each eye. (See Figure 131, p. 146.)

Feather patterns are also important in separating some closely related species. See Comparisons of Similar Species for Spotted Owl versus Barred Owl, Long-eared Owl versus Great Horned Owl, and Boreal Owl versus Northern Saw-whet Owl. False eye spots on the backs of both pygmy-owl heads are unique to these species, and Northern Hawk Owl's dark feather lines on its wide spotted crown and facial disc border are distinctive and helpful patterns.

HABITAT USE: Some owls are found only in certain habitats, and knowing their habits and preferences may be your best chance to see them. Even with careful research and preparation, a measure of luck is often needed. Other owls are generalists and inhabit a variety of habitats, including Great Horned Owl, Eastern and Western Screech-Owls, Barn Owl, and Ferruginous Pygmy-Owl. During migration, owls may be found in atypical habitats, although many owls are nonmigratory or migrate only when food supplies are low (mostly northern owls, such as Great Gray, Northern Hawk, and Boreal Owls).

VOCALIZATIONS: Owl vocalizations are helpful for locating them, and for correctly identifying similar species. Typical owl vocalizations include a variety of hoots, screeches, and whistles. Barn Owl has a

FIGURE 130. SPOTTED OWL AND BARRED OWL (QUIZ PHOTO)
These two species of large, dark-eyed owls are closely related. Southwestern Spotted Owls are paler than the Pacific subspecies shown in this photo. ID information is provided in the text. Can you identify these birds? Answers are in the appendix, page 271.

call reminiscent of a bloodcurdling shriek, a telltale sign of this ghostly owl's presence. Many species have extended songs or series of notes given only during the breeding season but are mostly quiet otherwise. Others vocalize throughout the year, especially nonmigratory species, but typically less during the nonbreeding season.

COMPARISONS OF SIMILAR SPECIES

Spotted Owl and Barred Owl

These two large woodland owls have dark eyes, which is a feature seen in only one other North American owl (the small Flammulated Owl).

UNCHANGING CHARACTERISTICS: Barred Owl is larger (21 in. long) than Spotted Owl (17 in. long), but structural features are very similar.

SUPPLEMENTAL CHARACTERISTICS AND NON-BBI DETAILS: Barred Owl is paler overall and has a slightly paler gray facial disc and yellower bill. Separating plumage details include a barred upper breast and streaked underparts in Barred versus scattered spots against a dark upper breast and uneven rows of bold, pale whitish spots against dark underparts

on Spotted Owl. Southwestern Spotteds are paler than the Pacific subspecies shown in Figure 130, above.

Long-eared Owl and Great Horned Owl

These two owls are often mistaken for each other owing to superficial similarities of their color and feather patterns.

UNCHANGING CHARACTERISTICS: Great Horned Owl is a large, bulky owl (22 in. long) with stout, widely spaced ear tufts. Long-eared Owl is smaller and more slender (15 in. long) with proportionally longer wings and tail, and its more closely set ear tufts are longer and thinner than Great Horned's shorter ones. (See Figure 131, p. 146.)

SUPPLEMENTAL CHARACTERISTICS AND NON-BBI DETAILS: Great Horned Owl has a rounded, buff-colored facial disc and thin, dark, horizontal barring on its underparts, while Long-eared's facial disc is more vertical in shape and its underparts are a mix of vertical dark streaks and barring. Black vertical stripes border the inner part of Long-eared's facial disc and cut through each eye. Because of the

FIGURE 131. LONG-EARED OWL AND GREAT HORNED OWL (QUIZ PHOTO)
These two owls share similar plumage coloration and ear tufts but differ in size, body shape, and plumage patterns. ID information is provided in the text. Try to identify which bird is which. Answers are in the appendix, page 271.

vertical facial disc, small eyes, and black vertical stripes through each eye, Long-eared may impart a surprised expression, while Great Horned's larger eyes and rounded facial discs give it a perceived calmer expression.

Northern Saw-whet Owl and Boreal Owl

These small forest owls are mostly nocturnal, though Northern Saw-whet Owl is sometimes found perched in thickets during daylight, and it may hunt at dawn and dusk.

UNCHANGING CHARACTERISTICS: Boreal Owl is larger (10 in. long) and has a bulkier body structure and wider head than Northern Saw-whet Owl (8 in. long).

SUPPLEMENTAL CHARACTERISTICS AND NON-BBI DETAILS: Boreal Owl has a darker crown with fine white spots versus a paler brownish crown with fine white streaks in Northern Saw-whet. Boreal also has a

pale gray bill versus a dark one on Northern Saw-whet, and a blackish border to a whitish gray facial disc versus a brownish border to a buff-white facial disc in Northern Saw-whet. Northern Saw-whet is more uniformly streaked below, while Boreal has a mix of spots and streaks.

NIGHTJARS AND NIGHTHAWKS

Nightjars and nighthawks belong to the family Caprimulgidae and are collectively referred to as "goatsuckers," which is a translation of their scientific family name. All are mostly nocturnal, although some nighthawks may actively hunt throughout the day over open spaces.

PHYSICAL PROFILE

Nightjars and nighthawks have elongated, rounded body shapes with very short legs and tiny feet. They all have tiny bills that can open exceptionally wide when they are catching flying insects. (See Figure

FIGURE 132. NORTHERN SAW-WHET OWL AND BOREAL OWL (QUIZ PHOTO)
These two small nocturnal owls are superficially similar in structure and plumage. ID information is provided in the text. Can you identify these birds? Answers are in the appendix, page 271.

133, p. 148.) Nightjars have large, blocky heads and broad, rounded wings, while nighthawks have smaller, rounder heads and thinner, angular, pointed wings. While they share physical attributes with other nightjars, Common Poorwill and Buff-collared Nightjar have shorter, more compact bodies than other species. (See Figure 134, p. 149.)

LOOK-ALIKE BIRDS

Larger nightjars may exhibit a falconlike flight when migrating, and when flying in a direct fashion. Kevin once initially misidentified a few Chuck-will's-widows as Merlins as they flew toward shore off the Gulf of Mexico in migration during daylight hours.

BIRDING BY IMPRESSION INFORMATION

SIZE: The six nightjars range from Common Poorwill at 7¾ in. long (slightly smaller than European Starling) to Chuck-will's-widow at 12 in. long (about the size of Mourning Dove). Common Poorwill's very short tail and wings account for its small measurement; the other five species are separated by only a few inches.

The three nighthawk species range from 8½ to 9½ in. long (about the size of Inca Dove), and there is wide variation between larger females and smaller males within the same species. These differences occasionally result in overlap measurements between similar species.

STRUCTURAL FEATURES: Nightjars have very large, dark eyes and fairly heavy body structures compared with nighthawks' smaller eyes and more slender body structures. Nighthawks have fairly long, notched tails compared with nightjars' short to long, rounded tails, with Common Pauraque having the longest tail of all the nightjars. (See Figure 134, p. 149.) While all goatsuckers have tiny feet incapable of tightly gripping perches, they often sit horizontally on branches or phone wires by sitting with their bodies arranged in the same direction as the wire or branch.

BEHAVIOR: All species forage by catching insects in flight. Nightjars are generally nocturnal hunters, but they also forage at dawn and dusk. Nighthawks hunt by day and night with long sustained flights over open areas. Both groups nest on the ground or on flat roofs.

FIGURE 133. COMMON NIGHTHAWK CATCHING AN INSECT
Nightjars and nighthawks feed by opening their mouth wide and using it like a funnel to catch moths and other insects in flight.

Because of their very short legs and tiny feet, goatsuckers spend little time walking on the ground. They are usually seen either flying or sitting quietly during daytime hours. Most nightjars are identified when they are sitting, since their foraging flights are typically short and localized. Nightjars often hunt in the light of streetlights at night, and you have a good chance of getting a good look at them there.

Because nightjars have wings that are broader and have rounded tips, their flight style differs from that of nighthawks. Nightjars give a powerful, steady flight impression in direct flight, while foraging nighthawks have a lighter, more buoyant flight style, with frequent changes of direction. While hunting on territory, however, nighthawks typically make short sallies from favorite perches, often in swirling and acrobatic flights that could be described as "mothlike."

Nighthawks are open-country birds that often fly for long periods when foraging, especially at dawn or dusk near breeding sites. All three nighthawk species can be seen during migration flying conspicuously at low to midrange heights over water and land. During migration it is not uncommon to see dozens of nighthawks flying together just before a cold front.

PLUMAGE PATTERNS AND GENERAL COLORATION: Goatsuckers are cryptically colored with muted earth tones that include black, gray, buff, rust, and white feather patterns. Sexes are similar, except for white (male) versus buff to gray (female) throat patches in nighthawks, and white tail corners on male nightjars versus buff ones on females.

A few species of nightjars have two color morphs that include rufous plumage tones versus gray and buff ones. Chuck-will's-widow has the most striking example of this rufous morph, while Eastern Whip-poor-will has a more muted rufous plumage condition. (See Figure 134, p. 149.) Mexican Whip-poor-will, split from Eastern Whip-poor-will in 2010 (the two were previously considered a single species, Whip-poor-will), has only a gray plumage condition that is virtually identical to that of gray-morph Eastern Whip-poor-will, and is best separated by its discrete geographic range. Vocalizations of the two whip-poor-will species also differ. Common Poorwill has dark and light plumage states.

Although nighthawks have cryptic plumage patterns and coloration similar to nightjars, there is marked variation in Common and Antillean Nighthawks that results in a possible similar plumage appearance to all three nighthawk species. Evaluation of general coloration and plumage patterns for nighthawks is rarely diagnostic by itself, except to eliminate Lesser Nighthawk from cold gray–plumaged Common Nighthawk.

HABITAT USE: Some nightjars are reliably found in specific habitats and geographic areas. Common Pauraque is found only in extreme south Texas in thorny, brushy habitats within open woods, while Buff-collared Nightjar is found in southeast Arizona in brushy desert canyons.

Three species are widespread summer residents of the United States, with Chuck-will's-widow and Eastern Whip-poor-will inhabiting open forested areas, and Common Poorwill found in open, arid habitats. Mexican Whip-poor-will occurs only in southwestern mountain regions.

With only three species of nighthawks in North America, and breeding ranges mostly segregated from each other, most nighthawks spotted away from dry southwestern habitats or extreme southern Florida can safely be identified as Common Nighthawk. Habitat is not a reliable feature for separating nighthawks in southern areas during migration and winter, but sparsely vegetated, arid southwestern locations are typically good habitats for Lesser Nighthawk.

VOCALIZATIONS: Vocalizations are distinctive among goatsuckers and often the deciding factor for some migrant birds or for similar species that occur in the same geographic area. Nightjars give a variety of loud, penetrating whistles and trills distinctive to each species. Most vocalize near breeding sites, but year-round residents may call earlier and later than seasonal migrants. Common Pauraque gives a loud, distinctive song throughout the year, but it is typically longer and more complex during the breeding season.

Nighthawks give a variety of quieter insectlike buzzes, notes, and trills. Common and Antillean Nighthawks give distinctive low, buzzy calls in flight, with some birds vocalizing during migration and in winter. These different calls are often the deciding ID factor where both species occur together in south Florida. Lesser Nighthawk gives a low, whistled trill near the breeding grounds.

COMPARISONS OF SIMILAR SPECIES

Chuck-will's-widow, Eastern Whip-poor-will, and Mexican Whip-poor-will

Chuck-will's-widow (Chuck) and Eastern Whip-poor-will (Eastern Whip) are the most similar nightjars in appearance, and they share a good portion of breeding range. Eastern Whip is the more northerly breeder, while Chuck extends farther south into the central and eastern United States.

Mexican Whip-poor-will occurs only in southwestern montane pine–oak forests south into Mexico. It has markedly different vocalizations from the typical explosive whistled *whip-poor-will* call

of northern and eastern birds, but is very similar in appearance to gray-morph Eastern Whip. ID criteria for Eastern Whip also applies to Mexican Whip-poor-will; they are best separated by voice.

UNCHANGING CHARACTERISTICS: Chuck is noticeably larger and heavier bodied than Eastern Whip, even when seen alone. It has longer, more pointed wings and a larger, flatter, blockier head compared with the smaller, rounder head of Eastern Whip. (See Figure 134, below.)

SUPPLEMENTAL CHARACTERISTICS AND NON-BBI DETAILS: Eastern Whip averages grayer plumage tones overall, even on rufous-morph birds. (See Figure 134, below.) Separating plumage features include Eastern Whip's dark throat and dark median crown stripe compared with a uniformly colored, dark-streaked crown and buff throat on Chuck.

Lesser, Common, and Antillean Nighthawks

The three species of nighthawks are often difficult to identify, even with extended views of some birds in flight. Geographic range allows for reliable identification of most birds, but Lesser Nighthawk has expanded its wintering range eastward to south

FIGURE 134. NIGHTJARS COMPARISON

Four species of regularly occurring nightjars, *clockwise from top left:* Eastern Whip-poor-will, Chuck-will's-widow, Common Pauraque, and Common Poorwill. ID information is provided in the text. Note the smaller size and shorter wings and body of Common Poorwill.

Florida, which further complicates the ID picture.

UNCHANGING CHARACTERISTICS: Lesser Nighthawk differs from Antillean Nighthawk by its proportionally longer tail, which extends past the folded wings on sitting birds, and from Common Nighthawk by its more rounded wingtips. Some Antilleans can have similar rounded wings that reach only the tail tip on sitting birds. Common's wings are typically more pointed and extend noticeably past the tail.

Another helpful ID feature on sitting birds is the length of the outer primary feather. On Lesser, the outer (last) primary is shorter than the next-to-last primary. The outer primary is longer on Common and Antillean. This feature is sometimes visible on a folded underwing and is illustrated in Figure 135, right-hand column.

Lesser typically has a more direct flight style with shallower, stiffer wingbeats than Common or Antillean. While all three species can occasionally have somewhat similar flight styles, the more fluttery quality of Lesser is best compared when it hunts for insects at dawn and dusk with Common in winter in south Florida. Common and Antillean have similar flight styles, and often show a distinctive rocking motion that Lesser does not, with very deep wing strokes, giving a somewhat buoyant flight impression.

SUPPLEMENTAL CHARACTERISTICS AND NON-BBI DETAILS: Lesser Nighthawk averages more buff in overall plumage tones than gray-plumaged Common Nighthawks, but Lesser's plumage may overlap with that of Antillean or of a few rufous Common subspecies. Lesser typically shows plainer, paler upperparts and lacks the bold, dark patterning of Common and Antillean.

One reliable detail that helps separate Lesser from warm-plumaged Common and Antillean is the location of the pale primary wing patch. In flight, this patch is seen closer to the wingtips on Lesser and farther in on the wing on Common and

outer primary shorter than next inner primary

FIGURE 135. LESSER NIGHTHAWK

This bird appears grayer than most Lesser Nighthawks because it is sitting in deep shade, without the warm tones of natural light. Solid field marks for this species include the presence of the white wing patch past the longest tertial feather and the outer primary being shorter than the next inner primary. Wingtips, visible here, are more rounded than Common Nighthawk's. This photo shows the first record of this species for New Jersey.

Antillean. On sitting Lessers, the wing bar is situated beyond the tertial tips and is nearly straight across (see Figure 135, above), while Common and Antillean have a diagonally oriented wing bar that is located well short of the tertial tips and is often hidden under the tertials. (See Figure 136, below.)

Common Nighthawk and Antillean Nighthawk

There is very limited published information concerning the separation of these two species as of 2013.

UNCHANGING CHARACTERISTICS: Antillean Nighthawk is smaller and has slightly to much shorter wing and tail measurements than most Common Nighthawk subspecies. These measurements support the subtly different impressions of body shape and structure between these two species, with Common's longer

FIGURE 136. COMMON NIGHTHAWK AND ANTILLEAN NIGHTHAWK (QUIZ PHOTO)

Extensive coverage of these two species, including varied color morphs, is provided in the text. All three birds shown here are males (the white throat is not always visible on perched birds). Try to identify the two species in these three photos. Warning: One bird is tricky. Answers are in the appendix, page 271.

tail and wings resulting in a more attenuated overall shape and a longer-winged look on sitting birds. (See Figure 136, p. 150.) While overlap occurs with wing length in the small subspecies *Chordeiles minor chapmani* of Common Nighthawk (which occurs in the southeast United States) and male Antillean Nighthawk, other subspecies of Common show no overlap in measurements and a more obvious difference in body shape.

On average, a perched Antillean appears proportionally smaller headed with a less attenuated overall shape than Common, because of Antillean's shorter tail and wings. The wingtips are more rounded on Antillean, similar to those of Lesser Nighthawk. Common's longer, more pointed wings and longer primary projection add to its longer, more tapered rear shape.

Antillean's shorter tail has a less pinched appearance at the base than Common's, which gives Antillean a subtly different appearance in overhead flight. A shorter tail length of 3.5 to 4 in. in Antillean versus 4.13 to 4.68 in. in Common adds to the longer, slimmer look of Common's tail in some overhead flight profiles.

Vocalizations of Common and Antillean are diagnostic for their ID, with Common typically giving a nasal, one-syllable *peent* in flight, while Antillean males give a two- or three-syllable *pity-pit, pity-pit-pit* or *killi-ka-dik*. Antillean calls are not as emphatic as those of Common, and often have a plaintive, insectlike quality.

SUPPLEMENTAL CHARACTERISTICS AND NON-BBI DETAILS: Although most popular field guides portray male Antillean Nighthawk with only a warm, rufous plumage (with some guides allowing for a gray-morph female), some male Antilleans have a mostly grayish morph that is similar to gray-morph Common Nighthawks. (See Figure 136, p. 150.) While male rufous-morph Antilleans may be more common than gray morphs, at least in the northern migratory subspecies, both color morphs exist.

An additional plumage feature useful in separating these two species is the density of underparts barring. The black bars average narrower on Antillean (1–2.5 mm) than on Common (1.5–3.5 mm). This narrower dark barring accentuates the buff coloration on Antillean's underparts, especially on birds with the narrowest bars. While overlap in bar width exists, the extreme ranges are recognizable.

Both species can have a similar rich buff color to the upper breast area below the throat patch, but buff-toned male Commons lack the contrasting paler buff coloration to the central breast area that occurs in male rufous-morph Antilleans.

Other plumage differences between the similar buff-toned Common subspecies *C. m. chapmani* and Antillean were noted by Kevin in careful study of museum skins. Both male and female Antillean (5 male and 4 female skins) had a rich buff coloration to the undertail coverts, while 29 museum skins of both sexes of *C. m. chapmani* showed little or no buff color in this area.

At first glance, these two bird families don't seem at all related, but they share several physical features and collectively belong to the taxonomic order Apodiformes. This name, derived from a Greek word meaning "without feet," describes the tiny feet of birds in both families. While hummingbirds have the ability to perch, swifts do not, and they use their feet only to cling to vertical surfaces at nesting and roost sites.

HUMMINGBIRDS

Fourteen species of hummingbirds regularly breed in North America, with six of these occurring only in extreme southern regions of the United States (Lucifer, Violet-crowned, Buff-bellied, Broad-billed, Blue-throated, and Magnificent Hummingbirds). An additional four species are regular vagrants in southeastern Arizona (Plain-capped Starthroat, Green Violet-ear, White-eared Hummingbird, and Berylline Hummingbird), with some breeding in small numbers from year to year. Only one species (Ruby-throated Hummingbird) breeds in eastern North America.

PHYSICAL PROFILE

Hummingbirds have relatively slender, tubular bodies that taper strongly near the rear and range from compact to elongate in shape. They have relatively large heads; long, tapered wings; short legs with tiny feet; and short, broad tails. The most obvious structural feature for all hummingbirds is their long, needlelike bill, which they use for probing deep into flowers for nectar. (See Figure 137, below.)

LOOK-ALIKE BIRDS

No other birds look like hummingbirds, but hummingbird moths (a type of clearwing moth) approximate a hummingbird's size, structure, and coloration. These diurnal moths also nectar on flowers while hovering in place. (See Figure 138, p. 153.)

BIRDING BY IMPRESSION INFORMATION

SIZE: Hummingbirds range in size from Calliope Hummingbird, at 3 to 3¼ in. long (about 25 percent smaller than Golden-crowned Kinglet), to Magnificent Hummingbird, at 5¼ in. long, which is the same size as Black-and-white Warbler.

Because hummingbirds are tiny and share a narrow size range (10 of the 14 North American species are 4 in. long or smaller), even 1 in. of size difference can represent up to a 30 percent difference in overall size. It is surprising how large a 4-in.-long hummingbird looks compared with a 3¼-in. one, and a 5-in.-long hummingbird looks like a giant compared with most of the smaller ones.

STRUCTURAL FEATURES: Structural features are often helpful in narrowing your ID choices of similarly plumaged hummingbirds. For example, the two species of *Archilochus* hummingbirds (Ruby-throated and Black-chinned) have small heads, thin necks, and slender bodies (see Figure 139, p. 155), while three species of *Selasphorus* hummers (Broad-tailed, Allen's, and Rufous) have larger and blockier heads, thicker necks, and rounder body shapes. For this reason, we provide a comprehensive table that compares the size, body shape and structure, bill, wings and tail, and important plum-

---

FIGURE 137. HUMMINGBIRDS (QUIZ PHOTO)

Hummingbirds are the smallest birds in the world, and their hovering flight and feisty nature make them some of the favorites in the world of birds. Try to identify these colorful hummingbirds. Answers are in the appendix, page 271.

FIGURE 138. HUMMINGBIRD MOTH
Hummingbird moths (L) resemble hummingbirds, especially when hovering to nectar on flowers. Differences include the long antennae and legs on hummingbird moths, and the very long proboscis they use to nectar on flowers. On the right is a male Calliope Hummingbird.

age details for similar female and immature hummingbirds. See Table 3, p. 154.

BEHAVIOR: Hummingbirds are the only birds able to fly backward. They spend a good amount of their lives hovering in front of flowers or sugar-water feeders while feeding. They are especially aggressive for their size, often chasing away other hummingbirds as well as much larger birds that cannot cope with the speed of hummingbirds. Besides feeding on natural and artificial nectar, hummingbirds routinely capture insects from vegetation and in the air, especially when feeding young. When not feeding, hummingbirds quietly perch near their favorite food source or nest site. Some species exhibit a unique "dive-bombing" display during breeding season or when defending territory.

PLUMAGE PATTERNS AND GENERAL COLORATION: Most male hummingbirds are distinctive because of their unique plumage, especially the color and shape of their bright gorgets (throat feathers). ID problems occur when colorful gorgets are not lit and appear blackish.

Other ID problems involve similar-looking males that share winter ranges, such as Ruby-throated and Broad-tailed Hummingbirds, but these instances are usually resolved with careful evaluation of pertinent structural features or plumage details.

Eight species of hummingbirds consistently cause ID problems, especially females and immatures. Table 3, p. 154, lists these species and outlines

the features that are important to a conclusive field ID.

VOCALIZATIONS: Hummingbirds give a variety of chips, ranging from sharp, flat ones to resonant, metallic ones. If you spend enough time with a single species, its call notes or staccato buzzing songs will become recognizable. Some hummingbirds produce sounds with their wings or tails, such as the trilling of male Broad-tailed Hummingbird's wings in flight (absent in fall because of worn primaries).

HABITAT USE: Habitat preferences for individual species are helpful for identification during nesting season but are of little use when hummingbirds congregate at feeders or groups of flowers at wintering and migratory locations. Hummingbirds occupy all possible habitats that support flowering plants, and knowing their favorite flowers is helpful when trying to locate a particular species.

COMPARISONS OF SIMILAR SPECIES

Immature and Female Ruby-throated Hummingbird and Black-chinned Hummingbird
These two species are nearly identical to each other in size and structure.

UNCHANGING CHARACTERISTICS: Female Ruby-throated Hummingbird averages shorter billed and longer tailed than female Black-chinned Hummingbird, whose tail projects slightly past its wingtips. When

Hummingbirds are divided into two sections of four species each since these are the birds that resemble each other the most.

Species	Size (Length)	Body Shape and Structure	Bill	Wings and Tail	Plumage Details
Anna's Hummingbird (similar to Costa's, Black-chinned, and Ruby-throated)	3½–4 in.	Longish, tubular body; stocky and large headed, with long, sloping fore-crown.	Short to medium length; straight.	Adult female's wings are slightly shorter than tail; immature's wings are noticeably shorter than longer tail.	Mostly greenish upperparts; whitish (adults) to grayish (immatures) underparts with grayish green spotted flanks; white line over eye, wider at rear of eye.
Costa's Hummingbird (similar to Anna's, Black-chinned, and Ruby-throated)	3–3½ in.	Small and dumpy with hunched posture; round head; thick neck.	Short, slightly decurved.	Wingtips project just past short tail.	Mostly greenish above; whitish underparts; pale eye line; gray cheek patch; slight gray mottling on dusky flanks.
Black-chinned Hummingbird (similar to Ruby-throated, Costa's, and Anna's)	3½–3¾ in.	Slender with small head and thin neck.	Medium length to long (longer in female); mostly straight.	Wings slightly shorter than tail in immature female; primary tips are broad and rounded.	Greenish upperparts; grayish crown and cheek patch contrast less with throat than in Ruby-throated; pale spot behind eye; dusky flanks and dull whitish underparts.
Ruby-throated Hummingbird (similar to Black-chinned, Costa's, and Anna's)	3½–3¾ in.	Slender with small head and thin neck (nearly identical to Black-chinned).	Similar to Black-chinned's but averages shorter.	Tail is slightly longer than wings in females; primary tips are narrow, pointed, and saber-shaped.	Green upperparts; green crown and dark cheek contrast strongly with white throat; white spot behind eye; greenish flanks and whitish underparts.
Calliope Hummingbird (similar to Rufous, Allen's, and Broad-tailed)	3–3¼ in.	Compact body; foreshort-ened appearance to rear body on perched birds.	Short; straight.	Wingtips extend slightly past short, rounded tail.	Greenish upperparts; pale buff underparts; lightly streaked pale throat; thin white line over bill; pale spot behind eye.
Broad-tailed Hummingbird (similar to Rufous, Allen's, and Calliope)	3½–4 in.	Long, graduated body; large head; thick neck.	Medium length; straight.	Long, broad tail with squared-off tip extends well past wingtips; broad tail is noticeably larger than on Rufous or Allen's, much longer than on Calliope.	Green upperparts and crown; strong buffy flanks; neatly spotted throat and cheeks; pale eye-ring.
Allen's Hummingbird (similar to Rufous, Calliope, and Broad-tailed)	3¼–3½ in.	Small, compact body.	Medium to long; straight.	Short winged; longish, graduated tail extends noticeably past wing-tips; tail feathers are narrower than in Rufous; adults have narrower rectrices than female and immature.	Mostly green upperparts, with rufous uppertail covert edging on some adult females; dusky flecking to whitish throat; heavy buff wash to flanks and undertail; white spot behind eye.
Rufous Hummingbird (similar to Allen's, Calliope, and Broad-tailed)	3¼–3¾ in.	Nearly identical to Allen's but averages slightly larger.	Similar to Allen's but averages longer and marginally more decurved.	As in Allen's, short wings fall well short of tail tip on perched birds; tail is long and tapered; female and immature have broader outer tail feathers than Rufous.	Similar to Allen's, but adult female lacks rufous edging to uppertail coverts.

FIGURE 139. BLACK-CHINNED HUMMINGBIRD AND RUBY-THROATED HUMMINGBIRD, FEMALES (QUIZ PHOTO)
ID information on these two very similar species is provided in the text, and in Table 3 on page 154. Can you identify these birds? Answers are in the appendix, page 271.

a female Ruby-throated is perched, its tail projects noticeably past the wingtips.

An important separating feature is the shape of the primary flight feathers. Ruby-throated has narrow primaries that angle sharply to a strongly pointed outer tip in a saberlike fashion. Black-chinned has broader, more evenly shaped primaries and noticeably rounded wingtips.

SUPPLEMENTAL CHARACTERISTICS AND NON-BBI DETAILS: Female Ruby-throated Hummingbird has a green crown and upperparts (sometimes tinged with gold) and a gray cheek that contrasts with a white spot behind the eye and a white or gray throat. Female Black-chinned Hummingbird has a gray forecrown and more heavily gray-washed cheek that shows less contrast with its throat. Ruby-throated's whitish underparts are washed with gray-green color on the flanks and sometimes a tawny wash of color, while female Black-chinned averages duller, duskier underparts.

Immature Female Anna's Hummingbird and Adult Female Costa's Hummingbird
UNCHANGING CHARACTERISTICS: Anna's Hummingbird is slightly larger than Costa's Hummingbird (4 in. vs. 3½ in. long on average) and has a longer, more tubular body shape compared with Costa's more compact, dumpy shape. (The Anna's in Figure 140 has fluffed body feathers and does not show the typical tubular body shape. It is important to recognize when a hummingbird has fluffed body feathers and thus presents an atypical profile.) Anna's longer body results in its wings falling short of the tail tip on perched birds, while Costa's wings project

just beyond the tail tip. Anna's has a short, straight bill and a long, sloping forehead, while Costa's has a short, slightly decurved bill and a more rounded head shape.

SUPPLEMENTAL CHARACTERISTICS AND NON-BBI DETAILS: Immature Anna's has grayish underparts with dense, greenish spotting, while Costa's has mostly whitish underparts and only slight, grayish mottling on the flanks.

Immature Female Anna's Hummingbird and Female Ruby-throated and Black-chinned Hummingbirds
(See Figure 139, above, and Figure 140, p. 156.)

UNCHANGING CHARACTERISTICS: Ruby-throated and Black-chinned Hummingbirds are very different structurally compared with Anna's Hummingbird. Ruby-throated and Black-chinned—*Archilochus* hummers—have small, rounded heads; thin necks; slender shoulders; and slim, tapered bodies. Anna's, a *Calypte* hummer, has a larger, stockier body; a much bigger head with a thicker neck; and a shorter, typically straighter bill than both of these species. On perched birds, Anna's tail projects noticeably farther past the wings than in Black-chinned, but this projection is similar to that of female Ruby-throated.

SUPPLEMENTAL CHARACTERISTICS AND NON-BBI DETAILS: Female Anna's Hummingbird typically has grayer underparts than Ruby-throated Hummingbird, and has heavier green mottling on the entire underparts versus lighter greenish to dusky (Black-

FIGURE 140. ANNA'S HUMMINGBIRD AND COSTA'S HUMMINGBIRD, IMMATURE AND ADULT FEMALES (QUIZ PHOTO)
Immature female Anna's and female Costa's Hummingbirds resemble each other physically, and require careful assessment of their structural and plumage differences. Adult female Anna's has a longer tail compared to its wings, so they are not included in this comparison. Try to identify these birds using the information provided in the text. Answers are in the appendix, page 271.

chinned Hummingbird) mottling on the flanks of both Ruby-throated and Black-chinned. A greenish gray crown on Anna's differs from Ruby-throated's green crown but may be similar to Black-chinned's.

SWIFTS

Swifts are expert aerialists, and spend most of their waking hours chasing insects or flying acrobatic sorties with their fellow swifts. Unable to perch, they cling like bats to vertical surfaces at roosts and nest sites.

PHYSICAL PROFILE

Swifts have generally tubular bodies with long, curved wings. They have short legs, and their tiny feet make them incapable of perching on branches. Bills are tiny, but wide gapes enable swifts to efficiently catch insects in flight. (See Figure 141, p. 157.)

LOOK-ALIKE BIRDS

While similar in habits, swallows generally have a broader base to their straighter wings and a less choppy flight than swifts. (See Figure 141, p. 157.) The Cliff Swallow in Figure 141 shows straight wings during a pause in flaps, but it can show angled wings that are somewhat similar to those of swifts. (See Figure 164, p. 191.) Swifts' wing shapes rarely change, even during glides.

BIRDING BY IMPRESSION INFORMATION

SIZE: Four species range in size from Vaux's Swift at 4¾ in. long (about the size of Nashville Warbler) to Black Swift at 7¼ in. long, which is similar in size to White-crowned Sparrow.

STRUCTURAL FEATURES: Besides their "flying cigar" impression, Vaux's and Chimney Swifts have deeply curved, pointed wings and short tails with squarish tips.

Black Swift and White-throated Swift have more elongated, tubular bodies, similar to those of swallows. The wings of Black Swift (not shown) are similar in shape to those of Chimney and Vaux's but are much longer and broader based with a proportionally longer hand, or outer wing. Its tail is longer and broader as well, and may show a slight notch.

White-throated Swift has long wings with a broad base and more slender primaries than the other three swift species. It also has a long, thin, forked tail that is often held in a tapered, pointed shape. (See Figure 141, p. 157.)

BEHAVIOR: Vaux's, Chimney, and White-throated Swifts nest on concealed vertical walls in chimneys, cliff crevices, and hollow trees. Black Swift nests on ledges behind waterfalls in the western United States. Swifts carry food for their young in expand-

FIGURE 141. SWIFTS (QUIZ PHOTO—TOP)
Three species of common North American swifts: Vaux's Swift, Chimney Swift, and White-throated Swift (bottom L). ID information for separating Chimney and Vaux's Swifts is provided in the text. Try to identify these two similar species (top photos) based on this information. Answers are in the appendix, page 271. The bottom right bird is a Cliff Swallow, shown to compare the differences in the wing shapes of swallows and swifts.

able throat pouches. All but White-throated are highly migratory and leave North America for the winter.

PLUMAGE PATTERNS AND GENERAL COLORATION: Swifts are grayish black to grayish brown overall with no other patterning, except for White-throated Swift, which has a white throat and belly, white sides to its rump, and white trailing secondary feathers.

HABITAT USE: Black Swift is associated with waterfalls and other moist cliff habitats in western mountains and northwestern coastlines. Chimney Swift is found in urban and suburban habitats because of its primarily chimney-nesting habits. Vaux's Swift is found mostly in forested montane habitats and lowland areas of the western United States. White-throated Swift is commonly found in the foothills and mountains of the western United States, especially near cliffs and outcroppings.

VOCALIZATIONS: Chimney and Vaux's Swifts both give a series of twittering notes that can be separated with practice. (See Comparisons of Similar Species, below.) Black Swift is generally silent but may give bursts of low chipping or clicking notes. White-throated Swift is vocal and gives a loud, rapid series of short, shrill notes that drop slightly in pitch.

COMPARISONS OF SIMILAR SPECIES

Vaux's Swift and Chimney Swift

Although the breeding ranges of these two species do not overlap, they may occur together in tropical areas during migration and winter, or as vagrant birds. Both species are wholly migratory, and sexes are similar.

UNCHANGING CHARACTERISTICS: Vaux's Swift is slightly smaller (4¾ in. long, 12-in. wingspan) than Chimney Swift (5¼ in. long, 14-in. wingspan), but these differences are difficult to notice with a single species. Both look like flying cigars, with long, arcing wings, small heads, and short, blunt tails. Subtle structural differences include longer, narrower wings in Chimney and a slightly longer rear body and tail that result in the wing placement being more forward on the body than on Vaux's. Chimney also tends to glide more and flap more slowly than Vaux's. (See Figure 141, p. 157.)

The best way to separate these two species is by their vocalizations. Chimney gives a series of hard chips that often run together into rapid twittering, while Vaux's gives sharp, higher-pitched, insectlike chipping sounds that often run together into buzzy trills.

SUPPLEMENTAL CHARACTERISTICS AND NON-BBI DETAILS: Plumage differences include Chimney Swift's gray-brown to dark brown throat, which usually contrasts with darker underparts, versus Vaux's Swift's more uniform underparts with a pale whitish to gray-brown throat, which extends through the breast. Chimney has more uniformly colored upperparts and a gray-brown rump that is only slightly paler than the back, versus a paler rump in Vaux's that contrasts more noticeably with the back. (See Figure 141, p. 157.)

Kingfishers are fish-eating birds that hunt from perches or in hovering flight. Only one species (Belted Kingfisher) is widespread throughout North America, with Ringed Kingfisher found in extreme south Texas, and Green Kingfisher a permanent resident of south to central Texas and extreme southeast Arizona.

PHYSICAL PROFILE

Ringed and Belted Kingfishers have fairly robust bodies with a "chesty" shape. Green Kingfisher is more slender and petite. All show flat backs when perched. They have large heads, short necks, short legs, and medium-length tails. All possess strong bills, with Ringed's massive bill much larger than Belted's evenly proportioned one. Green has a very long bill in relation to its head and body size. (See Figure 142, below.)

LOOK-ALIKE BIRDS

Belted Kingfisher and Blue Jay share similar colors and crested appearance. Blue Jay is slimmer and longer tailed, and never plunges into the water to catch fish. Belted Kingfisher is always found near water.

BIRDING BY IMPRESSION INFORMATION

SIZE: The three kingfishers range in size from Green Kingfisher at 8¾ in. long (the size of a Red-winged Blackbird) to the much larger Ringed Kingfisher at 16 in. long, which is slightly larger than Fish Crow. Belted Kingfisher is in between, at 13 in. long.

STRUCTURAL FEATURES: Belted Kingfisher shows the most prominent bushy crest when excited, while Ringed Kingfisher has much shorter crest feathers. Green Kingfisher has a prominent pointed crest on the rear of its head. All species can flatten their crests at will.

BEHAVIOR: All three kingfishers perch adjacent to water while hunting for fish. Belted and Ringed Kingfishers also hover in flight to spot fish, after

---

FIGURE 142. KINGFISHERS

All three commonly occurring kingfishers in North America are shown here. *Top, from left to right:* Female Ringed Kingfisher, male Belted Kingfisher, and male Green Kingfisher. Photos are scaled to size. *Bottom:* Kingfishers fly with an arrowlike profile. Male Ringed Kingfisher (L) and female Belted Kingfisher (R).

which they plunge head-first into the water to catch them. Green Kingfisher typically sits on small, hidden branches close to quiet bodies of water waiting for fish to swim by. It then plunges a short distance into the water to catch the fish. Green Kingfisher is usually hard to spot without hearing its ticking call notes, and it never hovers in the air like other kingfishers.

PLUMAGE PATTERNS AND GENERAL COLORATION: Ringed and Belted Kingfishers have varying amounts of blue, rust, and white, depending on the sex and age of the bird. Green Kingfisher's black wings have small white spots, and its white collar separates the green of its head from that of its back.

HABITAT USE: Ringed and Belted Kingfishers typically forage in small ponds and open bodies of water, including brackish bays (Belted). Belted frequently (Ringed less commonly) sits on power lines while scanning nearby bodies of water for prey. Green Kingfisher is found on sheltered creeks, ponds, rivers, and drainage ditches.

VOCALIZATIONS: Ringed and Belted Kingfishers both give loud, raucous calls, especially when flying across a body of water. Belted has a long, uneven rattle similar to that of a Hairy Woodpecker, while Ringed gives a loud, penetrating rattle on one pitch that resembles the sound of a machine gun. Green Kingfisher gives a series of quiet, dry notes that sound like two pebbles clicking together, usually in one or two notes.

This chapter covers the "tree huggers." Birds in these three families spend much of their time climbing up or down tree trunks and along limbs in search of their specialized food source.

WOODPECKERS

Woodpeckers cling to the sides of tree trunks as they forage for food. They use their chisel-like bills to excavate cavities for nesting and food gathering. Their skull and neck muscles are adapted to reduce brain impact from hammerlike blows of their bills. Woodpeckers reside in virtually every forested habitat in North America, as well as in the desert Southwest.

PHYSICAL PROFILE

Most woodpeckers have rounded bodies that taper strongly near the rear, and a flat-back profile. All have stiff tails that are used as props for shimmying up and down tree trunks and other structures. Legs are short with four strong, divided toes used for clinging to vertical surfaces (two species of woodpeckers have only three toes). All have stout, pointed bills used for excavating holes. (See Figure 143, p. 162.)

BIRDING BY IMPRESSION INFORMATION

SIZE: The 22 species of North American woodpeckers range from Downy Woodpecker, at 6¾ in. long (slightly larger than Song Sparrow), to the very large Pileated Woodpecker, at 16½ in. long (about the size of American Crow). Since many woodpeckers share a narrow size range from 7¼ to 9¼ in. long, a difference of 1 in. or so is noticeable.

STRUCTURAL FEATURES: Woodpeckers in the same genus generally share similar body shapes and structural features. Six species in the genus *Melanerpes,* including Red-bellied, Acorn, and Red-headed Woodpeckers, show gently rounded heads and have longer bodies and wings (see Figure 143, p. 162) than nine species of woodpeckers in the genus *Picoides,* which have blockier heads and more compact body shapes (see Figure 144, p. 164). Among the species in the genus *Picoides* are Hairy, Downy, Ladder-backed, and Three-toed Woodpeckers. Lewis's Woodpecker differs slightly from other *Melanerpes* woodpeckers with its long, broad wings and longer tail.

Four sapsucker species share structural features of slender, very pointed bills and rounded heads with a rear peak. (See Figure 146, p. 167.) Two species of flickers have long, powerful bodies; large heads; and long, stout bills. Springy legs and strong toes help with their ground-feeding habits. Pileated Woodpecker is the oddball with its large size; long, crowlike body shape; very long, broad wings; deep, hammerlike head with large rear crest; and long, powerful bill. (See Figure 143, p. 162.)

BEHAVIOR: All woodpeckers cling to the sides of trees or other structures in an upright posture, which is an immediate ID clue. The way they use their stiff tail as a prop results in a herky-jerky motion that is also distinctive and recognizable. Woodpeckers typically land feet-first against a vertical surface.

In flight, many woodpeckers pull their wings to their body after several flaps and descend noticeably before rising again with several wing flaps. This flight pattern results in a distinctive, repetitive undulating motion that only several other families share, and often with less dramatic rises and falls.

A small number of woodpeckers fly with a rowing motion of their wings and lack any consistent undulating movements. These include the larger Pileated and Lewis's Woodpeckers, which fly in a style similar to crows, and the medium-sized Acorn and Red-headed Woodpeckers, whose flight is similar to that of jays. These woodpeckers pause after several wingbeats, which results in a slight vertical drop in flight motion, but this irregular descent is nothing like the obvious repetitive undulation of other woodpeckers.

Woodpeckers excavate nest cavities in trees, cacti, and other vertical structures, including telephone poles. While foraging they will pick away at bark and sometimes create large holes in trees. Unlike other woodpeckers, sapsuckers drill concentric rows of shallow holes around a tree trunk, and return later to drink the oozing sap and feed on insects that are attracted to it.

Some woodpeckers, especially Acorn, drill holes in trees or utility poles to store nuts and seeds. Flickers regularly feed on the ground and probe the soil for grubs and their favorite food source, ants. Pileated Woodpeckers sometimes forage on fallen logs, where they strip bark in search of grubs, worms, and beetles.

PLUMAGE PATTERNS AND GENERAL COLORATION: Most woodpeckers are cryptically patterned. Some, however, including Red-headed and White-headed Woodpeckers, are distinctive, with bold areas of color and shading differences. Many have varying amounts of barring on their backs and underparts, including black, tan, brown, and white bars. Several

FIGURE 143. WOODPECKERS
Three striking members of the genus *Melanerpes*, and our largest woodpecker, Pileated, *clockwise from top left:* Red-headed Woodpecker, Pileated Woodpecker, Red-bellied Woodpecker, and Acorn Woodpecker. The genus *Melanerpes* has some of the most dramatic plumages of all woodpeckers.

show bold white wing patches that flash in flight (Acorn, Red-headed, Pileated, and the four species of sapsuckers).

Sexes are similar in most woodpeckers except for subtle markings on the head, nape, or face. Williamson's Sapsucker is an exception, with the female having a brown head and barred back and the male a black head with white stripes and a solid black back. Some immature woodpeckers look different than the adults, especially Lewis's and Red-headed Woodpeckers and all four sapsuckers.

Flickers are unique, with pale brown backs that have narrow black bars; pale underparts with bold, dark spotting; and a strong, oval-shaped black bib. Gilded and "Yellow-shafted" Northern Flickers have bright yellow underwings and undertails, while "Red-shafted" Northern Flicker has red instead of yellow coloration in these areas. (See Figure 147, p. 168.)

Seven species of *Picoides* woodpeckers have black-and-white plumage patterns with variable amounts of barring on the back and flanks. Most have variable black-and-white stripes on their heads, with males having red or yellow patches on their crowns or napes. (See Figure 144, p. 164, and Figure 145, p. 165.)

The brown coloration of Arizona Woodpecker differs from the typical black, white, and gray patterns of other *Picoides* woodpeckers.

HABITAT USE: While woodpeckers are mostly associated with forested habitats, some species are specialists. Gila Woodpecker and Gilded Flicker are found only in southwestern deserts, where they nest in trees and saguaro cacti. White-headed Woodpecker is found primarily in far western ponderosa and Jeffrey pine forests, and rarely wanders from these locations. Red-cockaded Woodpecker is found only in mature southeastern pine forests where diseased trees are available for nest holes.

VOCALIZATIONS: Woodpeckers are generally quiet, though they regularly give call notes throughout the year and loud vocalizations and drumming during courtship. Most woodpecker call notes are short and sharp, and fairly easy to recognize.

Another sign of woodpeckers' presence is loud drumming on tree trunks and other objects by territorial or foraging birds. Sapsuckers and the two three-toed woodpeckers (Northern and Black-backed) tap quietly on tree trunks, and the softness of their drumming or scraping bark is a clue to their presence.

Several groups of woodpeckers have distinctive, quiet calls that lack the penetrating quality of others. Three sapsucker species (Red-breasted, Yellow-bellied, and Red-naped) give drawn-out, nasal mewing calls quite unlike other woodpecker vocalizations, and which are unforgettable once learned. Red-cockaded Woodpecker gives an easy-to-overlook, sharp, nasal, squeaky call and an infrequent low rattle. Northern Three-toed Woodpecker has a quiet, flat *pwik* call note, similar to Downy Woodpecker's but more hollow in tone. Several of the *Melanerpes* woodpeckers (Red-headed, Red-bellied, Golden-fronted, and Gila) give wheezy or drawn-out nasal calls that are similar in quality to those of flickers.

COMPARISONS OF SIMILAR SPECIES

Downy Woodpecker and Hairy Woodpecker

These two very common woodpeckers have similar plumage patterning and crown color markings, so size and structural differences are the best way to separate them. Both differ from other woodpeckers with their vertical white back patches. Some western populations of both species have reduced or no white spotting on their wings, but similarities in plumage are consistent with geographic populations.

UNCHANGING CHARACTERISTICS: Hairy Woodpecker is noticeably larger than Downy Woodpecker in direct comparison (9¼ vs. 6¾ in. long), but single birds may be hard to evaluate. Hairy has a longer, heavier body structure that could be described as "rangy," while Downy has a smaller, more compact one. Hairy also has a distinct neck extension on relaxed perched birds, while Downy has somewhat of a "no-necked" appearance unless it is in an alert posture. (See Figure 144, p. 164.) Hairy has a more graceful flight style, with its long wings and more extended undulations different from Downy's quicker wingbeats and choppier flight.

BILL: Hairy Woodpecker's bill is noticeably longer and sturdier than Downy Woodpecker's, and typically more than half the width of its head. Downy's bill is usually shorter than half the width of its head, but bill size is slightly longer in males and may approach half of the head width. (See Figure 144, p. 164.) With practice, a quick evaluation of bill length combined with body structure is usually sufficient to form a confident ID of either species. Care should be exercised with juvenile Hairy, whose bill is incompletely formed and closely resembles Downy's bill in size and shape.

VOCALIZATIONS: Downy Woodpecker has a shorter, flatter *pik* call note, which differs from Hairy Woodpecker's louder, sharp *peek* note. Downy's rolling, laughing-like rattle song is distinctly different from Hairy's rapid series of one-pitch rattle notes, which is reminiscent of a Belted Kingfisher but higher pitched.

FIGURE 144. HAIRY WOODPECKER AND DOWNY WOODPECKER (QUIZ PHOTO)
Two different populations of Hairy and Downy Woodpeckers. The top photos represent the eastern forms of both species, which have denser white back spotting, while the two bottom photos show the Rocky Mountain populations (Rocky Mountain Hairies have darker backs and blacker facial markings). Can you identify both species? ID information is provided in the text, and answers are in the appendix, page 271.

SUPPLEMENTAL CHARACTERISTICS AND NON-BBI DETAILS: Both species have a similar black-and-white spotted or barred plumage, with males showing a red rear crown patch (small numbers of male Hairy Woodpeckers have a yellow crown patch). Hairy differs from Downy Woodpecker by having a tail that lacks faint dark bars on the white outer tail feathers. Interior West Hairy also has a darker overall facial pattern compared with Downy's broader white facial stripes.

Downy, Ladder-backed, and Nuttall's Woodpeckers

Downy Woodpecker is somewhat similar to Ladder-backed and Nuttall's Woodpeckers in size and structural features, so plumage differences and vocalizations are the best way to separate them. Ladder-backed is the south-central to southwest counterpart of Downy, and Nuttall's is a California relative close to both species. Downy and Ladder-backed have bred together in eastern Texas, and the hybrid offspring showed features of both species.

UNCHANGING CHARACTERISTICS: All three species are small, compact woodpeckers with short tails. Nuttall's Woodpecker is the largest at 7½ in. long, with Ladder-backed Woodpecker 7¼ in. long and Downy Woodpecker the smallest at 6¾ in. long. Since they are rarely seen with each other, size differences are hard to notice on single birds. Call notes and rattle songs are somewhat similar in all three species, but careful study of all these vocalizations may result in recognition of subtle differences in tone and timbre. Ladder-backed and Nuttall's have slightly larger bills and more sloping forecrowns than Downy.

SUPPLEMENTAL CHARACTERISTICS AND NON-BBI DETAILS: Downy Woodpecker has a conspicuous white back patch that immediately separates it from Ladder-backed and Nuttall's Woodpeckers, which have black backs with conspicuous white barring. The dark cheek marking on Ladder-backed and Nuttall's connects with the dark lower cheek marking and does not continue to the nape, as it does in Downy. This results in the white supercilium continuing around the entire cheek and connecting with the dark shoulder marking. Downy's dark cheek continues to the nape and does not connect with the dark lower cheek marking, which isolates the white supercilium. (See Figure 145, below.)

In addition to having a different geographic range, Ladder-backed averages whiter on the face and lacks the solid black upper back of Nuttall's. Male Ladder-backed also has a broader red crown that extends forward to the eye, while male Nuttall's shows red only on the rear crown.

Nuttall's has a white nasal bristle tuft and white breast with black spots, while Ladder-backed has a buff nasal bristle tuft with a buff-colored upper breast and black streaks. Nuttall's also has sparse black

---

FIGURE 145. LADDER-BACKED, NUTTALL'S, AND DOWNY WOODPECKERS (QUIZ PHOTO)
These three small woodpeckers in the genus *Picoides* share mostly similar size, structural features, and plumage patterns, but several plumage differences help separate them. After reading the ID information in the text, try to identify these birds. Answers are in the appendix, page 271.

spots on white outer tail feathers, while Ladder-backed has black bars.

Red-naped Sapsucker and Yellow-bellied Sapsucker

Red-naped Sapsucker is the Rocky Mountain counterpart to Yellow-bellied Sapsucker, which breeds widely across the continent at more northern latitudes. Yellow-bellied is the most migratory of all sapsuckers, and regularly flies over Atlantic and Gulf waters in migration.

UNCHANGING CHARACTERISTICS: Size, body shape, and structural features for these two species are virtually identical.

SUPPLEMENTAL CHARACTERISTICS AND NON-BBI DETAILS: Yellow-bellied Sapsucker has more extensive white barring on the back and limited red on the throat, with a more extensive black border than Red-naped Sapsucker. Red-naped usually has a distinct red patch on the nape, but this feature is sometimes absent, and is present in small numbers of Yellow-bellieds. Eastern-breeding Red-naped and western-breeding Yellow-bellied are most similar in plumage, and hybrids occur where breeding ranges overlap, with some birds best left unidentified. (See Figure 146, p. 167.)

Gilded Flicker and Northern Flicker ("Yellow-shafted" and "Red-shafted" Subspecies)

Except for the larger Pileated Woodpecker, flickers are the largest and heaviest North American woodpeckers. Major declines in population of "Yellow-shafted" Northern Flicker over the last 20 years may be attributed in part to European Starlings' relentless thefts of "Yellow-shafted's" nest holes in the more densely populated eastern United States.

UNCHANGING CHARACTERISTICS: All flickers have long, slightly decurved bills; very broad wings; long, thick necks; and long, slender heads. Northern Flicker is larger than Gilded Flicker (12½ vs. 11 in. long) and longer winged (20 in. vs. 18 in.).

SUPPLEMENTAL CHARACTERISTICS AND NON-BBI DETAILS: Gilded and both Northern Flicker subspecies have uniformly gray to brown heads; pale brown upperparts and wings with narrow black bars; a black upper breast patch; boldly spotted, pale underparts; and yellow or red underwing color. (See Figure 147, p. 168.)

All three flicker populations have distinct geographic ranges with narrow overlap zones, and only slight plumage differences on the head and face separate these closely related birds. Gilded is most similar to "Red-shafted" Northern Flicker, with a gray face and red malar stripe in males, compared with a brown face and black malar stripe in "Yellow-shafted" Northern Flicker males. Gilded differs from "Red-shafted" by a brighter cinnamon forehead, yellow underwings and wing linings versus reddish in "Red-shafted," and an all-brown crown and nape versus a brown forecrown and gray rear crown and nape on "Red-shafted." Hybrids occur regularly in the overlap breeding zone.

"Yellow-shafted" differs from "Red-shafted" with its brown versus gray face, gray versus brownish crown, red nape crescent in both male and female (lacking in "Red-shafted" and Gilded), and black malar stripe versus a red one in male "Red-shafted" and Gilded. Intergrades between "Red-shafted" and "Yellow-shafted" are very common in their overlapping breeding range, and these birds have some features of each subspecies. (See Figure 147, p. 168.)

NUTHATCHES

Nuthatches creep along tree trunks and limbs, often while upside down, and forage for food under bark and in crevices of tree trunks. All are cavity nesters.

PHYSICAL PROFILE

Nuthatches have compact, plump bodies with large heads, short tails, and relatively long, pointed bills. Legs are short with large, strong toes, and wings are broad based and rounded. (See Figure 148, p. 169.)

BIRDING BY IMPRESSION INFORMATION

SIZE: Four species of nuthatches share a narrow size range, from Pygmy Nuthatch, at 4¼ in. long (about the size of Ruby-crowned Kinglet), to White-breasted Nuthatch, at 5¾ in. long, which is slightly larger than Carolina Wren. Red-breasted and Brown-headed Nuthatches are both 4½ in. long.

STRUCTURAL FEATURES: Nuthatches have a somewhat compact, stocky shape. Their oversized bills are the most obvious physical feature, especially on Brown-headed and Pygmy Nuthatches. (See Figure 148, p. 169.) Red-breasted Nuthatch has a more slender body structure than other nuthatches, with a smaller, rounder head and proportionally smaller bill, while White-breasted Nuthatch has a longer body and much longer wings than other nuthatches. Nuthatches don't use their short tails for support like woodpeckers and Brown Creeper do; they use their strong toes to cling to vertical tree trunks.

BEHAVIOR: Brown-headed Nuthatch is one of only a few bird species in the world to use a tool while foraging. It sometimes holds a piece of bark in its bill and uses it to flake off other sections of bark. Pygmy Nuthatch exhibits unusual breeding

FIGURE 146. SAPSUCKER COMPARISON
Four species of common North American sapsuckers: Yellow-bellied (top L) and Red-naped (top R) Sapsuckers are closely related and share similar plumage colors and patterns. ID information is provided in the text. Hybrids of these two species occur regularly in the geographic overlap zone. Male Williamson's Sapsucker (bottom R) and Red-breasted Sapsucker (bottom L) are both striking and distinctive woodpeckers.

FIGURE 147. GILDED FLICKER AND NORTHERN FLICKER COMPARISON (QUIZ PHOTO)
Distinct plumage differences are the best way to separate these similar woodpeckers. Detailed ID information is provided in the text. Try to identify the Gilded Flicker, "Red-shafted" and "Yellow-shafted" subspecies of Northern Flicker, and one commonly found intergrade shown here. Answers are in the appendix, page 271.

FIGURE 148. NUTHATCHES (QUIZ PHOTO)
All four North American nuthatches. Detailed ID information is in the text on page 166. Try to identify all these birds. Answers are in the appendix, page 271.

behavior whereby relatives assist breeding pairs in the nesting process. Mated pairs and juvenile Pygmy Nuthatches often roost together, and groups of 10 or more birds may roost together in winter, when large flocks form cooperative foraging groups.

Brown-headed and Red-breasted Nuthatches also form flocks in winter, but White-breasted Nuthatches are typically seen alone or in pairs. Brown-headed and Pygmy Nuthatches are nonmigratory, and only Rocky Mountain White-breasted migrates on a regular basis, moving to the Great Plains after breeding. Some northern-nesting birds disperse

south throughout their range in harsh winters. Red-breasted is truly a migratory species, with large numbers moving south during years of poor food sources in northern areas.

PLUMAGE PATTERNS AND GENERAL COLORATION: All nuthatches have a blue-gray back color. Differences among species include different head and facial markings, and underparts coloration that ranges from white (White-breasted Nuthatch) and buff and gray (Pygmy and Brown-headed Nuthatches) to orange (Red-breasted Nuthatch). Sexes

FIGURE 149. BROWN CREEPER

Brown Creeper is North America's only treecreeper species. Detailed ID and natural history information is provided in the text.

are similar in Pygmy and Brown-headed, while White-breasted and Red-breasted females have duller plumage features than males. (See Figure 148, p. 169.)

Pygmy and Brown-headed are the most similar in plumage color and patterns. Pygmy differs by having a grayish olive versus brown crown, a smaller white nape spot, and buffier undertail coverts. Both species have a black mask that cuts through the eye and forms dark lores.

Red-breasted is unique with a belly and vent that are rich reddish orange in males and pale orange in females, and a complex head pattern. White-breasted has a distinctive mix of white breast, face, and neck that contrasts with a black (male) to gray (female) crown and nape. Gray to buff flanks and rust undertail coverts complete an unmistakable plumage, which includes a large dark eye set against a totally white face. (See Figure 148, p. 169.)

HABITAT USE: Brown-headed Nuthatch is found in pine forests of the Southeast, while Pygmy Nuthatch frequents long-needled pine forests in the West. There is no overlap in their permanent ranges. Both forage mostly high in trees among the outermost needles of pine boughs. Because of this feeding behavior, it is often difficult to spot these small birds as they disappear among pine needles. Nesting birds are more easily observed, and both species may excavate nest holes at low levels.

Red-breasted Nuthatches normally nest in mature forests dominated by spruce and fir trees, but during migration and winter they use a wide variety of habitats, including backyards, where they exhibit very tame behavior around bird feeders. White-breasted Nuthatch is another common visitor to backyard bird feeders throughout much of its range. It prefers a variety of open deciduous and mixed-forest habitats, especially oak woodlands that supply a ready food source of nuts.

VOCALIZATIONS: Nuthatches are best located by their vocalizations, which are typically given throughout the year. Red-breasted Nuthatch has a loud, penetrating nasal *yank-yank* call that sounds like a tin bicycle horn. White-breasted Nuthatch has a similar but louder *yank* call that is occasionally accompanied by repeated short, whistled notes, *whi-whi-whi-whi-whi,* especially during the breeding season. Pygmy Nuthatch gives a high, penetrating peeping call that is usually heard in chorus by flocks, while Brown-headed Nuthatch has a squeaky, repetitive two-note call that resembles a toy rubber duck, *KEW-deh.*

BROWN CREEPER

Brown Creeper is the only member of the treecreeper family in temperate North America.

PHYSICAL PROFILE

Brown Creeper has an elongated body with a bulging, rounded chest; flat back; and slender rear end. It has a relatively long, spiky tail and a very thin, pointed, and curved bill. Stocky, broad wings are useful for navigating forest habitats, and very short legs and strong toes are well suited for endless creeping motion.

BIRDING BY IMPRESSION INFORMATION

SIZE: Brown Creeper is 5¼ in. long (slightly smaller than Chipping Sparrow).

STRUCTURAL FEATURES: Brown Creeper uses its long tail as a prop for shimmying up tree trunks, and its thin, curved bill for probing under tree bark and other hard-to-reach areas for food items.

BEHAVIOR: Brown Creeper typically spirals up tree trunks while foraging, which it does with a smoother lurching motion than woodpeckers. It also forages with a more continuous style and fewer pauses than woodpeckers. Once it reaches a certain height, it usually flies to the base of another tree to begin the upward motion once again. Flight is undulating and woodpecker-like. While Brown Creeper is a resident species throughout its range, many birds migrate south after breeding, especially during harsh winters.

PLUMAGE PATTERNS AND GENERAL COLORATION: Brown Creeper is a cryptic brown-, buff-, and white-speckled bird that blends in remarkably with tree bark. It has a wide, pale supercilium; a mostly white throat and underparts; and a pale buff vent. (See Figure 149, p. 170.) Its rich, warm brown tail color contrasts with its grayish brown back and wings.

HABITAT USE: Mature woodland is the preferred habitat for Brown Creeper, but during migration it can be found in any wooded or shrubby location.

VOCALIZATIONS: Song is a series of accelerating high, thin, cascading notes. Calls include a single or double high-pitched *seet* note.

This large group of reasonably conspicuous, upright-perching, insect-chasing birds contains some of the most difficult ID challenges in North America. A bird's age and plumage state and the location, time of year, and viewing conditions can all factor into the ID solution. Sexes are similar in most cases, with major exceptions being Vermillion Flycatcher and Rose-throated Becard.

PHYSICAL PROFILE

Smaller flycatchers typically have slender, elongated bodies with relatively small heads and bills, while larger flycatchers are stockier with larger bills and "chestier" body structures. There is considerable physical variation within this group, though most species in the same genus share similar structural features, which are important to narrowing your ID choices. See Table 4, p. 176.

BIRDING BY IMPRESSION INFORMATION

SIZE: The 37 regular occurring North American flycatcher species (35 breeding) range in size from Northern Beardless-Tyrannulet, at 4½ in. long (slightly larger than Ruby-crowned Kinglet), to the adult male Scissor-tailed Flycatcher, whose tail accounts for more than half of its 15-in. measurement. Great Kiskadee is the largest-bodied flycatcher at 9¾ in. long, about the size of American Robin. (See Figure 150, below.)

Flycatchers can be divided into two general sizes: small and large. Small flycatchers include 15 species that range from 4½ to 6¼ in. long, including 11 species of *Empidonax* flycatchers ("empids"). Large flycatchers include 22 species that range from 7 to 9¾ in. long, as well as the very long-tailed Scissor-tailed and Fork-tailed Flycatchers, which have much

---

FIGURE 150. TYRANT FLYCATCHERS (QUIZ PHOTO)

Try to identify these flycatchers, which are among the most diverse group of birds in North America. Answers are in the appendix, page 271.

larger overall measurements but whose body size is comparable to that of 8-in. flycatchers. Though we group flycatchers into two size categories, the size range difference within each group is not extreme, and a confident ID is often the result of looking at structural features, behavior, and plumage details together.

STRUCTURAL FEATURES: Flycatcher ID can be difficult because many species in the same genus appear superficially similar. However, if you have only a few similar species to compare based on shared structural features and relative size, your ID process is not as complicated as trying to make sense of multiple species in several genera that share similar plumage patterns and color. (See Figure 151, below.)

Table 4, p. 176, lists the important structural features for 36 of the 38 flycatcher species, in six genera. The remaining two species (Vermillion Flycatcher and Rose-throated Becard) belong to two separate genera and pose few ID problems.

BEHAVIOR: Flycatchers tend to perch upright on exposed perches while scanning for insects or other prey, including small reptiles, mammals, and fish (Great Kiskadee). They will make a quick sallying flight to grab prey before returning to the same perch or finding a different one. Flycatchers also eat a variety of fruits and berries, especially during migration and in winter.

Foraging behavior and overall demeanor vary greatly among flycatchers, with some species being shy and retiring and others unwary and visible. For example, pewees and Olive-sided Flycatcher are visible birds that sit on conspicuous, open perches while hunting. After flying out to catch an insect in the air, they typically return to the same perch.

Some flycatchers regularly fly to the ground from exposed perches to grab suitable prey, such as insects or lizards. Kingbirds and *Myiarchus* flycatchers practice this hunting behavior, as do phoebes, Great Kiskadee, Scissor-tailed Flycatcher, and Vermillion Flycatcher.

Empidonax flycatchers are small birds of forested areas that often use inconspicuous perches when foraging. They are also nervous birds that don't generally allow close approach by humans, so they may give you only a few seconds' view before flying away, especially during migration. The bold, open-perch behavior of Eastern and Western Wood-Pewees helps separate them from similarly plumaged empids.

PLUMAGE PATTERNS AND GENERAL COLORATION: Most flycatchers in a particular genus share a number of general coloration and plumage pattern features. For example, pewees and Olive-sided Flycatcher have mostly gray-brown plumage tones with varying gray wash on the underparts. *Myiarchus* flycatchers have brownish upperparts, grayish breasts, yellow bellies, rufous wing margins, and rufous undertails (except Dusky-capped and some La Sagra's). (See Figure 150, p. 172.) Slight to obvious differences in the intensity and location of the color and shading in each group can often help separate similar species.

HABITAT USE: While flycatchers use a wide variety of habitats, most species within a genus share similar habitat preferences. For example, kingbirds and both long-tailed flycatchers (Scissor-tailed and

FIGURE 151. THREE FLYCATCHERS IN THE GENUS *TYRANNUS* (QUIZ PHOTO)

We saw these three similar-sized flycatchers in the same location in Limón, Costa Rica, in December 2013. Two of them were not shown in the region's field guide range maps. To reach an ID of all three species, concentrate on structural differences, refer to Table 4, page 176, and consult your field guides to compare plumage differences. Answers are in the appendix, page 271. Hint: All are first-winter birds.

Fork-tailed), which are in the genus *Tyrannus*, are birds of open spaces, as are phoebes, in the genus *Sayornis*. Pewees and Olive-sided Flycatcher, in the genus *Contopus*, use forested areas with adjacent clearings for hunting, which is also preferred habitat for most *Myiarchus* flycatchers. Ash-throated is the exception among the *Myiarchus*, using open, arid habitats for breeding.

Empidonax flycatchers are birds of forests, shrublands, and riparian zones, though some species are found in more open woodland habitats and nearby clearings. Great Kiskadee is a bird of thickets with adjacent open spaces, often with water bodies nearby, and Vermillion Flycatcher prefers open spaces with ample exposed perches for hunting.

VOCALIZATIONS: Flycatchers give a wide variety of songs, call notes, and phrases at all times of the year, and these can be the deciding factor to settle an ID dilemma between very similar species.

COMPARISONS OF SIMILAR SPECIES

Eastern Wood-Pewee and Western Wood-Pewee

Eastern and Western Wood-Pewees are two similar species that have long been considered identical in size, shape, and plumage, with calls the only reliable way to separate them. Several plumage and bare-parts features have recently been proposed as helpful for separating these birds, but occasional overlap of these features still makes ID of some silent birds impossible. Noticeably longer, more pointed wings, a reduced eye-ring, lack of tail flicking, and a peaked rear crown are features of both species that help separate them from similar *Empidonax* flycatchers. (See Figure 152, p. 175.)

UNCHANGING CHARACTERISTICS: Physical features are identical on both species, although some Western Wood-Pewees appear shorter tailed and slightly longer winged than Eastern Wood-Pewees.

SUPPLEMENTAL CHARACTERISTICS AND NON-BBI DETAILS: Western Wood-Pewee differs from Eastern Wood-Pewee by having slightly grayer versus olive-gray upperparts, and darker, more complete gray underpart shading. Eastern has variable gray shading to the underparts, with a pale vertical line running down the breast center. These features are variable within each species, however, and overlap may occur. Western also has less yellow on the lower mandible on average, with a larger dark bill tip. Both species can show somewhat defined pale wing bars in late summer and fall, so care should be taken to assess the other important field marks and structural features to separate pewees from *Empidonax* flycatchers.

Empidonax Flycatchers

Empidonax flycatchers (empids) remain one of the hardest dilemmas in bird identification, because of a lack of obvious differences in size, structure, and plumage details. These similarities are compounded by an active feeding style and the tendency of empids to disappear before any serious study can be conducted. Often photos of the same bird show marked variation in color and shading in different lighting conditions.

A good starting point is to make sure you are looking at an empid and not one of the more common look-alikes, such as Eastern or Western Wood-Pewee. (See the wood-pewee comparison in the left-hand column, and Figure 152, p. 175.) Most empids have noticeable eye-rings and wing bars, rounded heads, shorter wings than pewees, and are very active feeders, often changing perches after chasing a flying insect. Empids also tend to flick their wings and tails when perched and foraging for food.

GENERAL ID TIPS FOR SEPARATING EMPIDONAX FLYCATCHERS

UNCHANGING CHARACTERISTICS: Assess the wings and tail. Are they proportionally long compared with the body, or are they especially short? You can really only learn to evaluate these features through careful, repetitive field observation. One way to quantify long or short wings is to compare how far the wings extend down the tail, or how far they project past the longest tertial feather. This sounds confusing, but once you grasp the concept you can look for these features and they will help in most instances. (See Figure 152, p. 175.)

Tail length is another helpful field impression. Once you have carefully assessed a Willow or Alder Flycatcher's longer, broader tail, the tail of a Least or Hammond's Flycatcher appears shorter and thinner in comparison.

SUPPLEMENTAL CHARACTERISTICS AND NON-BBI DETAILS: If you feel confident that you are looking at an empid, note the general coloration of the back, underparts, and head. Are the upperparts greenish or a shade of olive or gray? Next determine if the underparts have dusky shading to the upper breast or flanks, and if there is any yellowish color present. Note the extent and shape of the eye-ring. Is it slim, round, and uniform, or does it have a teardrop shape behind the eye? Only five species of empids have this exaggerated teardrop-shaped eye-ring (Least, Acadian, Yellow-bellied, Cordilleran, and Pacific-slope), and combining this with other features helps narrow your choices. Also note if the eye-ring is absent or broken. Willow Flycatcher tends to have a thin or incomplete eye-ring.

Underpart color is often not reliable for some

FIGURE 152. PEWEES AND *EMPIDONAX* FLYCATCHERS (QUIZ PHOTO—BOTTOM)

Top: ID information for Eastern Wood-Pewee (L) and Western Wood-Pewee (R) is provided in the text. Wood-pewees have noticeably longer, more tapered primaries than *Empidonax* flycatchers (empids), and darker, more peaked crowns. *Bottom:* These birds show the typical large-headed, big-eyed *Empidonax* flycatcher look, with whitish eye-rings and wing bars found in most empids. Note the larger head and body, and longer tail and wings on the left bird. For an expert-level quiz, try to identify these common *Empidonax* flycatchers. Answers are in the appendix, page 271.

empids because freshly molted and immature birds may look brighter than worn adults. However, Yellow-bellied, Pacific-slope, and Cordilleran Flycatchers have yellower bellies than other empids, along with a dusky wash to the upper breast. Combine these plumage features with a teardrop-shaped eye-ring, and your choices are narrowed to three species. Geographic probability further reduces your choice to one or two species.

Willow Flycatcher and Alder Flycatcher

These two species of *Empidonax* flycatchers were formerly grouped into one species called Traill's Flycatcher, and even today some of these birds are still called "Traill's" because of their difficult ID, even in the hands of bird banders. Willow Flycatcher has an eastern and western subspecies, with minor differences between them.

Some observant birders have recently proposed

TABLE 4—QUICK COMPARISON GUIDE: FLYCATCHERS

Two flycatchers are listed in the "small" category, even though their length measurements overlap with or are larger than some flycatchers in the "large" category. This is because two species (Olive-sided Flycatcher and Greater Pewee) occur in the same genus as and resemble truly "small" flycatchers (the pee-wees).

SMALL FLYCATCHERS

Genus and Species	Size (Length)	Body Shape	Structural Features	Plumage Details
Empidonax (12 species) Cordilleran, Acadian, Yellow-bellied, Willow, Alder, Least, Dusky, Gray, Hammond's, Yellow-bellied, Pacific-slope, and Buff-breasted Flycatchers	5¼–6 in.	Varies from compact and foreshortened to elongated and slender.	Small heads and bills; relatively short wings; short to medium-length tails; heads are mostly rounded in shape, with slight differences among species.	Obvious wing bars; eye-rings; mostly drab plumage; variable yellow underparts on some juveniles and adults.
Contopus (4 species) Eastern and Western Wood-Pewees, Greater Pewee, Olive-sided Flycatcher	6¼–8 in.	Elongated, slender (peewees); stocky, compact (Olive-sided).	Long wings and tails; peaked crowns.	Gray to brown plumage; pale wing bars; weak to absent eye-rings; dusky underparts.
Camptostoma Northern Beardless-Tyrannulet	4¼ in.	Slender body with rounded chest; often mistaken for empid.	Tall bushy crest; short, narrow tail; short, blunt-tipped bill.	Olive-gray upperparts; gray head and breast; pale yellow belly and vent; two dull wing bars.

LARGE FLYCATCHERS

Genus and Species	Size (Length)	Body Shape	Structural Features	Plumage Details
Sayornis (3 species) Eastern, Say's, and Black Phoebes	7–7½ in.	Stocky, "chesty."	Large, blocky heads; slender bills; long tails.	Eastern and Black Phoebes are black, white, and gray; Say's has ochre belly, gray chest and upperparts.
Myiarchus (6 species) Great Crested, Ash-throated, Brown-crested, Dusky-capped, Nutting's (rare), and La Sagra's (rare) Flycatchers	7¼–8¾ in.	Elongated, "chesty."	Large heads with peaked rear crowns; medium-length, pointed bills; relatively short wings; long tails.	The 4 common species have yellow bellies and gray upper breasts; brownish gray crowns and backs; rufous undertails (except Dusky-capped).
Tyrannus (7 kingbird species) Gray, Eastern, Western, Tropical, Thick-billed, Couch's, and Cassin's Kingbirds	**Kingbirds** 8½–9½ in.	Elongated, with bulky chests.	Large, round heads; stocky bills.	Four kingbirds have yellow bellies and gray heads; 3 have white underparts and gray or black upperparts.
(2 "long-tailed" flycatcher species in the genus *Tyrannus*) Scissor-tailed and Fork-tailed Flycatchers	**Flycatchers** 10–15 in. (juvenile to adult male size values)	Slender.	Small, round heads; small, delicate bills; very long tails (see Figure 151, p. 173). Female and juvenile have shorter tails.	Scissor-tailed has salmon belly, white head, pale gray back, and black wings; Fork-tailed has gray upperparts, white underparts, and a black cap.
Large Tropical Flycatchers (2 species) ***Myiodynastes*** Sulphur-bellied Flycatcher	8½ in.	Husky, rounded bodies.	Large heads; stout bills; relatively short tails. Narrower, more pointed wings than Great Kiskadee.	Streaked above and below; rusty rump and tail; dark cheek and malar stripe separated by a wide, white lower cheek.
Pitangus Great Kiskadee	9¾ in.	Slightly more slender than Great Kiskadee.	Long, rounded wings.	Yellow below with rusty wings and tail; black crown and mask are highlighted by a white supercilium and throat.

FIGURE 153. WILLOW FLYCATCHER AND ALDER FLYCATCHER (QUIZ PHOTO)
These two very similar flycatchers were listed as a single species (Traill's Flycatcher) until the 1970s. They are still very difficult to separate, with some birds still best labeled as "Traill's." Refer to the extensive ID information in the text, and try to separate these birds. Both photos were taken in mid-September in New Jersey. Answers are in the appendix, page 271.

helpful structural features and plumage details that allow the ID of some silent birds in the field if they are seen well and long enough. When compared with most other empids, Willow and Alder Flycatchers both exhibit a larger body; longer, wider tail; bigger head and bill; and longer primary projection. (Acadian Flycatcher has a similar long tail and slightly longer wings.) Much of the following information was provided by Tony Leukering.

UNCHANGING CHARACTERISTICS
BILL LENGTH AND HEAD SHAPE: While Alder Flycatcher averages a shorter bill than Willow Flycatcher, the difference is quite small. However, this bill difference is usually accentuated by the posture and crown shape differences between the two species. Willow tends to exhibit a more gently sloping forecrown than Alder, with the crown slope of Willow being uniform from the peak of the crown to the base of the bill.

Alder tends to show an angle in the crown between the peak of the crown and the bill base—a feature that is well illustrated in *The Sibley Guide to Birds*. Recognizing this feature may be difficult, however, because of the constant head feather rearrangement by empids, and it often requires extended views for you to be certain. (See Figure 153, above.)

PRIMARY PROJECTION: Alder Flycatcher has a longer primary projection than the western subspecies of Willow Flycatcher, but it is similar to that of the eastern subspecies of Willow.

MIGRATION TIMING IN THE UNITED STATES AND CANADA: In spring, Alder Flycatcher is a slightly later migrant than Willow Flycatcher (this is related to Alder's more northerly breeding range). In fall, the extensive and northerly breeding range of Alder makes for a more protracted migration that extends longer into the fall. For example, in Cape May, NJ, most "Traill's Flycatchers" seen after early September are presumed to be Alder Flycatchers until proven otherwise.

SUPPLEMENTAL CHARACTERISTICS AND NON-BBI DETAILS
CROWN–BACK CONTRAST: Alder Flycatcher generally has a darker crown contrasting with a greener back, while Willow Flycatcher typically has a paler crown and a mix of gray and olive upperparts (adults).

EYE-RING: A "Traill's Flycatcher" completely lacking an eye-ring is probably a Willow Flycatcher, while one with a complete, bold eye-ring is more likely an Alder Flycatcher, although some Willows show a thin, complete eye-ring. Most Willows have eye-rings that encircle less than 50 percent of the eye, and the vast majority of Willows with significant eye-rings have them broken in the front.

AURICULARS–THROAT CONTRAST: Alder Flycatcher tends to have dark auriculars (cheeks) that contrast more sharply with the throat than in Willow Flycatcher; this difference is stronger in juveniles than in adults.

OVERALL COLOR: Alder Flycatcher tends to be a bit greener than "Eastern" Willow Flycatcher, and is much greener than western Willow. However, both species are much duller and less green than the truly green empids (Yellow-bellied Flycatcher, Pacific-slope Flycatcher, Cordilleran Flycatcher, and Acadian Flycatcher).

Caution: These two species are so difficult to ID that a variety of factors need to be considered for every silent bird. These include age, plumage, location, date, and lighting conditions. The more features and details you use for your ID, the better your chance of getting it right.

Myiarchus Flycatchers

Myiarchus flycatchers are another group of flycatchers that are notoriously difficult to identify. While songs and call notes are diagnostic, silent birds sometimes pose major ID challenges. Comparative photos of the three most similar native species and a regular Caribbean stray are shown in Figure 154, below, with important undertail patterns depicted.

UNCHANGING CHARACTERISTICS: Great Crested and Brown-crested Flycatchers are the largest of all *Myiarchus* flycatchers (8¾ in. long). Brown-crested may appear heavier bodied and longer billed than Great Crested, and it has shorter wings, much larger feet, and a proportionally longer tail.

Ash-throated Flycatcher (8½ in. long) has a smaller head and bill and more slender overall body shape than Great Crested and Brown-crested.

La Sagra's Flycatcher is a rare but regular vagrant from the Bahamas and Caribbean Islands to Florida, with one record from Louisiana. It is smaller than all North American *Myiarchus* except for Dusky-capped Flycatcher (both species are 7¼ in. long) and has a large, bulky head and dark, bushy crest. Noticeably shorter primaries and a proportionally larger head are good structural differences to separate La Sagra's from the somewhat similar Ash-throated.

Dusky-capped (not illustrated) has a similar size and body structure as La Sagra's but has a slightly smaller, more rounded head and lacks the obvious bushy crest of La Sagra's.

SUPPLEMENTAL CHARACTERISTICS AND NON-BBI DETAILS: Great Crested Flycatcher has the brightest yellow belly and lower breast of all *Myiarchus*, and the strongest demarcation between yellow underparts and gray upper breast. Great Crested also has the most extensive rufous color to the undertail feathers, including the entire inner web of each feather, as shown in Figure 154, below. It also has dark flight feathers with crisper and more contrasting white tips and edges—especially the tertials—than other *Myiarchus*.

Brown-crested Flycatcher has fairly extensive rufous color to the undertail feathers, and it extends in a straight line from the base of each feather to the tip. Outer edges to the outer tail feathers

---

FIGURE 154. *MYIARCHUS* FLYCATCHER COMPARISON (QUIZ PHOTO)

Four species of somewhat similar *Myiarchus* flycatchers: Ash-throated, Great Crested, La Sagra's, and Brown-crested Flycatchers. Use a combination of undertail patterns, size, wing and tail length, structural features, and plumage patterns to identify these birds. Detailed ID information is provided in the text. Answers are in the appendix, page 271.

FIGURE 155. COUCH'S KINGBIRD AND TROPICAL KINGBIRD (QUIZ PHOTO)
Recent study of head and bill shapes has enabled some silent birds to be accurately identified. In a relaxed posture, a wider, flatter head and a longer, flatter bill on Tropical Kingbird differ from a smaller, higher-profile head and shorter, stockier bill on Couch's Kingbird. Can you identify these two species using these physical features? Answers are in the appendix, page 272.

show more brown shading than on Great Crested. Brown-crested's throat and upper breast are more extensively paler grayish than Great Crested's, and this extends into and blends with a paler yellow belly. Brown-crested's paler flight feathers and tertials that lack the bold white edges of Great Crested help separate these two species, as does a browner back in Brown-crested versus an olive back in Great Crested.

Ash-throated Flycatcher has a paler yellow belly than Brown-crested and Great Crested, and it blends into a grayish white breast and a whiter throat. Ash-throated has a distinctive undertail pattern, with an extensive rufous-orange inner web showing a unique dark, teardrop-shaped pattern on the lower third of the outer tail feather near the tip. This pattern is easily observed on perched birds, and reliable on all but extremely worn birds. This is a good feature to separate Ash-throated from the similar La Sagra's Flycatcher as well as the vagrant Nutting's Flycatcher, both of which have a tail pattern similar to Brown-crested's.

La Sagra's underparts have limited to almost no pale yellow color on the belly, and very short primaries that reach to only the uppertail coverts. The undertail pattern is variable, with some birds showing only about 10 percent orange-rufous color on the inner webs, and others showing color on about 70 percent of the inner web, like the bird pictured in Figure 154, p. 178. A subspecies found in Cuba

and the Cayman Islands has little to no color on the undertail feathers, especially the outer rectrices.

Dusky-capped Flycatcher (not pictured) has a size and body structure similar to La Sagra's, but fresh-plumaged birds have brighter yellow bellies and virtually no rufous-orange color on the undertail feathers, except for fresh juvenile birds in fall, which have rufous edges only. These two species do not overlap in range.

Couch's Kingbird and Tropical Kingbird

These two very similar kingbirds have traditionally been considered inseparable in the field unless they're heard calling. Recent field study has given us a few structural guidelines that are useful in separating some silent birds.

UNCHANGING CHARACTERISTICS: Some Tropical Kingbirds have noticeably longer and flatter bills than Couch's Kingbird, which has a shorter, deeper bill on average. (See Figure 155, above.) Some Tropicals, however, have small bills, making them closely resemble some Couch's with very large bills.

Head shape is a fairly reliable feature that can be used along with bill size and shape to ID some silent birds. Many Couch's have a steep forehead that rises to a proportionally rounded crown versus a shallow forehead on Tropical that extends to a flatter crown and deeper head profile from front to back. Usually this deeper head shape on Tropical corresponds to birds with a larger, more obvious bill and very forked tail, confirming ID of a Tropical.

Tail shape is another helpful feature for separating these birds. Some Tropicals have noticeably forked tails, while some Couch's can show either slightly forked tails or square-tipped tails, like the bird in Figure 155, p. 179. This feature, combined with the extremes of bill length and shape, can be used to identify a good number of silent kingbirds. Silent birds that don't exhibit extreme bill size and head shape and have slightly forked tails are best left unidentified.

Vocalizations of these two species are distinctive, with Tropical giving a rapid series of high-pitched notes that rises abruptly near the end. If you run your finger along a metallic comb from the thick teeth to the thin ones, the sound, with its trill-like quality, will resemble Tropical's call. Couch's gives a series of slower *kip-kip* notes or a plaintive, descending *queer*.

SUPPLEMENTAL CHARACTERISTICS AND NON-BBI DETAILS: Tropical and Couch's Kingbirds are essentially the same in plumage, though Tropical usually has a darker mask and greener back, but these details are variable and often not helpful.

These two families of birds have historically been grouped together because of their similar genetics and hook-tipped bills. Lifestyles and behaviors are very different, though.

SHRIKES

Shrikes prey on other songbirds, reptiles, insects, and lizards, and often impale their prey on sharp objects for later feeding.

PHYSICAL PROFILE

Northern and Loggerhead Shrikes have somewhat rounded bodies and flat backs. Their heads are large and blocky with strong, hooked bills. Broad wings and relatively long tails combine for speed and maneuverability. Many other predatory birds use sharp talons and strong feet to capture and hold prey, but shrikes do not use their thin legs and small toes with long nails to kill prey.

LOOK-ALIKE BIRDS

Northern Mockingbird is often misidentified as a shrike because of its similar plumage. The mockingbird's smaller head and bill, longer tail, and thinner, more elongated body help separate it. Both shrikes usually exhibit a more upright posture than does Mockingbird. (See Figure 156, below.)

BIRDING BY IMPRESSION INFORMATION

SIZE: Both species of North American shrikes are about the size of American Robin, with Northern Shrike (10 in. long) a bit longer than Loggerhead Shrike (9 in. long).

STRUCTURAL FEATURES: Northern Shrike has a marginally larger bill, longer tail, and slightly longer, more slender body than Loggerhead Shrike's stockier one.

BEHAVIOR: Shrikes impale their prey on barbed wire or long thorns to hold it stationary while eating, or for later dining, which earned them the nickname "butcherbirds." Northern Shrike feeds mostly on rodents and birds, while Loggerhead Shrike prefers large insects and lizards. Northern occasionally hovers while hunting.

PLUMAGE PATTERNS AND GENERAL COLORATION: Shrikes have gray upperparts and indistinct pale-barred whitish underparts, with black wings, tail, and mask. A bold white primary wing patch is obvious in flight.

HABITAT USE: Both species hunt in open spaces from elevated exposed perches, with Northern Shrike occasionally foraging in bushes and thickets. Loggerhead Shrike occurs in a variety of habitats, including deserts, suburban habitats, and open forest clearings, and frequently hunts from utility wires along roadsides.

VOCALIZATIONS: Both species give harsh, sharp call notes (*kee, kaak, shak*) and songs that include soft, catbird-like trills, chirps, squeaks, warbles, mews, and so on.

FIGURE 156. LOGGERHEAD SHRIKE AND NORTHERN SHRIKE
Note the larger, longer body and longer wings and tail on Northern Shrike (C) compared with Loggerhead Shrike (L). Loggerhead also has a broader, more extensive black mask that extends over the bill and a whiter throat that contrasts more strongly with pale gray underparts. A look-alike Northern Mockingbird (R) differs with a longer tail, more slender and attenuated body, and smaller head and bill.

COMPARISONS OF SIMILAR SPECIES

Northern Shrike and Loggerhead Shrike

Northern Shrike breeds in high northern latitudes and overlaps with Loggerhead Shrike only at the southern edge of its wintering range. Loggerhead is a mostly resident species of southern and western locations, with migratory populations in more northern areas disappearing fast. Its numbers are declining noticeably throughout its range.

UNCHANGING CHARACTERISTICS: Northern Shrike's slightly longer, more slender body, and longer wings and tail give it a more tapered overall impression than Loggerhead Shrike in both perched and flying birds. Northern also has a slightly longer bill with a strong hook at the tip compared with Loggerhead's shorter, stubbier bill with variable overlapping tip. (See Figure 156, p. 181.)

Northern tends to sit more upright when relaxed, and it has slower wingbeats and a more buoyant flight style, similar to that of Mountain Bluebird because of its longer wings and tail. Loggerhead has quicker, choppier wingbeats that are spurty in nature because of its short, rounded wings.

SUPPLEMENTAL CHARACTERISTICS AND NON-BBI DETAILS: Loggerhead Shrike averages darker gray on the upperparts, and often has less defined underpart barring than Northern Shrike. Northern has a narrower dark mask that does not extend across the forehead, and since the lores are mostly pale in Northern, the dark mask narrows in front of the eye. Loggerhead's wide black mask extends through the eye and continues to the bill, where it extends thinly across the forehead. (See Figure 156, p. 181.)

VIREOS

All vireos belong to the genus *Vireo,* and thus there are only minor differences in size, body shape, and structure. Sexes are mostly similar, except for the noticeable plumage differences of male and female Black-capped Vireos, and subtle differences in richness of head color between male and female Blue-headed and Yellow-throated Vireos.

PHYSICAL PROFILE

Vireos have fairly stocky bodies on average compared with many warblers' slender bodies. Most have relatively large, rounded heads and bulky necks, and somewhat thick, blunt, hooked bills (see Figure 157, p. 183) that differ noticeably from warblers' thinner, more pointed ones (see Figure 160, 185). Strong legs enable methodical foraging movements from branch to branch.

LOOK-ALIKE BIRDS

Female and immature Tennessee Warblers resemble Philadelphia and "Eastern" Bell's Vireos but differ by having sharply pointed bills, dark legs, and more active behavior. (See Figure 160, p. 185.) Ruby-crowned Kinglet is similar to Hutton's Vireo, but Hutton's has a thicker bill, thicker bluish legs, and lacks the black patch below the lower wing bar on Ruby-crowned Kinglet. (See Figure 174, p. 203.)

BIRDING BY IMPRESSION INFORMATION

SIZE: Fifteen species of vireos share a narrow size range of 4½ to 6¼ in. long, which is slightly larger than Ruby-crowned Kinglet on the smaller end of the scale and about the size of Song Sparrow on the larger.

While the 1¾ in. that separate the smallest and largest vireos might not seem like much, it represents an almost 30 percent size difference! Larger vireos such as Red-eyed and Black-whiskered, at 6 to 6¼ in. long, appear much larger than many smaller vireos.

STRUCTURAL FEATURES: Red-eyed, Black-whiskered, and Yellow-green Vireos have long, stocky bodies; large heads; and heavy bills, which add to their larger size impression. Blue-headed, Cassin's, Plumbeous, and Yellow-throated Vireos have large, rounded heads; thick necks; and chunky bodies, which give them a subtly different structural impression.

A few other vireos have distinctive physical features, especially Hutton's Vireo. This small, stocky vireo (5 in. long) looks like a Ruby-crowned Kinglet with its proportionally large head, "no-necked" appearance, and short wings. (See Figure 174, p. 203.) Bell's Vireo has a slender body, smallish head, and long tail and resembles Tennessee Warbler at first glance. Gray Vireo has a distinctive, very rounded head; short wings; and a long, thin tail.

BEHAVIOR: Most vireos forage and move in a deliberate fashion, often pausing between changes of location to scan for food. They regularly glean insects and larvae from the undersides of leaves, sometimes while hovering in the air. These slower movements with pauses contrast noticeably with warblers' more active, flitting behavior.

Hutton's Vireo flicks its wings like a Ruby-crowned Kinglet, while Bell's Vireo regularly bobs its tail up and down. Black-capped and Gray Vireos are active feeders, but Gray raises and whips its tail like a gnatcatcher while foraging.

PLUMAGE PATTERNS AND GENERAL COLORATION: Most vireos are typically gray or green above and

FIGURE 157. VIREOS
Three colorful vireos, *from left to right:* Yellow-throated Vireo, male Black-capped Vireo, and adult White-eyed Vireo.

white or yellowish below. A few notable exceptions are the drab, all-gray Gray Vireo and the black-hooded Black-capped Vireo. Helpful ID features include the absence or presence of wing bars, spectacles—or eye-rings—supercilia, and lateral crown stripes. All vireos have bluish gray legs and feet, which help separate them from warblers.

HABITAT USE: All species prefer some sort of vegetative cover and rarely frequent open spaces. They use a wide variety of habitats for foraging and nesting, but most are specific to one or two habitat types at all seasons. Some are partial to low, dense thickets and brush (Bell's, White-eyed, Black-capped, and Gray Vireos), while others forage high in forested treetops (Yellow-throated, Warbling, and Red-eyed Vireos). During migration, vireos use a variety of wooded and brushy habitats.

VOCALIZATIONS: Vireos often sing continuously and are also proficient mimics. They learn their songs in the months after hatching, and often pick up other birds' songs and vocalizations from their breeding area. Some have a simple series of notes repeated in either couplets or random fashion, and others involve a jumble of notes or phrases strung together in wrenlike fashion. Most vireos give an emphatic nasal call note when agitated (*cheh* or *ehhh*), and many have an emphatic, scratchy fussing call that resembles those given by wrens.

COMPARISONS OF SIMILAR SPECIES

Red-eyed Vireo and Black-whiskered Vireo
These two very similar species occur together only in south Florida from spring to fall, with Black-whiskered Vireo being the Caribbean counterpart of Red-eyed Vireo.

FIGURE 158. RED-EYED VIREO AND BLACK-WHISKERED VIREO
Red-eyed Vireo (L) is similar in appearance and size to Black-whiskered Vireo (R), but Black-whiskered has a dark malar stripe and lacks the dark sublateral crown stripes that border the gray crown of Red-eyed.

FIGURE 159. BLUE-HEADED VIREO AND CASSIN'S VIREO (QUIZ PHOTO)
ID information for separating these two difficult species is provided in the text. Try to identify these birds using the information. Answers are in the appendix, page 272.

UNCHANGING CHARACTERISTICS: These two large vireos are very similar in size and structure, although Black-whiskered is slightly larger (6¼ in. long vs. 6 for Red-eyed) and has a subtly larger bill. However, these features are hard to separate in the field with only one species in view. (See Figure 158, p. 183.)

Songs and calls are distinctly different. Black-whiskered's song is an often-repeated two- or three-note phrase separated by a distinct pause. Red-eyed sings a series of short, robinlike phrases that lack the deliberate pauses of Black-whiskered's song. Call notes differ as well, with Red-eyed giving a whiny, down-slurred, nasal *myahh,* while Black-whiskered gives a thin, unmusical *mew.*

SUPPLEMENTAL CHARACTERISTICS AND NON-BBI DETAILS: Red-eyed Vireo differs from Black-whiskered Vireo by the presence of dark, sublateral crown stripes above a pale supercilium, which are lacking in Black-whiskered. Red-eyed lacks the dark black "whisker" mark that is present along both sides of the chin in Black-whiskered. (See Figure 158, p. 183.) Red-eyed also has greener upperparts compared with Black-whiskered's olive ones.

Blue-headed Vireo and Cassin's Vireo
These two species, along with Plumbeous Vireo, were formerly considered a single species (Solitary Vireo), which accounts for the occasional field ID problems.

UNCHANGING CHARACTERISTICS: Size, body shape, and structural features are similar in these species.

SUPPLEMENTAL CHARACTERISTICS AND NON-BBI DETAILS: Bright eastern Blue-headed Vireos are distinctive, with a striking blue-gray hood, green back, bold white spectacles, and yellow-green flanks that strongly contrast with white underparts. At the western part of their range, however, some duller Blue-headed Vireos resemble the more muted plumage tones of Cassin's Vireo, which includes a grayer, less contrasting hood and less color to the flanks. (See Figure 159, above.) Some birds from this overlapping breeding zone are best left unidentified because of variation in each species.

A few plumage guidelines are helpful for separating a dull Blue-headed from Cassin's. If a bird has a bluish cast to the head, it is a Blue-headed. Cassin's has a lead gray to olive-gray head, and a greenish head in immature females. Blue-headed typically has contrasting crisp white underparts, especially along the transition line from its dark head to white throat. Cassin's has a dingy appearance to the underparts and a more blended transition between the darker cheek and whitish throat. This feature is harder to assess in some western Blue-headed Vireos, but it is a good guideline for many other Blue-headeds.

Warbling Vireo and Philadelphia Vireo
Warbling and Philadelphia Vireos nest in different habitats, but they can be found together during migration.

UNCHANGING CHARACTERISTICS: Warbling and Philadelphia Vireos are similar in size and structure. Philadelphia is slightly smaller (5¼ in. long vs. 5½ for Warbling), and has a shorter tail and more rounded head, but these differences are subtle and often hard to discern in the field. (See Figure 160, p. 185.)

SUPPLEMENTAL CHARACTERISTICS AND NON-BBI DETAILS: Both species are plain in appearance with no wing bars or outstanding field marks. A reliable field

FIGURE 160. WARBLING, PHILADELPHIA, AND BELL'S VIREOS AND TENNESSEE WARBLER (QUIZ PHOTO)

Top: These two vireos (Philadelphia Vireo and Warbling Vireo) are similar in size and structure but show different plumage patterns. Can you identify these birds? ID information is provided in the text, and answers are in the appendix, page 272. *Bottom:* Eastern Bell's Vireo and female Tennessee Warbler appear similar at first glance, but a heavier bill and a proportionally longer tail on Bell's Vireo help separate them. Try to identify these birds using this information and your field guide. Answers are in the appendix, page 272.

mark for Philadelphia Vireo is a dark line that extends through the eyes to the bill. Warbling Vireo has a blank-faced appearance, with pale lores and little to no dark eye line. Philadelphia also has a darker gray cap that contrasts with a greenish olive back. Warbling has mostly grayish green upperparts that blend with its grayish cap. (See Figure 160, above.)

Yellow underparts color and its placement are also helpful for separating these two species. Philadelphia typically has more yellow coloration to the underparts, especially in spring when many Warblings are mostly grayish overall. Some worn spring Philadelphias may not have any appreciable yellow coloration, however, and other field marks need to be noted. (See Figure 160, above.)

Problems occur with fresh-plumaged fall birds. Warbling has yellow restricted mostly to the flanks and undertail in fall, while Philadelphia is uniformly yellow below, including the central breast and throat. Philadelphia also has brighter and darker green upperparts in fall and darker primary wing coverts.

Corvids are medium-sized to large birds that possess high intelligence and a mischievous nature. They are omnivorous and range across most of North America. All species belong to the family Corvidae.

JAYS, CLARK'S NUTCRACKER, AND MAGPIES

All species in this group are gregarious and often form small to medium-sized social groups. They are wily and cunning by nature, and often try to outsmart other birds, and each other, when gathering food.

PHYSICAL PROFILE

Jays have elongated, tubular-shaped bodies, with a few species having stockier body shapes than others (Gray Jay, Pinyon Jay, and Clark's Nutcracker). Most jays have long tails, except Pinyon Jay and Clark's Nutcracker, which have short, square tails. (See Figure 161, below.)

Magpies have slender, tubular bodies, similar to those of jays. They have very long, segmented tails with much longer central tail feathers. Jays and magpies have strong, springy legs and short to medium-length, straight, pointed bills.

BIRDING BY IMPRESSION INFORMATION

SIZE: North America's eight jays and Clark's Nutcracker share a narrow size range of 10½ to 12 in. long, which is slightly larger than American Robin. Only the larger geographically isolated Island Scrub-Jay, at 13 in. long, and the now rare Brown Jay (16½ in. long), with its very long tail, occur outside these narrow size parameters.

Black-billed Magpie (19 in. long) and Yellow-billed Magpie (16½ in. long) have long measurements, but almost half of that is their very long tails; their body size is similar to that of the larger jays.

STRUCTURAL FEATURES: All jays and Clark's Nutcracker have broad, rounded wings with distinct emarginated primaries ("fingers"), which are best seen in flight. Two species of jays have prominent,

FIGURE 161. JAYS, CLARK'S NUTCRACKER, AND MAGPIES

Jays and magpies show a variety of colors and distinctive plumage patterns. *Clockwise from top left:* Green Jay, Steller's Jay, Blue Jay, Black-billed Magpie, Clark's Nutcracker, and Gray Jay. Clark's Nutcracker, like Pinyon Jay (not shown), lacks the long-tailed look of most jays.

pointed crests and slightly shorter tails (Steller's Jay and Blue Jay). Gray Jay has a bulky, rounded chest and a smaller, stubbier bill than other jays (see Figure 161, p. 186), while Pinyon Jay and Clark's Nutcracker have longer, extremely pointed bills.

BEHAVIOR: Jays often participate in mobbing behavior when raptors or other predators appear in their territories, and most are regular visitors to backyard feeders. A good number of jays and Clark's Nutcracker adapt to human presence and can be quite tame while foraging or begging for food, especially at rest stops, campgrounds, and parking lots. All but Pinyon Jay and Clark's Nutcracker hop rather than walk on the ground, with these two species opting to walk like crows when it suits them. All bounce and spring about when foraging together.

The flight of jays is strong and buoyant, with wingbeats having a circular, rowing motion. All are omnivorous and eat just about anything, including other birds' eggs and young, but nuts and seeds are a favorite food source. Magpies are especially terrestrial when foraging, and walk deliberately while searching for a wide variety of food.

Many jays are mimics, and often replicate raptor vocalizations, especially when they want to clear feeding stations of other birds.

PLUMAGE PATTERNS AND GENERAL COLORATION: Seven jay species show considerable blue plumage tones, with Gray Jay and Clark's Nutcracker having mostly gray plumage and Brown Jay (not shown) being mostly brown with a white belly. Green Jay is the oddball with its gaudy green, blue, and yellow plumage tones. (See Figure 161, p. 186.) Three species of scrub-jays (formerly one species) are somewhat similar in plumage, but all are nonmigratory and geographically separated.

Magpies have black hoods and vents, blue wings and tails, and white underparts. Bold white scapulars are obvious on perched birds, while bright white primaries with black tips are conspicuous in flying birds. The main difference between these two species is a yellow bill and yellow skin below the eye on Yellow-billed Magpie versus a black bill and dark facial skin on the slightly larger Black-billed Magpie.

HABITAT USE: Jays are ubiquitous and occur in a wide variety of habitats, including forests and other vegetated locations as well as suburban areas. A few species are specialists and found only in particular locations. Pinyon Jays are nomadic birds that occur only near pinyon pines that are producing nuts, while Clark's Nutcracker is found only in mountainous coniferous forests.

VOCALIZATIONS: Jays, magpies, and Clark's Nutcracker are noisy, vocal birds. The crested jays and scrub-jays have harsh calls that resemble loud screams or angry squawks, or a softer, clear, whistled call. Mexican, Gray, and Pinyon Jays have uncharacteristically soft calls, while Brown Jay sounds like a screaming Red-shouldered Hawk. Clark's Nutcracker has an unmusical, grating, buzzy call.

COMPARISONS OF SIMILAR SPECIES

There are no significant ID problems with jays, magpies, and Clark's Nutcracker, although the three species of scrub-jays show similar plumages. However, all are geographically separated with no chance of occurring together. Any scrub-jay seen in Florida is a Florida Scrub-Jay, and Island Scrub-Jay occurs only on the island of Santa Cruz off the California coast. Scrub-jays seen elsewhere in North America are Western Scrub-Jays.

CROWS AND RAVENS

Crows and ravens are gregarious, and typically seen in pairs or small to very large groups. Some wintering flocks may number in the thousands. They are intelligent, curious, and mischievous, and will steal food and belongings from humans at public areas, including parking lots and picnic areas. They also rob other bird nests of eggs and young.

PHYSICAL PROFILE

Crows and ravens have heavy, bulky body shapes, with crows more slender overall than ravens. They have big, blocky heads with strong, powerful bills; long, broad wings; and relatively long tails. All species have springy, powerful legs and large feet. (See Figure 162, p. 188, and Figure 163, p. 189.)

LOOK-ALIKE BIRDS

All-black grackles are smaller bodied and more streamlined than crows and have much smaller heads and bills and noticeably longer tails.

BIRDING BY IMPRESSION INFORMATION

SIZE: Four species of crows range from the Tamaulipas Crow, at 14½ in. long (slightly larger than Rock Pigeon at 12½ in. long), to American Crow at 17½ in. long, which is about the size of Red-shouldered Hawk (see Figure 7, p. 9). Chihuahuan Raven averages 19½ in. long (similar to Red-tailed Hawk), while Common Raven averages 24 in. long (slightly larger than Ferruginous Hawk).

STRUCTURAL FEATURES: While crows and ravens both have long, broad wings, ravens have longer, narrower wings; longer, heavier bills; and proportionally longer bodies. While not as bulky as ravens,

FIGURE 162. AMERICAN, FISH, AND NORTHWESTERN CROWS
While you might notice subtle differences in shape and bill structure here, all species are variable, and identification of North American crows is best done by voice. Fish Crow (C), at 15 in. long, is smaller than American Crow (L), at 17½ in. long, and typically has shorter legs and neck. Northwestern Crow (R) averages 16 in. long. Some extreme individuals are identifiable in the field by careful birders who assess familiar structural features.

crows have a more foreshortened body shape. American and Northwestern Crows have relatively short tails, while Fish Crows and Tamaulipas Crows (not shown) possess longer tails. Ravens have longer, more wedge-shaped tails than crows, a feature that is best seen on flying birds.

BEHAVIOR: Crows fly with a distinctive rowing motion, while ravens have shallower wingbeats and often resemble raptors in flight. Ravens also soar for long periods, often in the company of raptors, while crows never do. This simple behavioral difference helps identify large black soaring corvids as ravens and not crows.

Crows are some of the most recognizable birds in the world, thanks to their cosmopolitan nature and ever-present visibility. They are omnivorous and scavengers, with landfills and garbage dumps favorite places to congregate. Ravens are also scavengers and opportunistic feeders that will eat virtually anything. Common Ravens are typically seen in pairs or small groups, but winter foraging flocks may number in the hundreds.

PLUMAGE PATTERNS AND GENERAL COLORATION: Crows and ravens are all black, including their legs, bills, and feet. Chihuahuan Raven has white-based neck feathers that are visible when blown by the wind.

HABITAT USE: Crows thrive in the presence of humans and are found in urban, suburban, and rural areas. Chihuahuan Raven is a resident of arid, desert areas and dry, open grasslands with scattered trees and shrubs. Common Raven prefers hilly or mountainous areas but also inhabits a wide assortment of habitats, including tundra, grasslands, for-

ests, farmsteads, and cities. Ravens benefit from human habitation, and many nest in human-made structures in remote areas without trees.

VOCALIZATIONS: Crows give a variety of loud, hoarse calls, which are often the best way to identify some birds where two species occur. (See Comparisons of Similar Species.) Ravens have a variety of loud calls, ranging from Common Raven's deep baritone croaks and high-pitched bell-like notes to Chihuahuan Raven's higher-pitched, crowlike croaks, which can also be duplicated by Common Raven. Both ravens also give growling sounds.

COMPARISONS OF SIMILAR SPECIES

American, Fish, and Northwestern Crows

Only these three crows are seen regularly in North America, with Tamaulipas Crow being a rare summer-nesting species in the southern Rio Grande Valley in Texas. Tamaulipas might be mistaken for male Great-tailed Grackle because of its similar size, but its long wings, short tail, and dark eyes immediately set it apart. Because of variation in size and physical features in each of the three highlighted species, vocalizations and geographic range are the best ways to separate them.

UNCHANGING CHARACTERISTICS: American Crow is slightly larger than Northwestern Crow (17½ vs. 16 in. long) and flaps its wings slightly more slowly, but the two species are virtually identical in shape and structural features. Voice is the best way to separate the two species in the narrow zone where their ranges overlap in coastal Washington State and British Columbia.

American typically gives a hoarse *caw-caw-caw* call. Northwestern has a similar call that is dis-

FIGURE 163. COMMON RAVEN AND CHIHUAHUAN RAVEN (QUIZ PHOTO)
ID information for separating these two similar birds is provided in the text. Try to separate them using this information. Answers are in the appendix, page 272.

tinctly lower pitched and more nasal. A subspecies of American (*hesperis*) that occurs near Northwestern's range has vocalizations similar to those of Northwestern, and more closely resembles it in size and structure.

American and Fish Crows are very similar, and occur together in the eastern and southeastern United States. Observant birders who evaluate subtle size and structural differences can identify some birds at the extreme range of their size and structural features.

American averages larger than Fish (17½ vs. 15 in. long), and often shows longer legs, larger feet, a heavier bill, and proportionally shorter wings and tail. Smaller Fish are somewhat distinctive and appear shorter legged, stockier bodied, and thinner billed than American. Some Fish appear "no-necked" when sitting at rest. (See Figure 162, p. 188.)

Vocalizations immediately identify these two species. Fish Crow gives a short, nasal *eh*, or *eh-eh* call, which descends noticeably in pitch on the second syllable. Its throaty, rattle *grrrrr* call is higher pitched and more nasal than American Crow's. Juvenile Americans give a higher-pitched call that resembles Fish's single-note call.

SUPPLEMENTAL CHARACTERISTICS AND NON-BBI DETAILS: There are no plumage or bare-parts differences that help separate these species.

Common Raven and Chihuahuan Raven

Most ravens can be safely identified by geographic ranges or habitat preferences (see Habitat Use above), but some Common Ravens occur in Chihuahuan Raven's preferred habitats where ranges overlap.

UNCHANGING CHARACTERISTICS: Common Raven averages larger and bulkier overall than Chihuahuan Raven (24 vs. 19½ in. long) and typically has a heavier bill and shaggier neck feathers. Common also has longer, narrower wings and a longer, more wedge-shaped tail. Chihuahuan's shorter, stouter bill also has longer nasal bristles than Common's and they extend more than halfway down the upper mandible, but this feature requires fairly close views or a photo. (See Figure 163, above.)

SUPPLEMENTAL CHARACTERISTICS AND NON-BBI DETAILS: White-based neck feathers of Chihuahuan Raven versus gray ones in Common Raven are the most reliable separating features, but these are seen only in preening birds or when the wind blows the feathers.

Swallows and Purple Martin are expert aerialists that catch flying insects. Mixed flocks of swallows can be dizzying as you try to follow their quick changes of direction and swooping flights.

PHYSICAL PROFILE

Swallows and Purple Martin are generally slender with elongated bodies. They have long, pointed wings; small, rounded heads; tiny, pointed bills with wide gapes; and very short legs with tiny feet. Their tails range from short and square-tipped to long and forked. (See Figure 164, p. 191.)

LOOK-ALIKE BIRDS

In mixed flocks, or when flying alone, swifts may be mistaken for swallows because of similar insect-chasing behavior, but swifts have a choppier, less fluid flight style, and swallows have straighter wings that lack the arcing shape of swifts' wings. (See Figure 141, p. 157.)

BIRDING BY IMPRESSION INFORMATION

SIZE: Six of the swallow species share a very narrow range of 5¼ to 5¾ in. long (similar to Yellow-rumped Warbler), with Barn Swallow having a longer measurement (6¾ in. long) because of its long tail. Purple Martin is larger, at 8 in. long, which is slightly smaller than Eastern Kingbird.

STRUCTURAL FEATURES: Though size differences among swallows are minimal, differences in body structure and wing shape help separate them.

Tree Swallow's slightly larger size; stocky body; broad, angular wings; and wide, slightly forked tail are helpful features to separate it from other eastern swallows.

Bank Swallow is visibly the smallest swallow, with thinner wings and a long, narrow tail. Rough-winged Swallow has broader wings and a stockier body than Bank, but has a short, squared-off tail and long undertail coverts that cover almost the entire undertail of flying birds.

Cliff Swallow and Cave Swallow are stockier than other swallows. They have relatively broad, rounded wings; short, square tails; and broad, square heads that project noticeably in front of their wings in flight. Barn Swallows are unique with their very slender, tapered bodies; long, angular wings; and long, forked tails.

Purple Martin is the largest swallow, but the appreciable size difference may be hard to notice when it is seen flying alone. It is more robust overall with a longer neck as well as a noticeably larger head and bill. Purple Martin has longer, angular,

broad-based wings that are most similar to those of Tree Swallow, but with a proportionally much longer hand (outer wing). Its slender rear body and long tail extend farther behind the wings, and its head and long neck project farther in front of the wings than on any swallow.

BEHAVIOR: While most swallows and martins are insectivorous, Tree Swallow also eats berries, and can winter much farther north than other species. Other swallows and Purple Martin undergo some of the longest migrations of all passerines. Post-breeding and migratory behavior includes lining up on wires in large numbers and foraging in huge flocks numbering in the thousands, often with other swallow and swift species.

PLUMAGE PATTERNS AND GENERAL COLORATION: A wide variety of colors and plumage patterns occurs within this small group of birds, but most of them are distinctive enough to create only minimal ID problems. Female and juvenile Tree and Violet-green Swallows are the most similar species. (See Comparisons of Similar Species, p. 191.)

Cliff and Cave Swallows are somewhat similar in plumage, but Cliff has a whitish forehead, black throat patch, and deep orange cheek versus Cave's deep orange forehead and pale orange throat and cheek. Most swallow ID problems occur with distant birds or with compromised views when distinctive field marks are hard to see.

HABITAT USE: Swallows and Purple Martin use a wide variety of habitats. The colonial-nesting Purple Martin uses mostly human-made nest condominiums, although western birds regularly use natural cavities. Tree and Violet-green Swallows regularly use nest boxes but also use cliff crevices and natural cavities such as old woodpecker nest holes. Violet-green often uses manmade structures for nesting in suburban areas, such as pipes and holes in buildings.

Northern Rough-winged and Bank Swallows inhabit holes in sand banks, while Cliff and Cave Swallows breed colonially under human-made structures, in caves, on cliff walls, or in culverts. Barn Swallow typically builds a small mud and grass nest on ledges in or under human-made structures, such as barns or eaves of buildings.

VOCALIZATIONS: Vocalizations range from Purple Martin's sweet, liquid gurgling to Bank and Rough-winged Swallows' series of dry, repeated, scratchy notes. Tree and Violet-green Swallows give similar

FIGURE 164. SWALLOWS AND PURPLE MARTIN

Top: Male Purple Martin (L) and female Purple Martin (R). *Bottom, from left to right:* Tree Swallow, Cliff Swallow, Barn Swallow, and Rough-winged Swallow. All four of these swallows are noticeably smaller than Purple Martin. Note the stocky body shape and broad wings of Tree Swallow and Cliff Swallow. Barn Swallow has longer, more pointed wings and long tail streamers. Rough-winged Swallow shows uniform brown upperparts; a bulky body shape; long, broad, pointed wings; and a short, square tail.

sweet whistles and chirping sounds, while the other species have a mix of strung-out, disjointed squeaky or nasal notes.

COMPARISONS OF SIMILAR SPECIES

Immature and Female Tree Swallow and Violet-green Swallow

Males of these two species are distinctive because of their unique plumage color differences, but females and immatures can pose ID problems. Violet-green Swallow is the western counterpart to Tree Swallow, but both breed widely in the western United States, often in the same locations.

UNCHANGING CHARACTERISTICS: Tree Swallow is larger than Violet-green Swallow (5¾ vs. 5¼ in. long) and has a bulkier body shape, broader wings, and longer, wider tail. With good looks, these features may be noticeable, but fast-flying birds with acrobatic movements are often hard to evaluate with respect to these subtle structural differences, unless they are seen together. Both species have long, pointed wings and compact body structures.

SUPPLEMENTAL CHARACTERISTICS AND NON-BBI DETAILS: Immatures and females of both species have brownish upperparts and whitish underparts, although juvenile Tree Swallow usually has a dusky breast-band and white underparts, while juvenile Violet-green Swallow has uniformly dusky underparts. (See Figure 165, p. 192.) One of the best ways to separate females and immatures of these species is by Violet-green's white sides of the rump that extend well onto the top rump area versus Tree Swallow's small white crescents on the rump sides that do not extend noticeably onto the top of the rump. Another helpful difference is female Tree Swallow's cleaner white throat with strong demarcation to dark cheeks versus Violet-green's dusky chin that blends into dark cheeks.

FIGURE 165. TREE SWALLOW AND VIOLET-GREEN SWALLOW, FEMALES (QUIZ PHOTO)
Females of these closely related species are very similar in appearance, with a few plumage details neces-sary to separate them. ID information is provided in the text. Try to identify these birds based on this information. Answers are in the appendix, page 272.

All species in these groups are relatively small and have mostly drab plumage. Short legs and short, strong bills are other shared features.

CHICKADEES AND TITMICE

Chickadees and titmice are inquisitive, fairly to very tame, and travel in small, social groups. They are arguably responsible for entertaining more backyard birdwatchers than any other bird species.

PHYSICAL PROFILE

Chickadees have compact, rounded bodies with fairly large, rounded heads and short, sharply pointed bills. They have short, rounded wings and long tails. Titmice are more elongated and have bulkier chests than chickadees. They have distinctive crested crowns; large, blocky heads; thick necks; and broad wings and tails. Small, stocky, pointed bills and medium-length springy legs are features of all titmice. (See Figure 166, p. 194.)

BIRDING BY IMPRESSION INFORMATION

SIZE: The seven species of chickadees range from 4¾ to 5½ in. long, about the size of most warblers. Bridled Titmouse is the smallest of five titmice species, at 5¼ in. long, and Tufted Titmouse and Black-crested Titmouse are the largest, at 6½ in. long, slightly larger than Song Sparrow. Most titmice are larger than chickadees; this is especially noticeable when they are seen together in feeding flocks and groups of mobbing birds. Bridled Titmouse is the same size as Black-capped Chickadee.

STRUCTURAL FEATURES: Bridled Titmouse (not shown) has a slimmer overall structure than the other four titmice, and often appears similar to a chickadee when seen only briefly.

BEHAVIOR: Chickadees and titmice regularly mob predators, including owls, raptors, and snakes. When they encounter a predator, they scold it, and the high-pitched fussing alerts other birds to the nearby danger.

Although chickadees are essentially nonmigratory, some move south or away from higher elevations during harsh winters.

PLUMAGE PATTERNS AND GENERAL COLORATION: All chickadees have a dark cap and bib, large white cheek patch, and grayish to whitish underparts. Several species have buff to rust flanks (Black-capped, Gray-headed, Chestnut-backed, and Boreal Chickadees), and a few have brown (Boreal Chickadee) to rust backs (Chestnut-backed Chickadee).

Titmice are mostly gray and white overall. A large, dark eye surrounded by a plain, pale face influences the general impression of all but Bridled Titmouse. Bridled is distinctive, with a unique black-and-white-striped facial pattern and chickadee-like black bib. Tufted and Black-crested Titmice have orange flanks, with Black-crested showing a black central crown and crest. While Tufted has a small black forecrown, Black-crested has a white one. (See Figure 166, p. 194.)

HABITAT USE: Chickadees occur in a wide variety of habitats, from mature woodlands, desert scrub, and high mountain forests to urban parks and suburban neighborhoods. They are cavity nesters and often use old woodpecker holes or human-made nest boxes for breeding.

Oak and Juniper Titmice are found in open dry woods of the western United States, while Bridled Titmouse inhabits higher-elevation oak woodlands in southern Arizona and New Mexico. Tufted and Black-crested Titmice are found in a variety of broadleaf woodlands and brushy habitats.

VOCALIZATIONS: Black-capped, Carolina, and Mountain Chickadees have clear, whistled songs, while the other four species give a variety of short phrases, chips, and trills. Titmice give a variety of clear whistled songs and fast, scratchy, scolding calls that they often repeat when they're agitated.

COMPARISONS OF SIMILAR SPECIES

Black-capped Chickadee and Carolina Chickadee
Black-capped and Carolina Chickadees are the two most similar chickadee species. They occupy distinct but overlapping geographic regions, with Black-capped occurring in northern and central North America, and Carolina in the southcentral and southeastern United States. Their songs differ subtly and are often a reliable feature for distinguishing the two species.

In areas where the two species overlap and often interbreed, chickadees can have features of both species and sing songs that are atypical of either species. In such areas, and with some vagrants in winter, vocalizations are not helpful to their ID. This is because their songs and call notes are learned from adults rather than genetically influenced.

UNCHANGING CHARACTERISTICS: Black-capped Chickadee is larger than Carolina Chickadee (5¼ vs. 4¾ in. long), with a bigger head and longer tail. Songs

FIGURE 166. CHICKADEES AND TITMICE (QUIZ PHOTO)

Top: ID information for Carolina and Black-capped Chickadees (L and C) is provided in the text. Try to separate these birds using that information. Answers are in the appendix, page 272. A Mountain Chickadee (R) is shown for comparison. *Bottom:* Tufted and Black-crested Titmice (L and C) were formerly considered the same species but now are separate. ID information for these two species is provided in the text, page 193. Try to identify both species. Answers are in the appendix, page 272. An Oak Titmouse (R) is shown for comparison.

and vocalizations of Carolina have more notes than those of Black-capped, and are higher pitched and more rapid. If you regularly see and hear one species, structural and vocal differences are noticeable when you visit the other species' range.

SUPPLEMENTAL CHARACTERISTICS AND NON-BBI DETAILS: Plumage differences include Black-capped Chickadee's darker tail and wings with brighter white feather edges. A complete white cheek on Black-capped differs from a pale gray rear cheek on Carolina Chickadee, and a greener back with buff flanks on Black-capped is unlike the grayer back with less contrasting buff flanks on Carolina. This last feature can be unreliable, as plumage varies when feathers are worn rather than fresh. (See Figure 166, above.) Confusing birds from the overlap zone may be hybrids, and a solid ID may be hard to come by.

VERDIN AND BUSHTIT

Verdins and Bushtits are very small, active birds that inhabit a variety of low, brushy habitats.

PHYSICAL PROFILE

Verdin has a slender body shape like that of Lesser Goldfinch, with a small, rounded head; small, sharply pointed bill; short, rounded wings; and relatively long tail. Bushtit has a more compact, rounded body, similar to that of chickadees. It has a very tiny, pointed bill; large, flat-topped head; "no-necked" appearance; and very long, slender tail.

BIRDING BY IMPRESSION INFORMATION

SIZE: Verdin and Bushtit are tiny birds at 4½ in. long, which is slightly larger than Ruby-crowned Kinglet.

STRUCTURAL FEATURES: Both species have spindly but strong legs. Also see Physical Profile, above.

BEHAVIOR: Verdins are often seen alone or in pairs, while Bushtits typically forage in small to medium-sized flocks in a frenetic fashion. Groups of Bushtits move from bush to bush in unison and constantly call while gleaning insects and larvae from every part of the leaves. (See Figure 167, p. 195.) They often hang upside down while foraging.

Verdins build a large, basketlike nest in thorny vegetation, and often vocalize from within thorn thickets. They readily respond to pishing or squeaking.

PLUMAGE PATTERNS AND GENERAL COLORATION: Adult Verdin has a bright yellow head and a rust shoulder patch, but juveniles lack these distinctive field marks and can create ID confusion. Interior

FIGURE 167. VERDIN AND BUSHTIT

Top: Bushtits (L) are some of North America's smallest birds, and this photo of a foraging flock imparts their frenetic, noisy feeding behavior. These coastal Pacific birds have a brown crown (versus a gray crown on the interior subspecies), and both males (dark eyes) and females (light eyes) are shown here. A female coastal Pacific Bushtit (R) shows a distinctive long tail, small bill, and rounded crown. *Bottom:* Verdins are residents of southwest arid brush habitats. This adult female has a partial yellow head; males have a full yellow head.

Bushtits have gray caps, while coastal Pacific birds have brown ones. Male Bushtits have dark eyes, while females have pale ones. (See Figure 167, above.)

HABITAT USE: Verdins occupy dry, arid brushlands and deserts of Texas and the southwestern United States. Bushtits are birds of chaparral and open western woodlands, and are often found foraging in weedy fields and brush thickets.

VOCALIZATIONS: Verdin gives a high, piercing call and a lower-pitched strong whistle. Often a sharp, nasal *kleeu* from within dense thorny brush gives this tiny bird's presence away. Bushtit has a variety of calls, including a scraping buzz ending with several high, clear chips. It also gives a high, thin series of buzzy notes.

Wrens are mostly small, active, brownish birds. They are often heard more than seen, because of their skulking behavior.

PHYSICAL PROFILE

Wrens have narrow heads and long, slender, pointed bills (except Sedge Wren, which has a short bill). Tails range from short to relatively long and are frequently raised above the back. (See Figure 168, below.) Strong, springy legs and long toes help wrens with their foraging behavior. Wrens have variable body shapes that range from short and compact (Winter and Sedge Wrens) to longer and more tapered (Bewick's, House, and Canyon Wrens). Carolina Wren has a heavy, chunky body shape, while Cactus Wren has an elongated, rounded body.

LOOK-ALIKE BIRDS

Cactus Wren may be mistaken for a Sage Thrasher because of similarities in size and spotting on the chest. Sage Thrasher, however, is shy and retiring, while Cactus Wren is outgoing and visible and shows little to no fear of humans. (See Figure 169, p. 197.)

BIRDING BY IMPRESSION INFORMATION

SIZE: Eight species of wrens range in size from Winter Wren, at 4 in. long (similar to Golden-crowned Kinglet), to Rock Wren, at 6 in. long (slightly smaller than Song Sparrow). Cactus Wren is a larger ninth species at 8½ in. long, about the size of Gray Catbird.

STRUCTURAL FEATURES: Bewick's Wren has a very long tail compared with other wrens, and Canyon Wren (not shown) has a very long, skinny, slightly decurved bill that differs from those of other wrens. Wren tails are rounded at the tip, and they take on a wide, fan shape when birds are agitated or in flight.

BEHAVIOR: Wrens are active yet secretive birds. They skulk and creep through dense vegetation, brush piles, and rock rubble and are often heard more than seen. Winter Wren is reminiscent of a mouse when it is foraging. Most species engage in aggressive scolding behavior when agitated or threatened. Tail cocking is typical wren behavior and may occur at any time, especially when a bird is alarmed or excited.

FIGURE 168. WRENS

Clockwise from top left: Carolina Wren is the largest and bulkiest of the six species shown here. Bewick's Wren (eastern subspecies) has a long tail, brownish plumage tones, and a prominent white supercilium. Winter Wren is tiny and mouselike in habits. Sedge Wren is shy and secretive, with distinctive buff coloration. Marsh Wren (western subspecies) has a bubbling song and lives in marsh habitats. House Wren (eastern subspecies) has barred flanks and checkered wings and is the most widespread wren of all.

FIGURE 169. CACTUS WREN AND SAGE THRASHER
Sage Thrasher (L) and Cactus Wren (R). These two species are found in the same arid western habitats. They are the same size and superficially similar in appearance, but the Cactus Wren's outgoing, curious behavior differs noticeably from that of the shy Sage Thrasher, and Cactus Wren's bill is longer, heavier, and slightly decurved.

PLUMAGE PATTERNS AND GENERAL COLORATION: North American wrens have a mostly brownish plumage that is darker above and paler below. Some species or subspecies have reddish or grayish plumage tones and distinct whitish supercilia, which is helpful to their ID. Cactus Wren is unique with heavy, dark spotting below, and Canyon Wren is distinctive with a rufous belly and white throat. Other wrens are mostly unmarked below or have variable dark bars on the flanks.

HABITAT USE: Some species are exclusive to certain habitats, such as Canyon Wren near steep cliffs or rocky slopes, Cactus Wren in desert habitats with cactus or thorny shrubs, Rock Wren near talus slopes, and Marsh Wren in marshes or wet-grass habitats. Others are found in a variety of habitats throughout the year.

VOCALIZATIONS: Wren songs are varied, and range from the long, melodic songs of Winter Wren and House Wren to the grating, unmusical songs of Cactus Wren. Canyon Wren gives a mesmerizing series of cascading clear whistles, while Sedge Wren has a series of dry, staccato chips. Many wrens give a variety of harsh scold notes that range from soft and nasal to loud and raspy. These scold notes are similar to those of several other bird species, including vireos, titmice, and gnatcatchers.

COMPARISONS OF SIMILAR SPECIES

There are no serious ID challenges with wrens, although compromised views of some birds may result in an inconclusive identification. Two species that might cause a few ID problems are Carolina Wren and the eastern subspecies of Bewick's Wren.

Carolina Wren and Bewick's Wren
UNCHANGING CHARACTERISTICS: Carolina Wren is a stocky bird with a large head and thick neck. Bewick's is a slender bird with a smaller head and longer neck. The most obvious difference is the very long tail of Bewick's, which the bird constantly flips sideways, versus Carolina's shorter tail. Bewick's often resembles a sparrow as it skulks through dense brush with its long tail cocked upward. Both species have slender, decurved bills. (See Figure 168, p. 196.)

SUPPLEMENTAL CHARACTERISTICS AND NON-BBI DETAILS: Both Bewick's Wren and Carolina Wren have strong, white supercilia and brownish upperparts, though Carolina typically has more reddish plumage tones. A major difference is the strong, buff tones to Carolina's underparts versus dingy gray underparts with rust lower flanks in Bewick's. In summer and early fall, however, worn Carolinas can be quite pale and washed out underneath and more closely resemble Bewick's in plumage. Bewick's tail differs from Carolina's by being more boldly barred with distinct segmented tail feathers of various lengths, and by the speckled white corners to the three outer tail feathers.

Three pipits and one wagtail breed in North America, and one native lark species (Horned Lark) occurs almost everywhere as a breeder, migrant, or winter visitor. Eurasian Skylark (not shown) is an introduced species that has a viable population in a very small area near Vancouver, BC. Wagtails are rarely seen in North America away from the Arctic breeding sites of Yellow Wagtail, which migrates to Asia after breeding.

PHYSICAL PROFILE

Most species in this group have slender, tapered bodies except for Sprague's Pipit and Red-throated Pipit (not shown), which are slightly stockier and have rounder chests. All have small, thin, pointed bills and relatively long, spindly legs. (See Figure 170, p. 199.) Eurasian Skylark and Sprague's Pipit have short tails, while all others have proportionally long tails of varying lengths. All have fairly long, broad wings.

LOOK-ALIKE BIRDS

In migration and winter, American Pipits may be confused with streaked sparrows such as Savannah Sparrow and Vesper Sparrow, but pipits walk instead of hop, and they typically forage in open spaces instead of in the cover of tall grass and thickets that sparrows prefer. (See Figure 171, p. 200.)

BIRDING BY IMPRESSION INFORMATION

SIZE: Horned Lark and Eurasian Skylark are 7¼ in. long, which is slightly larger than White-crowned Sparrow. Sprague's Pipit, American Pipit, and Yellow Wagtail are 6½ in. long, while Red-throated Pipit is slightly smaller at 6¼ in. long, which is similar in size to Song Sparrow.

STRUCTURAL FEATURES: Fairly long legs and long toes and nails are shared features of these terrestrial birds, and unusual for most other songbirds. Wagtails have more slender bodies than pipits, and longer, thinner tails. Horned Lark's long tail is often hidden behind its long wings when it is standing, and American Pipit has the longest tail of the three pipit species. Sprague's Pipit has a stocky bill and big eye compared with the thin bills and small eyes of the other species.

BEHAVIOR: All species are ground-dwelling birds that walk deliberately while foraging. They prefer to walk away from casual danger by quickly slipping into nearby grassy areas, but faced with imminent danger they use quick, vertical escape flights, often accompanied by emphatic vocalizations.

Most pipits and wagtails wag their tails when walking, and also bob their heads like chickens. Sprague's Pipit rarely, if ever, wags its tail. All fly in a strong, undulating fashion. Some species form small to large flocks in winter, although wagtails and Sprague's Pipit are often seen alone or in very small groups.

PLUMAGE PATTERNS AND GENERAL COLORATION: Most species have brownish or sandy-colored upperparts and whitish to earth-tone underparts that blend in with their surroundings. Nonbreeding Red-throated Pipit (rare, not shown) is best distinguished from American Pipit by its heavily streaked upperparts and underparts and bold mustachial stripe. Pipits and wagtails have white outer tail feathers that are easily seen on flying birds, while Horned Lark has a dark tail with pale central tail feathers.

HABITAT USE: All species are found primarily on the ground either in open, sparsely vegetated areas or in contiguous grasslands (Sprague's Pipit). Horned Lark regularly perches on fenceposts and logs. Wagtails are birds of open spaces that frequent wetland borders and agricultural areas in winter.

VOCALIZATIONS: Eurasian Skylark has a sweet, warbling song that is famous for its liquid tones and length. Horned Lark gives a series of weak, high-pitched tinkling notes, often in flight, while pipits have songs that include a series of high-pitched jingling phrases. Flight calls of wagtails include Yellow Wagtail's vibrant, buzzy *tzeer* and Black-backed and White Wagtails' dry, staccato *jijik*. American Pipit gives a distinctive dry flight call, *pipipit*, especially when flushed. Sprague's gives a rising *squeet* call in flight and when flushed.

COMPARISONS OF SIMILAR SPECIES

American Pipit, Sprague's Pipit, and Juvenile Horned Lark

UNCHANGING CHARACTERISTICS: Sprague's Pipit somewhat resembles American Pipit in shape, but it has a more compact body structure, shorter tail, and heavier bill. American Pipit has slightly longer legs; a longer, thinner bill; and a noticeably longer tail. It is more tolerant of humans than Sprague's, and much easier to study in open spaces. Sprague's often stands upright when nervous or alarmed, with only its head and upper breast rising above the grass. (See Figure 170, p. 199.)

Sprague's creeps around in dense, grassy areas

FIGURE 170. LARKS, PIPITS, AND WAGTAILS
Birds in these three groups are terrestrial by nature, and they forage by walking deliberately while looking for insects and seeds. *Clockwise from top left:* A young male Horned Lark from southern Texas, a White Wagtail (a rare vagrant from Europe and rare nesting species in northern Alaska), breeding Sprague's Pipit, and breeding American Pipit.

and often flushes before you can get a good look. It then flies very high in a vertical fashion before spiraling back to the ground like a lead-weighted torpedo in the same general vicinity from whence it came. During these flights, it gives a distinctive loud *squeet* call that rises sharply on the last part of the long call note. American Pipit gives a familiar two-note call that resembles the pipit name (*pip-it*).

Juvenile Horned Lark somewhat resembles Sprague's Pipit in plumage but is slightly larger and has a more slender body shape; smaller bill; and noticeably longer wings and tail. (See Figure 171, p. 200.)

SUPPLEMENTAL CHARACTERISTICS AND NON-BBI DETAILS: Sprague's Pipit has a scaly back pattern versus a mostly plain, faintly streaked back on American Pipit. Most American Pipits have a dark malar stripe and cheek, which Sprague's lacks, giving it a blank-faced look. A large, dark eye in a plain face adds to Sprague's characteristic appearance. (See Figure 171, p. 200.)

American Pipit has a distinctive breeding plumage that includes warm, lightly streaked orange-buff underparts and a plain, faintly streaked back. This plumage does not resemble Sprague's strongly patterned breeding plumage. (See Figure 170, above.) Nonbreeding American Pipit has whitish

FIGURE 171. AMERICAN PIPIT, SPRAGUE'S PIPIT, AND JUVENILE HORNED LARK (QUIZ PHOTO)
ID information for separating American Pipit, Sprague's Pipit, and juvenile Horned Lark is provided in the text. Try to identify these birds. Answers are in the appendix, page 272. The bottom right bird is an Ipswich Savannah Sparrow. Note its stockier bill and shorter tail.

underparts that are usually heavily streaked, which differs from nonbreeding Sprague's mostly unstreaked flanks. Pacific American Pipits have mostly unstreaked underparts that more closely resemble those of Sprague's, but they don't occur in the same geographic area.

Juvenile Horned Lark has plumage patterns simi-lar to those of Sprague's Pipit and is often mistaken for this species in late spring and summer. Separating plumage details include juvenile Horned Lark's dark malar smudge and buff-spotted back versus Sprague's plain-faced appearance and streaked back. Another helpful difference is the black outer tail feathers and brown central tail of Horned Lark.

American Dipper and Wrentit are two species that have no relatives in North America. American Dipper is a unique aquatic passerine, while Wrentit belongs to the Old World babbler family. There are no serious ID problems with these two distinctive species.

PHYSICAL PROFILE

American Dipper has a chunky, foreshortened body that is wrenlike in structure and a short tail that is often cocked upward. Long, springy legs are well suited for its rock-hopping behavior.

Wrentit has a rounded body that tapers toward the tail, and combined features of wrens and titmice. These include a large, round head; short, stout, pointed bill; and very long rounded tail. (See Figure 172, below.)

BIRDING BY IMPRESSION INFORMATION

SIZE: American Dipper is 7½ in. long (about the size of Wood Thrush). Although it measures 6½ in. long, Wrentit is a much smaller-bodied bird since its long tail comprises almost half of its measurement.

STRUCTURAL FEATURES: American Dipper has a thick neck, large head, short wings, and a slender, narrow bill. Wrentit has short, rounded wings and a thick, short, stocky neck.

BEHAVIOR: American Dipper spends its entire life near rushing streams and rivers. It acquires food by submerging its head or body underwater, or by swimming underwater against the current. Preferred nest sites are under human-made bridges, which protect the nest from bad weather and predators—and also help birders locate nest sites during the breeding season.

Wrentit is a social creature that lives in extended family groups. It skulks through dense chaparral habitats and is usually heard before it is seen.

PLUMAGE PATTERNS AND GENERAL COLORATION: American Dipper is dark gray overall with a brownish head. Immatures lack the contrasting brown head. Wrentit is either plain brownish or grayish with a pinkish blush to its upper breast.

HABITAT USE: American Dipper is found only in and around fast-moving streams and rivers in western North America. Wrentit is a resident of chaparral and foothills from southern Washington to southern California.

VOCALIZATIONS: American Dipper gives a repeated series of high whistled or trilled phrases. Wrentit has a distinctive song of clear, popping whistles that resemble an accelerating bouncing ball.

FIGURE 172. AMERICAN DIPPER AND WRENTIT

These two species are the only representatives of their families found in North America. They have very little in common, with American Dipper (L) being an aquatic songbird that lives in fast-moving streams, and Wrentit (R) being a western species of chaparral and brushy habitats.

These two groups of birds are characterized by their very small size and active feeding behavior. All are found in a variety of habitats throughout the year.

GNATCATCHERS

Gnatcatchers are very active birds. Their constant, flitting foraging behavior is accompanied by cocking and waving of their long tails in a wrenlike fashion.

PHYSICAL PROFILE

Gnatcatchers have slender, elongated bodies with very long, thin, graduated tails. Other features include fairly large, rounded heads; thick necks; and very thin, pointed bills. (See Figure 173, below.)

BIRDING BY IMPRESSION INFORMATION

SIZE: The three species of regularly occurring gnatcatchers in North America are quite small at 4½ in. long, which is slightly smaller than House Wren. A fourth species of the same size, Black-capped Gnatcatcher (not shown), occurs rarely as a breeding species.

STRUCTURAL FEATURES: All gnatcatchers have short, rounded wings and relatively long, spindly legs.

PLUMAGE PATTERNS AND GENERAL COLORATION: Gnatcatchers have a plain, muted plumage with grayish upperparts and paler gray to whitish underparts. Important differences include undertail patterns and varying dark markings on the heads of some male gnatcatchers, especially in breeding plumage.

BEHAVIOR: During migration and winter, gnatcatchers regularly forage in small to large feeding flocks with warblers, vireos, and titmice.

HABITAT USE: Blue-gray Gnatcatcher is the most widespread of the gnatcatchers and is found in a variety of woodland habitats across much of the United States. California and Black-tailed Gnatcatchers are birds of dry, brushy desert habitats of southern California and the southwest United States. Black-capped Gnatcatcher is a very rare occasional breeder in the arid desert canyons of extreme southern Arizona near the Mexico border.

VOCALIZATIONS: Gnatcatchers have a nasal, wheezy quality to their calls and songs. California Gnatcatcher gives a nasal mewing call, while Black-tailed Gnatcatcher has a dry, hissing call similar to a harsh scolding call of a House Wren. Blue-gray Gnatcatcher sings a series of thin, wheezy notes interspersed with high chips and slurs, and has a common call of thin, nasal buzzy notes that it gives year-round.

COMPARISONS OF SIMILAR SPECIES

Blue-gray Gnatcatcher and Black-tailed Gnatcatcher

UNCHANGING CHARACTERISTICS: These two species are similar in size and behavior. Black-tailed Gnatcatcher is slightly more delicate in body structure, with a smaller, rounder head; less pointed wings; and a thinner bill.

FIGURE 173. BLUE-GRAY GNATCATCHER AND BLACK-TAILED GNATCATCHER (QUIZ PHOTO)
ID information to separate these two species is provided in the text. Try to identify these birds based on this information. Note the undertail patterns on the left and right birds to help with your ID, and the extent of the white tertial edges on the female bird in the center photo. Answers are in the appendix, page 272.

FIGURE 174. RUBY-CROWNED KINGLET AND GOLDEN-CROWNED KINGLET
A female Golden-crowned Kinglet (L) lacks the red highlights in the yellow crown that males have. Ruby-crowned Kinglet (C) has a longer bill than Golden-crowned. Male Ruby-crowned has red crown feathers that are not visible until it raises the crown feathers when excited. Female Ruby-crowned lacks red crown feathers, so this bird cannot be sexed. Hutton's Vireo (R) resembles Ruby-crowned Kinglet but has a bigger bill with a hooked tip, and lacks the dark patch below the lower wing bar near the center of the folded wing.

SUPPLEMENTAL CHARACTERISTICS AND NON-BBI DETAILS: Black-tailed Gnatcatcher differs from Blue-gray Gnatcatcher by its mostly black undertail with bold, white feather tips versus a mostly white undertail on Blue-gray. Outer tail feathers on Blue-gray are mostly white, with inner tail feathers black, but it is the outer two whitish feathers that are primarily seen on a folded undertail.

Black-tailed has more graduated tail feathers than Blue-gray, with white tips only on the graduated outer rectrices versus Blue-gray's complete white outer rectrices. Breeding male Black-tailed also has a black cap, which differs markedly from the bluish crown and thin black eye-line stripe of breeding male Blue-gray.

Nonbreeding male Black-tailed has a thin, black line over the eye, which is lacking in nonbreeding Blue-gray but present in California and Black-capped Gnatcatchers. Females are similar to each other, but differences include a pale bill and mostly whitish visible undertail on Blue-gray, and a dark bill and dark undertail with bold white spots on Black-tailed. Blue-gray of both sexes has a bolder, more complete eye-ring compared with a thinner, less prominent eye-ring in Black-tailed. (See Figure 173, p. 202.)

KINGLETS

Kinglets are tiny, active songbirds that feed mostly on insects, often hovering near the tips of leaves and branches while gleaning food.

PHYSICAL PROFILE

Kinglets have plump, rounded bodies and rounded heads, and often show a "no-necked" look. Both species have sharply pointed bills and needle-thin legs that are surprisingly strong and springy. (See Figure 174, above.)

LOOK-ALIKE BIRDS

Ruby-crowned Kinglet closely resembles Hutton's Vireo. Differences include Hutton's thick, stocky bill with hooked tip versus a very thin, pointed bill in Ruby-crowned, and the absence of a dark patch below the lower wing bar in Hutton's that is present in Ruby-crowned. Hutton's also has bluish gray legs versus Ruby-crowned's black ones. (See Figure 174, above.)

BIRDING BY IMPRESSION INFORMATION

SIZE: Kinglets are some of the smallest songbirds in North America. Golden-crowned Kinglet is 4 in. long (similar to Winter Wren), and Ruby-crowned Kinglet is slightly larger, 4¼ in. long.

STRUCTURAL FEATURES: Ruby-crowned Kinglet has a rounder, stockier chest and a more elongated appearance overall than Golden-crowned Kinglet. Ruby-crowned also has a larger, blockier head and longer bill compared with Golden-crowned's smaller, rounder head and smaller, thinner bill.

PLUMAGE PATTERNS AND GENERAL COLORATION: Both kinglets are mostly grayish olive overall. Male Ruby-crowned Kinglet has a fiery red crest that is hidden beneath gray crown feathers unless a bird is agitated or excited. Golden-crowned Kinglet's yellow (female) to golden orange (male) crown with black border is easily seen if the bird is below eye level. Like the male Ruby-crowned, the male Golden-crowned can raise its crest to reveal red feathers. Golden-crowned also has a pale face with a prominent dark eye line and malar stripe. (See Figure 174, above.)

BEHAVIOR: Ruby-crowned Kinglet often joins mixed flocks of warblers and other songbirds in migration and winter, while Golden-crowned Kinglet does not generally associate with other species. Golden-crowned gleans insects and larvae from conifer needles and from under bark.

HABITAT USE: Ruby-crowned Kinglet breeds in mature forests and is found in migration and winter in a variety of habitats, including tall-grass fields and thickets. Golden-crowned Kinglet breeds in coniferous habitats, and typically frequents conifers throughout the year. While Golden-crowned is often seen from underneath, in migration both species are often seen in large numbers feeding near or on the ground in grassy areas with scattered bushes.

VOCALIZATIONS: Ruby-crowned Kinglet has a long, warbling song and a sharp, dry call note (*jit*) that is strung together in a fussing call when agitated, similar to that of a House Wren. Golden-crowned Kinglet's song includes a rising series of high, thin notes followed by a tumbling, chickadee-like chatter. Its typical call is a high, thin buzzy note (*zree*), which may be repeated two or three times.

BLUEBIRDS, TOWNSEND'S SOLITAIRE, AND NORTHERN WHEATEAR

Birds in these three groups share a number of physical features, including the shape of the head, bill, and wings and a prominent dark eye.

PHYSICAL PROFILE

Bluebirds and Northern Wheatear have a rounded body shape, especially the undercarriage. (See Figure 175, below.) Mountain Bluebird is longer and more slender than Eastern and Western Bluebirds. Townsend's Solitaire has a more slender, elongated, gently rounded body shape.

All species have rounded heads and short, thin, pointed bills. Wings are long and rounded, and necks are short and thick. Townsend's Solitaire has a long, slender tail, while Northern Wheatear has a short tail and long legs.

FIGURE 175. BLUEBIRDS, TOWNSEND'S SOLITAIRE, AND NORTHERN WHEATEAR
Clockwise from top left: Male Mountain Bluebird, Northern Wheatear, Townsend's Solitaire, and male Eastern Bluebird.

SIZE: Eastern and Western Bluebirds are 7 in. long, which is similar to White-crowned Sparrow. Mountain Bluebird is slightly larger, at 7¼ in. long. Northern Wheatear is much smaller, at 5¾ in. long (slightly larger than Palm Warbler), while Townsend's Solitaire is 8½ in. long, similar to Gray Catbird.

STRUCTURAL FEATURES: Bluebirds' structural features are covered in Comparisons of Similar Species (below). Townsend's Solitaire structurally resembles a Northern Mockingbird but has a larger, rounder head; shorter legs; and slightly rounder body shape. (See Figure 175, p. 205, and Figure 179, p. 211.) Northern Wheatear has a compact, stocky appearance overall, with a short tail, thick neck, longer legs, and a large, blocky head.

BEHAVIOR: Bluebirds and Townsend's Solitaire regularly sit on conspicuous, exposed perches and use these vantage points to hunt insects. Mountain Bluebird often hovers while hunting insects, and drops quickly to the ground to snatch its prey. Northern Wheatear is a terrestrial species that forages in open spaces. All species also feed on fruits and berries.

Away from breeding areas, bluebirds are typically found in small foraging groups, while Townsend's Solitaire and Northern Wheatear are mostly solitary. At breeding sites, all species are found in pairs.

PLUMAGE PATTERNS AND GENERAL COLORATION: Male bluebirds range from Mountain Bluebird's mostly sky blue color to Eastern and Western Bluebirds' deep blue upperparts and orange underparts.

Male Western Bluebird has a blue head and throat, orange breast, and gray belly, while male Eastern Bluebird has a blue head, orange throat and breast, and white belly. Townsend's Solitaire is mostly gray overall with a strong white eye-ring and a bold, tawny wing stripe.

Northern Wheatear has gray upperparts, black wings and tail, and whitish underparts with a buff upper breast in breeding plumage. Breeding males have a strong black mask. Nonbreeding female and first-winter Wheatears are mostly cinnamon-buff overall with grayish upperparts. All ages and sexes have a white rump with a strong, contrasting black tail band.

HABITAT USE: Bluebirds are birds of forest edges and fields with scattered bushes. Mountain Bluebird frequents open fields and agricultural areas in winter, where it hunts either from exposed perches or on the ground. Northern Wheatear is typically found in sparsely vegetated, open spaces. Townsend's Solitaire is a bird of mountain forests in summer and foothills during winter.

VOCALIZATIONS: Bluebirds give a series of resonant whistles and dry chatters, with each species having its own distinctive pattern and tonality. Townsend's Solitaire has a long, disjointed, finchlike song and a clear, soft whistled call. Northern Wheatear has a rapid, warbling song and a weak, high-whistled call note.

COMPARISONS OF SIMILAR SPECIES

Eastern, Western, and Mountain Bluebirds, Females

UNCHANGING CHARACTERISTICS: Eastern and Western Bluebirds are similar in size and shape, with stocky

---

FIGURE 176. FEMALE BLUEBIRDS (QUIZ PHOTO)

Female bluebirds are similar in plumage, with Eastern Bluebird and Western Bluebird comparable in size, body shape, and structure. Mountain Bluebird is longer and lankier overall and has longer wings. Try to identify each species. ID information is provided in the text, and answers are given in the appendix, page 272.

bodies; large, rounded heads; and short wings and tails. Mountain Bluebird differs with its more slender body; longer wings, tail, and legs; and in its hovering behavior. However, some dull female Easterns and Westerns may be mistaken for Mountains, with structural features and wing length the best way to separate them.

The primary projection on Mountain is noticeably longer than on other bluebirds. Mountain also has a shallower forehead that slopes up to a peak on its forecrown versus a more uniformly rounded crown on Eastern and Western, but these features are subtle and require familiarity with all species to be effective. (Western and Mountain share a substantial winter range in the Southwest, and all three species occur together in winter from western Texas to New Mexico.)

SUPPLEMENTAL CHARACTERISTICS AND NON-BBI DETAILS: Female Mountain Bluebird differs from Eastern and Western Bluebirds by its mostly gray underparts compared with rusty breasts in the other two species. Sky blue wings and tail on Mountain also differ from the deeper blue coloration in Eastern and Western.

Female Eastern differs from Western by its orange breast that extends to the sides of the neck, white throat, and bright white belly versus Western's orange breast and gray throat, neck sides, and belly. Female Eastern also has more extensive rufous flanks versus mostly grayish flanks in Western, but these plumage details vary with feather wear.

Nine species of regularly occurring thrushes make up this group. Because of the similarities in the spotted thrushes, those six species are treated separately.

AMERICAN ROBIN, CLAY-COLORED THRUSH, AND VARIED THRUSH

These three species represent the largest breeding thrushes in North America. American Robin and Clay-colored Thrush, both in the genus *Turdus*, have similar physical features and foraging behavior.

PHYSICAL PROFILE

All three species have rounded bodies, especially the undercarriage. They have long, rounded wings; relatively long, springy legs; large heads; thick necks; and short, slender bills. (See Figure 177, below.)

BIRDING BY IMPRESSION INFORMATION

SIZE: American Robin is the largest in this group, at 10 in. long, with Varied Thrush 9½ in. long and Clay-colored Thrush the smallest, at 9 in. long.

STRUCTURAL FEATURES: Clay-colored and Varied Thrushes are a bit more slender than the pot-bellied American Robin. American Robin and Clay-colored Thrush have long tails, while Varied Thrush has a short tail.

BEHAVIOR: The feeding style of American Robin and Clay-colored Thrush is similar to that of plovers: run, stop, pluck. Varied Thrush is a shy bird that feeds on the ground in mature forests. Although at times it shares a similar feeding style with the other species, it is not a bird of open spaces, and prefers to forage in more secluded areas. Varied Thrush looks for worms and grubs by probing under the ground and by digging under leaf litter with its strong legs and feet. During migration and in winter, all three species supplement their diets with fruit and berries.

PLUMAGE PATTERNS AND GENERAL COLORATION: While all three of these thrushes have a degree of buff, orange, and rust to their plumage, the patterns are distinctly different. (See Figure 177, below.) American Robin is orange below and gray above, with a black head in males. Clay-colored Thrush is sandy colored below with brownish upperparts. Varied Thrush has orange underparts and supercilium and gray upperparts and tail. Its gray wings show an intricate, pale orange pattern that is striking on flying birds, and males have a strong black breast-band, which is muted gray in females.

HABITAT USE: Both American Robin and Clay-colored Thrush forage on open lawns and fields, although in south Texas, where Clay-colored now nests, it is more often found in thickets. Varied Thrush is a bird of moist, conifer-dominated northwestern forests.

VOCALIZATIONS: American Robin and Clay-colored Thrush give similar musical, whistled notes in a deliberate fashion, while Varied Thrush sings long, single notes on one pitch, like those of an off-pitch tuning fork. Call notes vary for each species.

FIGURE 177. LARGE THRUSHES

Three large thrushes, *from left to right:* American Robin, Clay-colored Thrush, and Varied Thrush.

SPOTTED THRUSHES:
Wood Thrush, Veery, Swainson's Thrush, Gray-cheeked
Thrush, Bicknell's Thrush, and Hermit Thrush

Five species of thrushes in the genus *Catharus* and Wood Thrush, in the genus *Hylocichla*, are somewhat similar in physical features, plumage, and behavior, and present consistent ID problems for birders.

PHYSICAL PROFILE

The five species of spotted *Catharus* thrushes have rounded chests and elongated rear bodies. They have fairly large, rounded heads with short, thick necks and short, thin bills. Wood Thrush differs slightly, with a bulkier body structure and a longer, stockier bill. Other shared features include long wings; somewhat longish, springy legs; and proportionally long tails. (See Figure 178, p. 210.)

BIRDING BY IMPRESSION INFORMATION

SIZE: All six of these species are noticeably smaller than American Robin, ranging from Hermit Thrush, at 6¾ in. long (similar to White-throated Sparrow), to Wood Thrush, at 7¾ in. long (slightly larger than Brown-headed Cowbird).

STRUCTURAL FEATURES: These spotted thrushes have somewhat similar structural features, so the general impression they give when standing or walking along the forest floor may be quite similar to some birders. It takes a good amount of careful study to separate them. (See Comparisons of Similar Species, right-hand column.)

BEHAVIOR: Spotted thrushes have a retiring nature and forage mainly on the ground in forested areas with a start, stop, and pluck style similar to that of American Robin. When they pause in their feeding, they stand upright like plovers. During migration and in winter, food sources regularly include berries.

PLUMAGE PATTERNS AND GENERAL COLORATION: The five *Catharus* thrushes show various shades of brown in the head, back, and tail, with some having rust tones to their plumage. Underparts consist of a whitish background with variable amounts of dark defined or diffused spots on the breast. The western subspecies of Hermit and Swainson's Thrush and Veery (not shown) appear somewhat different in plumage than their eastern counterparts. Separation of these confusing birds requires a careful review of subtle plumage differences combined with an assessment of structural differences.

Wood Thrush differs with a rusty head and nape and warm brownish rust back. It also shows heavy, dense, dark spotting on most of the underparts, and a grayish black, striated cheek patch. (See Figure 178, p. 210.)

HABITAT USE: Spotted thrushes breed in mature deciduous or coniferous forests. In migration and winter, they may be found in a variety of wooded or brushy habitats.

VOCALIZATIONS: The spotted thrushes have clear, musical songs, with some giving flutelike phrases on or near the breeding grounds. All species also give distinctive flight notes during nocturnal migration and identifying call notes in winter.

COMPARISONS OF SIMILAR SPECIES

Wood Thrush, Veery, Swainson's Thrush, Gray-cheeked Thrush, Bicknell's Thrush, and Hermit Thrush

UNCHANGING CHARACTERISTICS: Wood Thrush is noticeably larger and has a heavier body structure and larger bill than other spotted thrushes. Hermit Thrush is slightly smaller than other *Catharus* thrushes and has proportionally shorter wings and a more compact, rounded body structure. Hermit also has a regular habit of slowly raising its tail and lowering its wings after taking a few steps during feeding forays. This unique, repeated behavior is not shared by other *Catharus* thrushes (some may raise their tails after landing or stopping in place, but not repeatedly like Hermit Thrush).

Gray-cheeked Thrush, at 7¼ in. long, is slightly larger and longer winged than other *Catharus* thrushes, but these features are hard to recognize in single birds. Bicknell's Thrush is a recent species split from Gray-cheeked and is slightly smaller and has shorter wings and a smaller bill. It may appear similar to Hermit in body proportions and bill size, and in these cases would appear chunkier and more compact than the alert bird shown in Figure 178. Birds that are alert or nervous often show different body shapes and structural features, so try to assess physical features on relaxed birds.

SUPPLEMENTAL CHARACTERISTICS AND NON-BBI DETAILS: Wood Thrush differs from other spotted thrushes with its rufous upperparts and boldly spotted underparts. Hermit Thrush has a unique reddish to reddish brown tail and complete, thin, white eyering. Eastern birds have reddish brown upperparts and buff flanks, while a variety of western subspecies have brownish to gray upperparts and gray flanks. All subspecies show strong, black spotting on the upper breast and a bold, black malar mark.

Gray-cheeked Thrush differs from the similar Swainson's Thrush by its plainer gray face that

FIGURE 178. SPOTTED THRUSHES (QUIZ PHOTO)

Six species of medium-sized, spotted thrushes are a constant source of ID confusion because of similarities in plumage and variability among subspecies of Veery and Hermit and Swainson's Thrushes. Try to identify the six species shown here. ID information is provided in the text, and answers are given in the appendix, page 272.

lacks buffy tones, and by its partial whitish eye-ring with just a pale smudge in front of the eye compared with buff spectacles in Swainson's. Swainson's is similar to Gray-cheeked and the western subspecies of Veery but has distinct buff spectacles, with buff lores extending to the bill, and a slight buff wash to the sides of the neck. An olive back color sometimes resembles that of the drab western Veery, but Swainson's differs with more distinct breast spotting compared with Veery's weakly diffused upper breast spotting. Swainson's also shows more olive-colored flanks versus pale gray ones in western Veery.

Veery is similar to other *Catharus* thrushes in size and shape but typically has a warmer-colored head, face, and upperparts and more weakly spotted upper breast and throat stripe. Eastern Veery has warm, reddish brown upperparts and crown, and diffused breast streaks within a buff wash to the sides of the throat, upper breast, and lower flanks,

while western Veery has a grayer brown color that lacks any rich, reddish tones. Western Veery more closely resembles Gray-cheeked, but the spotting on the upper breast is less distinct, and it lacks the olive-shaded flanks of Gray-cheeked. Western Veery typically has plain gray flanks.

Bicknell's Thrush is similar to Gray-cheeked but has a bill with more extensive yellow color on the lower mandible (variable) and a warmer overall coloration. Warmer, reddish-toned tail and wing edging in adult birds, shown in this early May photo in Figure 178, are fairly reliable plumage features, but variability within Bicknell's and Newfoundland Gray-cheeked may cause confusion.

Both Bicknell's and Gray-cheeked have brownish red primaries and tail in fresh fall plumage. Lighting conditions also influence perception of color tones. A slightly browner cheek in Bicknell's is a helpful field mark.

These three groups of birds belong to the family Mimidae and are casually referred to as "mimids." While Northern Mockingbird is well known for its perfect replication of many other birds' songs and calls, some thrashers and Gray Catbird can also mimic other bird vocalizations, although not as accurately or consistently as Northern Mockingbird.

PHYSICAL PROFILE

All species have slender, elongated bodies and rounded chests. They have long tails, short wings, rounded heads, and strong, springy legs.

LOOK-ALIKE BIRDS

Bahama Mockingbird is a resident of the Bahamas with a handful of vagrant records from Florida since 1973. (See Figure 179, below.) It differs from Northern Mockingbird with a brownish overall color, streaks on the underparts, and a longer tail. A few of these vagrants have hybridized with Northern Mockingbird in Florida. Some thrashers may be confused with the spotted thrushes, but thrashers have much longer tails and stouter bills.

BIRDING BY IMPRESSION INFORMATION

SIZE: Eleven species range from Sage Thrasher, at 8½ in. long (about the size of Red-winged Blackbird), to California Thrasher, at 12 in. long (slightly smaller than Common Grackle).

STRUCTURAL FEATURES: Both mockingbirds, Gray Catbird, and Sage Thrasher have short, slender,

---

FIGURE 179. MOCKINGBIRDS, CATBIRDS, AND THRASHERS

Birds in this group spend most of their time on the ground or in low thickets, and all have strong legs and bills. *Clockwise from top left:* Northern Mockingbird, Gray Catbird, Crissal Thrasher, and Bahama Mockingbird.

FIGURE 180. CURVE-BILLED, BENDIRE'S, BROWN, AND LONG-BILLED THRASHERS (QUIZ PHOTO)
Look at structural and plumage differences in these four birds. ID information is provided in the text. Try to identify these birds. Answers are in the appendix, page 272.

pointed bills, while Brown, Long-billed, and Bendire's Thrashers have longer, heavier, mostly straight bills. The remaining thrashers (Curve-billed, California, Crissal, and Le Conte's) have the longest and most decurved bills of all mimids. Thrashers also have strong legs and feet, which they use for scratching the ground for food and for running quickly from danger.

BEHAVIOR: While Northern Mockingbird is a conspicuous bird that is found around human residences as well as rural areas, other species in this group tend to be a bit shier, residing in dense thickets and shrubbery. All sing from open perches during the breeding season. When alarmed or excited they raise and lower their tails. Northern Mockingbird is a fierce defender of its territory when young are fledging, and will attack pets and people who venture too close to their young.

PLUMAGE PATTERNS AND GENERAL COLORATION: Northern Mockingbird is gray above and white below, while Gray Catbird has a uniformly rich, gray plumage with a black cap and rufous vent. Brown

and Long-billed Thrashers are rufous to brownish above with heavy, dark streaking below. (See Figure 180, above.) Five species of mostly southwestern thrashers are gray to brownish in tone, with Bendire's and Curve-billed Thrashers showing diffused spots on their breasts. (See Figure 180, above.) Crissal Thrasher has the darkest rust undertail coverts of all thrashers. (See Figure 179, p. 211.)

HABITAT USE: Northern Mockingbird and Gray Catbird are cosmopolitan by nature and found in a variety of suburban to semiwild habitats. Other members of this group use many habitats, including open woodlands, thorny subtropical scrub, deserts, and Pacific coastal brushlands. Sage Thrasher uses sagebrush habitats during the breeding season.

VOCALIZATIONS: Northern Mockingbird is the king of all songbirds, with some individuals able to perfectly mimic more than 100 other bird songs and calls, usually in triplet cadence. It also mimics car alarms as well as other bird sounds, such as the wing-boom noise of a diving Common Nighthawk. Gray Catbird gets its name from the mewing sound it commonly makes. Brown Thrasher occasionally mimics other birds' vocalizations fairly well, usually in couplets. Other mimids typically give a series of original repeated phrases and notes with varied musical quality, or rough imitations of other birds' calls.

COMPARISONS OF SIMILAR SPECIES

Bendire's Thrasher and Curve-billed Thrasher

UNCHANGING CHARACTERISTICS: Bendire's Thrasher is slightly smaller than Curve-billed Thrasher (9¾ vs. 11 in. long) and has a shorter, straighter bill. (See Figure 180, p. 212.) Bendire's and Curve-billed are found in a variety of Texas and southwestern desert habitats, though Bendire's prefers more open, grassy areas, while Curve-billed is found in thorny scrub locations.

SUPPLEMENTAL CHARACTERISTICS AND NON-BBI DETAILS: Bendire's Thrasher shows small triangular breast spots versus more rounded spots on Curve-billed Thrasher. Curve-billeds from Arizona and California have blurry, diffused spots, while birds in the eastern part of the species' range—Texas and New Mexico—have more defined spots. Bendire's has paler yellow eyes compared with deeper orange eyes in Curve-billed, and often shows a pale base to its shorter, thinner bill.

Brown Thrasher and Long-billed Thrasher

UNCHANGING CHARACTERISTICS: Long-billed Thrasher has a slightly heavier body structure than Brown Thrasher and a longer bill that shows a slight downturn near the tip. Otherwise, these two species are physically very much alike. (See Figure 180, p. 212.)

SUPPLEMENTAL CHARACTERISTICS AND NON-BBI DETAILS: Brown Thrasher differs from Long-billed Thrasher by having redder tones on the upperparts and thinner, less bold streaks on the underparts. Long-billed has darker orange eyes than Brown's yellowish ones, and a longer, more decurved dark bill compared with Brown's straighter, pale-based bill. (See Figure 180, p. 212.)

All of these species are distinctive in appearance and rarely mistaken for anything else, except for Cedar and Bohemian Waxwings, which can be confused with each other. (See Figure 182, p. 215.)

PHAINOPEPLA AND WAXWINGS

These unrelated families are grouped together because of their superficial structural similarities. Phainopepla is a silky-flycatcher and represents the only species of this family in North America. Cedar Waxwing is one of the most widespread birds in North America, and occurs from the lower Canadian provinces south to Mexico and Cuba.

PHYSICAL PROFILE

Phainopepla has a long, slender body and small head with a raised rear crest, long tail, rounded wings, and short, slender bill. (See Figure 181, below.) Waxwings have more compact, rounded bodies with big, squarish heads with long rear crests; long, slender, pointed wings; very short, squared-off tails; and short, stocky bills. (See Figure 181, below.)

BIRDING BY IMPRESSION INFORMATION

SIZE: Phainopepla is 7¾ in. long, slightly larger than Brown-headed Cowbird. Cedar Waxwing is slightly smaller, at 7¼ in. long. Bohemian Waxwing is

---

FIGURE 181. PHAINOPEPLA, WAXWINGS, EUROPEAN STARLING, AND COMMON MYNA
Clockwise from top left: Male Phainopepla, European Starling, Common Myna, and Cedar Waxwing. European Starling and Common Myna are similar in size and structure, while Phainopepla is the only silky-flycatcher found in North America.

FIGURE 182. CEDAR WAXWING AND BOHEMIAN WAXWING
Cedar Waxwing (L) is smaller (7¼ vs. 8¼ in. long) and lacks the rufous-tinged face and undertail coverts of Bohemian Waxwing (R). Cedar also lacks the pale primary streaks and white spots on Bohemian's wing. Note both species in the center photo (Bohemian is the top bird).

larger, at 8¼ in. long, about the size of Red-winged Blackbird.

STRUCTURAL FEATURES: See Physical Profile, above.

BEHAVIOR: Phainopepla is a graceful bird of open woods that feeds mainly on berries, but also flycatches from exposed perches in dry, open spaces and deserts. Waxwings also flycatch for moths and insects during the summer months, but otherwise glean berries and fruit for the majority of their diet. Waxwings are social but nomadic birds that travel in small to very large flocks when not breeding.

PLUMAGE PATTERNS AND GENERAL COLORATION: Male Phainopepla is all black with red eyes and has bold white wing patches that are best seen in flight. The female is grayish with orange eyes and white edges to its wing feathers. Waxwings are elegant birds that have a combination of soft buff underparts and heads and grayish underparts. A slender, angled black mask with pale or rust borders adds a mysterious element to their appearance. Both species have varying amounts of black on their throats. (See Figure 182, above.)

HABITAT USE: Phainopepla is a bird of open mesquite brushlands, riparian woodlands, and dense mesquite thickets in the southwestern United States and California. Waxwings breed in open woodlands, with Bohemian Waxwing preferring conifer-ous habitats. Winter locations include a variety of wooded habitats that contain fruits and berries.

VOCALIZATIONS: Phainopepla gives a distinctive, low-pitched, whistled *wurp* that rises like a question near the end. Cedar Waxwing gives a high-pitched, trilled *zeeee*, while Bohemian Waxwing has a similar call that is lower pitched and more distinctly trilled than Cedar's.

COMPARISONS OF SIMILAR SPECIES

Cedar Waxwing and Bohemian Waxwing
UNCHANGING CHARACTERISTICS: Bohemian Waxwing is noticeably larger than Cedar Waxwing and has a bulkier, rounder body structure and longer wings. Because of Bohemian's heavier, rounder body, its head appears proportionally smaller than Cedar's.

SUPPLEMENTAL CHARACTERISTICS AND NON-BBI DETAILS: Bohemian Waxwing has grayish underparts and belly compared with Cedar Waxwing's pale yellow belly and warm brown chest. Bohemian also has bold, rust undertail coverts versus Cedar's white ones, and a rusty wash to its forehead and cheek versus Cedar's warm brown tone.

Bohemian has white tips to its secondary flight feathers and upperwing coverts that show up as two white patches on the wing in sitting birds, and bold yellow or whitish internal markings on its primaries. All of these obvious field marks are lacking in Cedar.

EUROPEAN STARLING AND COMMON MYNA

Both of these species were introduced from the Old World. European Starling now occupies most of temperate North America, especially around populated areas. Common Myna is an Asian species that is now well established in southern Florida.

PHYSICAL PROFILE

Both European Starling and Common Myna have stocky, compact body shapes with big, rounded heads and short, square tails. Each has a pointed bill, but European Starling's is medium length, tapered, and straight while Common Myna's is short and thick. (See Figure 181, p. 214.)

BIRDING BY IMPRESSION INFORMATION

SIZE: European Starling is 8½ in. long (about the size of Gray Catbird), and Common Myna is 9¾ in. long, slightly smaller than American Robin.

STRUCTURAL FEATURES: Both species have strong, springy legs and powerful toes that are well suited for their terrestrial foraging behavior. European Starling's wings are triangular shaped and pointed in flight, while Common Myna has broad, rounded wings.

BEHAVIOR: European Starling forms huge flocks in winter that are impressive in flight as birds twist and twirl in unison. Common Mynas are often seen in pairs and sit conspicuously on signs and other human-made structures.

PLUMAGE PATTERNS AND GENERAL COLORATION: European Starling is mostly dark plumaged with pale speckling and a glossy purple head in breeding birds. Juveniles are mostly pale grayish brown. Common Myna has a black-and-brown plumage with a bold white wing patch, yellow legs and bill, and a bold yellow crescent behind the eye.

HABITAT USE: Both species thrive around human habitation and are found near malls, parking lots, fast-food restaurants, and warehouses. European Starling can also be found around agricultural areas and near livestock pens. Both are cavity nesters.

VOCALIZATIONS: Both species are accomplished mimics and replicate a variety of bird calls and unrelated sounds. Common Myna gives loud, slurred whistles and short grating notes, while European Starling gives harsh rattling notes with high, thin whistles.

Warblers are small, mostly Neotropical songbirds that grace our woodlands with sweet songs during spring and summer months. These active songsters are favorites of birders everywhere, and a migrant fallout in spring or fall can be a magical experience.

TIPS FOR WATCHING WARBLERS

Beginning birders are often frustrated by warblers, since these birds usually don't stay in one place for very long. By the time you raise your binoculars, the warbler has disappeared.

A helpful tip for viewing warblers is to keep your binoculars raised to chin level while following a moving warbler with your eyes. As the bird moves to a new perch, quickly raise the binoculars to your eyes, which are still trained on the bird, and the warbler should be in view. This will take only a second or two, instead of three to four seconds if you have to raise the binoculars from your waist or shoulder.

It also helps to focus your binoculars on the general location where warblers are present, which saves a few more crucial seconds of focusing time.

Try to relax your focal concentration while scanning vegetation where you have heard or briefly seen a warbler, and then wait for a sudden movement to disrupt the relative stillness of the scene. Now raise your prefocused binoculars to the general area.

Keep tracking the warbler, even if you can't see it completely. Often you can build a mental picture of a warbler by combining glimpses of its body parts and behavior. With luck, it might preen or catch an insect and remain still for a minute or so.

During spring migration when birds are in breeding plumage, few birders take time to look at a warbler's physical features. Instead, they concentrate on colors, feather patterns, and songs. In the fall, most of these cues break down. Drab plumage replaces the bright colors, and songs turn into chips, but the birds still move quickly through vegetation. It now becomes more important to pay attention to general size, structure, and behavior to enable the "fall warbler" experience to be as rewarding as the spring one.

FIGURE 183. WARBLERS
An assortment of colorful warblers, *clockwise from top left:* Male Chestnut-sided Warbler, male Hooded Warbler, Painted Redstart, and male Black-throated Blue Warbler.

light, which differs from the browner overall look of Northern.

Immature Female Bay-breasted Warbler and Immature and Nonbreeding Blackpoll Warbler

UNCHANGING CHARACTERISTICS: Both species share very similar size and structural features, but Bay-breasted Warbler tends to have a heavier bill and slightly thinner and more pointed primaries.

SUPPLEMENTAL CHARACTERISTICS AND NON-BBI DETAILS: Plumage is muted and somewhat similar in immature birds. Nonbreeding adult Bay-breasted Warbler, however, has a rufous wash to the flanks, buff undertail, streaked greenish back, and a greener head. Nonbreeding Blackpoll Warbler has a grayer crown and upper back, with adults showing prominent back streaks and sparse, defined dark streaks on the upper breast. Adult Blackpoll also has yellowish to olive flanks and white undertail coverts.

Both species have dark wings and two white wing bars, but Bay-breasted tends to have darker black wings while Blackpoll's are olive. Immature Bay-breasted has an unstreaked buff to yellowish upper breast with dingy, unmarked underparts, including buff flanks and grayish white vent. Immature Blackpoll differs by showing grayish sides of the neck and a buff-yellow upper breast with diffused streaks that contrast with a whitish belly and vent. Both species have muted eye stripes and supercilia, but Bay-breast shows more prominent pale eye-arcs. (See Figure 185, p. 219.)

A helpful ID feature is the color of the feet. Bay-breasted has gray legs and feet, while Blackpoll has yellowish feet and variable yellowish legs in adults and young males. Immature female Blackpolls may have pale gray legs and dull yellow feet that have bright yellow color only on the soles.

Cape May Warbler and Pine Warbler, Immature Females

UNCHANGING CHARACTERISTICS: Pine Warbler differs by having a longer tail and much heavier bill compared with Cape May Warbler's very slender, slightly down-curved bill and short tail. Pine also has a heavier body structure versus Cape May's slender one, and shows a slightly larger head with a thicker neck and less rounded crown compared with Cape May's smaller head and sometimes peaked crown.

SUPPLEMENTAL CHARACTERISTICS AND NON-BBI DETAILS: Immature female Pine Warbler has grayish to brownish overall plumage compared with Cape May Warbler's grayish green color. Immature female Cape May typically has noticeably blurry streaks on the breast and flanks, but this feature may be reduced in some birds. (See Figure 187, p. 221.) Pine may have limited blurry streaks on the upper breast but regularly shows clean, grayish brown underparts.

Helpful plumage features include a greenish rump in Cape May versus a grayish brown rump in Pine, as well as a noticeably bolder eye-ring in Pine. Most immature Cape Mays show a yellowish crescent behind the cheek, but this feature may be subtle and hard to see on some birds unless you are looking for it. (See Figure 187, p. 221.)

Wilson's, Hooded, and Yellow Warblers, Immature Females

These three female warblers can cause consistent ID problems for birders because of possible similar plumage coloration and patterns.

UNCHANGING CHARACTERISTICS: Hooded Warbler differs from the other two species by its larger size, noticeably heavier body structure, and distinctly bigger head and bill. Wilson's Warbler differs slightly from Yellow Warbler by its minimally smaller size and longer tail, which is accentuated by its shorter wings. These structural differences are often hard to pick out on fast-moving birds. Eastern Wilson's Warblers show a smaller, more delicate bill than Yellow's, but Western Wilson's may have a bill similar to Yellow's, like the bird from Arizona pictured in Figure 188, p. 221.

SUPPLEMENTAL CHARACTERISTICS AND NON-BBI DETAILS: Immature female Wilson's Warbler differs from female Yellow Warbler by its prominent yellow supercilium and from Hooded Warbler by its olive cheek patch and pale lores. Immature female Hooded has dark lores and a yellow face framed by an olive crown and nape. Immature female Yellow has whitish edges to its tertials and primary tips; these are yellowish in Wilson's and pale in Hooded. Immature female Yellow can have a white eye-ring, while Hooded and Wilson's have a yellow one.

Wilson's and Yellow have muted yellow wing bars, while Hooded has none. A defining feature for female Hooded is the bold white tail spots that are conspicuous when the tail is fanned and flicked sideways, which is common behavior for Hoodeds. (See Figure 188, p. 221.)

Connecticut Warbler and Common Yellowthroat, Immature Females

These two species have very similar plumage but differ noticeably in structural features and behavior.

UNCHANGING CHARACTERISTICS: Connecticut Warbler is noticeably larger than Common Yellowthroat

FIGURE 186. OVENBIRD STRUTTING
Ovenbird walks instead of hops as it searches for food amidst leaf litter. This ground-nesting warbler has a unique habit of strutting in a herky-jerky fashion with its tail raised and head lowered.

FIGURE 187. CAPE MAY WARBLER AND PINE WARBLER, IMMATURE FEMALES (QUIZ PHOTO)
Muted gray fall plumage contributes to ID confusion with these two immature female warblers. ID information is provided in the text. Can you identify these birds? Answers are in the appendix, page 272.

FIGURE 188. WILSON'S, HOODED, AND YELLOW WARBLERS, IMMATURE FEMALES (QUIZ PHOTO)
Similar plumage color and patterns cause ID problems with these three immature female warblers. ID information is provided in the text. Try to identify these birds using this information. Answers are in the appendix, page 272.

TABLE 5—QUICK COMPARISON GUIDE: WARBLERS

This table follows the 2010 American Ornithologists' Union (AOU) taxonomic order. which we feel is more useful than the AOU 2012 taxonomic order for comparing similar structural features among warbler genera. The new listing breaks warblers with similar physical features into different genera based on genetic information, which is not helpful for comparing similar physical features. All popular field guides published before 2014 show older taxonomic orders, including the one that we use here, and thus this table conforms to the genus listings found in your favorite guide (at least for the short term).

Genus and Species	Size (Length)	Structural Features	Behavior	Plumage	General Habitat
Vermivora Tennessee, Orange-crowned, Nashville, Virginia's, Colima, Lucy's, Blue-winged, and Golden-winged Warblers	4¼–5 in.	Slender bodies; thin, pointed bills; short, narrow tails.	Fairly active to active while feeding; often found in mixed winter flocks.	Variable.	Variable in breeding and migration; often found in forests and forest edges in both arid and humid habitats.
Parula Tropical Parula and Northern Parula	4½ in.	Slender, compact bodies; short necks; thin, pointed, slightly decurved bills; short tails.	Active feeders; tree-tops in spring, all levels in fall and winter; often sing variable song year-round.	Greenish back patch.	Variable in breeding, migration, and winter.
Dendroica Yellow, Magnolia, Chestnut-sided, Yellow-rumped, Cape May, Cerulean, Blackpoll, Bay-breasted, Blackburnian, Kirtland's, Townsend's, Prairie, Black-throated Green, Black-throated Gray, Black-throated Blue, Palm, Golden-cheeked, Pine, Hermit, Yellow-throated, and Grace's Warblers	4¾–5¾ in.	Slender, evenly proportioned bodies; straight, thin to moderately thick bills; medium-length wings and tails.	Variable, but none are secretive or retiring. Palm is a ground feeder; most eat berries or fruit in fall migration; most are found in mixed warbler flocks.	Most have wing bars and variable flank streaking.	Variable; many are found in conifers, while others use a variety of habitats; Palm is found in small groups on open ground in fall and winter; others in variable habitats in fall and winter; Pine, Cape May, and Grace's are found mostly in conifers.
Helmitheros Worm-eating Warbler	5¼ in.	Stocky, compact body; flat head; large bill; short, broad tail.	Forages on ground, in suspended dead leaves, or in tree crotches; not shy, but inconspicuous.	Black-and-tan-striped head; brown and tan overall; buff throat.	Open, mature deciduous woods; open understory; variable in migration.
Prothonotaria Prothonotary Warbler	5½ in.	Broad, rounded body with thick neck; large head and bill; short, broad tail with long undertail coverts.	Obvious and methodical feeder; not shy; responds well to pishing and squeaking.	Brilliant golden yellow with bluish upperparts.	Cavity nester in moist, low woodlands; usually found near water.
Mniotilta Black-and-white Warbler	5¼ in.	Slender body with rounded head; long, thin, decurved bill; short, squared-off tail; long toes.	Unique, nuthatch-like creeping behavior; often creeps upside down on tree trunks or limbs.	Streaked black-and-white.	Deciduous or mixed woods; common in fall and winter in mixed feeding flocks.
Setophaga American Redstart	5¼ in.	Slender, streamlined body; small, rounded head; flat bill; long, narrow tail.	Spreads tail and droops wings while foraging; also hunts flycatcher style for insects, or drops from perch in pursuit of prey; not shy; common in feeding flocks.	Adult male is black and orange year-round; broad orange (male) or yellow (female and immature) tail base.	Open woodland; in migration and winter, a wide variety of habitats.

TABLE 5 CONT.—QUICK COMPARISON GUIDE: WARBLERS

Genus and Species	Size (Length)	Structural Features	Behavior	Plumage	General Habitat
Myioborus Painted Redstart	5¾ in.	Slender body; rounded crown with slightly peaked look; long tail.	Active and animated, with wing and tail flashing; not shy.	Male and female show similar black and red plumage and bold white wing patch; black tail has broad white edges.	Pine–oak woods in foothills and mountains of southwest U.S.
Limnothlypis Swainson's Warbler	5½ in.	Bulky body with thick neck; large, flat head; very long, pointed bill; short tail with long undertail coverts.	Secretive ground dweller; often difficult to observe; forages by shuffling through leaf litter; easiest to see in spring when singing; does not join feeding flocks.	Plain brownish overall, with paler buff, unmarked underparts.	Dense, vegetated wet woods and swamps; similar habitat in winter and migration.
Seiurus Ovenbird, Northern Waterthrush, and Louisiana Waterthrush	6 in.	Ovenbird has an elongated body with a rounded chest, thick neck, and big head; waterthrushes have long bodies with shallow, rounded heads and short tails; all three species have long legs.	Ground dwellers that walk, not hop like other warblers; Ovenbird struts when walking, with long tail sometimes cocked up; waterthrushes bob tails and crouch when walking. All three may be seen alone or with migrant and winter flocks.	Ovenbird has large, dark eye, white eye-ring, orange crown with black borders, and long tail; waterthrushes have brown upperparts, heavily streaked underparts.	Ovenbird is found on open forest floors; Northern Waterthrush prefers bogs, swamps; Louisiana Waterthrush prefers stream or river edges.
Oporonis Kentucky, Mourning, Connecticut, and MacGillivray's Warblers	5¼–5¾ in.	Heavy bodied; long legs; long undertail coverts (except MacGillivray's, which has longer tail and shorter undertail coverts).	Secretive and skulking; all have loud, ringing songs and heavy chip notes; Connecticut walks unlike other *Oporonis*, which hop; all but MacGillivray's are uncommon in migration and do not join feeding flocks.	Yellow underparts with brown to gray hoods (except Kentucky, which has a black mask); pink legs.	Found on or low to ground in dense cover; only MacGillivray's responds readily to pishing.
Geothlypis Common Yellowthroat	5 in.	Dumpy body with short neck; small bill; long, rounded tail; short, rounded wings.	Secretive but easily seen and not shy when feeding or agitated; responds strongly to pishing or squeaking; sings on open perches; joins foraging flocks in migration but not in winter.	Male and female have bright yellow throat and vent with white belly; male has black mask.	Prefers marshes and brushy or wetland habitats; forages within dense, low vegetation, often oblivious to nearby people.
Cardellina Red-faced Warbler	5½ in.	Long, slender body; small, rounded head; small bill; long tail.	Not shy; forages without reservation by gleaning insects from foliage; also flycatches for insects.	Distinctive red head with black helmet; gray back; white underparts.	Found in mixed coniferous/ deciduous southwest montane forests during breeding season.

TABLE 5 CONT.—QUICK COMPARISON GUIDE: WARBLERS

Genus and Species	Size (Length)	Structural Features	Behavior	Plumage	General Habitat
Wilsonia Wilson's, Hooded, and Canada Warblers	4¾–5¼ in.	Wilson's has a compact, rounded body with a long, thin tail and small bill; Canada and Hooded are heavier bodied with larger heads and bills.	Wilson's is a very active feeder, often flycatching for insects; Hooded and Canada are less active foragers, moving slowly through low brush; all join feeding flocks.	All-yellow underparts year-round; Canada has black necklace; male Hooded has complete hood, female has variable to no dark hood; male Wilson's has black cap.	Wilson's is usually found in dense brush near water; Canada and Hooded are in open woods with low brush cover; often low in migration.
Icteria Yellow-breasted Chat	7½ in.	Large, rounded body; big head; thick bill; long, rounded tail; rounded wings; unmistakable when seen well.	A skulker, except when male sings in spring and performs display flights; heard more than seen in winter; does not join foraging flocks.	Rich yellow chest; white lower belly and spectacles; olive upperparts.	Dense, sunny brush thickets are typical year-round habitats.
Peucedramus Olive Warbler	5¼ in.	Similar to _Dendroica_ warblers in shape; long, slender bill; heavily notched tail.	Flicks wings like a kinglet when foraging; feeds deliberately without reservation; not shy.	Male has orange head with black mask; female has yellow head with muted dark mask; bold white wing bars.	High-elevation coniferous forests in southwest U.S.; mixed oak–conifer woods in winter.

FIGURE 189. CONNECTICUT WARBLER AND COMMON YELLOWTHROAT, FEMALES (QUIZ PHOTO)
These two warblers are often mistaken for each other because of plumage similarities, but size, structural differences, and different motion immediately separate them (Connecticut walks; Common Yellowthroat hops). ID information is provided in the text. Try to identify these birds using that information. Answers are in the appendix, page 272.

(5¾ vs. 5 in. long) and is bulkier overall with a larger head, thicker neck, and bigger, heavier bill. Connecticut also has longer wings and very long undertail coverts that extend well onto the underside of its tail. Common Yellowthroat has short wings and undertail coverts. Connecticut differs greatly with its deliberate walking motion and very large feet, while Common Yellowthroat does not walk but hops and has noticeably smaller feet. (See Figure 189, above.)

SUPPLEMENTAL CHARACTERISTICS AND NON-BBI DETAILS: Immature female Connecticut Warbler has a brownish hood with a whitish to buffy throat and pale yellow underparts, while female Common Yellowthroat has a brownish head, yellow throat, and dingy buff to gray underparts with brownish flanks. Females of both species have a complete bold white eye-ring.

These medium-sized songbirds add a splash of color and sweet songs to the forest or brushy locations they inhabit.

TANAGERS

Tanagers are slow-moving, colorful songbirds of forests and forest edges. Often tanagers are seen in the forest canopy, where they sing in spring and summer.

PHYSICAL PROFILE

Tanagers have elongated bodies with rounded chests. Hepatic and Summer Tanagers have large heads and stout bills, while Western and Scarlet Tanagers have smaller, rounded heads and shorter, thinner bills. All have relatively broad, rounded wings. (See Figure 190, p. 226.)

LOOK-ALIKE BIRDS

The all-red Summer Tanager might be mistaken for a Northern Cardinal, but it lacks the prominent pointed crest and black facial pattern of Northern Cardinal. (See Figure 190, p. 226.)

BIRDING BY IMPRESSION INFORMATION

SIZE: Four species of regularly occurring tanagers range in size from Scarlet Tanager, at 7 in. long (similar to White-crowned Sparrow), to Hepatic Tanager, at 8 in. long (slightly smaller than Gray Catbird).

STRUCTURAL FEATURES: Western (not shown) and Scarlet Tanagers are more diminutive overall than Hepatic and Summer Tanagers, and have slightly shorter tails. See Comparisons of Similar Species, right-hand column, for structural differences between Hepatic and Summer Tanagers.

BEHAVIOR: Tanagers often sit still while scanning for bees and other insects. Despite their bright colors, they can be very hard to locate among the leaves. Tanagers also glean fruit and berries from trees and shrubs.

PLUMAGE PATTERNS AND GENERAL COLORATION: Summer and Hepatic Tanagers vary in plumage by sex, with males red and females yellowish buff. Male Western and Scarlet Tanagers are very different in breeding plumage from their respective females, but nonbreeding males and females have somewhat similar plumages. Immatures more closely resemble nonbreeding adult females because their wings are not black like those of adult males.

Male Hepatic and Summer have similar reddish plumage color, but Hepatic differs by having a dark cheek and grayish wash to its back, wings, and flanks. Male Western differs from other tanagers by having a red head that contrasts strongly with a yellow body and black wings, tail, and back. All Westerns differ from other tanagers by having distinct wing bars.

HABITAT USE: Scarlet Tanager is a resident of mature eastern deciduous forests, while Summer Tanager is found in mixed woodlands and has a more southerly and western range. Hepatic Tanager is a resident of southwestern mountainous pine–oak forests, while Western Tanager resides in a variety of wooded habitats in the western United States.

VOCALIZATIONS: Tanager songs include a series of deliberate, musical notes that somewhat resemble an American Robin's song, but without the deliberate pauses between notes. Call notes are distinctive for each species.

COMPARISONS OF SIMILAR SPECIES

Summer, Hepatic, and Scarlet Tanagers, Females
UNCHANGING CHARACTERISTICS: Hepatic Tanager has a large, blocky head that lacks the rounded rear crown of Summer Tanager, which can show a peak in the rear when excited or stressed. Hepatic also has a somewhat stockier bill with a distinct notch on the lower border of the upper mandible about halfway to the tip that is lacking in Summer. Scarlet Tanager has a shorter, thinner, more pointed bill in comparison, and a smaller, more compact, rounded body shape with a more diminutive rounded head. (See Figure 191, p. 227.)

SUPPLEMENTAL CHARACTERISTICS AND NON-BBI DETAILS: Female Hepatic Tanager has grayer lores, cheeks, and crown than female Summer Tanager, and a dark gray bill with paler lower mandible compared with Summer's overall pale bill. Hepatic also has grayish flanks and a contrasting yellow throat compared with Summer's overall yellowish underparts. Scarlet Tanager has more lemon-colored underparts with contrastingly dark wings and an overall olive-green crown and back.

FIGURE 190. TANAGERS, NORTHERN CARDINAL, AND PYRRHULOXIA

Tanagers are colorful songbirds of mature forests. Northern Cardinal and Pyrrhuloxia are birds of thickets and scrub habitats. *Clockwise from top left (all males):* Summer Tanager, Pyrrhuloxia, Northern Cardinal, and Scarlet Tanager. The especially rounded body shape and raised crown feathers on the Summer Tanager are a result of this bird resting and conserving energy during migration. All birds respond to this stress by fluffing their feathers.

FIGURE 191. SUMMER, SCARLET, AND HEPATIC TANAGERS, FEMALES (QUIZ PHOTO)
Female Summer, Scarlet, and Hepatic Tanagers are somewhat similar in size, shape, and coloration but show subtle structural and plumage differences. ID information is provided in the text. Can you identify these species? Answers are in the appendix, page 272.

FIGURE 192. NORTHERN CARDINAL AND PYRRHULOXIA, FEMALES
Female Northern Cardinal (L) is mostly buff colored with an orange bill; reddish wings, tail, and crest; and distinctive black border to its bill. Female Pyrrhuloxia (R) differs by its shorter, more rounded, grayish-yellowish bill and grayish overall plumage. It also has a more pointed crest.

NORTHERN CARDINAL AND PYRRHULOXIA

Northern Cardinal is one of the most widely known birds in North America, even to nonbirders. Pyrrhuloxia shares a south-central/southwest range with Northern Cardinal, but it has more muted plumage features and a few physical differences.

PHYSICAL PROFILE

Both species slightly resemble tanagers, with elongated bodies and rounded chests. They have short, heavy, conical bills; long, pointed crests; and broad, rounded wings. (See Figure 190, p. 226.)

BIRDING BY IMPRESSION INFORMATION

SIZE: Northern Cardinal and Pyrrhuloxia are similar in size at 8¾ in. long, which is about the size of Red-winged Blackbird.

STRUCTURAL FEATURES: See Comparisons of Similar Species, p. 228.

BEHAVIOR: Northern Cardinal tends to be less shy than Pyrrhuloxia and is a frequent visitor to backyard feeders. Both species sing from open perches during the breeding season.

PLUMAGE PATTERNS AND GENERAL COLORATION: Male Northern Cardinal is one of the most recognized birds in North America with its bright red plumage and black facial mask. Male Pyrrhuloxia is mostly cool gray overall with rosy red face, crest, chin, and central breast. (See Figure 190, p. 226.) Females are discussed in more detail under Comparisons of Similar Species, below.

HABITAT USE: Pyrrhuloxia is a bird of dry, arid, brushy habitats in southern Texas and extreme southwestern United States. Northern Cardinal frequents thickets and forest edges with open spaces in many of the same locations as Pyrrhuloxia, as well as most of the eastern half of the United States.

VOCALIZATIONS: Northern Cardinal and Pyrrhuloxia have similar, loud, clear whistles and sharp, flat call notes.

COMPARISONS OF SIMILAR SPECIES

Northern Cardinal and Pyrrhuloxia, Females

Females of these two species are superficially similar, but a few physical and plumage differences allow for a fairly easy ID. Juveniles are more similar, so structural differences are more useful for identifying them.

UNCHANGING CHARACTERISTICS: Female Pyrrhuloxia differs from female Northern Cardinal by its shorter, more rounded bill and more pointed crest compared with Northern Cardinal's shorter, bushier crest and longer, more slender bill. (See Figure 192, p. 227.)

SUPPLEMENTAL CHARACTERISTICS AND NON-BBI DETAILS: Female Northern Cardinal is mostly buff colored with an orange bill that has a distinctive black border and with reddish wings, tail, and crest. Female Pyrrhuloxia has a grayish overall plumage with less red in the wings and tail. It has a reddish crest tip and grayish yellow bill. Juvenile Pyrrhuloxia is mostly gray, while juvenile Northern Cardinal has browner upperparts and buff-orange underparts.

These two groups of birds range from small (buntings) to medium-sized (grosbeaks), and have strong conical bills that are well suited for cracking open seeds and nuts.

PHYSICAL PROFILE

Black-headed and Rose-breasted Grosbeaks have identical heavy, stocky bodies with big, blocky heads; large, conical bills; broad, rounded wings; and relatively short tails. Blue Grosbeak shares a similar bill and wing shape but is more slender overall with a slightly rounded chest; a smaller, rounded head; and a long, rounded tail.

Buntings have slender to stocky body shapes with rounded chests; small, rounded heads; small, conical bills; and broad, rounded wings. (See Figure 193, below.)

BIRDING BY IMPRESSION INFORMATION

SIZE: The three regularly occurring grosbeaks range from Blue Grosbeak, at 6¾ in. long (similar to White-throated Sparrow), to Black-headed Grosbeak, at 8¼ in. long (slightly smaller than European Starling). Four species of buntings are all sparrow sized at 5½ in. long.

STRUCTURAL FEATURES: See Physical Profile, left-hand column, for grosbeaks. Detailed structural information on the four species of buntings is in Comparisons of Similar Species, p. 230.

BEHAVIOR: Grosbeaks are typically slow-moving and relatively shy, while buntings are more conspicuous. Buntings often sing from open perches during the breeding season.

PLUMAGE PATTERNS AND GENERAL COLORATION: Adult male Black-headed and Rose-breasted Grosbeaks are distinctive in plumage and pose no ID problems. Females and immatures can be similar in plumage (see Comparisons of Similar Species). Male Blue Grosbeak is also distinctive and differs

FIGURE 193. GROSBEAKS AND BUNTINGS

These two bird groups are composed of colorful males and muted females. *Clockwise from top left (all males):* Blue Grosbeak, Painted Bunting, Indigo Bunting, and Black-headed Grosbeak.

from Indigo Bunting by its bold rufous wing bars and black facial border. (See Figure 193, p. 229.) Adult male buntings are also distinctive in plumage, whereas the plain-colored females and immatures can be problematic and are described in detail in Comparisons of Similar Species, right-hand column.

HABITAT USE: Black-headed and Rose-breasted Grosbeaks prefer mature forests, while Blue Grosbeak is a bird of thickets with scattered trees. Buntings are found in weedy and brushy areas, often near wooded edges.

VOCALIZATIONS: The two large grosbeaks sing warbled whistles. Black-headed Grosbeak's song is faster, higher-pitched, and choppier than Rose-breasted Grosbeak's song, which sounds like a fast American Robin song that lacks the obvious pauses between phrases. Blue Grosbeak sings a fast, jumbled warbling song, similar to Purple Finch's. Call notes are strong and metallic in tone and are distinctive for each species. Buntings sing a variety of slow to fast warbling songs, with some species giving deliberate, repetitive phrases. Call notes are similar, but slight differences help the trained ear separate them.

COMPARISONS OF SIMILAR SPECIES

Black-headed Grosbeak and Rose-breasted Grosbeak

UNCHANGING CHARACTERISTICS: Structural features are identical in these two species.

SUPPLEMENTAL CHARACTERISTICS AND NON-BBI DETAILS: Nonbreeding adult female Black-headed Grosbeak and first-winter male Rose-breasted Grosbeak are similar in plumage, but Rose-breasted typically shows more streaking on the center of a buff-colored breast and has pink versus yellow underwing linings. Rose-breasted also has a uniformly pale pinkish bill, while Black-headed's is bicolored—light gray on the lower mandible and darker on the upper mandible. Black-headed also has darker head markings on average. (See Figure 194, below.)

Nonbreeding female Rose-breasted and dull-plumaged female Black-headed are also similar in plumage, but Rose-breasted has more distinct streaking on the underparts, especially the breast center, and more uniformly whitish underparts, while female Black-headed has buff-tinged underparts. Black-headed female has lemon yellow underwing linings, while female Rose-breasted has buff-yellow ones.

FIGURE 194. BLACK-HEADED GROSBEAK AND ROSE-BREASTED GROSBEAK (QUIZ PHOTO)
Immature male Rose-breasted Grosbeak can have a plumage similar to that of nonbreeding female Black-headed Grosbeak. ID information for separating these birds is provided in the text. Try to identify these birds. Answers are in the appendix, page 272.

FIGURE 195. FEMALE AND IMMATURE BUNTINGS AND FEMALE BLUE GROSBEAK (QUIZ PHOTO)
Four species of female or immature buntings and female Blue Grosbeak. Detailed ID information is given in the text. For an expert-level quiz, try to identify the five species in this photo. Two photos are of the same species but different-aged birds, and two birds show remnants of juvenile plumage (streaks) on the underparts. Answers are in the appendix, page 272.

Female and Immature Buntings and Female Blue Grosbeak

Occasionally buntings will hybridize and complicate the ID process, and these birds are best left unidentified. The most common hybrids occur between Lazuli and Indigo Buntings.

UNCHANGING CHARACTERISTICS: All four species of buntings are a similar size (5½ in. long) and have somewhat similar structural features. Indigo and Lazuli Buntings are the most similar, and their structural differences are hard to discern without careful comparison of both species. All exhibit a big-eyed look that is accentuated by dark eyes and plain, unmarked faces.

Lazuli Bunting averages longer winged and longer tailed than Indigo and has an overall more slender, tapered appearance. Indigo has shorter wings and tail, a slightly heavier bill, a more chest-heavy body structure, and a slightly larger, blockier head. Take care when evaluating female and immature Lazulis that are fluffed up because of cold weather, as these birds may appear larger and bulkier than normal, and may more closely resemble Indigos in structure.

Immature and female Painted Buntings have similar structural features as Lazuli and Indigo, but differ with a slightly longer bill that has a more curved culmen (top of the upper mandible). Varied Bunting differs from other buntings by having a stockier, heavier bill with a curved culmen, a more rounded body shape, and a shorter primary wing projection. Its slightly larger head is another helpful structural feature.

Female Blue Grosbeak is larger (6¾ in. long) than buntings and has a noticeably bigger head and a much larger, heavier bill.

SUPPLEMENTAL CHARACTERISTICS AND NON-BBI DETAILS: IMMATURE AND FEMALES: Lazuli Bunting has a slightly different plumage color and pattern from other buntings. It is slightly grayer overall, with two distinct whitish to buff wing bars. The young Lazuli in Figure 195, above, shows traces of juvenile plumage in this early August photo, but most immature birds away from breeding areas don't show these juvenile streaks on the underparts and have a plainer overall appearance.

Adult female Lazuli shows a buff wash to the upper breast, and a grayish brown belly and head. Bluish tail color is shared by female and immature Lazulis and adult female Indigo Bunting. Immature male Lazuli is somewhat similar to adult females in first-winter plumage. Breeding adult female Indigo is browner overall with a whitish throat, streaked chest, and indistinct dark malar stripe.

Immature Indigo has two pale, indistinct buff wing bars and a cinnamon wash on the breast in first fall plumage. Nonbreeding female Indigo has indistinct, blurry streaks on the breast, while immature Lazuli has some blurry streaks only until late summer. (See Figure 195, p. 231.)

Female and immature Painted Buntings have uniformly greenish upperparts and dull grayish buff underparts, with immature males brighter on the crown and upperparts than females. The juvenile Painted photographed in early August in Figure 195, p. 231, is grayer than older juvenile birds, with only slight greenish feathering on the upperparts. A bold white eye-ring and lack of definitive wing bars are helpful plumage details.

Female and immature Varied Buntings show a more uniformly drab, brownish gray plumage than other buntings and lack the pale tertial fringes of both Lazuli and Indigo. The worn female photographed in early August in Figure 195, p. 231, is duller than fresh-plumaged birds in fall and winter.

Female Blue Grosbeak is similar in plumage to female Indigo and Lazuli Buntings but differs by having dark wings with a broad, buff median wing covert patch. Immature Blue Grosbeaks in fall and winter have a rich rufous-brown plumage that differs from that of all buntings except some especially rich, warm-plumaged immature Indigos.

These two unrelated seed-eating birds somewhat resemble buntings and finches.

PHYSICAL PROFILE

Dickcissel has a stocky body with a rounded chest; large head; strong, conical bill; broad, rounded wings; and short tail. White-collared Seedeater has a compact, rounded body with a proportionally large, rounded head that gives it a "no-necked" look. It has short wings and tail and a stubby conical bill with a curved culmen. (See Figure 196, below.)

BIRDING BY IMPRESSION FEATURES

SIZE: Dickcissel is 6¼ in. long, similar to House Sparrow. White-collared Seedeater is 4½ in. long, slightly larger than Ruby-crowned Kinglet.

STRUCTURAL FEATURES: See Physical Profile.

BEHAVIOR: Dickcissel is a nomadic species that breeds in a variety of central U.S. locations. White-collared Seedeater is fairly easy to see in most of its range, throughout Central and South America, but often difficult to see in the tall-grass habitat it prefers in the Lower Rio Grande Valley of Texas.

PLUMAGE PATTERNS AND GENERAL COLORATION: Adult male Dickcissel, like the one in Figure 196, below, is distinctive with bold rust wing patches, yellow eyebrows and breast patches, and a black V-shaped collar. Some molting birds show only an undefined black patch on the throat. The plumage of first-winter females resembles that of House Sparrows. (See Figure 197, p. 234.)

Adult male White-collared Seedeater has a unique plumage that poses no ID problems. Females are mostly grayish brown overall and similar to female buntings, but their very small size and stubby bill immediately separate them as seedeaters. (See Figure 196, below.)

HABITAT USE: Dickcissel occurs in grassy or weedy fields with nearby brush. White-collared Seedeater frequents dense grass near patches of tall cane in a small area near the Mexico border in south Texas.

VOCALIZATIONS: Dickcissel sings a series of short, dry, insectlike notes that phonetically resemble its name. Call note is a hard, dry *chek*. Flight call is a memorable buzz that is reminiscent of a popular imitation of flatulence, achieved by vibrating a protruding tongue. White-collared Seedeater has a sweet song similar to Yellow Warbler's, and variable rising, husky call notes.

COMPARISONS OF SIMILAR SPECIES

Immature Female Dickcissel and Female House Sparrow

UNCHANGING CHARACTERISTICS: These two species are identical in size (6¼ in. long) and have somewhat similar structural features. Dickcissel is more slender overall with a proportionally longer bill and more pointed wingtips. House Sparrow typically shows a larger, puffier head shape. (See Figure 197, p. 234.)

FIGURE 196. DICKCISSEL AND WHITE-COLLARED SEEDEATER
These two species don't really fit cleanly into any taxonomic bird group, but straddle the lines between buntings, finches, and blackbirds. *From left to right:* Adult male Dickcissel, adult male White-collared Seedeater, and adult female White-collared Seedeater.

FIGURE 197. IMMATURE FEMALE DICKCISSEL AND FEMALE HOUSE SPARROW (QUIZ PHOTO)
These two species are the same size (6¼ in. long) and somewhat similar in overall plumage, body structure, and bill shape. ID information is provided in the text. Try to identify these two birds. Answers are in the appendix, page 272.

SUPPLEMENTAL CHARACTERISTICS AND NON-BBI DETAILS: Dickcissel has a narrower, yellow supercilium (tan on House Sparrow) that does not broaden past the eye, and also extends to the bill in front of the eye, unlike on House Sparrow. Dickcissel shows a white lower eye-arc and fine streaks on the flanks, which House Sparrow lacks. A spotted crown on Dickcissel differs from a plain, drab brown crown on House Sparrow. Upperpart shading and markings on immature female Dickcissel are grayer and less boldly patterned than on House Sparrow.

All four groups included here belong to the family Emberizidae. Species in these groups are ground-dwelling, often shy birds that have a mostly brownish plumage and short, conical bills. Some male towhees and longspurs have colorful plumage patterns.

TOWHEES

Towhees have larger bills and heavier bodies than other members of these groups. Their heads are noticeably larger as well.

PHYSICAL PROFILE

Towhees have robust bodies with rounded chests. They have fairly large, rounded heads; thick necks; long tails; and short, pointed, conical bills. (See Figure 198, below.)

BIRDING BY IMPRESSION INFORMATION

SIZE: Five of North America's six towhees are noticeably larger than sparrows, and range from Spotted and Eastern Towhee, at 8½ in. long (slightly smaller than Red-winged Blackbird), to Abert's Towhee, at 9½ in. long (slightly smaller than American Robin). Green-tailed Towhee is 7¼ in. long (slightly larger than White-crowned Sparrow).

STRUCTURAL FEATURES: Green-tailed Towhee differs from other towhees by its slender body shape, and it more closely resembles a large sparrow. See Table 6, p. 241.

BEHAVIOR: Towhees frequent brushy areas, where they noisily scratch the ground with their feet in search of seeds and insects. Flight is usually low to the ground, with several flaps alternating with short glides.

PLUMAGE PATTERNS AND GENERAL COLORATION: Towhees are fairly distinctive, with somewhat similar plumage only between Eastern and Spotted Towhees, and between Canyon and California Towhees. However, the similar species in these pairs

FIGURE 198. TOWHEES

Towhees are members of the family Emberizidae. *Clockwise from top left:* Male Eastern Towhee, Abert's Towhee, Green-tailed Towhee, and Canyon Towhee.

are geographically separated. Spotted has white spotting on its back and wings that are lacking in Eastern, and Canyon has a rusty cap, buff throat with spotted necklace, and pale lores and eye-ring that are lacking in California.

Only Spotted and Eastern show differences between males and females, with males having a black head and wings while females have grayish brown (Spotted) to brown (Eastern) head and upperparts. Green-tailed Towhee has a distinctive mix of colors and gray shading (see Figure 198, p. 235), while California, Canyon, and Abert's Towhees all show a muted gray-brown plumage with brownish orange undertail coverts.

HABITAT USE: Towhees frequent dense brush in a variety of different habitat types, including deserts, foothills, open woodlands, and forest edges.

VOCALIZATIONS: Towhees are vocal birds that sing a variety of songs composed of whistled notes, trills, and accelerated chip notes. Call notes are distinctive for each species.

SPARROWS

Sparrows are the birds responsible for the popular phrase "little brown jobs," or LBJs. Their predominately brown plumage, small size, and mostly shy nature create ID problems for many birders, although recent attention to differences in size and structure have eased some of this confusion.

TIPS FOR VIEWING SPARROWS

The best way to find sparrows is to look for them in appropriate habitats, especially fields and brushy areas. While this may sound overly simple, it is because sparrows can be secretive and easily overlooked, especially in winter. Large feeding flocks in fall and winter may contain many species, providing great opportunities for direct comparisons of similar sparrows.

Initial encounters with sparrows can be unnerving. Many birders have painful memories of small, brown, ground-hugging birds disappearing into dense grass or brush at the slightest noise or disruptive movement. Typical comments include "They all look the same!" and "How will I ever get a good look at these birds?" A good starting point is to become familiar with species you might see before venturing into the field.

MINIMIZE YOUR PRESENCE IN THE FIELD: Wear muted, earth-tone clothing to minimize your presence, and take your time. Walk slowly and quietly through the grass, stopping often to allow sparrows to get used to your presence. Keep your binoculars raised to your chin when stalking sparrows, so you don't lose precious time raising your binoculars; sparrows need only a few seconds to slip away.

When sparrows flush, watch their retreat to a general area. Then scan the bushes or grass tops for perched birds. After a while, they usually return to the ground a bit farther away and begin feeding again. Now approach them slowly and repeat the process.

COAXING SPARROWS TO YOU: After locating sparrows and positioning yourself for good looks, try quietly "pishing" or "squeaking" to get them to perch in the open. "Pishing" is done by pushing air through a narrow opening in your lips with a short air burst using the letters "pssh." Squeaking is accomplished by pressing your lips on the back of your hand and drawing air into your mouth in short bursts, which creates a high, squeaking sound. Both of these sounds mimic birds' distress calls and often cause sparrows to come out of cover to see what the fuss is about.

Another way to view sparrows is to place some bird seed near the edge of a thicket or woodland. If sparrows or other seed-eating birds are present, they will soon venture into the open near the edge to feed. This simple strategy works well during spring and fall migration, and even better during winter, when sparrows have established feeding territories. After a few days, even shy birds come to feed with the group.

PHYSICAL PROFILE

Sparrows have a variety of body shapes, from compact and rounded to elongated and slender. All have short, conical bills of varying thicknesses and strong legs and feet. (See Figure 199, p. 237.) Members of each genus share a fairly consistent variety of structural features. See Table 6, p. 241.

LOOK-ALIKE BIRDS

A number of unrelated species resemble sparrows.

Red-winged Blackbird, female: This bird is often mistaken for a sparrow because of its heavily streaked appearance and pointed bill. Larger than most sparrows, it walks (not hops) on the ground and forms large flocks in swamps, marshes, and wetlands. (See Figure 207, p. 246.)

Indigo Bunting, female and immature: This sparrowlike bunting feeds in brushy fields alongside sparrows, but it has a heavy, conical bill and flies strongly with a characteristic buzzy call when flushed. It also calls when perched, often in the open. (See Figure 195, p. 231.)

Bobolink, female and immature: This small blackbird with sparrowlike streaking has a large, blocky head and pointed wings, and flies strongly

FIGURE 199. SPARROWS

These four sparrows belong to different genera, and show differences in body shape and structural features. *From left to right:* Breeding Golden-crowned Sparrow, nonbreeding Swamp Sparrow, "Large-billed" Savannah Sparrow, and Grasshopper Sparrow.

when flushed, often with a distinctive, metallic *bink* call note. (See Figure 207, p. 246.)

House Finch, female (and other finches) (see Figure 216, p. 256): The muted gray- to brown-streaked plumage of some female finches resembles that of sparrows, but most finches differ by having a heavy, conical bill with a curved culmen, and the habit of perching in high, open branches for long periods. Flight and ground calls are also different.

House Sparrow, female (see Figure 197, p. 234): This introduced European weaver finch is a common species in North America, and resembles typical sparrows in size and appearance.

BIRDING BY IMPRESSION INFORMATION

SIZE: The 35 species of North American sparrows (including juncos) range in size from Grasshopper, Le Conte's, Henslow's, and Nelson's Sharp-tailed Sparrows, at 5 in. long (similar to American Goldfinch), to Harris's Sparrow, at 7½ in. long (similar to Brown-headed Cowbird).

Smaller sparrows appear truly diminutive when seen next to the larger ones, with size differences of up to 40 percent. After you've spent some time comparing several different-sized sparrows, you'll have a sense of sizes of various species, even in a brief sighting.

STRUCTURAL FEATURES: After noting distinctive structural features of different sparrows, such as the size and shape of the bill, tail, and head, you should be able to place many sparrows into genus by comparing these shared features. Even birds that fly away can often be narrowed down to a few possible species because of distinctive structural features, such as short, spiky tails versus long, rounded ones, and big, blocky heads and bills versus small, rounded heads and small, pointed bills.

BEHAVIOR: Sparrows are ground-dwelling birds that range from being somewhat tolerant of human presence to being very shy. Most sing on open perches during the breeding season, and many species respond to "pishing" and "squeaking" during migration and in winter.

Sparrows in the same genus often share certain behaviors, and these behaviors and the birds' movements can be helpful clues to their identification. (See Table 6, p. 241.) For example, sparrows in the genus *Ammodramus,* such as Le Conte's, Baird's, and Henslow's, are very shy and often hard to see, and run like mice through the grass during their escapes.

Others have distinct flight styles when flushed. Sparrows in the genus *Melospiza* (Song, Lincoln's, and Swamp) fly low when flushed from tall grass. They also briefly cock their tails upward and hold their wings against their bodies for a split second during these short escape flights, which adds a recognizable, repeated pause to the overall flight impression and an up-and-down motion to their tails.

Song Sparrow does this regularly and is the easiest to observe engaging in this behavior because of its long, broad tail and slow, deliberate escape flight. The flight style of Lincoln's Sparrow is not as obvious as Song's during these flights, and it often flies low and fast to get away. Swamp Sparrows often resemble small, dark, flying mice as they dive into grassy cover during low escape flights.

Savannah Sparrow also has a distinctive flight style when flushed. It flies a good distance in a fast, direct fashion, often twisting its body from side to side during the flight. Recognizing this flight style is helpful, since Savannah often sprints away right after landing.

Juncos are generally tame and easily viewed throughout the year, especially when they form large flocks in winter and feed in open spaces, including at backyard feeders. They often fly as a group into nearby tree cover or dense thickets when flushed instead of running on the ground or diving into tall grass. Vesper Sparrow also regularly flies into tall trees or shrubs during its escape flights, and often sits in the open after landing.

PLUMAGE PATTERNS AND GENERAL COLORATION: Most sparrows share a muted, earth-tone plumage of brown, gray, and rust, and some have dark streaks on the upperparts and underparts. A handful of sparrows have rich orange color on their heads and breasts. Eastern Fox Sparrow differs with its rich, rusty overall plumage. Adult juncos are easy to recognize with their gray to black hoods and upperparts, and white bellies.

HABITAT USE: Sparrows are found in a wide variety of habitats, including grasslands, woodland borders, deserts, open spaces, and foothills. Most prefer thickets, tall grasses, or thorny scrub habitats.

VOCALIZATIONS: Sparrows sing a wide variety of songs that include musical notes, trills, staccato chips, and dry hissing sounds. Many species have distinctive calls and chip notes. *Zonotrichia* sparrows (White-crowned, White-throated, and Golden-crowned) sing songs, or variations of them, throughout the year, while some species, such as Song and Fox Sparrows, may start to sing their spring songs on warm, late-winter days.

COMPARISONS OF SIMILAR SPECIES

Cassin's Sparrow and Botteri's Sparrow
UNCHANGING CHARACTERISTICS: Cassin's Sparrow typically has a smaller, shorter bill and averages a longer tail than Botteri's Sparrow, but these features are often hard to assess and not so obvious in the photo comparison in Figure 200, below. Both occur together in extreme southern Texas, southwestern New Mexico, and southeastern Arizona. Bot-

teri's has a very limited range in these areas, while Cassin's occurs widely from southern Texas and southeastern Arizona north to Colorado and Kansas. Songs and vocalizations are often the best way to reliably separate some birds where their ranges overlap.

SUPPLEMENTAL CHARACTERISTICS AND NON-BBI DETAILS: Cassin's Sparrow has a finely streaked brownish crown, while the crown of Botteri's Sparrow is dark and reddish. Cassin's also has distinctive dark, subterminal markings on upperpart feathers (lacking in Botteri's) and clean, pale edges on tertials and wing coverts. Cassin's has sparse streaks on the lower flanks, while Botteri's has clean, buff-colored flanks. The buff color on the face of Cassin's in the photo in Figure 200, below, is because of fresh plumage, and may be found on some Botteri's. The worn Botteri's was photographed in August, and the fresh Cassin's in February.

Clay-colored, Chipping, and Brewer's Sparrows
Breeding plumage for these three species is fairly distinctive, but immature and winter-plumaged birds pose ID problems.

UNCHANGING CHARACTERISTICS: These three sparrows in the genus *Spizella* are mostly similar in size, body shape, and structure, though Brewer's Sparrow has a slightly smaller bill and smaller rounded head. Clay-colored Sparrow averages smaller and smaller-billed than Chipping Sparrow, and more closely resembles Brewer's.

FIGURE 200. CASSIN'S SPARROW AND BOTTERI'S SPARROW (QUIZ PHOTO)
You'll need to look at subtle plumage differences to separate these species, with a few structural differences in the bill and tail also useful in separating them. ID information is provided in the text. Buff color on the face on this Cassin's is due to fresh plumage, and may occur on some Botteri's, but not on this worn bird. Try to identify these birds. Answers are in the appendix, page 273.

FIGURE 201. CLAY-COLORED, CHIPPING, AND BREWER'S SPARROWS (QUIZ PHOTO)

All of these sparrows in the genus *Spizella* have a number of similar plumage and structural features. Try to identify these similar birds in nonbreeding plumage. ID information is provided in the text. Answers are in the appendix, page 273.

SUPPLEMENTAL CHARACTERISTICS AND NON-BBI DETAILS: Chipping Sparrow differs from the other two species with its dark versus pale lores, gray versus brownish to buff rump, and muted malar and submustachial stripes versus bold in Clay-colored Sparrow and very thin but defined in Brewer's Sparrow. Nonbreeding adult Chipping has a reddish-toned crown, but first-winter birds like the one in Figure 201, above, show no red at all. Fall and winter Chippings have overall darker upperparts with chestnut tones versus buff and tan upperparts in the other species, although early first-winter Chippings can have upperparts closer in shading to those of Clay-colored and Brewer's.

Clay-colored shows the boldest dark malar stripe and submustachial markings that highlight a pale malar region, and has the strongest pale median crown stripe as well. Clay-colored typically shows warmer buff-toned underparts in fall and winter; a broader, pale supercilium; and a more contrasting gray nape. A dark lower border to a tan cheek immediately separates Clay-colored from Chipping, which has a grayish brown cheek that lacks a dark lower border.

In fall and winter, Brewer's is more similar to Clay-colored than to Chipping, but differs with a streaked nape versus gray nape in Clay-colored, grayish versus whitish submustachial region, and plainer, more subdued facial pattern with an indistinct median crown stripe versus a bold one in Clay-colored. Brewer's also has grayish buff underparts compared with Clay-colored's warm ones.

Song, Lincoln's, and Savannah Sparrows

UNCHANGING CHARACTERISTICS: Song Sparrow is the largest of these three species (6¼ in. long vs. 5¾ in. long for Lincoln's Sparrow and 5½ in. long for Savannah Sparrow) and has a noticeably rounder head; heavier, more conical bill with curved culmen; and longer, rounded tail, which it often cocks upward in short escape flights. (See Behavior, p. 237.)

With its shorter tail and tinier bill, Lincoln's gives a more delicate first impression than Song. Relaxed Lincoln's typically show a more peaked rear crown than the other two species, but the bird in Figure 202, below, is alert and shows a rounded crown like that of Song.

Savannah differs by having a thinner body structure, smaller head and bill, and noticeably shorter, notched tail than both Song and Lincoln's. The

FIGURE 202. SONG, LINCOLN'S, AND SAVANNAH SPARROWS (QUIZ PHOTO)

These three sparrows have somewhat similar plumage patterns and sizes. ID information is provided in the text. Can you identify these birds? Answers are in the appendix, page 273.

FIGURE 203. NELSON'S SHARP-TAILED SPARROW AND LE CONTE'S SPARROW (QUIZ PHOTO)
These two sparrows in the genus *Ammodramus* are similar in size and share some structural features and plumage patterns. Try to identify these birds using the ID information provided in the text. Answers are in the appendix, page 273.

shorter tail is noticeable in flight, and combined with a distinctive direct, twisting flight style helps quickly identify Savannah.

SUPPLEMENTAL CHARACTERISTICS AND NON-BBI DETAILS: All three species have brownish gray upperparts with rust color interspersed, and whitish to buff underparts that contain variable dark streaks and a central breast spot. Some helpful plumage differences include Lincoln's buff central crown stripe and upper breast versus whitish on Song and Savannah, and a yellowish supercilium in Savannah versus gray on Lincoln's and whitish on Song. Lincoln's has a noticeably grayer face than the other two species, especially the supercilium.

Savannah and Lincoln's both have finer streaks on the upper breast versus denser, blurrier streaks on the upper breast and belly of Song. Lincoln's also has a streaked rather than whitish throat, and a buff eye-ring versus white on Song and Savannah. All three can show a dark central breast spot, but Song's is usually larger and bolder. The plumage details for Savannah Sparrow do not include the "Ipswich" and "Belding's" subspecies.

Le Conte's Sparrow and Nelson's Sharp-tailed Sparrow

These two small sparrows (5 in. long) in the genus *Ammodramus* are both secretive away from breeding areas, and often allow only short glimpses before they disappear into dense grass. Saltmarsh Sparrow can be similar to Nelson's Sharp-tailed

Sparrow in appearance and structure, and the differences noted here for Nelson's can be applied to Saltmarsh as well.

UNCHANGING CHARACTERISTICS: While superficially similar to Le Conte's Sparrow, Nelson's Sharp-tailed Sparrow differs with its uniformly rounded head versus Le Conte's flat forecrown and rear peaked crown. Nelson's also has a more elongated body with a rounded chest versus Le Conte's more compact, rounded body. Nelson's has a longer bill compared with Le Conte's somewhat conical, pointed bill. (See Figure 203, above.)

SUPPLEMENTAL CHARACTERISTICS AND NON-BBI DETAILS: Nelson's Sharp-tailed Sparrow has a broad, gray crown stripe bordered by thin black lines versus Le Conte's Sparrow's brownish black streaked crown with a thin, whitish median stripe. Nelson's also has a broad, gray nape, while Le Conte's has a streaked nape with purplish lines. Nelson's has distinct white lines on its back versus straw-colored "cornrows" on Le Conte's back. (See Figure 203, above.)

LONGSPURS AND BUNTINGS

Four species of longspurs (Chestnut-collared, Lapland, McCown's, and Smith's) and three species of buntings (Snow, McKay's, and Lark) are specialists in habitat preference and lifestyles. Away from breeding areas, they form small to large flocks in open spaces.

TOWHEES

Genus and Species	Size (length)	Body Shape and Structure	Plumage	Behavior	Habitat
Pipilo Eastern, Spotted, Canyon, Abert's, California, and Green-tailed Towhees	7¼–9½ in.	Robust body shapes; blocky heads; short wings; long tails; stout feet.	Unstreaked brown or colorful plumage.	Somewhat shy, but sometimes seen foraging in the open.	Dense brush dwellers; noisily scratch for food.

SPARROWS

Genus and Species	Size (length)	Body Shape and Structure	Plumage	Behavior	Habitat
Arremonops Olive Sparrow	6¼ in.	Heavy body shape; short wings; long bill.	Plain grayish and unstreaked below; olive above.	Secretive and hard to see, except when singing in spring; often runs on ground.	Dense patches of thorny brush or tall grass.
Aimophila Cassin's, Rufous-crowned, Botteri's, Bachman's, Rufous-winged, and Five-striped Sparrows	6 in. on average	Fairly stocky body shapes; short, rounded wings; long, often rounded tails; variably short to long, heavy bills.	Unmarked, grayish underparts, except Five-striped, which has dark gray underparts with dark central spot.	Cassin's, Botteri's, and Bachman's are secretive, except when singing; others are less shy.	Variable, from open spaces with brushy areas to rocky, brushy hillsides.
Spizella Black-chinned, Field, American Tree, Chipping, Clay-colored, and Brewer's Sparrows	5½–6¼ in.	Slim body shapes; small, rounded heads; long, thin, slightly forked tails; small bills.	Adults have unstreaked underparts with variable amounts of buff and rust; Black-chinned has gray underparts and head.	Loose flocks in fall and winter; not secretive; often perch in plain view (except Black-chinned).	Most prefer open, brushy habitats; Black-chinned is also found in chaparral.
Pooecetes Vesper Sparrow	6¼ in.	Rounded body shape; long, notched tail; relatively small bill.	White eye-ring; strong double mustache pattern.	Small, loose flocks in fall and winter; not secretive; flushes into nearby trees and perches in the open.	Prefers open fields and pastures, often near trees.
Chondestes Lark Sparrow	6½ in.	Long, slender shape; long, rounded tail.	Bold head pattern; white-edged tail.	Not secretive; feeds in open spaces; forms flocks in winter; perches in open when flushed.	Lawns, fields, open woods, agricultural areas, mixed grasslands.
Amphispiza Sage, Bell's, and Black-throated Sparrows	5–6 in.	Long tails; pointed wings; small bills.	Strong, distinctive facial patterns; unstreaked underparts.	Sage and Bell's run on ground with tail raised; Black-throated is not shy, and forms small winter flocks.	Deserts with bare open ground; sagebrush deserts; coastal chaparral.
Passerculus Savannah Sparrow (about 6 subspecies)	5½ in.	Elongated, slender body; pointed wings; short, notched tail; small bill; "Ipswich" is slightly larger, bulkier, and larger headed with thicker neck; Large-billed is stockier, chestier, with much heavier bill.	Streaked on back and breast.	Ground feeder; not secretive, but inconspicuous; flight is low and twisting; runs on ground after landing.	Variety of open country habitats; grassy fields, beaches, farms, marshes, etc.

PHYSICAL PROFILE

Longspurs and buntings have fairly stocky bodies with rounded chests. Most species have fairly large, round heads; short, thick necks; and small, pointed conical bills. (See Figure 205, p. 244.) Lark Bunting, however, has a noticeably heavier bill, similar to that of a grosbeak. Longspurs and buntings have long, broad wings and short tails, although Chestnut-collared Longspur has shorter wings and Smith's Longspur a longer tail than other longspurs.

SPARROWS continued

Genus and Species	Size (length)	Body Shape and Structure	Plumage	Behavior	Habitat
Ammodramus Baird's, Henslow's, Seaside, Nelson's Sharp-tailed, Saltmarsh, Grasshopper, and Le Conte's Sparrows	5–6 in.	Compact body shapes; large heads; short wings; short, spiky tails.	Variable; some with distinctive buff or orange on head and breast.	Six species are secretive, with three of them (Baird's, Henslow's, and Le Conte's) being very secretive; hard to flush; many run like mice when threatened; Seaside is fairly easy to see in marsh grass habitats.	Four are in wet grasslands (Le Conte's, Nelson's Sharp-tailed, Saltmarsh, and Seaside); three are in dry grasses.
Passerella Fox Sparrow (4 geographically distinct subspecies)	6–7 in.	Stocky body shape; long wings; large, round head; large, conical bill.	Eastern subspecies is rusty; western is sooty colored; all are heavily marked below with central breast spot.	Sometimes hard to find in dense brush; responds well to pishing; sings on exposed perches; often sits still in open when alarmed.	Dense brush thickets with open areas; chaparral, brush piles, wet woods; feeds on ground.
Melospiza Lincoln's, Swamp, and Song Sparrows	5¾–6¼ in.	Short, rounded wings; long, rounded tails; Song is stocky and round-bodied with medium-length bill and longer tail; Swamp and Lincoln's are smaller and less robust with shorter tails, smaller, pointed bills, and smaller heads.	Streaked above and below; Swamp has rust on upperparts and plain gray underparts; Lincoln's has buff wash to face and breast; Song has bolder streaking below.	Song is widespread and the most visible of the three; often nests in backyards; Swamp and Lincoln's are shier but usually respond to pishing.	Song is found in any open, weedy, brushy habitat; others are found in grassy, weedy areas, often near water.
Zonotrichia White-crowned, White-throated, Golden-crowned, and Harris's Sparrows	6¾–7½ in.	Heavy bodied; long tailed; wings proportionally short; medium-length, conical bills.	All have striking crown or head markings.	Not very shy; all respond to pishing; fly to open bush when flushed, and often easily seen.	Brushy areas, swamps, open woods, hedgerows, backyard feeders.
Junco Yellow eyed Junco and Dark-eyed Junco (6 subspecies): "Oregon," "Pink-sided," "White-winged," "Slate-colored," "Red-backed," and "Gray-headed"	6¼ in.	Slender, compact body shapes; rounded heads; long tails; small, pointed bills.	Cleanly marked with hooded appearance; white to grayish bellies; variable white to color-shaded flanks; bold, white outer tail feathers.	Form small to large winter flocks; feed in open areas near wood line; not secretive or shy; common at feeders.	Breed in coniferous woods; common in open woods and brushy clearings in migration and winter.

LOOK-ALIKE BIRDS

Nonbreeding and female longspurs resemble sparrows, but distinctive tail patterns, behavior, and open-country habitat preferences help separate them. Nonbreeding and female Lark Buntings also resemble sparrows but are slightly larger and differ from sparrows in structure, voice, and plumage.

BIRDING BY IMPRESSION INFORMATION

SIZE: Chestnut-collared and McCown's Longspurs are 6 in. long, while Smith's and Lapland Longspurs are 6¼ in. long (similar to Song Sparrow). McKay's and Snow Buntings are slightly larger, at 6¾ in. long, while Lark Bunting is 7 in. long.

STRUCTURAL FEATURES: McCown's Longspur differs from other longspurs with its heavy, stocky body; large, squarish head with flat crown; very thick neck; short tail; and larger, heavier bill. Smith's and Lapland Longspurs are slimmer overall than McCown's and Chestnut-collared, and have smaller, rounder heads and longer tails. Chestnut-collared is our smallest longspur and has a short tail and wings and a small bill. (See Figure 205, p. 244.)

McKay's (not shown) and Snow Buntings have

FIGURE 204. FEMALE AND NONBREEDING LONGSPURS AND BUNTINGS (QUIZ PHOTO)
Nonbreeding and female longspurs and buntings resemble sparrows but have different structural features and plumage (see text). Shown here are a breeding female longspur and bunting and two nonbreeding longspurs. For an expert-level quiz, try to identify these birds. Look at structural features and plumage details to separate them. Answers are in the appendix, page 273.

identical structural features and very long wings. Lark Bunting has a larger, thicker conical bill and a bigger, broader head than longspurs and other buntings.

BEHAVIOR: All species are birds of open spaces, including short-grass prairies, overgrazed pastures, fields, beaches, and tundra. Because of their open-country habits, where they are more exposed to wind, weather, and a variety of predators, all are shy and frequently explode into flight at the slightest disturbance.

PLUMAGE PATTERNS AND GENERAL COLORATION: Breeding males and females of longspurs and buntings show distinctly different plumages. Breeding male longspurs are more colorful overall, and have more prominent, contrasting dark and light markings than breeding females. Breeding male Snow and McKay's Buntings are whiter overall than females, which have smudgy head markings and dark-streaked backs. Breeding male Lark Buntings, with their all-black plumage and bold white wing patches, differ greatly from breeding females, which have streaked plumage. Nonbreeding and immature buntings show subtle plumage differences from each other. (See Figure 204, above.)

VOCALIZATIONS: Songs given on breeding grounds include a variety of liquid, melodic, warbling phrases. Lark Bunting sings liquid, whistled notes interspersed with rattled notes. Flight calls are distinctive to each species and are helpful with the ID of flying birds.

LONGSPURS

Genus and Species	Size (length)	Body Shape and Structure	Plumage	Behavior	Habitat
Calcarius Lapland, McCown's, Smith's, and Chestnut-collared Longspurs	6–6¼ in.	Long, pointed wings; relatively short bills; McCown's and Chestnut-collared are stockier with short tails; Lapland and Smith's are slender with long tails.	Strongly dimorphic in breeding plumage, with males colorful and more boldly patterned than females.	Terrestrial; form large flocks in winter; nervous by nature; hard to approach in open spaces; feed on ground.	Barren open ground; pastures; short, dry grass; fields; beaches.

BUNTINGS

Plectrophenax and Calamospiza Snow and McKay's Buntings	6¾ in.	Chunky body shapes; rounded heads; long wings; short, notched tails; small, pointed bills.	Large, white wing patches.	Form large flocks in winter away from tundra breeding grounds; can be either tame or nervous.	Barren open ground; fields; beaches; tundra.
Calamospiza Lark Bunting	7 in.	Elongated, stocky body; bulky head; short tail; short, rounded wings; large bill.	Bold, white wing patch; male is all black in breeding plumage; female resembles "typical" sparrows.	Conspicuous on breeding grounds; forms large flocks in winter.	Arid grassy or brushy areas; in winter prefers dry brushless desert scrub, farms, grasslands.

FIGURE 205. LONGSPURS AND BUNTINGS

Longspurs and a few species of buntings in this group are birds of open grasslands, and all show strong sexual dimorphism with respect to plumage. *Clockwise from top left (all breeding males):* Chestnut-collared Longspur, Snow Bunting, Lark Bunting, and McCown's Longspur.

MEADOWLARKS, BOBOLINK, COWBIRDS, GRACKLES, BLACKBIRDS, AND ORIOLES

The family Icteridae—commonly called icterids—is a diverse group of birds that share a structural feature of slender, pointed bills. Otherwise, they differ in shape, behavior, and plumage color.

MEADOWLARKS AND BOBOLINK

Eastern and Western Meadowlarks and Bobolink are birds of open grasslands and prairie habitats.

PHYSICAL PROFILE

Meadowlarks have stocky bodies with rounded chests. Perched meadowlarks have a European Starling–like profile. Structural features include a large, flat head; sharply pointed bill; short, rounded tail; and broad, rounded wings. (See Figure 206, below.)

Bobolink has a compact, rounded body shape that is sparrowlike in appearance. It has a large, blocky head with a short, thick neck; a short, pointed bill; and long, pointed wings.

BIRDING BY IMPRESSION INFORMATION

SIZE: Eastern and Western Meadowlarks (9½ in. long) are slightly smaller than American Robin. Bobolink (7 in. long) is about the size of White-crowned Sparrow.

STRUCTURAL FEATURES: Meadowlarks have long, springy legs that allow them to cover large areas of open space while foraging for food. Bobolink has a unique blocky profile with a short, spiky tail. (See Figure 206, below.)

BEHAVIOR: Meadowlarks have a distinctive flight style of several quick wingbeats followed by protracted glides. They are mostly ground-dwelling birds that blend with their surroundings, but they often perch on and sing from exposed perches and fenceposts.

Except for male Bobolinks' exuberant and protracted display flights, which they perform on the breeding grounds, accompanied by bubbling songs, Bobolinks quietly skulk around under dense grass cover. Bobolinks and meadowlarks form small to large flocks in migration and winter.

PLUMAGE PATTERNS AND GENERAL COLORATION: Eastern and Western Meadowlarks have similar plumage. (See Figure 208, p. 247.) Male Bobolink is striking with its black body, yellowish nape, and white rump and scapulars. Female and nonbreeding birds are cryptically colored. (See Figure 207, p. 246.)

HABITAT USE: Meadowlarks are open-country birds that frequent grassy fields and agricultural areas in winter. Bobolink is a grassland species that relies on mature grasslands for breeding and migrates to South America for the winter.

FIGURE 206. MEADOWLARKS AND BOBOLINK
These members of the icterid family are birds of grasslands and open spaces. Both have sweet, gurgling songs and nest on the ground. *From left to right:* Eastern Meadowlark perched and in flight, and breeding male Bobolink.

FIGURE 207. BOBOLINK AND FEMALE RED-WINGED BLACKBIRD

These two species are often mistaken for sparrows. *From left to right:* Female Red-winged Blackbird, nonbreeding Bobolink, and breeding female Bobolink. The Red-winged's larger size (8¾ in. long) and long, pointed bill are features that help separate it from sparrows. At 7 in. long, the female Bobolink is slightly larger than most sparrows. Other separating features are its heavy, pointed, conical bill and very long wings. Both sexes of nonbreeding Bobolink have similar plumage.

VOCALIZATIONS: Meadowlarks sing a series of melodic, broken phrases, with Eastern Meadowlark giving clearer, higher-pitched notes that lack the guttural quality of Western Meadowlark's song. Bobolink males sing a long, cheerful, bubbling song of clear notes on different pitches, and both sexes give a distinctive, easily remembered musical *bink* flight call.

COMPARISONS OF SIMILAR SPECIES

Eastern Meadowlark and Western Meadowlark

Eastern and Western Meadowlarks are geographic counterparts, with a breeding range that overlaps from the eastern Great Lakes southwest to Arizona.

UNCHANGING CHARACTERISTICS: Since both species have similar physical features, meadowlarks are often best separated by their vocalizations, including Western Meadowlark's resonant, blackbird-like call note. Western's song is a variable combination of melodious notes that ends with guttural gurgles, while Eastern Meadowlark's is a series of clear, slurred whistles, clearer and higher pitched than Western's. Since young meadowlarks learn their songs on the breeding grounds, birds from overlap zones may sing songs similar to those of both species.

SUPPLEMENTAL CHARACTERISTICS AND NON-BBI DETAILS: Meadowlarks are similar in appearance, but a few guidelines are helpful in separating birds by plumage. In nonbreeding plumage, Eastern Meadowlark generally has a more contrasting head pattern with darker crown and eye stripes, buff flanks compared with Western Meadowlark's whitish ones, and more rufous-tinged upperparts with darker feather centers versus Western's pale gray-brown ones (except for "Lilian's," a subspecies of Eastern that is more similar to Western). Some birds are inseparable in the field, and may represent hybrids.

Breeding-plumaged birds are more easily separated, with Eastern showing a mostly white malar region versus yellow in Western; bold, dark flank streaks versus spots on Western; and darker, more complex upperpart markings versus paler, more uniform markings on Western. Head markings are also darker on Eastern. (See Figure 208, p. 247.)

COWBIRDS, GRACKLES, AND BLACKBIRDS

These three groups of birds often associate together in large winter flocks that forage in fallow agricultural areas, grassy fields, granaries, and livestock farms. Males share a partial to mostly black plumage, and most females are a muted brownish to gray. All have strong legs that are well suited for their terrestrial foraging behavior.

PHYSICAL PROFILE

Cowbirds generally have chunky, rounded bodies that are blackbird-like in structure, with conical bills and relatively short tails. Blackbirds have tapered bodies with rounded chests. Their heads are rounded with short, sharply pointed bills, and they have rounded wings and short to longish tails. Grackles have long, slender bodies with rounded

FIGURE 208. EASTERN MEADOWLARK AND WESTERN MEADOWLARK (QUIZ PHOTO)
Since size (9½ in. long) and structure are identical, a few subtle plumage details help separate these two species in breeding and nonbreeding plumage. ID information is provided in the text. Try to identify these birds. Two birds are in breeding plumage, while two are in nonbreeding plumage. Answers are in the appendix, page 273.

chests. They have relatively small heads with flattish crowns, very long tails, long wings, and longer, heavier bills than blackbirds. (See Figure 209, p. 248.)

BIRDING BY IMPRESSION INFORMATION

SIZE: The three cowbirds range from Brown-headed Cowbird and Shiny Cowbird (a Caribbean vagrant), at 7½ in. long (slightly larger than White-crowned Sparrow), to Bronzed Cowbird, at 8¾ in. long (similar to Gray Catbird). Five blackbird species range from Red-winged and Tricolored Blackbirds, at 8¾ in. long, to Yellow-headed Blackbird, at 9½ in. long (slightly smaller than American Robin). Three grackles range from female Common Grackle, at 12½ in. long (about the size of Mourning

FIGURE 209. COWBIRDS, BLACKBIRDS, AND GRACKLES

Eleven species of cowbirds, blackbirds, and grackles from the icterid family occur in North America. *Clockwise from top left:* Male Red-winged Blackbird displaying, male Brown-headed Cowbird, male Bronzed Cowbird, breeding female Rusty Blackbird, male Great-tailed Grackle, and male Yellow-headed Blackbird. Females of most species are brown to grayish.

Dove), to the largest male Great-tailed Grackle, at 18 in. long. (See Figure 209, above.)

Male blackbirds and male Common Grackle are slightly larger than females. Male Boat-tailed and Great-tailed Grackles are noticeably larger than females, but their longer tails account for much of their longer measurements.

STRUCTURAL FEATURES: Bronzed Cowbird differs from the two smaller cowbirds by having a blockier body and unique massive, blocky head with flat crown, very thick neck, and heavy, conical bill. Brewer's and Rusty Blackbirds have more rounded chests and heads than other blackbirds. Male Boat-tailed and Great-tailed Grackles have very long, segmented tails.

BEHAVIOR: Cowbirds are brood parasites that lay eggs in other birds' nests. During the breeding season, male blackbirds (except Rusty and Brewer's) oversee harems of females in marshy areas. Grackles are gregarious birds that thrive in many different locations. Great-tailed Grackles thrive around humans, and often roost in large flocks in parking lots, especially where palm trees are found. All three groups form large flocks in winter, and while these flocks can be made up of one species, they often include a mix of cowbirds, grackles, and blackbirds.

PLUMAGE PATTERNS AND GENERAL COLORATION: Male cowbirds are mostly black, with Brown-headed Cowbird having a warm, brown head. Females are mostly brownish gray. Blackbirds and most grackles are sexually dimorphic, with males differing from females in plumage. Common Grackle males and females are mostly similar, however.

HABITAT USE: Cowbirds are found in a variety of habitats, from open woodlands and grassy fields to agricultural areas and livestock farms in winter. Yellow-headed, Red-winged, and Tricolored Blackbirds are found primarily in marsh habitats from fall to spring. Rusty Blackbird prefers open, wet forests, while Brewer's Blackbird is found in a wide variety of habitats, including cities, suburbs, and agricultural fields. Grackles are found almost everywhere from natural wild areas to shopping malls and rest stops.

VOCALIZATIONS: Cowbirds give a variety of gurgling notes and squeaky phrases. Blackbirds give a

FIGURE 210. BREWER'S BLACKBIRD AND RUSTY BLACKBIRD, BREEDING MALES (QUIZ PHOTO)
Males of both species are similar in breeding plumage, with a few subtle differences in structure and plumage. Try to identify these birds. ID information is provided in the text. Answers are in the appendix, page 273. Puffed feathers on bird at left alters its typical body shape.

variety of gurgling, nasal, and buzzy songs, as well as distinctive *chack* or *kek* notes. Grackles have a wide variety of songs and notes, all of which are nonmusical; some are harsh and grating in quality.

COMPARISONS OF SIMILAR SPECIES

Breeding Male Brewer's Blackbird and Rusty Blackbird

Rusty and Brewer's Blackbirds are more closely related to grackles than to other blackbirds, and share some of their habits and breeding displays. Nonbreeding birds are distinctly different and pose no ID problems.

UNCHANGING CHARACTERISTICS: Rusty Blackbird has a smaller, thinner, slightly decurved bill with a mostly straight culmen, while the bill of Brewer's Blackbird is longer and thicker with a slightly curved culmen. Rusty also has a shorter tail and rounder crown with steeper forehead than Brewer's. (See Figure 210, above.)

SUPPLEMENTAL CHARACTERISTICS AND NON-BBI DETAILS: Breeding males of both species are all black, but Brewer's Blackbird shows an iridescent purplish gloss to its head and greenish blue cast to its body, while male Rusty Blackbird is mostly uniformly black. Breeding female Rusty has a mix of variable buff, brownish, and black tones (see Figure 209, p. 248) compared with female Brewer's plain, muted

dark gray and brown overall plumage. Almost all female Brewer's have dark eyes compared with pale ones in Rusty.

Female Common, Boat-tailed, and Great-tailed Grackles

Boat-tailed and Great-tailed Grackles were formerly a single species, with similar structural features that may be indistinguishable in some birds.

UNCHANGING CHARACTERISTICS: Female Common Grackle is noticeably smaller than the other two species and has a more compact body and shorter tail. Boat-tailed Grackles, especially males, show a rounder head because of their steeper forehead and more rounded forecrown. (See Figure 211, p. 250.) Boat-taileds also have a somewhat bulkier body structure, especially the chest and shoulders, and a slightly smaller bill. Boat-tailed is a resident of coastal salt marshes and freshwater wetlands from Connecticut south to Texas, while Great-tailed occurs in a wide variety of habitats mostly west of the Mississippi River to California. Boat-taileds also frequent rest stops, shopping malls, and restaurant dumpsters along the Atlantic Seaboard, especially in the Southeast and Florida.

SUPPLEMENTAL CHARACTERISTICS AND NON-BBI DETAILS: In western Gulf Coast areas where both species occur, male and female Boat-tailed Grackles have

FIGURE 211. GREAT-TAILED, BOAT-TAILED, AND COMMON GRACKLES, FEMALES (QUIZ PHOTO)
While this photo shows distinct physical differences between Great-tailed and Boat-tailed Grackles, some of these differences are due to fluffed crown and body feathers. Many individuals of both species can appear quite similar and create ID problems. ID information is provided in the text. Can you identify the three species (including two subspecies of one species) in this photo? Answers are in the appendix, page 273.

brown eyes, while Great-tailed Grackle has pale eyes. Care should be exercised with some first-year female Great-taileds that have dark eyes, which typically turn pale by late fall.

Female Atlantic Boat-tailed Grackles (central Georgia north to Connecticut) have pale yellowish eyes, which are somewhat similar to Great-tailed's. Geographic segregation removes this potential ID problem (at least for the time being; Great-tailed is currently moving eastward from Texas after colonizing Texas from western locations in a relatively short time).

Female Boat-tailed has an overall rich brownish color that is warmer than that of female Great-tailed, and that contrasts more with its dark blackish wings and tail. Female Great-tailed is brownish gray overall. Female Boat-tailed has an indistinct pale supercilium that blends into the rear crown and indistinct dark lateral throat stripes. Female Great-tailed differs by its fairly prominent supercil-

ium that accentuates a dark cheek patch and fairly distinct lateral throat stripes.

ORIOLES

Orioles are colorful icterids whose sweet songs are a welcome addition to backyards and natural areas.

PHYSICAL PROFILE

Orioles have slender, elongated bodies with rounded chests. They have rounded heads and short, sharply pointed bills. Wings are generally broad and rounded, and tails range from medium length to long. (See Figure 212, p. 251.)

BIRDING BY IMPRESSION INFORMATION

SIZE: Nine orioles share a relatively narrow size range, from Orchard Oriole, at 7¼ in. long (slightly larger than White-crowned Sparrow), to Altamira Oriole, at 10 in. long (similar to American Robin).

STRUCTURAL FEATURES: Hooded and Orchard Orioles have more slender and petite overall physical profiles than other orioles, while Altamira, Spot-breasted, Scott's, and Audubon's Orioles are larger, bulkier, and have bigger heads and longer tails. Baltimore and Bullock's Orioles share an evenly balanced body structure and head size with relatively short tails.

BEHAVIOR: Orioles are graceful songbirds that forage deliberately in many habitat types. Most build elaborate nests woven of grasses that resemble hanging baskets. Altamira, Spot-breasted, and Audubon's Orioles are nonmigratory in their extreme southern range.

PLUMAGE PATTERNS AND GENERAL COLORATION: Most orioles have orange or yellow body color and black heads or throats in males of migratory species and both sexes of nonmigratory subtropical species. Females of migratory species are a muted yellow and gray, with some having whitish bellies. Orchard Oriole male differs by having rich chestnut underparts and a black head, back, wings, and tail.

HABITAT USE: Orioles are birds of forests, open woodlands, suburbs, deserts, parks, and riparian thickets.

VOCALIZATIONS: Sweet songs and call notes often give away an oriole's presence. Their songs include

FIGURE 212. ORIOLES
Orioles are some of the most colorful songbirds, and their sweet songs liven up the forest in spring and summer. *Clockwise from top left:* Altamira Oriole, male Baltimore Oriole, male Orchard Oriole, and male Hooded Oriole.

a variety of whistled notes of varying tonal quality. Some inject warbling notes and chattering phrases into the songs. Most have distinctive call notes and chatters.

COMPARISONS OF SIMILAR SPECIES

Baltimore Oriole and Bullock's Oriole, Immature Females

Baltimore and Bullock's Orioles, two closely related species, are geographic counterparts. Hybridization of the two species readily occurs in a narrow geographic overlap zone, with male hybrids easily recognizable. Female and immature hybrids are not readily recognizable, and some immature female Baltimores that show plumages similar to female Bullock's may in fact be hybrids.

UNCHANGING CHARACTERISTICS: Baltimore and Bullock's Orioles share very similar structural features, with Baltimore averaging slightly smaller (8¾ vs. 9 in. long).

SUPPLEMENTAL CHARACTERISTICS AND NON-BBI DETAILS: Dull, immature female Baltimore Orioles and female and immature Bullock's Orioles share plumage features of a gray back, whitish belly, and yellow head and breast. (See Figure 213, below.) The location of the yellow coloration differs, being brightest on the sides of the neck and cheek in Bullock's and brightest on the breast in Baltimore.

Immature female Baltimore has a dusky cheek with an indistinct dark eye line versus Bullock's yellow face with a more defined dark, thin eye line.

The yellow of Baltimore's upper breast typically blends into a gray-buff belly, while in Bullock's this transition is more abrupt. Bullock's typically shows grayer flanks compared with Baltimore's buff flanks.

Most, if not all, immature female Baltimores have yellowish undertail coverts and a pale yellow rump, while Bullock's typically has gray undertail coverts (some can have yellow) and a grayish rump. Baltimore also tends to have darker feather centers on the mantle versus mostly gray centers on Bullock's.

A hard-to-notice plumage detail is the dark interior markings on the whitish median covert wing bars. They are typically pointed on Bullock's and rounded on Baltimore, but these markings may be hard to see in the field, and some Baltimores and hybrids show these pointed dark markings as well.

Hooded Oriole and Orchard Oriole, Females and Immature Males

UNCHANGING CHARACTERISTICS: Hooded Oriole is larger (8 vs. 7¼ in. long) and bulkier than Orchard Oriole. Hooded has a longer, more attenuated body structure, a more extended and graduated tail, and a longer, more decurved bill. Orchard's more delicate size and compact body structure, shorter tail, and mostly straight, pointed bill contribute to it often being mistaken for a large warbler at first glance. (See Figure 214, p. 253.)

SUPPLEMENTAL CHARACTERISTICS AND NON-BBI DETAILS: Female and immature male Hooded Orioles are

---

FIGURE 213. BULLOCK'S ORIOLE AND BALTIMORE ORIOLE, IMMATURE FEMALES (QUIZ PHOTO)
Young female Baltimore Orioles may show browner tones to the head and neck than this immature bird, as well as a paler yellow-buff face, neck, and breast. A general guideline is that Bullock's Oriole is brighter yellow on the face and head, while Baltimore is brighter yellow on its chest. More ID information is provided in the text. Can you identify these two similar species? Answers are in the appendix, page 273.

FIGURE 214. HOODED ORIOLE AND ORCHARD ORIOLE, FEMALES (QUIZ PHOTO)
These two small to medium-sized female orioles are somewhat similar in structure and plumage patterns, but a few structural features and plumage details help separate them. Try to identify these birds using the ID information provided in the text. Answers are in the appendix, page 273.

very similar in plumage to Orchard Orioles. Orchard shows two well-defined, thin white wing bars, while Hooded has a stronger upper white wing bar and an indistinct lower white wing bar.

Orchard also has a greener overall appearance, especially on its upperparts, compared with a drabber overall look to Hooded, including grayer up-

perparts. Orchard has dark bases to the secondaries versus uniformly gray secondaries on Hooded. (See Figure 214, above.) Immature males have the same differences noted here, but Hooded typically has a larger black throat patch that extends onto the upper breast versus a smaller black throat patch on immature male Orchard.

Finches are small to medium songbirds that have characteristic conical-shaped bills used for feeding on seeds. Nearly all species have short, notched tails. Old World Sparrows are introduced weaver finches that include House Sparrow and Eurasian Tree Sparrow.

GROSBEAKS, ROSY-FINCHES, AND *CARPODACUS* FINCHES

Two large grosbeaks (Pine and Evening) differ from other finches with their large size, big heads, bulky-chested bodies, and very large conical bills (Evening Grosbeak). (See Figure 215, p. 255.)

PHYSICAL PROFILE

Evening Grosbeak has a bulky, compact body shape with a bulging chest; very large, blocky head; thick neck; massive conical bill; and very short tail. Pine Grosbeak is more elongated with evenly rounded underparts, a large rounded head, smaller rounded bill, very long tail, and long wings.

Three species of rosy-finches have slender bodies with rounded chests, rounded heads, small conical bills, very long wings, and long, forked tails. *Carpodacus* finches (Purple, Cassin's, and House Finches) have chunkier bodies with rounded chests, short tails, and stout conical bills.

LOOK-ALIKE BIRDS

Male *Carpodacus* finches (Purple, House, and Cassin's Finches) have plumage features and red color similar to that of male Pine Grosbeak, but are much smaller overall with shorter tails, and they lack bold white wing bars. (See male Purple Finch in Figure 215, p. 255.)

BIRDING BY IMPRESSION INFORMATION

SIZE: Eight species range from Purple Finch and House Finch, at 6 in. long (slightly smaller than Song Sparrow), to Pine Grosbeak, at 9 in. long (slightly larger than Red-winged Blackbird).

STRUCTURAL FEATURES: See Physical Profile, above.

BEHAVIOR: Evening Grosbeaks move in small flocks and are usually seen feeding in treetops and at bird feeders. Pine Grosbeak feeds on fruits and their seeds in winter, in moderate-sized flocks. Rosy-finches are hardy birds that feed on open ground and tundra, often near snow fields. *Carpodacus* finches occur in small flocks in a wide variety of geographic locations and readily come to backyard feeding stations.

PLUMAGE PATTERNS AND GENERAL COLORATION: Male Pine and Evening Grosbeaks are unmistakable in appearance. Females have a muted grayish plumage. Female Pine has variable yellow on its head and rump, while female Evening has a yellow wash on its flanks and nape and under its wings. Each of the rosy-finches has a distinctive mix of black, gray, brown, and pink shading and unique plumage patterns. *Carpodacus* finches are similar in appearance, and are covered in detail in Comparisons of Similar Species.

HABITAT USE: Pine Grosbeak is a bird of far northern coniferous forests, while Evening Grosbeak frequents open woodlands. Rosy-finches are birds of high-elevation mountains where they often forage above the tree line near snowfields. In winter they retreat to lower elevations and visit feeders. *Carpodacus* finches occur in a wide variety of habitats. Most finches are common visitors to backyard feeding stations.

VOCALIZATIONS: Finches give distinctive flight calls that identify them to species. Evening Grosbeak rarely sings, but the other species give a variety of whistles and clear, warbling notes.

COMPARISONS OF SIMILAR SPECIES

Purple, Cassin's, and House Finches, Females
UNCHANGING CHARACTERISTICS: All three species share a narrow size range (6–6¼ in. long) and somewhat similar structural features.

Purple Finch is the stockiest of the three species, with a bulky body shape. It also has a short tail, stout bill, thick neck, and large, blocky head. Cassin's Finch is slightly larger than Purple and House Finches and has longer wings and a slightly longer bill with a straight upper mandible, which creates a more conical impression. (See Figure 216, p. 256.)

There are two subspecies of Purple Finch. "Eastern" Purple Finches have long primaries that extend noticeably past the longest tertial, while "Western" Purple Finches have shorter primaries and a shorter projection past the tertials. These differences are more relevant for separation of Purple Finch from Cassin's, which has very long primaries and longer projection past the tertials.

House Finch is a widespread resident of all the United States except for the Florida peninsula and southeast Texas. It differs structurally from the other two species by having a smaller, more slender

FIGURE 215. GROSBEAKS, ROSY-FINCHES, AND *CARPODACUS* FINCHES
Eight species of birds in four genera make up this group of finches, and the two species of grosbeaks represent some of the largest members of the finch family. *Clockwise from top left:* Male Pine Grosbeak, breeding male Brown-capped Rosy-Finch, male Purple Finch, and male Evening Grosbeak.

body; longer tail; and shorter, rounder wings. Other features include a rounder, more proportional head shape and shorter, stout bill with more rounded culmen. Purple and Cassin's have more distinctly notched tails than House, with Cassin's tail noticeably longer than Purple's and slightly shorter than House's.

SUPPLEMENTAL CHARACTERISTICS AND NON-BBI DETAILS: *Carpodacus* females have grayish brown upperparts, streaked underparts against pale backgrounds, and streaked crowns and backs. Female Purple Finch differs from the other species with its white undertail coverts that lack noticeable streaking. (See Figure 216, p. 256.)

Female "Western" Purple shows more similarities to female Cassin's than it does to "Eastern" Purple, including a weak facial pattern, drab greenish brown back with indistinct streaks, and diffused, blurry streaks below against an off-white background. "Eastern" Purple female has a bold brown and white head pattern, brownish back with distinct streaks, and bold, dark streaks against whitish underparts.

Female Cassin's differs from "Western" Purple and House Finch with its sparse, defined streaks on the flanks compared with Purple's dense blurry ones. Cassin's also has crisp, defined dark breast streaks that differ from female "Western" Purple and House's heavier, less defined streaking. Female

FIGURE 216. CASSIN'S, HOUSE, AND PURPLE FINCHES, FEMALES (QUIZ PHOTO)
Both males and females of three species of *Carpodacus* finches may cause ID confusion. You need to look at subtle structural features and plumage to separate females. ID information is provided in the text. Two subspecies are shown for one of these species. Try to identify all three female species and one subspecies in this expert-level quiz. Answers are in the appendix, page 273.

"Eastern" Purple has fairly distinct and bold breast and flank streaks, but it does not overlap in geographic range with Cassin's.

Female House is more grayish brown overall than the other two species, and it has a plain head and face that may show a thin, whitish eye-ring. The plain face differs from those of Purple and Cassin's, which have distinct pale eyebrows.

CROSSBILLS, REDPOLLS, SISKINS, AND GOLDFINCHES

Each group of these small finches has distinctive plumage features and behaviors.

PHYSICAL PROFILE

Crossbills have fairly long, heavy bodies with gently rounded chests. They have unique, odd overlapping

FIGURE 217. CROSSBILLS, REDPOLLS, SISKINS, AND GOLDFINCHES
These four groups represent the smallest finches in North America. *Clockwise from top left:* Male Common Redpoll, breeding male American Goldfinch, male White-winged Crossbill, and Pine Siskin.

bills that are suited for prying seeds from conifer cones. Redpolls have very compact, rounded bodies with small heads and tiny, conical bills.

Siskin and goldfinches are slender with rounded chests, with American Goldfinch showing a more rounded body shape. Pine Siskin has a small head, short tail, slender body, and very thin, pointed bill. Goldfinches have small, pointed, conical bills and small rounded heads. (See Figure 217, above.)

BIRDING BY IMPRESSION INFORMATION

SIZE: Eight species range from Lesser Goldfinch, at 4½ in. long (slightly larger than Ruby-crowned Kinglet), to White-winged Crossbill, at 6½ in. long (slightly larger than Song Sparrow).

STRUCTURAL FEATURES: Red Crossbill is heavier bodied and larger headed than White-winged Crossbill, and has a longer, heavier bill and shorter tail. Though small in size, redpolls have proportionally large heads and thick necks as well as thin, forked tails, and very small, pointed, conical bills.

Lawrence's and Lesser Goldfinches are more compact in structure than Pine Siskin, with small heads; short necks; short, forked tails; short, rounded wings; and shorter, more conical, pointed bills. American Goldfinch is the bulkiest goldfinch, with a larger, round head and thicker neck.

BEHAVIOR: Crossbills and redpolls are northern-breeding nomadic finches that disperse southward in search of food in winter. Pine Siskin is one of the most abundant finches in North America, and it disperses widely during winter in search of food. Goldfinches are small, delicate birds that are common at backyard feeders and in weedy fields and willow and birch trees.

All species form small to large feeding flocks in winter, and most perch conspicuously on tall, open treetop branches. Groups of crossbills, redpolls, and Pine Siskins shift from tree to tree in search of seed sources, and just as quickly fly away to other locations. Goldfinches are more consistent in their winter habits, and remain in a weedy feeding area until the seeds are exhausted. All are fairly tame and often allow good looks.

PLUMAGE PATTERNS AND GENERAL COLORATION: Males and females show marked plumage differences, except for redpolls and Pine Siskin, which show only subtle differences. Male crossbills are red with dark wings, while White-winged Crossbill has two bold white wing bars. Females of both species are a muted yellow-gold color with dark wings, with female White-winged having white wing bars and indistinct streaks on the underparts.

Redpolls have pale and brown-streaked upperparts, small black chins, and whitish underparts with variable streaks on the flanks. Males have a reddish blush to the chest. Common and Hoary Redpolls are somewhat similar in plumage. (See Comparisons of Similar Species.) Worn redpolls in summer are darker and more heavily streaked than winter-plumaged birds.

Pine Siskin is mostly brownish and heavily streaked overall. Males have a strong yellow wing bar, while females have a smaller white one and less whitish underparts background. All goldfinches have some degree of yellow to buff plumage, with females and immatures duller than males. Lawrence's Goldfinch is mostly grayish with a yellow chest patch and yellowish gray wing bars. Males have a strong black face and forecrown, and females just a dusky facial border near the bill.

American Goldfinch is yellow with black wings in breeding plumage, with males having a black cap. Lesser Goldfinch males are yellow below with black wings and a black cap. Some Texas and Southwest males are all black above. Female and juvenile American and Lesser Goldfinches may have a muted gray-buff plumage and are somewhat similar in appearance. (See Comparisons of Similar Species.)

HABITAT USE: Crossbills are finches of northern coniferous forests, although Red Crossbill is also a resident species in several widespread western mountain habitats south into Mexico. Both redpolls are found in birch and willow thickets in far northern regions, with some breeding in Arctic coastal tundra (Hoary). Pine Siskin is found in widespread coniferous forests, and goldfinches are found in a variety of grassy and open woodland habitats.

VOCALIZATIONS: Songs include sharp, hard notes; musical trills; clear warbling phrases; and jumbled, buzzy phrases. Call notes and flight calls are distinctive for each species, and all species frequently vocalize in flight.

COMPARISONS OF SIMILAR SPECIES

Common Redpoll and Hoary Redpoll
UNCHANGING CHARACTERISTICS: Common Redpoll is slightly smaller than Hoary Redpoll (5¼ vs. 5½ in. long) and has a more slender body and shorter tail. Hoary often appears fluffier, thicker necked, and more compact in structure than Common. Both species have short, pointed, conical bills, but Hoary's bill is smaller, stubbier, deeper-based, and has a straighter culmen compared with Common's longer bill with slightly decurved culmen.

Hoary's bill looks like a Common Redpoll's bill that was forcefully pushed back into its face, with the resulting appearance tinier and more triangular. This impression is further accentuated by a steeper forehead. (See Figure 218, p. 259.)

SUPPLEMENTAL CHARACTERISTICS AND NON-BBI DETAILS: Common Redpoll is typically darker and more heavily streaked than Hoary Redpoll, especially in winter, with males of both species paler and less streaked than their respective females. Winter male Hoary can be very pale, with almost no streaking on the underparts and a noticeably smaller black throat patch than Common. Some breeding Hoarys, especially females, can be brownish with heavy streaks, so care should be taken with this plumage. Hoary also shows fluffy nasal feathering adjacent to the bill, which is lacking in Common.

Male Common averages darker pink than Hoary on the underparts, and females of both species show little or no pink color to the underparts. Common also shows more streaks on the undertail coverts and lower flanks than Hoary. Some Hoarys have no streaks on the undertail coverts. (See Figure 218, p. 259.)

Lesser Goldfinch and American Goldfinch, Females and Immatures
UNCHANGING CHARACTERISTICS: American Goldfinch is a noticeably larger, bulkier bird with a bigger, rounded head; thicker neck; and longer wings and tail. Lesser Goldfinch has a short, stout bill, while American's is more sharply pointed. Both are conical.

FIGURE 218. HOARY REDPOLL AND COMMON REDPOLL (QUIZ PHOTO)
Hoary and Common Redpolls are somewhat similar in size, structure, and plumage, but a few subtle structural and plumage differences help separate them. Look carefully at the four photos and try to identify both species. ID information is provided in the text. Answers are in the appendix, page 273.

SUPPLEMENTAL CHARACTERISTICS AND NON-BBI DETAILS: Both male and female American Goldfinch differ from Lesser Goldfinch at all ages, having white undertail coverts while Lesser's are yellow or buff. Breeding female American and Lesser Goldfinches have similar plumage features, but Lesser differs with its slightly darker, greener back; two narrow, whitish wing bars versus American's two bolder wing bars, and by a bold white patch at the base of the primaries that is sometimes barely visible in American. Female Lesser also has a dark bill year-round versus a pink bill in breeding American Goldfinch, which turns gray to black in winter.

Nonbreeding American is much duller overall than nonbreeding Lesser, with grayish brown versus yellowish underparts, brownish gray upperparts versus lightly streaked greenish upperparts in Lesser, and two bold yellowish, buff, or white (adult male) wing bars, with the lower wing bar larger. Adult female Lesser appears similar year-round, although worn birds in late summer are paler and duller. (See Figure 219, p. 260.)

Juvenile and early first-winter Lessers are grayer overall than similar-aged juvenile Americans, and they have some buff or yellow tones to the underparts, and very narrow, almost indistinct, pale wing bars. Juvenile and early first-winter Americans are browner overall than Lessers with bold buff wing

FIGURE 219. LESSER GOLDFINCH AND AMERICAN GOLDFINCH, FEMALES AND IMMATURES (QUIZ PHOTO)
Males of these two species are distinctive, but females and immatures are harder to separate. Immature and nonbreeding females of both species are shown. Try to identify and age these birds. ID information is provided in the text. Answers are in the appendix, page 273.

bars and a warm buff wash to the flanks and upper breast. (See Figure 219, above.)

HOUSE SPARROW AND EURASIAN TREE SPARROW

Both of these species were introduced to the United States in the mid-1800s. While House Sparrow has spread to all of the lower Canadian provinces, the entire United States, and Mexico, Eurasian Tree Sparrow previously had a limited range near St. Louis, MO, but in recent years has expanded to nearby states and as a vagrant species to much further locations.

PHYSICAL PROFILE

Both species have husky, rounded bodies with large heads; short, thick necks; short, rounded wings; short tails; and conical bills. (See Figure 220, p. 261.)

BIRDING BY IMPRESSION INFORMATION

SIZE: House Sparrow is 6¼ in. long. Eurasian Tree Sparrow is 6 in. long.

STRUCTURAL FEATURES: House Sparrow has a longer, heavier bill than Eurasian Tree Sparrow.

BEHAVIOR: Both species form small flocks and nest in cavities near human habitation, including urban areas.

FIGURE 220. HOUSE SPARROW

House Sparrow is a European weaver finch that is now widespread throughout the United States, lower Canadian provinces, and Mexico. A breeding male is on the left, and a nonbreeding male is on the right. Female House Sparrow is shown in Figure 197 (p. 234).

PLUMAGE PATTERNS AND GENERAL COLORATION: Male House Sparrow is distinctive, with rust back, white wing patch, black bib and breast, and pale underparts. Females are relatively dingy gray-brown with a brown, buff, and black streaked back, a plain pale brown crown, and a buff rear supercilium. Female House Sparrow resembles female Dickcissel. (See Figure 197, p. 234.) Eurasian Tree Sparrow is a distinctive-looking weaver finch with rust cap, black cheek spot, small black chin, and dusky underparts. Sexes are similar.

HABITAT USE: Both species thrive in small to large flocks near human habitation, including densely populated urban areas. Both nest in natural and human-made cavities.

VOCALIZATIONS: Both species sing a song consisting of similar monotonous chirps, with Eurasian Tree Sparrow giving harder, clearer sounds. Calls include a husky, squeaky rising note and a series of rattling notes when excited.

ACKNOWLEDGMENTS

Special thanks to Pete Dunne, who provided important advice on how we should display our ideas, and whose input was instrumental to the final version of the book. Equally significant to the final version were the suggestions and professional resolve of Lisa White, our editor, who pushed us with questions and clarifications that helped refine how we presented the BBI approach.

A big thank-you to our good friend Brian Small, who provided many photos, especially at the final hour, that allowed us to accurately present comparative photo composites, and to comrade photographers Lloyd Spitalnik and Mike Danzenbaker, who helped with many hard-to-get images. Thanks also to the following photographers who helped elevate the visual impact of the book: Adrian Binns, Cameron Cox, Scott Elowitz, Bob Fogg, Jim Gilbert, Bruce Hallett, Julian Hough, Bill Hubick, Don Riepe, David Roemer, Brian Sullivan, Brian Taber, Scott Whittle, and Jim Zipp.

Manuscript accuracy and flow are better because of the work of Glen Davis, who reviewed the entire manuscript and offered key advice for clarifications. Special appreciation goes to Liz Pierson, whose attention to detail in the final copyediting contributed to the book's accuracy and flow. Thanks also to the following people who reviewed chapters and provided constructive criticism: Cameron Cox (waterfowl, seabirds, gulls), Bob Fogg (seabirds), and Adam Kent (sparrows). Also key to the final product were the friends and colleagues who gave personal advice and information about bird ID and how we should present it. These include Lloyd and Sandy Spitalnik, who provided special insight from an everyday birdwatcher's perspective; Glenn Olsen, who walks a similar ID path and leads organized field trips and workshops with Kevin; and to Richard Crossley and Michael O'Brien, who were responsible for Kevin's exposure to this different ID approach during the preparation and writing of *The Shorebird Guide*.

We are also grateful to the following people, who influenced how we look at birds and how we presented our thoughts: Bruce Anderson, Tim Barksdale, Jessie Barry, Gian Basili, Tony Bennett, Wes Biggs, Adrian Binns, Jeff Bouton, William J. Boyle, Michael Brothers, Jen Brumfeld, Paul and Fran Buckley, Bill Clark, George and Scarlet Colley, Mike Crewe, Jim and Mike Danzenbaker, Glen Davis, Jon Dunn, Scott Elowitz, Shawneen Finnegan, Bob Fogg, Doug Gochfeld, Jason and Laura Guerard, Pete Gustas, Catherine Hamilton, Keith Hansen, Julian Hough, Dave Irons, Alvaro Jaramillo, Tom Johnson, Kenn and Kim Kaufman, Adam and Gina Kent, Paul Lehman, Tony Leukering, Jerry Liguori, Tom Magarian, Becky Marvil, Jonathan Meyrav, Steve Mlodinow, Frank Nicoletti, Evan Obercian, Tom Reed, Melissa Roach, John Robinson, David Sibley, David Simpson, Jim Stevenson, Brian Sullivan, Pat and Clay Sutton, Peter Trueblood, Brian Wheeler, Chris Wood, Jim Zipp, and our late, dear friend Jason Starfire, whose tragic early passing a number of years ago extinguished one of the brightest lights in the birding community. Extra thanks to the many workshop participants we encountered on field trips and during workshops who provided valuable feedback and enthusiasm about the BBI approach, and to anyone whose name we inadvertently left off this list.

Dale offers special thanks to her former colleagues at New Jersey Audubon, Gordon Schultze and Rich Kane, for encouraging her interest in New Jersey birds, and to Pat Kane and Brian Vernachio for sharing their commitment and passion for learning and teaching. Also to her mom, Myra, and sisters, Donna and Diane, for their love and never-ending support. And finally, to her best friend, Shawneen Finnegan, with whom Dale has spent countless hours chatting, commiserating, crying, and most of all, laughing, and who shares in this passion for birds and the natural world.

Finally, overdue thanks to Bob Perna, who showed us "strange" birds with "funny" names (Yellow-bellied Sapsucker, Yellow-breasted Chat, Rufous-sided Towhee) some 36 years ago at Sandy Hook, NJ, and started us on this journey of watching, living, and breathing birds.

APPENDIX

FIGURE 1. Compromised Viewing Situations (page 3)
The two slender birds with long legs at rear left and right (1) are Lesser Yellowlegs. They are slightly smaller than the round-bodied bird at rear left (2), which we can tell is a Long-billed Dowitcher because of its rounded back, distended egg-shaped undercarriage, thick neck, and probing behavior. If the yellowlegs were Greater Yellowlegs, they would be noticeably larger than Long-billed Dowitcher. The medium-sized bird with the longish, drooping-tipped bill in the front right center (3) and the preening birds left of center (3) among the smaller Western Sandpipers (4) are Dunlin. Dunlin is similar to Western Sandpiper in structure but differs by its larger size and longer bill and legs. The largest bird in the center (5) is a "Western" Willet; note its large size; long, thick bill; and long legs. Greater Yellowlegs can be eliminated since it would have a longer, thinner neck, thinner bill, and more slender body shape.

FIGURE 5. Wetland Birds Comparison (page 7)
FROM LEFT TO RIGHT: Wood Stork, Great Egret, White Ibis, Purple Gallinule (rear R).

FIGURE 8. Comparative Sizing of Birds in Flight (page 9)
(Right photo) The large bird near the bottom left is a Bald Eagle (large, broad wings and big head and bill), and two much smaller crows flank it. Note the crows' distinctive, angled wings; small head; and longish tail. The Osprey in the top right shows the typical long, curved-wing, head-on profile that gives this slender-winged raptor its gull-like impression during relaxed flight. Note that the Osprey is larger than the crows but smaller than the eagle.

FIGURE 9. Assessing Comparative Size, Body Shape, and Structural Features (page 10)
In addition to size comparisons, it is helpful to note differing body and bill shapes and leg lengths. Some differences here are dramatic, ranging from the obvious large, orange, carrotlike bill of American Oystercatcher (3) and the odd-shaped red and black bill of Black Skimmer (4) to the short, stubby dark bill of Black-bellied Plover (5).

Body shape differences range from the bulky,

rounded bodies of American Oystercatcher and Black-bellied Plover to the slender, tapered bodies of Forster's Tern (6) and Laughing Gull (7; similar in size to Oystercatcher). Black Skimmer has a tapered, submarine-shaped body with very short legs. Terns have short legs, while Black-bellied Plover has medium-length legs.

Other species in this photo include Short-billed Dowitcher (8), Ruddy Turnstone (9), and Common Tern (10). This Common Tern was identified by its small, rounded head that shows a distinctive rear dark helmeted appearance compared with Forster's Tern's black mask that touches its eye, and because it is the only other medium-sized white tern in this location in late summer. This bird was identified from this photo, not in real life. The medium-sized shorebird (11) preening in front of the Ruddy Turnstone is a Sanderling. Although it is preening and its head is not visible, we can reach this ID conclusion because it is much larger than the Semipalmated Sandpiper (2) and slightly smaller than the Ruddy Turnstone (9), and because it is mostly gray and white in plumage and shows some retained dark-centered breeding feathers on its back. This is the only shorebird of this size in North America that shows these features. The location of the East Pond at the Jamaica Bay Wildlife Refuge in New York City helps eliminate some similar species that are rare to uncommon in August, such as Long-billed Dowitcher and American Golden-Plover.

FIGURE 12. Bill Shape Comparison (page 11)
The six bird groups represented here have different bill shapes and feeding styles. Top left is a Black-and-white Warbler, which has a slender, fine-tipped bill suited for gleaning insects. Top middle is a male Black-headed Grosbeak, whose heavy conical bill is perfect for cracking open seeds and nuts. Top right is a Red-tailed Hawk, whose powerful, hooked beak is suited for tearing flesh. Bottom right is a dabbling duck, American Black Duck, with a flat bill well suited for eating aquatic vegetation. Bottom middle is a wading bird, a Wood Stork, whose long, curved bill is configured for probing muddy substrates for aquatic creatures. Bottom left is a female Broad-

tailed Hummingbird, which inserts its long, slender, fine-tipped bill into flowers to gather nectar.

FIGURE 13. Leg Length Assessment (page 12)
Bonaparte's Gull (L) has short legs that barely show beneath its body feathers, with its upper leg (tibia) not visible at all. Medium-length leg values are a bit tougher to qualify, with this Eastern Meadowlark (C) showing a fairly long lower leg (tarsus) and a relatively short feathered upper leg. A white-morph Reddish Egret (R) has noticeably long legs that resemble those of stilts, and which cause awkward, gawky movements. Medium-legged birds move in a steady, uniform fashion, while short-legged birds take short, quick steps.

FIGURE 15. Kiptopeake Hawk Watch Models (page 13)
FROM LEFT TO RIGHT: American Kestrel, Merlin, Broad-winged Hawk, Cooper's Hawk, and Sharp-shinned Hawk.

FIGURE 20. Mixed Flock of Waterfowl (page 22)
The large white birds are Tundra Swans, and the next largest birds in the foreground, with orange legs and in flight, are Greater White-fronted Geese. Smaller ducks include American Wigeon (1), Northern Pintail (2), Ruddy Ducks (3), Northern Shoveler (4; one male), and Buffleheads (5; two males and one female).

FIGURE 22. Duck Look-Alikes (page 24)
FROM LEFT TO RIGHT: Common Loon, Double-crested Cormorant, American Coot, and Eared Grebe.

FIGURE 25. Greater Scaup and Lesser Scaup (page 26)
Greater Scaup are on the left—male above, female below.

Lesser Scaup are on the right—male above, female below.

FIGURE 26. Redhead, Canvasback, and Ring-necked Duck, Females (page 27)
FROM LEFT TO RIGHT: Ring-necked Duck, Redhead, and Canvasback females.

FIGURE 27. Blue-winged, Cinnamon, and Green-winged Teal, Females (page 27)
FROM LEFT TO RIGHT: Cinnamon Teal, Blue-winged Teal, and Green-winged Teal females.

FIGURE 30. Ross's Goose and Snow Goose (page 30)
TOP, FROM LEFT TO RIGHT: "Lesser" Snow Goose, white-morph Ross's Goose, and dark-morph Ross's Goose (rare).

FIGURE 37. Dusky Grouse and Sooty Grouse, Males (page 38)
Dusky Grouse (L) and Sooty Grouse (R).

FIGURE 39. Nonbreeding Loons (page 40)
CLOCKWISE FROM TOP LEFT: Juvenile Yellow-billed Loon, adult Common Loon, adult Pacific Loon, juvenile Red-throated Loon, adult Red-throated Loon, and juvenile Common Loon.

FIGURE 41. Nonbreeding Eared, Horned, and Red-necked Grebes (page 43)
FROM LEFT TO RIGHT: Horned Grebe, Eared Grebe, and Red-necked Grebe.

FIGURE 42. Western Grebe and Clark's Grebe (page 44)
TOP PHOTO: Clark's Grebe (L) and Western Grebe (R), in mostly nonbreeding plumage.

BOTTOM PHOTOS: Clark's Grebe (L) and Western Grebe (R), in breeding plumage.

FIGURE 44. Sooty Shearwater and Short-tailed Shearwater (page 47)
Sooty Shearwater (L) and Short-tailed Shearwater (R).

FIGURE 45. Black-vented, Manx, and Audubon's Shearwaters (page 48)
FROM LEFT TO RIGHT: Black-vented Shearwater, Audubon's Shearwater, and Manx Shearwater.

FIGURE 46. Storm-Petrels (page 49)
TOP, FROM LEFT TO RIGHT: Wilson's Storm-Petrel (note feet visible behind tail), Band-rumped Storm-Petrel, and Leach's Storm-Petrel (note slender, angular wings and forked tail).

FIGURE 50. Nonbreeding Long-billed, Marbled, and Kittlitz's Murrelets (page 53)
FROM LEFT TO RIGHT: Marbled Murrelet, Kittlitz's Murrelet, and Long-billed Murrelet.

FIGURE 56. Anhinga and Double-crested Cormorant in Flight (page 58)
Double-crested Cormorant (L), Anhinga (R). Note the Anhinga's thinner neck, longer tail, and headless look.

FIGURE 63. Black-crowned Night-Heron and Yellow-crowned Night-Heron, Juveniles, and American Bittern (page 66)
FROM LEFT TO RIGHT: Juvenile Yellow-crowned Night-Heron, juvenile Black-crowned Night-Heron, and American Bittern.

FIGURE 64. Snowy Egret and Little Blue Heron, Juveniles (page 67)
Birds on the left (top and bottom) are Little Blue Herons. Birds on the right are Snowy Egrets.

FIGURE 65. Medium-sized Herons and Egrets in Flight (page 68)
TOP, CLOCKWISE FROM TOP LEFT: Cattle Egret, Snowy Egret, Little Blue Heron, and Tricolored Heron.

BOTTOM SILHOUETTES, FROM LEFT TO RIGHT: Tricolored Heron, Snowy Egret, Little Blue Heron, and Cattle Egret.

FIGURE 67. Great Egret and White-morph Great Blue Heron (page 70)
Great Egret (L) and white-morph Great Blue Heron (R).

FIGURE 68. Nonbreeding Glossy Ibis and White-faced Ibis (page 71)
TOP: White-faced Ibis is the left dark ibis, and Glossy Ibis is the right one.

BOTTOM: Nonbreeding adult Glossy Ibis (L) and nonbreeding adult White-faced Ibis (R).

FIGURE 72. Virginia, Clapper, and King Rails (page 75)
CLOCKWISE FROM TOP LEFT: Female King Rail, Clapper Rail ("Gulf Coast" subspecies), Virginia Rail, and California Clapper Rail (light-footed s. CA subspecies).

FIGURE 75. Raptor Flight Profiles (page 78)
FROM LEFT TO RIGHT: Osprey, adult Red-tailed Hawk (buteo), juvenile Sharp-shinned Hawk (accipiter), Merlin (falcon), and adult male Northern Harrier.

FIGURE 78. Broad-winged Hawk and Red-shouldered Hawk, Juveniles (page 81)
FROM LEFT TO RIGHT: Lightly marked Broad-winged Hawk, Red-shouldered Hawk, and heavily marked Broad-winged Hawk. Note the bold, wide dark line on the throat of the Red-shouldered, and the thin dark line on the throat of the rightmost Broad-winged. Red-shouldered typically shows a much bolder throat marking than Broad-winged, which usually shows a narrow or indistinct dark throat line.

FIGURE 79. Red-tailed Hawk and Ferruginous Hawk (page 82)
CLOCKWISE FROM TOP LEFT: Adult light-morph Ferruginous Hawk (although they appear dark in this photo, note the reddish leg feathers on the upper legs near the wings), juvenile Ferruginous Hawk, adult "Eastern" Red-tailed Hawk with "Krider's" Red-tailed Hawk subspecies plumage traits, and juvenile "Eastern" Red-tailed Hawk.

FIGURE 82. Cooper's Hawk and Sharp-shinned Hawk, Juveniles (page 86)
TOP PHOTOS AND BOTTOM SILHOUETTES: Female Cooper's Hawk is the left bird, and Sharp-shinned Hawk (sex unknown, but possibly a female due to the long tail with narrow base and longish, tapered primaries) is the right one. Note that the lines inserted into the silhouettes and connecting the wrists cut through the rear of the head and neck on Cooper's and the front of the head on Sharp-shinned.

FIGURE 83. Kites and Osprey (page 88)
CLOCKWISE FROM TOP LEFT: Swallow-tailed Kite, female Snail Kite, White-tailed Kite, Osprey, and sub-adult male Hook-billed Kite.

FIGURE 84. Falcons and Crested Caracara (page 89)
TOP PHOTOS, FROM LEFT TO RIGHT: Male American Kestrel, adult male Merlin, and juvenile dark-morph Gyrfalcon.

FIGURE 85. Falcons in Flight (page 90)
FROM LEFT TO RIGHT: American Kestrel, Merlin, Prairie Falcon, and Peregrine Falcon.

FIGURE 89. Black-bellied Plover, American Golden-Plover, and Pacific Golden-Plover, Juveniles (page 97)
CLOCKWISE FROM TOP LEFT: Juvenile Pacific Golden-Plover, juvenile American Golden-Plover, presumed hybrid juvenile American Golden-Plover x Pacific Golden-Plover, and a gold-plumaged juvenile Black-bellied Plover.

Presumed American Golden-Plover x Pacific Golden-Plover Hybrid

UNCHANGING CHARACTERISTICS: Structural features on this bird are indeterminate for either species, but it has a slightly wider, blockier head shape like Pacific Golden-Plover, and a short, thin bill like American Golden-Plover. Leg length is indeterminate for either species but is more consistent with that of American Golden, which lacks the proportionally longer tibia (upper leg) of Pacific Golden. Body shape also favors American Golden.

SUPPLEMENTAL CHARACTERISTICS AND NON-BBI DETAILS: This bird has plumage traits that more closely resemble those of juvenile Pacific Golden-Plover, especially the golden tones to the head and breast, and coarsely streaked upper breast and plainer, buff belly. Narrow upperpart feather fringes are more typical of American Golden-Plover, but a supercilium that expands behind the eye and pale legs are more typical of Pacific Golden-Plover. This individual has an entire page in *The Shorebird Guide* (p. 312), where it is treated as a hybrid of the two species. It also gave calls typical of both species (fide Michael O'Brien), which supports the hybrid theory.

FIGURE 90. Piping, Snowy, Semipalmated, and Wilson's Plovers (page 99)
CLOCKWISE FROM TOP LEFT: Semipalmated Plover, Wilson's Plover, Piping Plover, and Snowy Plover. Both photos were taken in Texas in April. The Piping Plover in this photo is a first-winter inland subspecies bird that lacks a complete neckband, and the Snowy is a partial breeding-plumage bird from the Great Basin population.

FIGURE 95. Greater Yellowlegs and Lesser Yellowlegs (page 104)
TOP, FROM LEFT TO RIGHT: Greater Yellowlegs and Lesser Yellowlegs, in mostly breeding plumage.

BOTTOM, FROM LEFT TO RIGHT: Greater Yellowlegs and Lesser Yellowlegs, juveniles.

FIGURE 96. Solitary Sandpiper and Lesser Yellowlegs (page 105)
Lesser Yellowlegs (L) and Solitary Sandpiper (R). Both are in breeding plumage.

FIGURE 97. Western Sandpiper and Semipalmated Sandpiper (page 105)
TOP: Western Sandpiper (L) and Semipalmated Sandpiper (R).

BOTTOM: Juvenile Semipalmated Sandpiper (L) and juvenile Western Sandpiper (R). The Semipalmated has a smaller, rounder head and even weight distribution in front of and behind its legs. The Western has a blockier head shape and a chest-heavy weight distribution with a thicker neck. A narrow line of rust-colored scapulars is present on the Western's upper back. The pale greenish yellow legs on the Semipalmated are uncommon in a small number of young juveniles.

FIGURE 98. White-rumped Sandpiper and Baird's Sandpiper (page 106).
FROM LEFT TO RIGHT: Juvenile Baird's Sandpiper, mostly nonbreeding White-rumped Sandpiper, and juvenile White-rumped Sandpiper.

FIGURE 99. Dunlin and Stilt Sandpiper (page 107)
Dunlin (L) and Stilt Sandpipers (C and R). These birds were photographed on March 13 in Texas.

FIGURE 100. Long-billed Dowitcher and Short-billed Dowitcher (page 108)
TOP: Nonbreeding adult Long-billed Dowitcher (L) and nonbreeding adult Short-billed Dowitcher (R). Long-billed Dowitcher normally has a more rounded body with an egg-shaped undercarriage, while Short-billed has a rounded back and straighter undercarriage. This Long-billed, however, just arrived on its winter territory and is somewhat undernourished, which affects the obvious egg-shaped undercarriage and strongly rounded back seen on most Long-billeds. Long-billed has a more front-heavy body structure and thicker neck versus an evenly balanced weight distribution and thinner neck than Short-billed. A bolder lower white eye crescent is another supplemental ID field mark for Long-billed, compared with a uniformly thin eye-ring on Short-billed.

BOTTOM: Long-billed Dowitcher (L) and Short-billed Dowitcher (*hendersoni* subspecies; R) in early breeding plumage. Both birds were photographed in Texas on the same day in the same location. Short-billed has a more slender, evenly balanced body structure, with less rounded appearance to the back and undercarriage. It also has a thinner neck, although the thicker neck on Long-billed does not show in this photo because of the bird's posture. Short-billed's thick bill with deeper base does not taper evenly to the tip as in Long-billed, and often shows a slight "kink" near the tip, as if the bill got caught in a closing door. This feature is obvious in the photo.

FIGURE 101. Willet Comparison (page 110)
CLOCKWISE FROM TOP LEFT: Two "Eastern" Willets in mostly nonbreeding plumage (mid-March, Texas), nonbreeding "Western" Willet, juvenile "Western" Willet, and juvenile "Eastern" Willet. Male and female "Eastern" Willets are close in size, while female "Westerns" can be much larger than all "Easterns" and some male "Westerns," and on average have noticeably longer legs and longer bills with tapered, upturned tips. Since the bills on both juvenile birds pictured here may not be fully formed, this juvenile "Western" is best left unsexed from this single photo.

The "Western" Willet in the top right photo is probably a female, since the bill is slender and tapered near the tip, but this bill is near the short end of possible female "Western" bill sizes. This bird was also substantially larger than all the nearby "Eastern" Willets, which supports a female "Western." (All three of the birds at top were photographed within minutes of each other in Texas on March 12, 2005.)

FIGURE 105. Ring-billed Gull and Mew Gull (page 116)
Ring-billed Gulls (top and bottom L) and Mew Gulls (top and bottom R).

FIGURE 106. Laughing Gull and Franklin's Gull (page 117)
TOP: The center bird is a breeding Laughing Gull, and the right bird is a breeding Franklin's Gull. The sleeping bird at left is a Black-bellied Plover in spring transition plumage. Note its heavy, bulky body and blocky head shape, as well as its size, which is smaller than that of the gulls.

BOTTOM: The left bird is a nonbreeding adult Franklin's Gull, and the other two are nonbreeding adult Laughing Gulls. Note the larger size and bigger bill on the center male Laughing Gull compared with the slightly smaller, more slender female Laughing Gull at right.

FIGURE 107. California Gull and Western Gull (page 118)
This Western Gull (L) and California Gull (R) are both first-cycle birds. (February, CA)

FIGURE 109. First-cycle Glaucous Gull and Iceland Gull (page 120)
Iceland Gull (L) and Glaucous Gull (R).

FIGURE 117. Common, Arctic, and Roseate Terns, Nonbreeding (page 129)
FROM LEFT TO RIGHT: Roseate Tern, Common Tern, and Arctic Tern, all nonbreeding.

FIGURE 118. Common Tern and Forster's Tern (page 130)
TOP: Breeding birds in flight: Common Tern (L) and Forster's Tern (R).

BOTTOM: Transition-plumage birds. This first-year spring (early April) Forster's Tern (L) has replaced only some fresh gray back feathers and dark crown feathers from its juvenile plumage. It also shows worn, retained wing coverts, dark primaries, and characteristic dark-centered tertials, which are good separating field marks in worn first-spring birds versus the pale gray tertials on Common Tern (R). Note the distinct black mask within the incoming black crown and the longer orange legs on Forster's Tern. Common Tern has shorter reddish legs and a partial hood in juvenile and nonbreeding plumage.

Another helpful feature is a heavier, thicker bill on Forster's versus a longer, thinner one on Common, but these two birds show how subtle and variable this feature can be, with this Common's bill appearing to be just as heavy as the Forster's. A darker carpal bar is obvious on the upperwing of Common, with Forster's typically showing a pale, muted carpal bar in first-year birds.

FIGURE 121. Mixed Terns (page 133)
Obvious are the two large orange-billed terns in the top center (Royal Tern; 1). At their rear are two smaller, stocky terns with rounded crowns; short, heavy, dark bills; and bulky chests (Gull-billed Tern; 2). An even smaller, medium-sized tern (Forster's Tern; 3) is at far right, with its distinctive black mask, blocky head shape, heavier bill, and longer legs than the two similar-sized birds in the front of the main group. A slight carpal bar and blackish primaries on this Forster's Tern are a result of late first-cycle, or first-spring, plumage.

The two birds in the front of the main pack of terns have shorter legs and a beady-eyed look compared with the Forster's Tern at right. Combine these features with thinner bills and more rounded heads and you come up with an ID of transition-plumage Common Tern (4). The out-of-focus birds in the left foreground with a pinkish chest; long, dark bill with yellow tip; and flat, long, black crest are Sandwich Terns (5). You can just see the top of the head and crest of the rear Sandwich Tern.

The bird second from the right, directly in front of the right-hand Royal Tern, shows plumage features of nonbreeding Common Tern with a beady eye and similar dark crown pattern, and seems to have a thinner black bill, but it seems larger than the two Common Terns. Single photos can be hard to assess, but this is probably a transitional Common Tern (4), which can show silvery versus dark primaries in spring.

FIGURE 124. Common Ground-Dove and Ruddy Ground-Dove (page 136)
CLOCKWISE FROM TOP LEFT: Female Common Ground-Dove, female Ruddy Ground-Dove, male Ruddy Ground-Dove, and male Common Ground-Dove (eastern subspecies).

FIGURE 125. Black-billed, Mangrove, and Yellow-billed Cuckoos (page 138)
TOP, FROM LEFT TO RIGHT: Yellow-billed Cuckoo, immature Black-billed Cuckoo, and Mangrove Cuckoo (Caribbean subspecies found in Florida).

BOTTOM: Greater Roadrunner.

FIGURE 126. Smooth-billed Ani and Groove-billed Ani (page 139)
Although Smooth-billed Ani is very rare in Veracruz, Mexico, with fewer than 15 records overall (eBird 2013), the bird in the lower left photo seems to be a fairly standard Smooth-billed Ani based on the high, flared upper mandible and lack of grooves on the bill. Kevin initially identified this bird in the field as a Groove-billed Ani since the range map showed that only Groove-billed was possible in Veracruz in 2001.

FIGURE 130. Spotted Owl and Barred Owl (page 145)
Spotted Owl (Pacific Northwest subspecies) (L) and Barred Owl (R).

FIGURE 131. Long-eared Owl and Great Horned Owl (page 146)
Long-eared Owl, female (L), and Great Horned Owl (R).

FIGURE 132. Northern Saw-whet Owl and Boreal Owl (page 147)
Boreal Owl (L) and Northern Saw-whet Owl (R).

FIGURE 136. Common Nighthawk and Antillean Nighthawk (page 150)
FROM LEFT TO RIGHT: Common Nighthawk (western subspecies), rufous-morph Antillean Nighthawk (migratory Florida subspecies), and gray-morph Antillean Nighthawk (Caribbean subspecies). All are males.

FIGURE 137. Hummingbirds (page 152)
FROM LEFT TO RIGHT: Male Rufous Hummingbird, female Rufous Hummingbird, male Blue-throated Hummingbird, and male Ruby-throated Hummingbird.

FIGURE 139. Black-chinned Hummingbird and Ruby-throated Hummingbird, Females (page 155)
Ruby-throated Hummingbird (L) and Black-chinned Hummingbird (R).

FIGURE 140. Anna's Hummingbird and Costa's Hummingbird, Immature Females (page 156)
Female Costa's Hummingbird (L) and immature female Anna's Hummingbird (R).

FIGURE 141. Swifts (page 157)
Chimney Swift (top L) and Vaux's Swift (top R).

FIGURE 144. Hairy Woodpecker and Downy Woodpecker (page 164)
CLOCKWISE FROM TOP LEFT: Female eastern Hairy Woodpecker, male eastern Downy Woodpecker, interior West female Hairy Woodpecker, and interior West male Downy Woodpecker.

FIGURE 145. Ladder-backed, Nuttall's, and Downy Woodpeckers (page 165)
FROM LEFT TO RIGHT: Downy Woodpecker, Ladder-backed Woodpecker, and Nuttall's Woodpecker, all males.

FIGURE 147. Gilded Flicker and Northern Flicker Comparison (page 168)
CLOCKWISE FROM TOP LEFT (ALL MALES): "Yellow-shafted" Northern Flicker, "Red-shafted" North-ern Flicker, intergrade "Red-shafted" and "Yellow-shafted" Northern Flicker, and Gilded Flicker. The intergrade flicker, from British Columbia, has a red malar stripe like "Red-shafted" but a thin red V on the rear crown as on "Yellow-shafted," but much smaller than normal. Plumage shading on the head is more like "Yellow-shafted's," but wing and wing-pit color is red like "Red-shafted's." The bird was breeding with a female "Red-shafted" Northern Flicker.

FIGURE 148. Nuthatches (page 169)
CLOCKWISE FROM TOP LEFT: Male White-breasted Nuthatch, male Red-breasted Nuthatch, Brown-headed Nuthatch, and Pygmy Nuthatch.

FIGURE 150. Tyrant Flycatchers (page 172)
CLOCKWISE FROM TOP LEFT: Great Kiskadee, Say's Phoebe, Least Flycatcher, Ash-throated Flycatcher, Western Kingbird, and male Scissor-tailed Flycatcher.

FIGURE 151. Three Flycatchers in the Genus *Tyrannus* (page 173)
FROM LEFT TO RIGHT: Eastern Kingbird, Gray Kingbird, and Scissor-tailed Flycatcher. All three are first-winter birds. Note the smaller head and bill and more slender body on Eastern Kingbird compared with Gray Kingbird's longer, heavier bill, bigger head, and bulkier body shape. The young first-winter Scissor-tailed Flycatcher has an even smaller head and more slender body than Eastern Kingbird, and a longer tail than both other species. Gray Kingbird and Scissor-tailed Flycatcher are unusual vagrants to southern Costa Rica.

FIGURE 152. Pewees and *Empidonax* Flycatchers (page 176)
BOTTOM: "Eastern" Willow Flycatcher (L) and Least Flycatcher (R).

FIGURE 153. Willow Flycatcher and Alder Flycatcher (page 177)
Willow Flycatcher (L) and Alder Flycatcher (R). Note the more gently sloping forehead on Willow with a peak near the rear, versus a steeper fore-crown and more evenly rounded crown on Alder. This feature can be assessed only on relaxed birds and is often hard to differentiate.

FIGURE 154. *Myiarchus* Flycatcher Comparison (page 178)
FROM LEFT TO RIGHT: Great Crested Flycatcher, Brown-crested Flycatcher, Ash-throated Flycatcher, and La Sagra's Flycatcher (Caribbean subspecies).

FIGURE 155. Couch's Kingbird and Tropical Kingbird (page 179)
Couch's Kingbird (L) and Tropical Kingbird (R). Note the forked tail on Tropical and square tail tip on this "typical" Couch's. This supplemental ID feature is reliable only for Couch's with square tails; most Tropicals have an obvious forked tail, and some Couch's do as well.

FIGURE 159. Blue-headed Vireo and Cassin's Vireo (page 184)
Cassin's Vireo (L) and Blue-headed Vireo (R).

FIGURE 160. Warbling, Philadelphia, and Bell's Vireos and Tennessee Warbler (page 185)
CLOCKWISE FROM TOP LEFT: Warbling Vireo (May), Philadelphia Vireo (May), Tennessee Warbler (April), and Bell's Vireo (eastern subspecies) (December).

FIGURE 163. Common Raven and Chihuahuan Raven (page 189)
Chihuahuan Raven (L) and Common Raven (R).

FIGURE 165. Tree Swallow and Violet-green Swallow, Females (page 192)
Tree Swallow (L) and Violet-green Swallow (R).

FIGURE 166. Chickadees and Titmice (page 194)
TOP: Black-capped Chickadee (L) and Carolina Chickadee (C).

BOTTOM: Tufted Titmouse (L) and Black-crested Titmouse (C). Black-crested differs from Tufted by having a black crest and crown and white forecrown. Tufted has a black forecrown and gray crown and crest.

FIGURE 171. American Pipit, Sprague's Pipit, and Juvenile Horned Lark (page 200)
CLOCKWISE FROM TOP LEFT: Nonbreeding American Pipit, nonbreeding Sprague's Pipit, Savannah Sparrow ("Ipswich" subspecies), and juvenile Horned Lark.

FIGURE 173. Blue-gray Gnatcatcher and Black-tailed Gnatcatcher (page 202)
Breeding male Blue-gray Gnatcatcher (L) and female Blue-gray Gnatcatcher (C). The nonbreeding male Black-tailed Gnatcatcher (R) somewhat resembles a breeding or partial breeding male Blue-gray Gnatcatcher.

FIGURE 176. Female Bluebirds (page 206)
FROM LEFT TO RIGHT: Western Bluebird, Eastern Bluebird, and Mountain Bluebird.

FIGURE 178. Spotted Thrushes (page 210)
CLOCKWISE FROM TOP LEFT: Gray-cheeked Thrush, Swainson's Thrush, Eastern Veery, Eastern Hermit Thrush, Bicknell's Thrush, and Wood Thrush.

FIGURE 180. Curve-billed, Bendire's, Brown, and Long-billed Thrashers (page 212)
CLOCKWISE FROM TOP LEFT: Curve-billed Thrasher (interior form), Bendire's Thrasher, Long-billed Thrasher, and Brown Thrasher.

FIGURE 185. Northern Waterthrush and Louisiana Waterthrush; Blackpoll Warbler and Bay-breasted Warbler, Nonbreeding (page 219)
TOP: Northern Waterthrush (whitish variant; see text) (L) and Louisiana Waterthrush (R).

BOTTOM: Nonbreeding immature female Bay-breasted Warbler (L) and nonbreeding immature Blackpoll Warbler (R).

FIGURE 187. Cape May Warbler and Pine Warbler, Immature Females (page 221)
Pine Warbler (L) and Cape May Warbler (R).

FIGURE 188. Wilson's, Hooded, and Yellow Warblers, Immature Females (page 221)
FROM LEFT TO RIGHT: Yellow Warbler, Wilson's Warbler, and Hooded Warbler.

FIGURE 189. Connecticut Warbler and Common Yellowthroat, Females (page 224)
Common Yellowthroat (L) and immature Connecticut Warbler (R).

FIGURE 191. Summer, Scarlet, and Hepatic Tanagers, Females (page 227)
FROM LEFT TO RIGHT: Hepatic Tanager, Summer Tanager, and Scarlet Tanager.

FIGURE 194. Black-headed Grosbeak and Rose-breasted Grosbeak (page 230)
Immature male Rose-breasted Grosbeak (L) and nonbreeding female Black-headed Grosbeak (R).

FIGURE 195. Female and Immature Buntings and Female Blue Grosbeak (page 231)
CLOCKWISE FROM TOP LEFT: Juvenile/first-winter Lazuli Bunting, female Indigo Bunting, worn female Varied Bunting, female Blue Grosbeak, juvenile/first-winter Painted Bunting, and worn female Lazuli Bunting.

FIGURE 197. Immature Female Dickcissel and Female House Sparrow (page 234)
Immature female Dickcissel (L) and female House Sparrow (R).

FIGURE 200. Cassin's Sparrow and Botteri's Sparrow (page 238)
Cassin's Sparrow (L) and worn Botteri's Sparrow (R).

FIGURE 201. Clay-colored, Chipping, and Brewer's Sparrows (page 239)
FROM LEFT TO RIGHT (all in nonbreeding plumage): Brewer's Sparrow, first-winter Chipping Sparrow, and Clay-colored Sparrow.

FIGURE 202. Song, Lincoln's, and Savannah Sparrows (page 239)
FROM LEFT TO RIGHT: Savannah Sparrow, Song Sparrow, and Lincoln's Sparrow.

FIGURE 203. Nelson's Sharp-tailed Sparrow and Le Conte's Sparrow (page 240)
Le Conte's Sparrow (L) and Gulf Coast form of Nelson's Sharp-tailed Sparrow (R). Different postures in these birds result in different physical appearances, but both species have a similar body shape and structural features when their poses are the same.

FIGURE 204. Female and Nonbreeding Longspurs and Buntings (page 243)
CLOCKWISE FROM TOP LEFT: Breeding female McCown's Longspur, nonbreeding first-winter Lapland Longspur, female Lark Bunting, and nonbreeding Smith's Longspur.

FIGURE 208. Eastern Meadowlark and Western Meadowlark (page 247)
CLOCKWISE FROM TOP LEFT: Breeding Eastern Meadowlark, nonbreeding Western Meadowlark, nonbreeding Eastern Meadowlark, breeding Western Meadowlark.

FIGURE 210. Brewer's Blackbird and Rusty Blackbird, Breeding Males (page 249)
Rusty Blackbird (L) and Brewer's Blackbird (R).

FIGURE 211. Great-tailed, Boat-tailed, and Common Grackles, Females (page 250)
CLOCKWISE FROM TOP LEFT: Boat-tailed Grackle (Atlantic subspecies, Georgia northward), Common Grackle, Great-tailed Grackle, and Boat-tailed Grackle (Florida to Texas subspecies).

FIGURE 213. Bullock's Oriole and Baltimore Oriole, Immature Females (page 252)
Baltimore Oriole (L) and Bullock's Oriole (R).

FIGURE 214. Hooded Oriole and Orchard Oriole, Females (page 253)
Orchard Oriole (L) and Hooded Oriole (R).

FIGURE 216. Cassin's, House, and Purple Finches, Females (page 256)
CLOCKWISE FROM TOP LEFT: Female "Eastern" Purple Finch, female "Western" Purple Finch, female Cassin's Finch, and female House Finch. The very long primary projection on Cassin's Finch is shown here, and a short primary projection on House Finch is obvious compared with that of both Purple Finches.

FIGURE 218. Hoary Redpoll and Common Redpoll (page 259)
CLOCKWISE FROM TOP LEFT: Nonbreeding male Common Redpoll, nonbreeding female Common Redpoll, nonbreeding female Hoary Redpoll, and worn breeding Hoary Redpoll. Hoary typically shows a very small, triangular bill like the worn breeding male, but the nonbreeding female Hoary has a larger one that would not be very helpful for ID purposes. Note the more extensive white on the back, underparts, and wing coverts of the bottom right Hoary. This bird was banded and verified as a Hoary Redpoll by measurements.

FIGURE 219. Lesser Goldfinch and American Goldfinch, Females and Immatures (page 260)
CLOCKWISE FROM TOP LEFT: Juvenile Lesser Goldfinch (August), female American Goldfinch (September), female Lesser Goldfinch (August), and juvenile American Goldfinch (November).

PHOTOGRAPHER CREDITS

All photographs by Kevin Karlson with the exception of the following:

Adrian Binns: Figure 120 lower left

Cameron Cox: Figure 110 right center and right

Mike Danzenbaker: Figure 39 upper left, Figure 44 both, Figure 45 left and right, Figure 89 upper left, Figure 130 left, Figure 141 upper right, Figure 165 right, Figure 173 right, Figure 216 upper right

Scott Elowitz: Figure 148 lower right

Bob Fogg: Figure 43 upper left, upper right, and lower right, Figure 46 all four photos, Figure 49 right, Figure 71 left, Figure 112 left, Figure 113 left and center

Jim Gilbert: Figure 50 right

Bruce Hallett: Figure 136 right

Julian Hough: Figure 89 upper right

Bill Hubick: Figure 37 right

Don Riepe: Figure 113 right

David Roemer: Figure 30 lower right; cover photo lower right

Brian Small: Figure 72 lower right, Figure 129 upper right, Figure 134 lower left, Figure 140 left, Figure 145 right, Figure 146 lower left, Figure 147 lower left, Figure 159 left, Figure 163 left, Figure 166 lower right, Figure 170 lower right, Figure 172 right, Figure 174 right, Figure 177 right, Figure 179 lower right, Figure 191 left, Figure 201 left, Figure 203 right, Figure 208 upper right, Figure 214 right, Figure 216 lower right

Lloyd Spitalnik: Figure 71 right, Figure 98 right, Figure 109 left, Figure 117 center, Figure 128 right, Figure 189 right, Figure 191 right, Figure 194 left, Figure 196 left, Figure 209 lower right, Figure 212 upper right, Figure 215 lower right

Brian Sullivan: Figure 79 upper right, Figure 86 right

Brian Taber: Figure 15

Scott Whittle: Figure 57 lower center

Jim Zipp: Figure 81 upper right, lower right

GLOSSARY

attenuated. Tapering gradually, often to a slender point.

auriculars. Ear covert feathers or ear patch.

axillaries. Feathers in the wingpit of a bird (where the wings meet the body).

bare parts. Unfeathered parts of a bird, including the bill, feet, and eyes.

belly. Underparts below the breast and above the vent.

breast. Underparts below the throat and above the belly.

carpal bar. Marking on the upperwing (usually appearing as a long stripe) created by the contrast between the greater wing coverts and the rest of the wing.

clinal. Referring to a gradual change that occurs across a range of similar things; in bird morphology or physiology, it refers to gradual variation across a geographic region.

color morph. A regularly occurring genetic variant of a bird's plumage.

culmen. Upper ridge of a bird's upper mandible.

cycle. A period of molt; in aging terminology, a cycle represents a time period in which a bird shows a plumage characteristic of that age.

dimorphism. Having two distinct morphs, or appearances.

diurnal. Occurring or active during the day.

emarginated primaries. The outer primaries that appear separated during flight.

eye line (or eye stripe). Thin line of feathers extending both in front of and behind the eye.

eye-ring. Thin circle of feathers around the eye that contrasts in color with the surrounding feathers.

family. In taxonomy, a family includes a group of genera believed to share a common evolutionary ancestor.

flank. Area between the belly and wing.

gape. Area near the base of the bill where the upper and lower mandibles meet.

gonydeal angle. Pointed protrusion along the lower mandible of a bird's bill.

gorget. Brightly colored throat of a bird, such as the iridescent throat patch of male hummingbirds.

hand. The outer wing.

hybrid. The offspring of two different species.

immature. An age class between a juvenile and an adult.

life year. Time span between the date of hatching and one year later.

lores, loral area. Area between the eye and base of the bill.

malar stripe. Region where the lower portion of the face meets the throat.

mandible. One half of the bill, either the upper or lower.

mantle. Feathers that cover the back, scapulars, and upperwing.

median coverts. Row of feathers that lies between the lesser wing coverts and greater wing coverts.

molt. Regular replacement of one set of feathers by another.

nape. Area above the back and below the crown; the back of the neck.

nasal bristles. Stiff hairs situated near the nasal opening on a bird's bill.

Neotropical. Referring to the geographic area that includes southern Mexico, Central America, and South America.

passerine. A perching bird belonging to the order Passeriformes, which in taxonomy includes all species from tyrant flycatchers through weaver finches.

patagial mark. Marking on the front edge of the underwing that may be located between the shoulder and wrist.

pelagic. Referring to offshore ocean waters.

plumage. Coat of feathers, usually replaced one or two times per year.

plumage details. Markings on a bird's feathers. Conventional ID approaches rely primarily on plumage details.

plumage patterns. General coloration and overall appearance of a bird's plumage, such as streaking or spotting versus plain underparts, or reddish underparts versus plain gray ones. An assessment of plumage patterns is part of the BBI ID process.

polymorphic. Having two or more different adult appearances, or morphs.

precocial. Young that are active and mostly independent almost immediately after hatching.

primaries. Outer flight feathers on the outer half of

the wing. These feathers form the lower border of a folded wing.

primary extension. Degree to which the primaries extend beyond the tail on a standing bird.

primary projection. Degree to which the primaries extend past the tertials on a folded wing.

rectrix, rectrices (plural). Tail feather(s).

rump. Part of the upperparts that lie between the back and uppertail coverts.

scapulars. Rows of relatively large feathers on the shoulders that cover the base of the upperwing.

secondaries. Long flight feathers on the inner half of the wing. Secondaries are generally not visible on a folded wing.

structural features. Size, length, and shape of a bird's legs, bill, head, neck, wings, and tail. All of these parts, along with body shape, combine to provide a physical profile of a bird.

sublateral crown stripe. Line that runs between the supercilium and the crown along the width of the head.

subspecies. Geographically separate breeding population of a species that is distinguishable by plumage or other characters but that is not reproductively isolated.

subterminal. Referring to a marking inside the margin or tip of a feather.

supercilium. Pale line above the eye that separates the cap and cheek; the eyebrow.

supraloral. Region directly above the lores that usually extends from just above the eye to the base of the upper mandible.

tapered. Gradually becoming narrow at one end.

tertials. Innermost three flight feathers that cover the other secondary flight feathers on a folded wing. Tertials are relatively long and are situated beyond the scapulars.

undercarriage. A bird's lower body.

undertail coverts. Tract of feathers that lie below the vent and cover the base of the tail feathers on a bird's underparts.

uppertail coverts. Tract of feathers that cover the base of the tail feathers on a bird's upperparts.

vent. Part of a bird's underparts below the belly and above the undertail coverts.

wing bar. Stripe on the upperwing created by contrasting feather tips on wing coverts.

wing coverts. Rows or groups of relatively small feathers that cover the bases of the primaries, secondaries, and tail feathers, both on the upperside and underside of the wing.

wingspan. Measurement from wingtip to wingtip of a bird's outstretched wings.

wrist. Point on the leading edge of the wing about halfway to the tip where the wing bends. The wrist is situated at the base of the hand.

BIBLIOGRAPHY

Alderfer, Jonathan, ed. 2006. *National Geographic Complete Birds of North America*. Washington, D.C.: National Geographic Society.

Behrens, Ken, and Cameron Cox. 2013. *Seawatching: Eastern Waterbirds in Flight*. Peterson Reference Guide Series. Boston: Houghton Mifflin Harcourt.

Dunn, Jon L., and Kimball L. Garrett. 1997. *A Field Guide to Warblers of North America*. Peterson Reference Guide Series. Boston: Houghton Mifflin.

Floyd, Ted. 2008. *Smithsonian Field Guide to the Birds of North America*. New York: HarperCollins.

Gladwell, Malcolm. 2005. *Blink: The Power of Thinking Without Thinking*. New York: Little Brown.

Harrison, Peter. 1987. *A Field Guide to Seabirds of the World*. Lexington, Mass.: Stephen Greene Press.

Howell, Steve N. G., and Jon Dunn. 2007. *A Reference Guide to Gulls of the Americas*. Peterson Reference Guide Series. Boston: Houghton Mifflin.

Liguori, Jerry. 2005. *Hawks from Every Angle*. Princeton, N.J.: Princeton University Press.

O'Brien, Michael, Richard Crossley, and Kevin Karlson. 2006. *The Shorebird Guide*. Boston: Houghton Mifflin.

Sibley, David. 2000. *The Sibley Guide to Birds*. New York: Alfred A. Knopf.

Wheeler, Brian K. 2003. *Raptors of Eastern North America*. Princeton, N.J.: Princeton University Press.

———. 2003. *Raptors of Western North America*. Princeton, N.J.: Princeton University Press.

INDEX

Index pages in **bold** refer to photographs.

PETERSON FIELD GUIDES®

Roger Tory Peterson's innovative format uses accurate, detailed drawings to pinpoint key field marks for quick recognition of species and easy comparison of confusing look-alikes.

BIRDS

Birds of North America

Birds of Eastern and Central North America

Western Birds

Birds of Britain and Europe

Birds of Texas

Eastern Birds

Feeder Birds of Eastern North America

Hawks of North America

Hummingbirds of North America

Warblers

Western Birds' Nests

Eastern Birds' Nests

PLANTS AND ECOLOGY

Eastern and Central Edible Wild Plants

Eastern and Central Medicinal Plants and Herbs

Western Medicinal Plants and Herbs

Eastern Forests

Rocky Mountain and Southwest Forests

Eastern Trees

Western Trees

Eastern Trees and Shrubs

Ferns of Northeastern and Central North America

Mushrooms

North American Prairie

Venomous Animals and Poisonous Plants

Southwest and Texas Wildflowers

Wildflowers of Northeastern and North-Central North America

MAMMALS

Animal Tracks

Mammals

Finding Mammals

INSECTS

Insects

Eastern Butterflies

Moths of Northeastern North America

REPTILES AND AMPHIBIANS

Eastern Reptiles and Amphibians

Western Reptiles and Amphibians

PETERSON FLASHGUIDES®

Portable and waterproof, FlashGuides are perfect for those who want to travel light. Covering 50–100 species, with brief surveys of habit and habitat, each opens to two rows with twelve full-color, laminated panels on each side.

PETERSON FIRST GUIDES®

The first books the beginning naturalist needs, whether young or old. Simplified versions of the full-size guides, they make it easy to get started in the field, and feature the most commonly seen natural life.

PETERSON FIELD GUIDES FOR YOUNG NATURALISTS

This series is designed with young readers ages eight to twelve in mind, featuring the original artwork of the celebrated naturalist Roger Tory Peterson.

Backyard Birds

Birds of Prey

Songbirds

Butterflies

Caterpillars

PETERSON FIELD GUIDES® COLORING BOOKS®

Fun for kids ages eight to twelve, these color-your-own field guides include color stickers and are suitable for use with pencils or paint.

Birds

Butterflies

Dinosaurs

Reptiles and Amphibians

Wildflowers

Seashores

Shells

Mammals

PETERSON REFERENCE GUIDES®

Reference Guides provide in-depth information on groups of birds and topics beyond identification.

Seawatching: Eastern Waterbirds in Flight

Gulls of the Americas

Molt in North American Birds

Behavior of North American Mammals

Birding by Impression

PETERSON AUDIO GUIDES

Birding by Ear: Western

Birding by Ear: Eastern/Central

More Birding by Ear: Eastern/Central

Bird Songs: Eastern/Central
THIRD EDITION

PETERSON FIELD GUIDE / *BIRD WATCHER'S DIGEST* BACKYARD BIRD GUIDES

Identifying and Feeding Birds

Hummingbirds and Butterflies

Bird Homes and Habitats

The Young Birder's Guide to Birds of North America

The New Birder's Guide to Birds of North America

DIGITAL

Apps available on the App Store for iPad, iPhone, and iPod Touch.

Peterson Birds of North America

Peterson Birds Pocket Edition

Peterson Backyard Birds

E-books

Birds of Arizona

Birds of California

Birds of Florida

Birds of Massachusetts

Birds of Minnesota

Birds of New Jersey

Birds of New York

Birds of Ohio

Birds of Pennsylvania

Birds of Texas